The Wadsworth Guide
to Research

The Wadsworth

Guide

to Research

Susan K. Miller-Cochran
North Carolina State University

Rochelle L. Rodrigo
Mesa Community College

WADSWORTH
CENGAGE Learning

Australia • Brazil • Japan • Korea • Mexico • Singapore • Spain • United Kingdom • United States

WADSWORTH
CENGAGE Learning™

The Wadsworth Guide to Research
Susan K. Miller-Cochran
Rochelle L. Rodrigo

Publisher: Lyn Uhl

Development Editor: Marita Sermolins

Assistant Editor: Kelli Strieby

Editorial Assistant: Megan Power

Associate Media Editor: Emily Ryan

Executive Marketing Manager: Mandee Eckersley

Marketing Manager: Jennifer Zourdos

Senior Marketing Communications Manager: Stacey Purviance

Production Manager: Samantha Ross

Senior Content Project Manager: Lauren Wheelock

Senior Art Director: Cate Rickard Barr

Senior Print Buyer: Betsy Donaghey

Senior Rights Acquisition Account Manager – Text: Tim Sisler

Production Service: Lachina Publishing Services

Text Designer: Lisa Garbutt, Rara Avis Graphic Design

Senior Permissions Account Manager – Images: Sheri Blaney

Photo Researcher: Naomi Kornhauser

Cover Designer: Lisa Garbutt, Rara Avis Graphic Design

Compositor: Lachina Publishing Services

For product information and technology assistance, contact us at **Cengage Learning Customer & Sales Support, 1-800-354-9706**

For permission to use material from this text or product, submit all requests online at **www.cengage.com/permissions.** Further permissions questions can be emailed to **permissionrequest@cengage.com**

Library of Congress Control Number: 2008931219

ISBN-13: 978-0-495-79966-5

ISBN-10: 0-495-79966-1

Wadsworth
20 Channel Center Street
Boston, MA 02210
USA

Cengage Learning products are represented in Canada by Nelson Education, Ltd.

For your course and learning solutions, visit **www.cengage.com**

Purchase any of our products at your local college store or at our preferred online store **www.ichapters.com**

Printed in the U.S.A.
3 4 5 6 7 13 12 11 10

Contents

PART 2: CONDUCTING RESEARCH 61

chapter four: Finding Resources through Secondary Research 63

PART 4: FORMATTING YOUR RESEARCH 245

chapter twelve: MLA Citation Style Guidelines 247

chapter thirteen: APA Citation Style Guidelines 289

appendix: Invention Activities 389

Research. Ick.

Sound familiar?

Nothing sounds more boring to students—more irrelevant to their every day lives—than research.

And yet we do research every day. We compare gas prices and cell phone plans, make grocery lists, and read movie reviews. We look up music lyrics, class schedules, headlines, weather reports, game scores, personal ads, and newspaper articles. And often we use the information we find to make decisions—and to persuade others to make decisions as well.

So . . . why are students so put off by the idea of doing research?

We are convinced that one of the reasons is because students don't realize that they already do research every day, and they can refine the skills they already have to conduct effective academic research. Research skills are transferable, but students have to understand that the context of their research impacts the kinds of strategies they will find useful and the results that they'll find.

What's more, academic research can be overwhelming. Students are often faced with big end-of-semester research projects, due at the same time as several other projects for different classes, all on topics that they don't know much about—yet they feel they must sound as if they are experts on the topics by the time they're finished. Anyone would be intimidated by such a situation, and students often don't know where to start. The short-term solution is generally to put the projects off until the last minute and then try to come up with something the night before they're due.

What's Different about This Research Guide?

This guide approaches research in a unique way—by helping students think about how to look for connections between the research they already do in their personal, academic, and perhaps even professional lives. By breaking research down into a set of smaller strategies that fit together into a research process for students, *The Wadsworth Guide to Research* makes the task of academic research more manageable, relevant, and—believe it or not—even enjoyable. Perhaps most importantly, this guide emphasizes that *context matters*. Research strategies are affected by the rhetorical situations in which we research—the audiences we write to, the topics we write about, the purposes for which we're writing, and the background and perspective of the author who is doing the writing and researching.

Research is a complex process, and it needs to be adapted to the situation surrounding it. Yet the leading texts that teach research-based writing tend to treat the research process as *one* process—a step-by-step plan that will work in any situation—without acknowledging the ways that context influences research or the fact that research takes place in settings outside of academia. This book presents a different approach to research-based writing, one that encourages students to think critically about the situation surrounding a research project and how that context shapes and influences the decisions they make in their research.

Specifically, we ask students to think about how the purpose, audience, topic, and perspective of the author connect and influence the research they conduct:

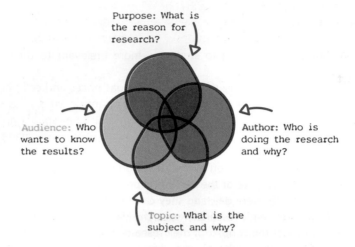

Purpose: What is the reason for research?

Audience: Who wants to know the results?

Author: Who is doing the research and why?

Topic: What is the subject and why?

The driving philosophy behind this textbook is that all research takes place in a certain place at a certain time, and the context surrounding the research project impacts the process. Successful researchers learn to identify what is important in their research situation and weave those elements into their research process. They also have a variety of different tools at their disposal that they can draw on in order to match their context with the needs of their research project. Research-based writing is about choices, and our goal is to provide students with tools to make effective choices—not to make all of the choices for them.

In addition, this text is based on the premise that all research projects are undertaken for a purpose and they often must present a position on a topic—a concept that students sometimes fail to understand. Therefore, we have included a detailed discussion of how to use research to construct an effective, persuasive argument.

Finally, the text has been updated to conform to the latest guidelines in the seventh edition of the *MLA Handbook for Writers of Research Papers*.

How Is the Guide Organized?

Are there common steps that most researchers take when working through a research project? Absolutely! The key is that these steps are "common," but not necessarily "identical." The steps and activities are similar enough to be considered common, but they need to be adapted to a specific project. Other research textbooks tend to present research as one, monolithic process without acknowledging that researchers adapt their approaches, and sometimes rearrange the steps, depending on the situations they encounter. *The Wadsworth Guide to Research* is organized to walk students through some of the common elements of a research process while allowing them to adapt those steps to the project they are tackling. The various strategies are organized into four sections:

Part One: Preparing for Research. Rubber bands start out small and eventually stretch to fit around whatever they're holding together. Generating ideas works much the same way. And to help guide students through that process as it relates to research, Part One walks students through the process of identifying a topic that they would like to research (usually the most daunting task for students), formulating a research question, and writing a research proposal.

 Part Two: Conducting Research. We've all had trouble getting organized in our lives at some point. Using a paperclip can help hold meaningful items together. With research, organization is key, and Part Two guides students through the gathering of data and resources that will help them respond to their research question. Having students respond to their own research question gives them a sense of ownership and investment.

 Part Three: Reporting on Research. Sending the results of our research out into the world can be intimidating, but it can be less so if we have the right tools and strategies for communicating our message. And a paper airplane folded the right way can fly much farther than a flat sheet of paper. Part Three guides students through the process of putting research results into an appropriate format so that they can share their research effectively with others to achieve their intended purpose.

 Part Four: Formatting Your Research. Research is most effective when it follows expected conventions for a particular rhetorical situation. Part Four offers students the "nuts and bolts" of how to use different academic citation systems to document their research, helping them to communicate persuasively and clearly to their intended audience.

As students work through the different sections of the book, the features and activities help them identify the specific rhetorical situation of their own research, while also understanding how research Is conducted in and adapted to different contexts.

🖎 Each chapter in the first three sections opens with a **Research in Action** scenario that gives students a specific example of how the principles introduced in that chapter might work in a specific rhetorical context.

> *Why use this feature?* These quick case studies can be used as classroom discussion starters, and they can provide a starting point for having students practice analyzing the context of research.

🖎 The **˃ reflect ˂** activities ask students to think about prior research they've done and the potential connections between research they have done or are doing in different contexts.

> *Why use this feature?* These activities ask students to explore aspects of the rhetorical situation of their own research project.

preface

- The `...write...` activities walk students through the steps of actually writing about and drafting a report of their research.

  Why use this feature? These activities break the research process down into manageable pieces for students to tackle one at a time.

- The `techno_tip >` activities offer suggestions and instructions for how students might use various technological tools in their own research. Even though many students now are familiar with using technology, they likely haven't used technology extensively to conduct effective academic research.

  Why use this feature? The Techno Tips can be a powerful way for students to make connections between what they already know and what they can learn to help strengthen their research practices. Students will learn to use technology for many purposes—from generating ideas to getting organized to finding sources. Even if you or your students don't already know how to utilize these technologies—don't worry! At the Online Resource Center, interactive tutorials demonstrate how to make use of the tips in your research with guided demos. These tips focus on several different Web-based applications that students can use at various stages of their research, and they emphasize open source and freeware applications wherever possible.

- Many instructors agree that the most typical research assignments are a research proposal, a review of prior research, and a researched argument. To help students understand what's required of them for these common assignments, the **Research in Progress** sections at the end of each part of the guide sum up and make use of all the skills explained in the chapters prior to.

  Why use this feature? Each Research in Progress section includes a specific assignment and two student samples, the first showing teacher comments to highlight strengths and weaknesses. The assignments build on each other to walk students through the entire process of developing an extended research project.

- Finally, the **Online Resource Center** [⇗] provides a variety of tools for you and your students to supplement the work they'll do in your class.

  Why use this feature? You'll find a user-friendly documentation guide that allows students to search for examples of how to cite a variety of sources in the same way that they might do a Google or Wikipedia search. You'll also find additional sample student papers and online activities that will support your classroom instruction.

Why Should You Use This Research Guide?

Everyone is a researcher. The text used in a class that teaches research-based writing should help students realize that research is a necessary part of their personal, academic, and professional lives and prepare them for the kinds of research they'll need to do. Unfortunately, most research textbooks continue to emphasize only one approach and fail to make research relevant to students. *The Wadsworth Guide to Research* can help you make those connections with your students and prepare them to conduct effective research, both in college and beyond.

The Wadsworth Guide to Research is designed to be used in any class that has a research component, and it can also be a tool for research outside of academic contexts. The activities and principles in the book walk readers through a specific research project, or projects, regardless of the approach used in the class:

- **I assign one research paper throughout the entire semester. How can I keep students interested the whole way through?**

    o *The Wadsworth Guide to Research* walks students through three different projects that help them develop an effective, well-researched argument and a complex understanding of an issue. The first project carefully guides students through the process of choosing a topic that is relevant and interesting to them—one in which they're invested—that will help them maintain a semester-long interest in their research.

- **I assign two or more research papers a semester. How could I use this book?**

    o Students can work through the projects in *The Wadsworth Guide to Research* more than once during a semester. Consider spending more time on the assignments the first time through to give students a firm foundation in research. You could also emphasize different kinds of research each time through (i.e., research questions that arise from different disciplinary areas; gathering data and working with various technologies; or research questions that come from their personal, professional, and academic lives).

- **I assign a non-traditional research project that asks students to use new media to write in a multimodal format. How could my students benefit from this book?**

    o *The Wadsworth Guide to Research* could be an ideal fit for your class. No other book on the market helps students use as wide of a variety of technologies in their research process and assist them as thoroughly in documenting new media resources that they might use in their research.

Supplements

Cengage Learning offers many supplemental resources that will help you and your students as they develop their research projects.

Online Resource Center The Online Resource Center for *The Wadsworth Guide to Research* helps your students prepare for class more effectively using MLA, APA, CMS, and CSE citation examples; video activities; *Techno Tip* interactive tutorials; annotated student samples; and online versions of the *Reflect* and *Write* features. Instructor-specific material is also available, including activity options and suggestions for how to structure your class using *The Wadsworth Guide to Research.*

English21 The largest compilation of online resources ever organized for composition and literature courses, English21 is a complete online support system that weaves robust, self-paced instruction with interactive assignments. Easily assignable, English21 engages students as they become better-prepared and successful writers. English21 supports students through every step of the writing process, from assignment to final draft. English21 includes carefully crafted multimedia assignments; a collection of essays that amounts to a full-sized thematic reader; a full interactive handbook including hundreds of animations, exercises, and activities; a complete research guide with animated tutorials and a link to Gale's InfoTrac® database; and a rich multimedia library with hand-selected images, audio clips, video clips, stories, poems, and plays. To learn more, visit academic.cengage.com/english21.

Infotrac® College Edition with InfoMarks™ InfoTrac® College Edition, an online research and learning center, offers over 20 million full-text articles from nearly 6,000 scholarly and popular periodicals. The articles cover a broad spectrum of disciplines and topics—ideal for every type of researcher.

Wadsworth's InSite for Writing and Research™ This online writing and research tool includes electronic peer review, an originality checker, an assignment library, help with common grammar and writing errors, and access to InfoTrac® College Edition. Portfolio management gives you the ability to grade papers, run originality reports, and offer feedback in an easy-to-use online course management system. Using InSite's peer review feature, students can easily review and respond to their classmates' work. Other features include fully integrated discussion boards, streamlined assignment creation, and more. Visit academic.cengage.com/insite to view a demonstration.

Turnitin® This proven online plagiarism-prevention software promotes fairness in the classroom by helping students learn to correctly cite sources and by allowing instructors to check for originality before reading and grading papers. Visit academic.cengage.com/turnitin to view a demonstration.

CengageNOW™ for Writing This powerful and assignable online teaching and learning system contains diagnostic quizzing and multimedia tutorials that work with students to build personalized study strategies and help them master the basic concepts of writing. It features reliable solutions for delivering your course content and assignments, along with time-saving ways to grade and provide feedback. CengageNOW provides one-click-away results: the most common reporting tasks that instructors perform everyday are always just one click away wile working in the CengageNOW gradebook. For students, CengageNOW provides a diagnostic self-assessment and Personalized Study Plan that enables them to focus on what they need to learn and guides them in selecting activities that best match their learning styles. Visit academic.cengage.com/now to view a demonstration. To package access to CengageNOW for Writing with every new copy of this text, contact your Wadsworth representative.

Merriam-Webster's Collegiate® Dictionary, **11/e (Casebound)**
Available only when packaged with a Wadsworth text, the new 11/e of America's best-

selling hardcover dictionary merges print, CD-ROM, and Internet-based formats to deliver unprecedented accessibility and flexibility at one affordable price.

The Merriam-Webster Dictionary (Paperbound) Available only when packaged with a Wadsworth text, this high-quality, economical language reference covers the core vocabulary of everyday life with over 70,000 definitions.

Acknowledgments

Writing a textbook requires a tremendous amount of support and a great deal of patience, and we have been fortunate to have much assistance along the way from folks who have encouraged us—and pushed—when we needed it. First and foremost, we have been honored to work with Marita Sermolins, our top-notch development editor, who has had unending patience and many good ideas that have helped us shape the rough concept we had for this manuscript into a polished text. We're also grateful to Lyn Uhl, our publisher, who has been generously supportive of this project throughout the entire process. Jennifer Zourdos and Mandee Eckersley, marketing gurus extraordinaire, have never failed in their enthusiasm for this project and in their abilities to renew our excitement about it. Emily Ryan, Associate Media Editor, has helped to make our technological dreams a reality. Megan Power, Lauren Wheelock, and Annie Beck painstakingly guided the text through the production process, and Naomi Kornhauser and Timothy Sisler carefully tracked down the texts and images that we felt were essential to its message. To each of these people we owe a huge debt of gratitude—without them, our ideas would have no voice.

We are also extremely grateful to the students who were willing to share their writing in this book. Their examples are a critical component of the research guide, and their generosity in sharing their work truly appreciated.

We appreciate the outstanding comments and suggestions that we received from the following colleagues who took their time to review the manuscript while it was under construction:

Emory Reginald Abbott, Georgia Perimeter College
Susan Ariew, University of South Florida
Basak Tarkan-Blanco, Miami-Dade Community College—Kendall Campus
Richard Bogart, Essex County College
Arnold Bradford, Northern Virginia Community College
Eric Branscomb, Salem State College
Amy Braziller, Red Rocks Community College
Linda Brender, Macomb Community College
Carolyn Calhoon-Dillahunt, Yakima Valley Community College
Anita P. Chirco, Keuka College
Marisue Coy, Kentucky Wesleyan College
Barbara D'Angelo, Arizona State University
Kevin Eric DePew, Old Dominion University
Clark L. Draney, College of Southern Idaho
Don Erskine, Clark College
Elizabeth (Sharifa) Evans, Georgia Perimeter College
Douglas Eyman, George Mason University

Brian Fehler, Tarleton State University
Christina Fisanick, Xavier University
Cynthia Fischer, Harford Community College
Teddi Fishman, Clemson University
Letizia Guglielmo, Kennesaw State College
Christine Heilman, College of Mount Saint Joseph
Candy A. Henry, Westmoreland County Community College
Michael Hricik, Westmoreland County Community College
Greg Kemble, Yuba College
Cindy King, Berry College
Patricia Kohler, Syracuse University
Sharon L. Lagina, Wayne County Community College
Benjamin D. Lareau, Casper College
Gary Leising, Utica College
David C. Lowery, Jones County Junior College
Vickie Machen, Texas A&M University—Corpus Christi
Kate Mangelsdorf, University of Texas—El Paso
Janice Marshall, University of Wisconsin, Marathon County
Angela Megaw, Gainesville State College
Connie Mick, University of Notre Dame
Kathleen Mollick, Tarleton State University
Bryan Moore, Arkansas State University
Kris Muschal, Richland Community College
Fran O'Connor, Nassau Community College
Veronica Pantoja, Chandler-Gilbert Community College
Colleen A. Reilly, University of North Carolina at Wilmington
Janet Ridgeway, Syracuse University
Jenny R. Sadre-Orafai, Kennesaw State College
Jeff Simmons, Syracuse University
Jennie Stearns, Georgia Perimeter College
Jeremy Venema, Mesa Community College
Carol S. Warren, Georgia Perimeter College
Phillip Wedgeworth, Jones County Junior College
Anne Williams, Indiana University Purdue University Indiana
David Wilson-Okamura, East Carolina University
Cheryl Windham, Jones County Junior College

We are also personally grateful to our long-standing writing group members, Lisa Cahill and Veronica Pantoja, who helped us work through our ideas for this manuscript in the early stages and cheered us on as we wrote. And we're indebted to our colleagues at Mesa Community College and North Carolina State University, especially the members of the First-Year Composition Committee at MCC and the faculty in the First-Year Writing Program at NCSU, who have provided inspiration and guidance that continually encourage us to refine our approaches to teaching research.

And most importantly, we would like to thank our families—Stacey and Sam, and Tom—who have been patient, encouraging, and endlessly giving of their time and energy as we worked on this project. We could not ask for more supportive partners.

PART 1

▢ ▢ ▢ ▢ ▢ ▢ ▢ ▢ ▢ ▢ ▢ ▢

Preparing for Research

↓ ↓ ↓

[
RESEARCH IN PROGRESS:
Writing a Research Proposal
]

Why Research?

The word *research* often strikes fear into students' hearts. Why? Some students report that research is boring or that they're fearful of the grade that they'll receive when they turn in their assignments. Others are uncertain about their teachers' expectations, and they might be wary of the amount of time they'll have to put into a research assignment. These fears can be relieved if you understand how to do research, what the expectations are for your research, and how it will be assessed. In addition, choosing a topic in which you are interested and invested can make research helpful and enjoyable, even exciting, instead of boring. In Kendell's research scenario detailed on the next page, for example, she is interested in her topic, and she has experience with it. She will probably enjoy her research project because she sees an immediate purpose for the work she is doing. >

we'll explore → the rhetorical situation's effects on writing and research

reasons for conducting research

similarities and differences between academic research and research for other purposes

Research in Action

Author: As part of the service learning component of a class she is taking, Kendell decides to volunteer at a local soup kitchen.

Topic: Kendell wants to understand how to help homeless people in the soup kitchen who are also struggling with mental illness, so she starts to research schizophrenia and other serious psychological illnesses.

Audience: Kendell's original audience is her professor, but when the managers of the soup kitchen realize that she is doing the research, they ask Kendell to share the results with the other volunteers.

Purpose: Kendell needs to find reliable information that she can condense into manageable pieces to pass on to the other soup kitchen volunteers.

QUESTIONS

1. How do the elements of Kendell's situation help develop her research topic?

2. How might Kendell present her research results to her intended audience? How do the elements of her situation suggest this presentation or publication plan?

3. What other things might Kendell want to find out about her situation before beginning her research?

4. Can you imagine other aspects of the situation that would affect researching, writing, and publishing in this case?

Recognizing Research Contexts

You might be surprised to realize that you've been conducting research for a long time. Whenever you have a question to answer, you decide what kind of information you will need to find the answer; that is, you decide what kind of research you need to conduct to answer the question. In school, you might be used to thinking of research in terms of going to the library, searching for information on the Internet, or writing a report. Research happens in other contexts as well, though. For example, you might have conducted research about which college to attend, or you might research a particular company if you are applying for a job. Research certainly takes place in academic contexts, but it also takes place in our everyday lives. The goal of this book is to help you develop strategies for conducting research in all sorts of scenarios: college classes, work settings, and various personal situations. Sometimes research involves a large-scale investigation, but more often it is pretty informal.

All sorts of research have one thing in common, though—research is highly situational. For example, imagine that someone close to you is experiencing heart problems, and you want him or her to go to the best doctor available. Not only do you need to do research on the local doctors and their expertise, but you also have to research the person's resources (especially medical insurance coverage). Answering the question "Which heart doctor should my mother go to?" requires some research. And although the final product of your research may simply be the name of a specific doctor, the reading, writing, and thinking you put into the process is considerable and depends on multiple variables within the situation.

People encounter research questions every day—questions about which car to buy, whether to lease or purchase that car, whether to adopt a pet, where (and how) to apply for a specific job, which utility company to choose, where to apply for scholarships and financial aid for school, which store to purchase textbooks from at the beginning of the semester, or which classes to take. While you are in school, you'll also conduct academic research on a variety of topics. Even school assignments are situational, though; they depend on the teacher's expectations, the course, the discipline, and a variety of other factors, such as:

- topic chosen or assigned

- length of the paper or project

- whether you conduct primary research

- whether you interpret something or critique someone else's interpretation

- whether you develop a theory about a phenomenon or test someone else's theory

- the expected product: a developed argument? a report? a description of a methodology? a review of previous research on the subject?

You will continue to encounter research situations outside of the academic setting. In the workplace, you might encounter research questions—either ones that are assigned to you (What do we need to include in our proposal in order to win the contract?) or issues that intrigue you (What salary would be competitive and fair for the work that I will be doing in my new job?). Working through the activities and projects described in this book will help you with the everyday research that you already do, the academic research you'll be expected to do, and the workplace research that you'll want to do in the future.

Regardless of the purpose of the research, the general research principles remain the same, although the time and effort you put into your research might vary depending on the situation and context of your research. This book will guide you through developing your own research process and developing arguments that consider the **rhetorical situation**. The rhetorical situation is the context surrounding a particular research or writing task. In other words, we will ask you to consider how several contextual factors influence your research:

- **topic**—what you are researching

- **purpose**—why you are researching it

- **audience**—to whom you are writing (reporting results)

- **author**—who you are and the experience you bring to the issue you are researching

When you consider the rhetorical situation of your writing, you are considering these elements. These factors influence not only the research that you do and how you conduct it but also your conclusions and your presentation of those conclusions to your readers. Additionally, becoming more thoughtful about your own research process will make you a more careful reader of the research and arguments of others.

> reflect >

How Have You Conducted Research Before?

Think of a situation recently in which you had to conduct research to solve a problem. Perhaps you had to solve some transportation problems in getting to school, or maybe you had to come up with a solution to a challenge at work. You might even consider the choice that you made about where to enroll in classes or which degree to pursue. Answer the following questions about that experience.

1. Describe the situation. Why did you need to conduct research? What did you need to find out? Try to state your challenge as a question that you needed to answer.

2. Who was involved in the situation—just you, or did the research and conclusion(s) affect others? Did you conduct the research alone or with others?

3. How did you explore possible answers to your question? Where did you look for information? Did you ask anyone for advice? Did you look for information that others had written, or did you gather information by talking to people?

4. What conclusion(s) did you come to? How did you decide on that conclusion?

5. Were you satisfied that you had considered all the options or did you make a quick decision? If time was a factor, was there something you would have done differently if you had had more time?

6. How did you share the results of your research? Who wanted or needed the information and how did you present it to them?

Identifying Research Purposes

You might conduct research for a number of reasons, but each time you're essentially doing the same thing—answering a question. In other words, there are a multitude of purposes you may fulfill by answering research questions. You might choose which college to apply to or what car to buy. You might decide where to live or which name to choose for your baby. You might point out an often-overlooked reason for the start of World War II or propose a more efficient process for your company. Each of these personal, academic, and work-related situations requires that you ask a question and then find an answer.

The most traditionally understood purpose for research is to answer an academic question. For example, a history professor might ask the class to dig a little deeper into the history of World War II and to question the reasons that traditional textbooks give for the war. This research question requires the student not only to answer the question, "What are the traditionally cited reasons for the start of World War II?" but also to consider other possible causes of the war. After looking at numerous textbooks to understand which reasons are often cited, the student needs to access highly specialized references (history journals, discussion boards, even individual scholars) to search out other possibilities. Because this is an academic assignment, the student has access to traditional academic resources: library materials, databases, and professors. However, one student in the class may have a family member who fought on the European front in World War II. Another student's family may have emigrated from Japan after the war. These students may have access to personal and individualized resources that relate to the cultural situation at the beginning of and during World War II.

Such a research project is a fairly traditional example of the purpose and situation of a research assignment in a school setting. You will likely find that you will adapt your research process to the research question and the context in which you need to answer it. For any research question and context, it's important to be aware of the rhetorical situation.

How Do Research Processes Compare?

Think about two times you've conducted research in the past: one when you conducted research for a school project and one when you conducted research to answer a question for yourself. Think about the processes that you used in each situation and respond to the following questions.

	Academic Research	Personal Research
Why did you conduct this research? If you were given instructions, what were they?		
What questions did you ask?		
How did you start?		
What went right and what went wrong?		
What were the outcomes of your research?		
How would you conduct your research differently if you were to do it again?		

Considering Elements of the Rhetorical Situation

Whenever we conduct research, and especially when we share the results of our research, we must consider each element of the rhetorical situation of our research and writing: the topic, purpose, audience, and author. In the history project example, the professor requested that students write an essay about possible causes of World War II. Such an essay would require that the students demonstrate their understanding of both the generally mentioned causes of World War II and possible alternative causes. On the other hand, the professor might request that rather than write an essay, the students use the results of their research in a letter to the author of the course's history textbook, proposing that a lesser-mentioned reason be given more attention in the textbook's next edition. In this letter, students would have to demonstrate their understanding of World War II (the topic) and how and why content decisions are made for textbooks (the purpose is to influence this decision), while addressing the needs of the textbook author (audience) and keeping in mind their experience in studying with this textbook (author).

Each of the four elements of the rhetorical situation is shaped and influenced by the others. (See Figure 1.1.) The topic you choose to write about may be influenced by your purpose for researching, especially if you are assigned a research paper in a class. Or your topic might be influenced by who you are and what you are interested in as the author. The way you approach and narrow your topic might also be influenced by the audience for your research and that audience's expectations. Being aware of the rhetorical situation for your writing and research will help you to answer your research question effectively.

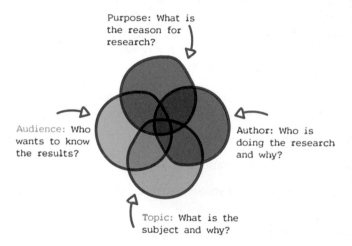

Figure 1.1   The Rhetorical Situation

Let's go back to Kendell's research situation outlined at the beginning of the chapter. If Kendell had been doing the research purely for her own interest, the author and audience for the research would completely overlap; in fact, they would be the same. (See Figure 1.2.)

Figure 1.2   Overlap of Author and Audience

As we know, though, Kendell's topic and purpose for researching originally arose out of the class she was taking. Therefore, Kendell's audience widens to include her professor; but her audience still overlaps somewhat with the author because Kendell is interested in the topic herself, too. (See Figure 1.3.)

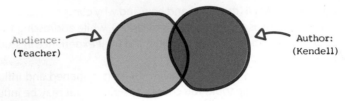

Audience:
(Teacher)

Author:
(Kendell)

Figure 1.3   Kendell's Audience Widens

When Kendell shared her research goals with managers of the soup kitchen, she found that other people were interested in her research. Kendell's audience widened even more. She must be aware of this because different audiences have different expectations.

The rhetorical situation of Kendell's research and writing affects the way she conducts her research and the kinds of resources she chooses. What types of resources might Kendell have assumed were appropriate for just personal knowledge? How might she change her research processes and the types of resources she looks for if she is going to present her information in a formal research paper? And how might those shift even further if she presents her research more informally to other volunteers at the soup kitchen?

As another example, imagine that you are applying for scholarships so that you can continue your education. First, you must conduct research to determine

- which scholarships to apply for, and

- what to write in your applications.

Imagine that in the first stage of your research you locate two scholarships for which you would like to apply:

1. One is sponsored by the institution you attend and is given by the alumni association to a student who demonstrates financial need and has a promising academic record.

2. One is sponsored by a local church and is given to a member who is actively involved in the church and demonstrates a commitment to both community service and academic achievement.

For both scholarship applications, you must conduct research to determine what each organization values and which aspects of your experience you should include in the application. What would be relevant for both scholarship committees to hear? In your application to the alumni association, you might discuss your previous success in school and include specific praise for the institution you are attending. In your application to the local church, you might include information about your school record, but it will also be important to include information about your involvement in community service. The expectations and values of your two audiences will most likely result in your writing two different scholarship applications, even though the purpose is the same (asking for money for school), the author is the same (you), and the topic (also you!) is the same. All elements of the rhetorical situation shape and affect your research and writing; any of the elements might carry more weight than the others in any given situation. (See Figures 1.4 and 1.5.)

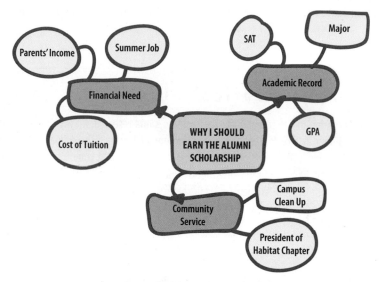

Figure 1.4   Cluster Map of Ideas for Alumni Scholarship Application

For more information about cluster maps and how to use them in your writing, see the appendix.

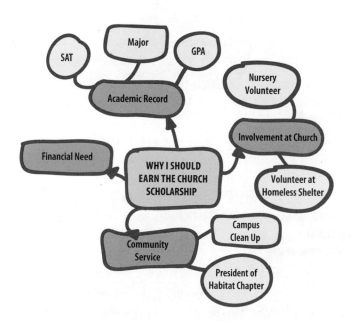

Figure 1.5   Cluster Map of Ideas for Church Scholarship Application

Considering the rhetorical situation of research and writing is central to the discussion of research in this book. You will be asked to reflect on your purpose for conducting research, your audience, your position and influences as the author, and the way your topic shapes (and is shaped by) your research. In addition, we will ask you to consider how each element of the rhetorical situation influences the others in the research you are conducting. Awareness of the rhetorical situation will help you conduct successful research and communicate the results of your research so that you can achieve your goals.

> reflect <

How Do Rhetorical Situations Compare?

Think of a situation in the recent past that required some research. Maybe you were planning a celebratory dinner at a restaurant and needed to look at menus, price ranges, locations, accommodations, and so on. Or you might focus on a research project that you completed for one of your courses. Think about the rhetorical situation of your research and fill in a Venn diagram like the following one with the four elements of your rhetorical situation. Try to pay attention to the size and placement of your circles based on the importance of and relationship between the different elements.

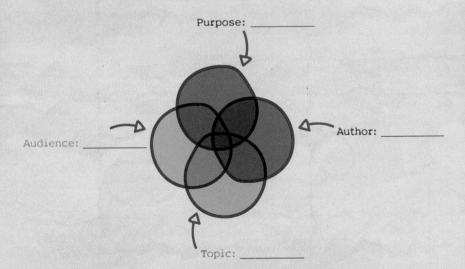

Purpose: _____

Author: _____

Audience: _____

Topic: _____

Compare and contrast your situation with other members of the class using the following questions:

1. What motivated you to conduct the research?

2. What was the topic, or subject, of your research? Was the topic rooted to a specific time and location? Why or why not?

3. Who was the audience for your research? Who was affected by the results? Who might have been an unintended audience that was affected by your research? How did knowing your audience affect your research?

4. As the author, what was your experience with this topic before you began to research it? What was your experience with the audience? How did your experiences affect your research?

5. How do your rhetorical situations compare with those of other members of your class? How do your processes for adapting to the specific rhetorical situations compare?

Entering a Conversation

As you can see, research does not happen in a vacuum. Research projects develop in a particular situation, from a question that someone asks. Sometimes it helps to think of your rhetorical situation as a conversation that you are entering—and you are entering that conversation by asking a question (or answering a question someone is asking you). So what does this mean exactly?

Imagine that a friend has invited you to a party and you're a little apprehensive about going because you don't know many of the people who will be there. Perhaps you feel a little out of your element at first when you walk in the door. You don't see many people that you know, and there are already several groups around the room having lively conversations. Your friend immediately sees people that he knows and runs over to say hello. You're left on your own. What do you do? Perhaps you would circulate through the room, listening to what's going on, until you find a conversation that sounds interesting to you.

You might listen for a topic or person you know about already, or you might listen for something that is interesting for another reason. As you join the circle of people in discussion, you might listen for a little bit before saying anything—you wouldn't want to say something inappropriate, and it's best to find out what has been said already. It is wise to listen to the ongoing conversation before jumping in and adding to it. Perhaps an entry point into that conversation is a question—and you might think of your research in the same way.

As you choose a topic to research and a question on which to focus, you are entering a conversation in progress. People have most likely been talking about this topic for a while, and you can learn by "listening" to what's been said already. You might do this by reading things that others have written, or you might interview people who are knowledgeable about the subject to learn what they know. The important thing is to remember that you're most likely jumping in mid-stream—the conversation has been going on already and you'll have some catch-up work to do before you can contribute to the discussion. Part of understanding the rhetorical situation of your research

Listening to Conversations in Progress.

techno_tip >

> Listen to Conversations in Progress Online <

For an interactive tutorial about listening to conversations in progress online, go to *Student Resources* on the online resource center at www.cengage.com/english/Miller-Cochran/WGTR.

With the prevalence of the Internet, many professional and academic conversations are occurring more quickly than ever, and a little less formally than in traditional print venues. A number of professionals have blogs, or online journals, in which they reflect and share their thoughts and processes on various topics. For example, Alan Levine, an instructional technologist, has published CogDogBlog for a number of years (http://cogdogblog.com/).

One way to start listening to conversations in progress is to read dynamic Internet materials produced in blogs. You can find blogs on a variety of topics at the following sites:

- ☐ BlogCatalog: http://www.blogcatalog.com
- ☐ BlogHub: http://www.bloghub.com
- ☐ Blogarama: http://www.blogarama.com
- ☐ Feedster: http://feedster.com
- ☐ Technorati: http://www.technorati.com

Find a blog that is interesting to you, read through some of the posts and comments, and respond to the following questions:

- ☐ What are people on this blog talking about?
- ☐ How do the different blogs relate to one another? How are they similar? How are they different?
- ☐ What subtopics did you learn about while following the conversations? Do some of the subtopics cause you to reconsider your understanding of the issue?

© Reprinted by permission of Alan Levine.

If you'd like to read more about blogs, see the discussion of blogs in Chapter 4.

In his blog, Levine reflects on various technologies and their incorporation into the education process. His peers read his blog as a way to keep up on innovative ideas for teaching with technologies. ☐

topic is learning what has already been said so that you can focus on how you want to enter the conversation.

Many people come to college with some experience and skill in everyday research in their personal lives; some people also come with experience in academic research. Instead of claiming to teach research, this book helps the experienced researcher (you are experienced, after all, because you've been asking and answering questions for many years) become a more proficient and effective academic researcher, especially in contexts that may be unfamiliar, such as a college course.

Research and Writing Processes

All writing and research has a rhetorical context. Just as the different elements of the rhetorical situation (purpose, audience, author, and topic) affect a topic or research question, the rhetorical situation influences research processes and the writing of their results. For example, if your instructor says that you will need at least two academic journal articles to support the argument you present in your paper, then your research will probably focus (at least at first) on finding academic journal articles. Similarly, in the example on the next page, if Qi knows that he wants to attend a school in New York City, his research will be limited to schools within that area.

You will also likely be influenced by the subject matter that you are researching and writing about. Imagine that you are conducting a research project in a physics class on the Doppler effect. Your research process will be influenced by the accepted research practices in the field of physics, and your final written product will probably need to follow a specified >

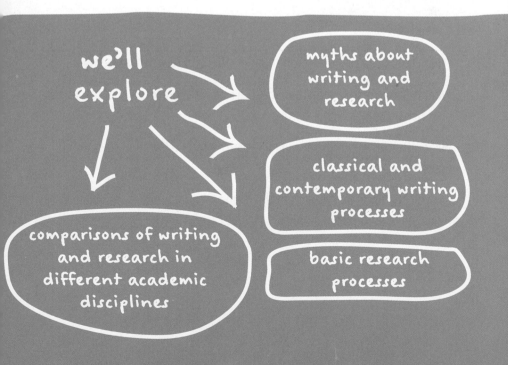

we'll explore

myths about writing and research

classical and contemporary writing processes

comparisons of writing and research in different academic disciplines

basic research processes

Author: Qi wants to come to the United States, New York City (NYC) specifically, to go to college. He has time to do research before coming to NYC, and he will be in NYC for six months before starting school.

Topic: Of the multitude of colleges in NYC that Qi could attend, which one should he choose and why?

Audience: Although Qi is the primary audience for his research and decision making, there are other stakeholders who are invested in his topic. Qi's family, especially if they are paying for a portion of his schooling, care tremendously about which school he attends. Also, many other international students who may want to come to the United States for college might be interested in his ultimate decision as well as his criteria and processes for selecting a college.

Purpose: Qi has to select the most appropriate college to attend with some of the following considerations: cost of tuition for an international student, language instruction and support because he is still learning English, commute time because he will not live in NYC proper, and curriculum—he wants to study to be an engineer.

QUESTIONS

1. What elements of Qi's rhetorical situation affect his research process?

2. What is going on in Qi's life that affects his research process? What resources does Qi have that will help him?

3. What obstacles might Qi have in his research process? What unexpected opportunities?

4. Can you imagine other aspects of the rhetorical situation that would affect researching, writing, and publishing in this case?

> format for a laboratory report. Knowing the rhetorical situation for your writing will likely influence the writing process, too. You would probably have an idea of the format your writing should follow (a lab report) and your subject matter, so your writing process would likely focus more on drafting and revising than on defining a topic.

Processes and Rhetorical Situations

Writing and research processes are often described in simple, one-size-fits-all formulas, but no formula will fit every writing and research situation you might encounter. Although it can be helpful to start a project by following a formulaic research and writing process, you will often discover that you need to repeat some steps, skip others, and occasionally loop back to the beginning again. Not all research follows the scientific method, and even when it does, the scientific method is often a much messier process than the charts in elementary school led us to believe. Similarly, not all writing follows the step-by-step process of prewriting, drafting, revising, editing, and publishing. You might get to the editing stage, show the paper to a friend, and then realize that you need to start over from square one. Writing and research processes need to be flexible enough to meet the needs of each rhetorical situation. This research guide will introduce you to a variety of strategies and tools that you can use in research and writing. Our hope is that you will adapt these tools to help you address your specific projects.

Myths about Writing and Research Processes

Before you get started, however, you should have realistic expectations of what your research and writing processes might look like. Many of us carry around common myths about writing and research in our minds, but those myths don't measure up to the reality of what we encounter as we start working. If you first recognize those myths as unrealistic, then you can avoid a lot of frustration later.

    ⊘ **Myth 1: You must complete each step in the writing process.** The writing process is often described as linear, as shown in Figure 2.1. In this representation, writing is a simple process where you start at the top, with prewriting (or invention), systematically work your way down through each step, and finish with a perfectly written product. Writing often does not happen this way, though. We don't intend to say that people cannot, or do not, sometimes follow these steps in this order and finish with an effective piece of writing. In fact, this textbook presents a process of working through a major research project that appears to be linear, presenting one step at a time, chapter by chapter. Although we have a plan in mind, most of the time the actual process is much messier. Sometimes we have to

Figure 2.1   Myth 1

revisit steps more than once, and sometimes we even skip steps (depending on the rhetorical situation) that we might return to later in the process.

You already know that many casual writing situations do not require every step outlined in Figure 2.1. For example, a grocery list might require revising, especially to make sure everything is on the list. If someone else is going to do the shopping, you might also proofread the list before giving it to him or her, revising the list for clarity based on the new audience. One way you can make the writing process flexible enough to work for a specific rhetorical situation is by following the steps that are needed for a given writing task. Give yourself the freedom to skip steps if they are not necessary or to repeat steps if some require additional time.

   Myth 2: Each step is equally important and time-consuming. Deleting steps is not the only way writing processes vary from one another. The linear image of the writing process from myth 1 also gives the faulty impression that each step involved in the process will take the same amount of time, energy, and work. Depending on the demands of the writing project and the rhetorical situation, you may spend lots of time in one area and very little in another (Figure 2.2). Not only can the steps of the process take varying amounts of time and energy, but your process can change or shift in the middle of the project as a result of the process itself and what you have found in your research so far.

   Myth 3: The steps are linear. The aforementioned myths refer to research and writing processes as more or less linear. Even if you skip steps in these processes, or if you spend more or less time on a certain step, the represented process still looks like a neat, clean line. Many people bounce back and forth among the steps, though (Figure 2.3). Some very common moves include going back to the invention, or the thinking and planning, stage once you've begun researching. Your initial research might bring up some issues you had not considered, and so you need to move to a different step in the process. Likewise, many writers find that once they start drafting, or once someone else looks over their project, a large gap becomes evident and they need to go back to the invention or research stage.

Although it is easier to teach and talk about writing and research as single, linear processes, in reality, writing and research processes are all variations on the theme of the mythical, linear process. Most researchers and writers start their projects with the linear process in mind, but once they get working, they usually start adapting. They also find that

Figure 2.2   Myth 2

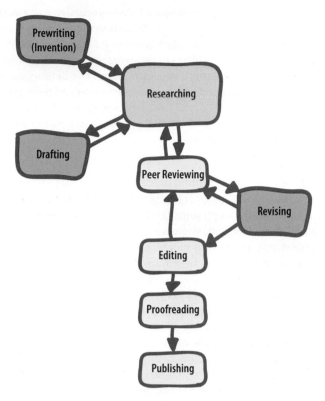

Figure 2.3 Myth 3

as a need arises, they might have to bounce a few steps back to repeat some work in a particular step. For example, if you were reviewing for your end-of-year exams, you might reread a chapter or two of material you did not understand and only skim the rest. And you might even reskim that chapter right before the test. You know what you need to study, or research, or write, so your process fits your needs.

This book will help you become a more *proficient* researcher, not necessarily an *efficient* researcher. Good research is a messy, and somewhat recursive, process. Your research and writing process might require you to revisit some steps out of order, or it might even require going back to the drawing board to refine, restate, or reconsider your topic. Very rarely does research happen in a linear fashion and when it does, the researcher has usually missed something. Take this example from everyday life: While answering "What do I need from the grocery store?" you might refer to the household's weekly menu and refer to cookbooks for items on that menu. However, if you do not also check what is, or is not, in the refrigerator or cupboard, you could find multiple trips to the grocery store in your future. You might go several times from the list, to the refrigerator, to a couple of recipes, and to the coupons in the newspaper before finally answering your original question.

Good writers and researchers are aware of these recursive steps and even more aware of their rhetorical situations. Effective writers and researchers allow the individual rhetorical situation to influence their process for every project and help them determine what step to take next. Writers have several processes to choose from when working on a writing project. The more you know about the options you have in tackling a research and writing project, the more successful you can be in completing it.

Writing Processes

You may have encountered descriptions of "the writing process" in classes you have taken. A listing of the steps of the writing process might include some of the following: invention or prewriting, researching, drafting, peer review, revising, editing, proofreading, and publishing. Some of these steps relate loosely to principles of classical rhetoric, and it is helpful to understand where some of these ideas came from first. As you develop your own successful writing processes, you might find that a combination of some of these approaches will work best in certain situations.

Foundations in Classical Rhetoric

Aristotle defined rhetoric as "finding the available means of persuasion." He acknowledged that although you may not use all of the information and materials you have discovered and developed, it is important to identify them all so that you have choices. Ancient Greek and Roman rhetoricians kept the purpose of writing (or speaking) in mind and the audience to whom it would be delivered, and this understanding of the rhetorical situation governed the ways they developed an argument. Ancient rhetoricians described the various aspects of discovering these "means of persuasion" through the Five Canons of Rhetoric.

- **Invention** refers to discovering and developing the possible arguments that might persuade an audience. Invention was of the utmost importance to ancient rhetoricians because it is the stage where the author discovers what he or she will say.

- **Arrangement** refers to the order in which an author might present the information found during the invention stage.

- **Style** addresses how the author says what he or she has to say.

- **Memory** refers both to the memorization of a speech that will be delivered or performed and to the memorization of the commonplaces that the author can recall to assist with the first stage of invention.

- **Delivery** deals with how something is presented, or delivered, to the audience. Today we might relate delivery to the publishing of a piece of writing. □

Publishing a piece of writing is discussed in Chapter 11, "Sharing the Results."

Each of these canons of rhetoric addresses an important aspect of writing that you will need to consider as you work on your own research project. Some of the canons may be more important to you than others, and in writing classes, we often use specific strategies to break them down into manageable chunks.

Invention

Aristotle's emphasis on finding the "available means of persuasion" places a high importance on the canon of invention, and this book helps you work through the stages of invention in your own research and writing. Invention is similar to what you might have referred to as prewriting, a stage where the author (or *rhetor*) brainstorms, researches, and "invents" possible ideas and arguments. In this book, we prefer the term *invention* to *prewriting* because these kinds of activities can be useful at several stages of the writing process—not just before you start drafting. If we return to Qi from the beginning of the chapter, he might do some brainstorming about schools that he has heard of or read about at the beginning of his research process. But imagine that he has started drafting a letter to his parents about his top three schools after arriving in the United States, and then a friend mentions another school and program that he has not heard of. He might go back to the invention stage and do a little more research before he continues to draft his letter.

Careful and thorough invention leads to effective writing. You might have noticed that much of the research process contributes to invention—research itself can be a means of discovering what you want to say. As you work through the activities in this text, you'll notice that many of the "Write" activities fall under the category of invention. We want to encourage you to think thoroughly about what you are going to say before you commit to a finished written product.

Ancient rhetors often practiced invention by using common topics to generate ideas. These topics were called *commonplaces*, or *topoi*. You may have been taught and asked to practice certain kinds of essays that have been developed from specific interpretations of the commonplaces. For example, you might have been asked to write definition, comparison, or cause/effect papers; these patterns of development were originally developed as commonplaces to generate ideas and arguments. Think about it—if you're developing an argument, it can be useful to think about how you might define your issue, what you might compare it to, and what the causes and effects are. As you construct your argument, you might find that one or more of these patterns of development will work well for your rhetorical situation. ▢

The patterns of argument are discussed in more detail in Chapter 11.

During invention, writers try to explore and focus their topics. Even with the common use of computers and word-processing programs like Microsoft Word®, many writers do a lot of their invention by hand with pen and paper. Because the purpose of many invention activities is to explore topics, they are often visual. Common invention activities that you might be familiar with include brainstorming or listing, journaling, freewriting, looping, cluster mapping, outlining, and asking journalistic questions. We'll ask you to try many of these activities as you develop your research project. More information is provided on these activities in the appendix.

Researching

Much like invention, research can be useful at any stage of your writing process. Research might include gathering information from resources found online or in the library, in the form of secondary research, or it might include gathering data first-hand through activities such as interviewing people, observing, or distributing and collecting questionnaires, as in primary research. ▢

These types of research are discussed in more detail in Chapters 4 and 5.

Drafting

Depending on your rhetorical situation and writing preferences, you might find that you like to start with drafting and that sitting down to write actually helps you generate ideas. Drafting includes any part of your writing process that involves generating text that you could imagine ending up in a final version. You might notice that there could be some overlap between drafting and invention—remember, the steps are not always linear, separate, easily identifiable categories. They are fluid steps, and you should feel comfortable moving from one to another, or combining them, whenever it suits your rhetorical situation.

As you draft, you might prefer to start with a blank screen. Or, you might take all of the relevant invention activities that you've completed and try to weave them together (thus avoiding the blank screen). Invention and drafting are very closely related, and if you are doing invention from the beginning of your writing process, you probably are doing some drafting as well.

> reflect <

How Do You Write Best?

Answer the following questions as you think about your writing preferences. You might consider all kinds of situations, but especially focus on intense writing tasks that you have completed such as academic writing and research assignments. Understanding your preferences might make it easier to tackle the drafting stage.

1. Where do you like to write? Do you like to write at home? in a certain room? Do you like to go somewhere specific to write? Would you rather write indoors or outdoors?

2. What kind of environment do you like to write in? Do you like to be around other people? Do you like to be alone? Do you like to have "noise" in the background (such as music, television, other people), or do you like to have a quiet environment?

3. When do you like to write? At what time of day do you like to write?

4. Do you prefer to write on the computer or on paper? Why?

5. If you prefer to write on the computer, what software program do you use? If you prefer to write on paper, what kind of paper do you use? Do you write in a notebook? Do you use pen or pencil?

6. Do you follow any special rituals when you write? Do you have a favorite place to sit? Do you like to have a cup of coffee next to you?

7. Do you generally share your writing with others? If so, at what stage? If not, why not?

8. If you share writing with others, what do you do with their comments? What kind of comments do you expect?

9. Do you like to outline your ideas first? Do you draft first? In other words, what is the first step you take when you write?

10. Where do you start writing? Do you start at the beginning? The end? Somewhere in the middle? If there's a title, do you write it first or last?

11. How do you know when you are finished writing?

Share your preferences with a classmate or friend, and see if you gather any new ideas about writing situations that might work well for you. Keep these preferences in mind as you draft because you'll do your best writing in *your* optimal circumstances.

Peer Review

During the peer review stage you get to see your writing through the eyes of your audience, or an approximated audience, a luxury that you often don't have when you hand in writing for an assignment or send it out to be published. In a peer review workshop, you might be asked to read and comment on the work of another classmate while he or she reads and comments on yours. If you are in a work environment, you might share what you have written with a colleague who is knowledgeable about your project or who will be able to help you imagine how your audience would respond to what you have written. You might even share writing with friends or family members for feedback. Anytime you have someone who is not formally evaluating your work read it with the intention of commenting on it or helping you to see it from another person's perspective, you are participating in peer review.

Peer review is not the same thing as proofreading. Peer review includes reading and commenting on more global features of a piece of writing, like the development of ideas or the evidence used to support an argument; proofreading generally focuses on surface features such as correct use of grammar and consistent adherence to a particular citation style. The three types of changes you might make to your draft as you polish and refine it for publication are typically revising, editing, and proofreading. Peer review could include gathering comments and feedback on all three of these areas.

You might already have experience with peer review from a previous class. Unfortunately, many students report having unfavorable impressions of peer review, often because they didn't receive useful feedback from their peers. If you have ever had a classmate write something like "This looks good to me," during a peer review, or if you've had peers give you conflicting feedback, you might have an unfavorable impression as well.

The key to good peer review is asking the right questions of your peers and helping them understand what kind of feedback you need. Depending on your stage in the writing process, you might need different kinds of feedback. If you are at an early stage of writing, or if you don't have any specific criteria for the project you are working on, you might try variations of the following questions:

- What works well in this piece of writing?

- What did you want to know more about as you read?

- What was unclear in this piece of writing?

- What suggestions would you make for a revision?

These questions will prompt peer reviewers to give a balanced response, discussing things that you did well and things to consider in a revision. You might also draft some questions based on the specifics of your rhetorical situation. For example, have you done an adequate job of addressing the interests and expectations of your audience? If you were writing an annual report for your job, did you provide the information your superiors would be expecting? Are there other issues they might want to see addressed in the report?

Try following these guidelines the next time you participate in a peer review:

- Ask for both positive comments and constructive feedback. It's helpful to know what you're doing well—not just what you should revise.

- Ask your peer to ask questions if there are things he or she finds confusing in the text. Questions invite a response, and responding to questions written on your draft during a peer review will help you begin revising.

- If you have specific criteria for an assignment or project you are working on, ask your peer to address each of the criteria in his or her review. If there are numerous criteria to consider, perhaps have several peers read your work and have each one look at separate criteria.

- Finally, offer to review your peers' work as well. When you write a response for one of your peers, write the kind of review that would be helpful to you.

techno_tip >

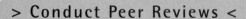

> Conduct Peer Reviews <

 For an interactive tutorial about peer reviewing technologies, go to *Student Resources* on the online resource center at www.cengage.com/english/ Miller-Cochran/WGTR.

Several technological tools can facilitate peer review, either in a classroom setting or in a work environment. If you have access to different kinds of technology, you might try one of the following variations on peer review:

- If you are using a software program such as Microsoft Word®, try using the "Insert Comment" feature to comment on specific parts of the text. If you have time, have several peers electronically comment on the same document. If you switch computers, be certain to enter your information under "User Information" in the word processor before entering your comments.

- If you have access to a closed discussion board for your class or workplace, you could post a draft of what you are working on with specific questions for peer review. Then your peers can post their responses.

- If you are comfortable using instant messaging software, you could schedule a chat with the peer(s) who read your writing. Chats work best one-on-one or, if you have access to a chat room, in very small groups. If you include more than four people, the feedback can be difficult to process in a chat environment.

Revising

Revising your writing generally refers to larger-scale changes you make to a document. As you revise, you will probably focus on the content of your writing. Revision can be challenging, especially when you have worked very hard on your original draft. You might be reluctant to delete things that you spent time writing, but revising is an act of refining. Sometimes revision will require the addition of ideas, sometimes movement, and sometimes deletion. The Nobel Prize-winning writer Elie Wiesel wrote that "Writing is not like painting where you add. . . . Writing is more like a sculpture where you remove, you eliminate in order to make the work visible." The important thing is to keep an open mind, and sometimes that requires having distance from what you have written. Having some time between drafting and revising will also help you to see your writing with new eyes (re-vision).

Editing

Similar to revision, editing is a way of refining and polishing your paper. When you edit, however, your focus is not on the larger-scale issues of content and organization but rather on issues of style and fluidity. Editing might include looking at your use of transitions, for example, to help the reader follow your train of thought in a piece of writing. You also might look at sentence variety in your writing or the overall tone of your piece. As you edit, you could pay attention to consistency in your writing. Try reading your essay out loud to "hear" how it sounds and how the language flows, or you might ask someone else to read it to you; either reading will help you to hear things that you otherwise might not notice when editing silently.

techno_tip >

> Read Your Writing Out Loud <

It can be helpful to read your own essay aloud to hear how it sounds, and it can sometimes be even more beneficial to hear someone else read it. If you feel uncomfortable having someone read to you, however, or if you simply don't have someone you can ask to do it, you can have your computer read your essay to you. Granted, it's not quite the same thing, and the computer is not going to tell you when something doesn't "sound right." The computer also won't stumble over things that are awkward—it will just plow right on through. But hearing the computer read your writing is a very different experience from reading it yourself. If you have never tried it, you might find that you notice areas for revision, editing, and proofreading that you didn't notice before.

You can download a free trial version of Read-Please, a software package that will read your writing to you, at http://www.readplease.com.

Proofreading

Many instructors combine editing and proofreading under one label. They are separated here, however, because we want to highlight that there are several different steps to polishing your writing. In addition to looking at issues of style and fluidity when you edit, you will also need to proofread your work, focusing on surface features such as grammar, punctuation, and citations. Obviously, you can do a first round of proofreading by yourself, perhaps referring to the spelling and grammar checkers that are built into most word-processing programs. However, you need to be aware that they will not catch all of the errors in your paper. For example, many of them are "dumb" and do not know whether your sentence needs *there*, *their*, or *they're*. Automated grammar and spelling checkers might be a good place to start proofreading your writing, but you won't want to stop there for most rhetorical situations. If you are working on a piece of writing that needs to be polished in its final draft, you definitely will want to proofread carefully yourself and also have someone else read your paper.

> reflect <

What Are Your Writing Idiosyncrasies?

Over time, most people realize that they have a writing style that tends to rely on certain words and sentence structures, and they tend to make the same errors over and over again. For example, when one of the authors was in college she had an instructor who repeatedly marked her papers for passive voice. She spent an entire semester focusing on learning what passive voice was, how it functioned in a sentence, how to identify it in a sentence, and how to correct it. Now she is very aware of when she uses passive voice and only uses it to make a specific point in her writing. This was a trouble spot that she identified and keeps track of in her writing.

Answer the following questions to start a list of the idiosyncrasies of your writing style.

☐ What have friends, family members, and instructors identified as strengths in your writing? What have they said that you do well?

☐ What words, phrases, or sentence styles do you find yourself repeating in your writing?

☐ What things do you always find yourself correcting in your own writing? What things have friends and family members politely corrected for you?

☐ If you still have them, pull out graded writing assignments from past classes. Read through the comments. What common themes run through the comments?

☐ What parts of your own writing (paragraphs, complex sentences, semicolons, passive voice, etc.) do you already know you should spend some time focusing on and improving?

If you know you have problems in a specific area, ask someone to pay close attention to it when he or she is peer reviewing your writing. If you tend to overuse certain words or sentence styles, consider checking to make sure that you add variety to your writing. Also use this list to help you select one aspect of your writing that you would like to work on improving during a specific amount of time (perhaps during a semester). Consider sharing this list with your instructor to discuss methods by which you might improve upon specific trouble areas.

Publishing

Once you have brainstormed, researched, drafted, revised, rethought, edited, drafted again, edited, and proofread (whew!), you will be ready to publish your writing. Publishing could include a variety of ways of presenting your writing to your readers. For example, you might print a paper and turn it in to your instructor. Or you might upload your research onto a Web site. Or you might send an article in to a newspaper. Or you might turn in a report to your supervisor at work. Your choice of publication method will be influenced, of course, by your rhetorical situation. The final "publication" of Qi's research and writing at the beginning of the chapter would likely be quite different from the final form of a paper that you might turn in for a class in school. ▢

Research Processes

Although *research* is listed as one of the possible steps in the list of contemporary writing processes, that step can be broken down into a series of smaller steps, or processes. And as we did with *writing processes*, we'll describe *research processes*; however, realize that individual research processes are just as rhetorically situated and variable. Although we present the steps as a list, and we put them in a specific order in this textbook, you should always adapt the approach you use for the specific writing/research project you are undertaking.

> Publishing occurs in many ways, and Chapter 11 talks about the different methods to present your research.

In Chapter 1 we mentioned that the simplest way to understand research is that research answers a question. Many writing tasks qualify as research because they require the answering of a question (like making a grocery list), even though they do not feel like major research projects. However, there are five basic steps in research that you should follow when you take on any research project larger than a grocery list:

1. Identify your topic/problem and develop a focused research question. (Chapter 3)

2. Assess what you know and what you need to know and develop a research plan. (Chapter 4)

3. Locate and document resources. (Chapters 4–8 and 12–15)

4. Analyze resources and develop the answer to your research question. (Chapters 9 and 10)

5. Present the answer to your research question while carefully citing your resources. (Chapters 10 and 11)

Many students make the mistake of simplifying their research process down to step 3, locating resources. Without the careful preparation of steps 1 and 2, however, as well as the careful analysis and presentation of the results of your findings in steps 4 and 5, the work in step 3 can be completely overwhelming and not well represented in the results of the research project. Another way in which many students simplify the research process is by assuming that the only product of their research is the final report or presentation of the results. We hope you noticed that each step above includes an actual product that researchers should be developing as they work through the step.

Disciplinary Approaches

The writing and research processes outlined so far in this chapter are fairly generic descriptions of the steps and procedures you might use for any given research project. We're sure it will be no surprise to you, however, that we want to emphasize the importance of adapting the process that you use to the specific situation in which you are writing and researching. One particular circumstance that we would like to address is the variety of approaches to writing and researching that you will encounter (and likely have already encountered) in school settings. From one class to the next you will come across different preferences, or what writing teachers often call conventions, for each discipline. As an extreme example, the writing that you do when completing an observational lab report in a biology class will be very different from the writing you do when completing a poetry assignment for a creative writing class. Similarly, your writing in a literary analysis paper will probably have significant differences from your writing in an experimental psychology report.

Of course, there are many similarities in the writing you will do in these contexts, too. Since they are all fairly formal assignments completed in an academic setting, you will thoroughly proofread and edit your work. Also, you will carefully cite resources that you use in your writing because the citation of others' ideas is an important part of writing in any academic setting. But there may be differences in style, organization, voice, and even the format for citing your sources, depending on the conventions of the discipline. You will even find that what counts as evidence for an argument can vary from one discipline to another. While a logically constructed argument defending a theory might count as evidence in one class, another class might require the collection of data through observation or experimentation to defend a claim.

Each discipline has conventions for the writing in that field. One of the best ways to discover the kinds of conventions that are expected is to look at examples of writing in that discipline, writing that you want to emulate. You'll notice certain patterns. For example, if you look at various observational and experimental reports in the natural sciences and social sciences, you might notice that many of them follow the same organizational pattern. Researchers and writers in these disciplines expect that reports, generally, will be organized as follows:

- introduction and review of relevant research

- description of the methodology used in the study

- presentation of the results of data collection

- analysis of the results

- discussion of the results and concluding comments

Of course, exceptions to this pattern exist, too, and part of being an effective writer is determining when to follow the conventions and when to break them. In order to make that decision, you have to know the conventions in the first place. Learning about the discipline in which you are writing is an important part of your rhetorical situation if you are writing in an academic setting. Table 2.1 shows some of the distinct characteristics of academic disciplines in three main categories, the types of research in those fields, and the usual citation styles, but always keep in mind that such distinctions aren't absolute.

You have a variety of resources to help you learn about the conventions of different disciplines. Your primary resource is your instructor. Ask your instructor about expectations for writing and research in your discipline. Ask for a list of academic journals to skim through so that you can see those patterns. You might even ask your instructor for a sample of the writing he or she has done in that discipline. In addition, you could look at one or more of the many textbooks and references devoted to discussing writing in various disciplines.

 For annotated Web links discussing writing in the various disciplines, go to *Student Resources* on the online resource center at www.cengage.com/english/ Miller-Cochran/WGTR.

Table 2.1.
Characteristics of Academic Disciplines

	Humanities	Social Sciences	Natural Sciences
Example areas of study	Literature, art, philosophy, dance, film studies, religious studies	Anthropology, sociology, political science, psychology, justice studies, economics, linguistics	Geography, biology, geology, engineering, computer science, nursing, physics
Primary areas of inquiry	Texts, artifacts, and other ways in which people create meaning and value	Society and social (especially human) interaction	The physical world
Primary role of the researcher	Interpreting and making meaning	Developing theories and looking for patterns	Investigating and reporting
Common citation styles	Modern Language Association (MLA), Chicago Manual of Style (CMS)	American Psychological Association (APA), Linguistics Society of America (LSA)	Council of Science Editors (CSE), American Psychological Association (APA)

...write...

Discover Disciplinary Patterns and Conventions

Begin by finding a teacher or professional that you could talk to in the discipline/major/career that you are interested in pursuing. You might talk to a professor that you know, or you might talk to someone who is currently in the kind of job you would like to have. Ask the following questions, and take careful notes on the responses you receive.

1. What kinds of writing are assigned in classes in this field? What kinds of writing do professionals in this field do on the job?

2. Are there specific patterns or conventions expected in the writing in this field? If so, what are they?

3. What are the most common problems that students or new writers in the field have? How could these problems be avoided?

4. What kinds of research are conducted most often in this field?

5. Are there specific research processes that people in this field/profession usually follow? How do they learn these processes?

6. What citation style is primarily used for research conducted in this field? Why is that citation style used? Are other styles sometimes used as well? If so, how should a new writer in the field choose an appropriate citation style?

7. Is there an example of writing in this field that you could share with me? (You might even ask to see something that the teacher or professional has written.)

If you do receive a piece of writing that you could analyze, look for the patterns and conventions that the teacher or professional identified for you. Then share your discoveries with your classmates. You might try filling out a table like Table 2.2 so that you can compare the similarities and differences among the disciplines you each investigated.

Table 2.2.
Research Patterns in Academic Disciplines

Discipline/ Major				
What kinds of writing are assigned in classes or done on the job?				
What patterns are followed by writers in these fields?				
What are the most common problems students have?				
What kinds of research are conducted most often?				
Are there specific research processes that people in this field usually follow?				
What citation style is primarily used?				

This textbook will provide you with strategies to approach writing and research in a variety of contexts, but you will need to adapt them to fit rhetorical situations. For academic writing and research projects, an important part of your rhetorical situation is the conventions and expectations of the discipline within which you are writing. Always try to ask questions and look at examples of writing in fields with which you are unfamiliar; you can discover a wealth of information from analyzing exemplary pieces of writing, and that will increase your chances of writing effectively.

Identifying a Topic

Any writing situations, academic as well as professional and personal, require that you select and narrow your own topic. For example, several community organizations might get a call for funding proposals from a federal agency. The agency's request for proposals might say it is willing to fund projects that help low-income, single mothers, but to receive the funding each organization must write a successful grant proposal asking for the money. So each organization has to figure out the specific challenge to resolve that would use the funding. Similarly, in a film studies class you may be asked to research and write about a particular director's work. Although you have a general topic, you need to narrow it further. You might focus on a contemporary director whose movies you have always enjoyed watching, or you might focus on a director whose work has been mentioned in your class and that you would like to learn more about. Then, depending on the number of films the director has completed, you might need to determine if you want to focus on a particular time period or theme in the director's body of work. In both cases, the writer is given a general topic with which to start; however, it is his or her responsibility to narrow it further to a manageable, focused topic. >

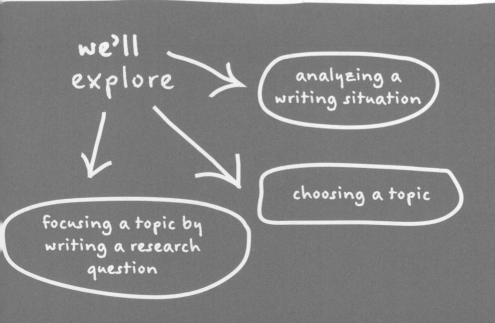

we'll explore

analyzing a writing situation

choosing a topic

focusing a topic by writing a research question

Author: Haley is taking a math course in college that is also designated as a writing-intensive course.

Topic: Haley's math professor assigns a writing project that asks her to report on an important person in mathematical history.

Audience: Haley's audience for the math assignment is her professor.

Purpose: Haley needs to focus on a particular topic for her research paper that will be interesting to her and to her audience while fulfilling the requirements of the assignment.

QUESTIONS

1. What questions should Haley ask herself to get started on finding a topic?

2. What strategies might she use to begin brainstorming a list of possible topics?

3. Have you ever been assigned a paper in a class where you were given relatively free rein on the topic? Have you ever been overwhelmed with picking a topic or needing to narrow a topic to make it manageable? What did you do?

Analyzing the Writing Situation

Research and writing projects usually develop out of a specific situation, with a certain problem that needs to be solved or a goal that needs to be obtained. An instructor might require you to research the chemical properties of a family of plants or your boss might ask you to research various shipping methods for a new product you are selling. In these cases, the context you are working and living in demands action; you have to write a paper to pass a class or you have to research shipping methods to keep your job. Many people are personally motivated to research. Whenever you are in a situation that presents the need to communicate, you experience **kairos**; you are in a "kairotic" moment.

Taking Advantage of Kairos

Kairos is a moment that inspires you or compels you to write. Elements of kairos are usually present in both time and space. Let's focus on an everyday example. Imagine that you are eating at a restaurant and things keep going wrong. Your friend arrives 20 minutes late, your niece spills a drink all over you, your food is cold, and then you realize at the end of dinner that you need the check to be split among everyone and you forgot to ask the server. The server could get frustrated with all of these complications and convey that frustration by taking a long time to bring the food to the table, appearing irritated with the customers, or not refilling drinks. However, imagine that in this situation the server goes above and beyond to help resolve all the issues (he keeps everyone's drinks filled as you wait for your friend, he immediately helps clean up the mess from the spilled drink, he brings out a new plate of food for you, and he quickly splits the check four ways) and keeps on smiling. In that moment, you may think that it would be good to take the time to write the restaurant a letter to say how well this server interacted with your group. However, you know it is very unlikely that you will take the time to do so. But to your surprise, and luck, there is a feedback form included with the receipt. Without taking too much time out of your schedule, you now have the opportunity to respond to this situation and commend the server for his performance. All of these contextual forces combining to both motivate and set the conditions for your communication are an example of kairos.

In other words, communication needs to take advantage of a timely issue (the great job of the server) and have the material components necessary (the feedback form). Successful communication, both written and oral, develops out of opportune times

Identify Kairos

Answer the following questions to explore what elements of kairos might shape your research.

1. What is your motivation for doing this research and writing? course assignment and grades? interest in topic? need to do/change something in your life?

2. What is going on around you that affects your understanding of this research

project and topic? school? work? home? community?

3. What has happened in the past and present, and what might happen in the future, that affects your understanding of this research project and topic?

and places—out of kairos. To research and write about a topic that your readers will actually want to read, you will need to be aware of and understand what is going on around you to find a topic that is both timely and appropriate.

Considering the Rhetorical Situation

You can revisit the definition of the rhetorical situation in Chapter 1, p. 6.

To understand kairos better, think about how and why it is related to the concept of the rhetorical situation. ⬚ Simply put, kairos presents the circumstance that then produces a rhetorical situation within which to research and write. By responding to the questions in Table 3.1, you can test the timeliness, the kairotic fit, of an issue by analyzing whether the rhetorical situation emerging around your proposed topic "fits."

Table 3.1.
Kairos in the Rhetorical Situation

Kairos in the Rhetorical Situation	Purpose	Audience	Author
Time	What has happened in the past, or is happening in the present, that motivates research and communication? What will happen in the future that will require research and communication?	What has happened in the past, or is happening in the present, that motivates this audience to care about this topic? What will the audience need to do in the future to motivate their reading and learning about the topic?	What has happened in the author's past, is happening in the present, or might happen in the author's future that motivates him or her to research and write?
Space	What persons, places, or things will be affected by the outcomes of this research?	What "real-world" things can the audience do to impact this issue based on the research and writing?	What resources does the author have to facilitate research, writing, and publishing on this topic?

Table 3.2 analyzes the example of Haley from the beginning of this chapter.

Table 3.2.
Kairos in a Specific Rhetorical
Situation: History Report in a Math Class

	Purpose	Audience	Author
Time	Haley was never good at math in high school, or college, and dreaded taking this last math class. Haley was also taking a women's studies course and had been learning that the achievements of many women had been erased throughout history.	Haley knew that her math instructor wanted the students to recognize that math has a history and has developed and changed over time. She also knew that the math instructor was very interested in the history of math in different cultures. Finally, Haley knew her women's studies instructor would probably also like information about women in the history of math.	Haley wants to survive this last math class, so she wants to do well on this report. She knows she wants to focus on a topic that keeps her interested so she does well in the class.
Space	Haley's math professor was very excited by Haley's idea. The professor told Haley that there are significantly fewer women in math and science majors and professions.	Haley's math professor mentioned that a report on a woman in the history of math might motivate women to take more math classes and possibly become math majors.	Haley is excited about her access to resources because she has been learning about various women's studies resources in her women's studies class. Her math instructor has also provided starting places for historical research in math. Finally, her first Google hit listed four books to check out!

As you can see from Table 3.2, Haley has many factors that help develop a kairotic moment for her math research project. One of the strongest elements is that she is also taking a women's studies class. And after she did a little exploratory research on the topic, including talking to her professors, she found that she has access to a variety of resources as well as a potential "real-world" purpose and audience. For Haley, this topic has moved beyond just a research report for a college class into something that can change people's lives. By taking the time to explore the timeliness of her topic, both for herself and for the community, Haley has now focused on a research topic that is exciting and will motivate her when the work gets tough.

...write....

Analyze the Rhetorical Situation

Start thinking about what is going on in your life and in your various academic, professional, and personal communities that might influence your understanding of possible research topics. Consider resources, both people and places, that you have access to while developing your research topic and/or during your research process. Focus on situations that would benefit from knowing more about your topic. How might your research impact the real world? Use the following grid to help analyze your research project's rhetorical situation, and use the questions in Table 3.1 to guide your response.

Kairos in the Rhetorical Situation	Purpose	Audience	Author
Time			
Space			

Generating Topics

A common element of the rhetorical situation for many students is that someone assigns a general topic to research. Like Haley's math professor, many instructors give students broad topics to research, usually based on the course's topics and/or themes. Your job in this situation, then, is to focus more carefully on a specific topic you are interested in researching within the guidelines of the assignment. However, if you are given free rein on your research topic, you may need to do a little searching for a general topic. Finding a general topic, and starting to narrow to a specific one, involves the same activities: finding out what is both important and motivating to you.

...write...

Find Out What's Important to You

Take some time to explore the various communities that you participate in:

- ☐ personal—home, family, leisure, and so on

- ☐ academic—school, past, present, and future

- ☐ professional—work and career, past, present, and future

- ☐ civic—community, political (local, national, global), and so on

Answer the following questions about these four communities you live in.

1. What discussions (in writing, on the Internet, verbally) engage you and other members of the community?

2. What events or experiences have happened that you still remember and that left you, or other members of the community, with questions or concerns?

3. What problems or concerns exist in this particular community?

Focus on one or two of your answers by digging deeper with the following questions.

4. Who, which individuals and groups, is involved in this discussion, event, or problem? Why are they involved?

5. When and where did/does the discussion, event, or problem take place?

6. What exactly is the topic of the discussion, event, or problem?

7. Why is the discussion, event, or problem significant to the community members?

8. How does the community usually start to resolve the discussion, event, or problem?

...write...

Generate Topic Ideas

As you think about topics to research, try writing down your responses to these steps.

1. Spend 3 to 5 minutes generating a list of topics that you find interesting and compelling (you might refer to your writing from the "What's Important to You?" activity). List 6 to 8 possibilities.

2. Go through your list and phrase each topic as a question. In other words, what would you like to find out? For example, if you listed "Parking at my school," then you might write, "How could the school provide more convenient parking options for students?" or "Why is the parking on campus so expensive?" You might even generate more than one question for a topic.

3. Now look at your list of questions and choose one that sounds particularly interesting to you. Freewrite for 5 minutes on why you think this topic is interesting and what you know about it.

4. Look at your freewriting and highlight or underline the most interesting idea you came up with. Copy (or copy and paste, if you're using a word-processing program) that idea below your freewriting and write about that idea for the next 5 minutes.

5. At this point, you might continue this exercise one or two more times until you find a focus that seems interesting to you. Or, if you find yourself stuck and think you might not want to research this topic, try one of your other questions and start the exercise at step 3 again.

...write...

Consider Audience and Purpose

As you make a final decision on your topic for research, freewrite for 5 minutes on each of the following two questions.

1. What might your audience be interested in? How could you relate your topic to your audience's experience?

2. Will this topic satisfy the purpose of your writing and research? What criteria must you keep in mind to make sure that you are meeting your writing goals?

Your answers to these questions might help you choose the best topic from several that you are considering.

   Selecting and narrowing a topic can be one of the most important things you do before engaging in a research process. Consider talking about your answers with friends, family, coworkers, and classmates. Try putting down the questions and answers and returning to them a couple of hours, or days, later. Do you have new ideas? Can you add to some of your older ideas?

You, the author, are an important part of the rhetorical situation. If you are not engaged by the topic and motivated to learn about it, you will have difficulty being successful with your research project. Before committing to a specific topic, it is important that you explore various possibilities for your research. This is an opportunity for you to explore your own understanding of the topic. What issues and events is the topic related to?

techno_tip >

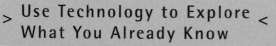

> **Use Technology to Explore** <
> **What You Already Know**

To explore what you already know about a research topic you are considering, try doing some exploratory freewriting. Open up a new word processing file on your computer. If you can (although some computers might not let you), turn off your monitor. Set a goal of writing for 5 to 10 minutes, and then write. Just write everything that comes to mind about your topic. If you wander off topic, that is okay. Just keep writing. Do not stop writing for the full period of time you allotted. If you get stuck, type the last word you typed over and over again until your mind slips into a new track of thinking.

You might realize that your mind wanders off track; however, some of those sidetracks might be interesting topics in their own right. This is a time to explore.

Exploring and Narrowing a Potential Topic

Once you have a general idea of a topic you are interested in researching, you will want to spend a little time exploring it further to see what specific elements within it interest you. You should explore your topic prior to committing to it for two reasons. First, you need to verify that there are resources out there (people, places, and resources in the library and online) to actually use in conducting the research. If you don't have access to the proper tools, you can't do the work! Usually the best person to help you identify resources for starting your research is your instructor or any other person who "assigned" the research project (a boss, a community leader, or a family member). Haley was able to find a wealth of information on her topic after talking to both her women's studies and math professors, for example.

A second reason you should explore your topic further before committing is to broaden your understanding of the topic. By gaining a better understanding of some of the complexities of the topic, you can identify subtopics of interest to further narrow your research focus. Beginning researchers should learn more about their topic so they can then focus on a smaller chunk of it. For example, when Haley searched online for "women in math history," she found a page that listed ten women with brief descriptions of their impact on math. As an English major, Haley was fascinated to find out that the poet Lord Byron's daughter might have been the first person to write computer code. By doing a little preliminary research, or exploration, of her topic, Haley may have found a specific

techno_tip >

> Use the Internet to Explore a Possible Topic <

 For an interactive tutorial about using the Internet to explore topics, go to *Student Resources* on the online resource center at www.cengage.com/english/Miller-Cochran/WGTR.

Depending on which of these descriptions best fits you, choose one of the following two activities to use the Internet to explore, or even find, a topic.

☐ **I think I know what I want to research.** In this case, we recommend a variation on an activity that you might have done in the first chapter of this book. Try finding some running discussions about your topic. With the explosion of the blogsphere, there are lots of blogs on just about any topic. You could also consider looking at what has been written in *Wikipedia* on your topic, but you should be wary of the reliability of any information you find in *Wikipedia*. ☐

> See Chapter 4 for a more thorough discussion of Wikipedia.

o Keep in mind that this is the exploratory stage; blogs and *Wikipedia* won't likely be the most reliable resources you'll find. But they can be good starting points for understanding what people are saying about your topic. Try answering the following questions as you read what you find about your topic.

o What discussions are emerging around your topic?

o Who are some of the key players and groups interested in your topic?

o What subtopics emerged in discussions of your topic?

☐ **I'm not sure what I want to research.** There are some resources that include lists of possible topics, and even include places to start reading about them.

o Web directories are a more linear way to search for resources on the Web. Instead of just dumping terms into a search engine, work your way through a Web directory. The directory starts with broad topic areas and allows you to continue narrowing down to subtopics. As you narrow, the directory will also provide resources to start reading. Try working through a couple of the following directories:

o The Open Directory Project http://dmoz.org/

o Google Directory http://directory.google.com/

o Yahoo Directory http://dir.yahoo.com/

o StumbleUpon is a useful resource for finding topics and resources that might interest to you. It works as a toolbar within Firefox, and you can try it out at http://www.stumbleupon.com.

o *CQ Researcher* is a publication for congressional leaders in their attempt to stay up to date on current events and issues. Forty-four weeks of the year a new report on a specific issue is published. The reports include lists of related issues, specific research questions with essays, and a list of resources to read more on the topic. *CQ Researcher* is published in both hard copy and in an electronic database. Most college libraries subscribe to one format or the other.

☐ Identify and read a few Web directories or *CQ Researcher* topics that you might be interested in. Then try answering the following questions.

o What discussions are emerging around your topic?

o Who are some of the key players and groups interested in your topic?

o What subtopics emerged in discussions of your topic?

subtopic she is very interested in; therefore, she is more motivated to do the research. Narrowing a larger topic, like the one Haley started with, to a more focused subtopic will make your research project, and your writing task, much more manageable.

Once Haley confirms that there are resources available on her topic and that other people are dialoguing about that topic, she needs to reassess whether her topic is appropriate for her rhetorical situation. Will her chosen topic be interesting to her audience? Is it appropriate for the assignment she was given? Will she be able to find enough information to meet the requirements of the assignment (or will she have too much information, which would mean she might need to narrow her topic further)?

How Can I Make a Topic Manageable?

When choosing a topic for writing, it is important to make sure that your topic is actually manageable and appropriate for the specific writing situation. Before continuing with your writing, take a moment to reflect on the topic you are working with by responding to the following questions.

1. How appropriate is this topic to the writing situation? In other words, will this topic fulfill the requirements of the assignment, if you are writing for a class? If you are motivated by a situation at work or in your personal life, will exploring this topic satisfy the need that first prompted you to explore this topic?

2. How interested are you in your topic? Will you be able to sustain your interest long enough to complete the writing and research necessary? Is there a specific aspect of your topic that holds more interest for you that would be a good place for you to focus?

3. How doable is your writing task? Consider how broad your topic is right now. Will you have time to explore this topic thoroughly? Is there too much information available about the topic? If so, you might need to narrow it further. Is it difficult to find information about your topic? If so, you might need to refocus or broaden your topic.

Haley found many resources on Lord Byron's daughter, Ada Lovelace, but she had no idea how to narrow the topic further to help her decide what she needed to focus on while researching and reading. Although she was excited about all the material she was reading, Haley was overwhelmed with information. She decided to talk to both her math and women's studies instructors. Both asked her questions that helped her to decide what she was really interested in, Lovelace's impact on the field of software development.

Focus Your Research Topic

...write...

Take 5 minutes to brainstorm a list of the things that people debate regarding your topic. Think of conversations that people would have about your topic and points of disagreement. You might think of these as subtopics within the larger topic you're exploring. If you are in a classroom setting, pass your list on to your classmates and have them add to it. If you don't have access to other students, ask your friends and family to add to the list.

Once you have your list of related topics and subtopics, try visually depicting your topic. Start by writing your topic in the center of a piece of paper. Write your various subtopics on branches. If you can break down any of the subtopics further, create additional branches that stem from the subtopics. You might see that some branches generate more ideas than others, and you may find that you are more interested in one or two branches than the others. These observations can help you pick a narrowed focus within your topic. You will probably want to focus your research and writing on one of the second- or third-generation branches away from your central, broad topic. ◻

If you'd like to explore using cluster mapping further for your invention, see the appendix.

Developing a Research Question

Once you have discovered a topic that fits your rhetorical situation, and you've narrowed it down to a workable subtopic, it's time to really begin your research. Sometimes it is difficult to determine where to start, however. One of the most effective ways to get started on your research is to think of your topic in terms of a question that you would like to answer: your **research question**. Your natural inclination when you hear a question is to respond to it, and phrasing your chosen topic as a research question can motivate you to begin thinking of ways to answer. If you were having trouble narrowing your focus on your topic, writing it in the form of a research question is another way to work on focusing your topic.

A research question should be clearly stated and provide the specific focus and scope of your research. For example, Haley might write a research question that looks something like this:

What influence did Ada Lovelace have on the development of computer code?

Try to avoid yes/no questions because they won't help you generate as much research and writing. For example, if Haley asked the following question,

Was Ada Lovelace the first person to write computer code?

then it could be answered either "yes" or "no," but she might not have much more to say. An exception to this rule might be if there were a controversy surrounding the answer; in that case, Haley could write about the controversy. Even so, a more accurate research question would be:

What is the controversy surrounding whether Ada Lovelace was the first person to write computer code?

Write a Research Question

1. To start developing possible research questions, begin with some basic question words. Try to write at least one question that someone might raise about your issue that starts with each of the following words: *who, what, when, where, how, why, should, would*.

2. Think about what your goal is in writing. Do you want to share information about your issue? Are you defining terms or aspects of your issue? Are you evaluating something or comparing/contrasting it with something else? Are you identifying a solution? Take a look at your questions and circle any that specifically match your goal. Cross out questions that do not fulfill that goal.

3. Go back to the writing and thinking you have done about your audience and purpose in writing. Who are you writing to? What are their interests? What is your purpose in writing?

4. Use your responses to these questions to consider each of your preliminary questions from number 1. Cross out questions that would not meet the needs of your audience or fulfill your purpose in writing.

5. Finally, choose the one remaining research question that interests you most. Are there any terms you should define more clearly? Show your question to someone else and ask if it is clear. You might exchange your question with a classmate, a friend, or a family member.

Situating the Writer in the Research

Throughout our discussion of research, we have talked about the importance of choosing something to research and write about that interests you. Furthermore, the activities in this chapter have encouraged you to choose a topic in which you are *invested*. In other words, you have a stake in the outcome of your research.

For example, if you are researching whether you should purchase a hybrid or a standard automobile, you have a stake in the outcome of your research. The answer you discover might determine what type of car you purchase. You are invested in your research because it will have an impact on you. You might be specifically invested in the topic because of various influences in your life—you might be living on a tight budget, so cost is a major factor to you. Or, you might be concerned about the environment and the emission of chemicals from standard automobiles. Any of these factors might influence the way that you conduct your research, the sources that you choose, the way you read and use those sources in your writing, and the criteria you develop for choosing the best answer to your research question. We call this **bias**, and it is the unique perspective that you bring to your research.

We are not using the term *bias* in a negative sense—everyone has bias. We all have unique experiences and backgrounds that influence the way that we see an issue. As you conduct your research, however, we want to encourage you to be *aware* of your bias and to consider how it might influence the way that you research and write about your topic. It's really not possible to be completely objective about an issue—we all see the world and the issues surrounding us through the lenses of our own perspectives, influences, and experiences. The audience that you envision for your research might not share your specific bias, though, and this is something that you will need to take into consideration if you are trying to persuade your audience to take action on your topic.

> reflect <

What Is the Writer's Place in the Rhetorical Situation?

Reflect on how and why you are interested in your narrowed issue and research question. Consider the following questions as you compose this reflection.

- ❑ What initially sparked your interest in this issue?
- ❑ What did you already know about the issue, and how well could you answer your research question right now?
- ❑ After conducting a preliminary exploration of the issue, have those interests been confirmed?
- ❑ What has surprised you as you've conducted the preliminary exploration?
- ❑ Why do you value this issue?

- ☐ What is your perspective on this issue?
- ☐ How might your values and perspective influence your research and writing on this issue?
- ☐ What specific experiences have you had with this issue (friends, family members, colleagues, community, news, movies, etc.)?

While answering these questions, you will want to be sure to explore past events that have molded your values and beliefs about this topic and issue. Do not simply discuss how you feel. Instead, focus on why you feel that way. What experiences have you had that make you believe what you believe? While discussing the experiences, use concrete details (sight, sound, smell, touch, taste, specific emotions, etc.) to make the reader feel like he or she has had the same experience.

Your Knowledge of Your Topic

If you have chosen a topic in which you are interested and invested, chances are that you already know something about it. You might not be an expert, but you will still find it helpful to reflect on what you already know about your topic before you begin to think about what other resources you will need to find.

Once you identify what you already know, look for different perspectives in order to understand the complexity and controversy surrounding the issue. If you are researching capital punishment, for example, find resources that discuss why some people believe that capital punishment is a valid punishment for extreme criminals and resources that disagree with that perspective. If you already have a specific opinion on the issue that you are researching, be very careful to find resources that both agree and disagree with your opinion. If you start with what you know and believe, however, you will be able to piece together a plan for what you still need to find out. The first step, though, is determining what you already know.

> reflect <

Take an Inventory of What You Know

As you make your final decision about the topic you will research and write about, take a personal inventory of what you know.

- ☐ What is the central issue that people debate when they talk about your topic or discuss your research question? In other words, what is the main controversy (or, what are the main controversies)? What do people disagree about?
- ☐ What do you believe about this topic? What evidence makes you believe this? Where did you find or learn about this evidence?

>>>

>>>

☐ What different people, or groups of people, are interested in your research question? What do you believe others think about this topic? What evidence do you believe they base their opinions on? Where do you think they found that evidence?

☐ Where do these people discuss their positions on your issue? In other words, where would you go to find out what people are saying?

☐ Based on what you already know, what perspectives do you need to learn more about?

Try conducting this activity more than once, returning to it numerous times as you research. And don't do this activity alone—get friends and family members to participate in a dialogue with you. This activity should not only help you figure out what you know, but it should also give you a sense of what you *think* you know but need to verify. Keep in mind that there is a difference between what we *know* as fact and what we *think* we know.

RESEARCH IN PROGRESS:
Writing a Research Proposal

At the beginning of any major research project, a researcher needs to identify the focus and purpose of the research, something you have been working towards through Chapters 1–3. Sometimes this is done in the form of writing a research proposal, especially if the researcher is seeking permission, funding, or approval of some sort to conduct the research. Depending on the nature of the research project and the rhetorical situation, a formal written proposal might or might not be necessary. Whether or not the researcher writes a proposal, though, it is always important to define the focus of the research, and the kinds of questions one might ask when working on a proposal are a good place to start. Therefore, this assignment can serve as a starting point for any major research project.

In this section, we offer guidelines and an assignment for writing a research proposal, but keep in mind that proposals can take many forms. The elements of the proposal assignment included in this book are designed to help you draw on the principles discussed and practiced in Chapters 1–3 and will pull together everything you learned into this one assignment. You or your instructor could adapt the assignment to fit your rhetorical situation, though.

The Assignment

The goal of this research proposal is to introduce the issue that you are interested in exploring in your major research project. This might be a topic that you will develop for a course (and perhaps for the entire semester), or you might eventually research and write about several topics in your class. You will want to narrow your focus to one issue that you could explore through this assignment, however. In this assignment, we will ask you to define the focus of your research by

- focusing your topic to one research question;

- designing a rhetorical situation for the project that includes

  - discussing your own interests and prior experience with the issue;

  - articulating your purpose in researching the specific issue;

o   focusing on a specific audience to which you will communicate the results of your research; and

o   discussing how all of these elements construct a rhetorical situation in which you will be researching and writing.

In your research proposal, you will define the focus of your research project and to whom you plan to present your final research.

The research proposal is an opportunity for you to define your research question and construct the rhetorical context in which you will be working as you research. A primary goal of this assignment is to focus on the specific audience that you will address in your final research paper and to determine the purpose of addressing your argument to that audience. The way in which you choose to present an argument is influenced by your individual experiences with the topic, by the audience to whom you address it, and by the purpose you hope to achieve.

In this assignment you will also explore the values and perspectives you already hold before you begin to research the available positions on the issue and what others are saying about it. Your experience and interest in the issue are part of your rhetorical context. Nobody looks at an issue entirely objectively, so this is where you will begin to define your unique position on the issue by describing the perspective you already bring to the table. For example, a single mother who chooses to write about the controversy over spanking might describe her struggle to determine the best way to discipline her own children and whether or not she chooses to spank them. She might describe her experience with discipline as a child, or she might choose to describe the influence of others on her decision. Finally, she would describe how these experiences influence her opinion on the issue of whether or not parents should spank their children.

Your final researched argument will be addressed to a specific audience whose thinking you want to influence. Your credibility as a reliable researcher will be very important in persuading this audience to adopt your evaluation of the issue or position, so you should take care to present yourself as someone who is well informed about the issue you are discussing. ▢ You might choose an audience that is open-minded about your evaluation, or, if you want to attempt something a bit more difficult, choose an audience that is skeptical or even hostile to you or your evaluation. If you are evaluating the merits of gun control, for example, you could imagine yourself writing to members of the National Rifle Association.

> For more information about developing your credibility, or *ethos*, as an author, see Chapter 9, "Constructing an Argument."

Features of a Research Proposal

You have multiple audiences for this assignment. If you are completing this proposal in the context of a class, one of your audiences is your instructor. You might also think of your fellow classmates as part of your audience. If you were assigned a research project for work, you may want to share this type of a document with your boss to be sure you both understand the requirements of the research project.

In addition, your audience is yourself—this is a chance to explore your own perspective on your issue and become more aware of the influences on that perspective. The proposal is also an opportunity to narrow down your research to a specific, guiding research question and focus. Generally, you would not need to use many, if any, outside resources for this proposal; your primary resource is your own experience and knowledge of the issue. You are exploring what you know, what you need to find out, what your focus is, and who your audience is.

Your response to this assignment should provide your audience with the following information:

- an overview of what the issue is that you are interested in;

- a focused research question;

- a discussion of how and why the topic is controversial;

- a reflection on what your specific experience(s) is/are with the issue (be specific, include concrete details);

- your purpose in researching and writing on the issue;

- your perspective and/or opinion on the issue right now;

- who your audience will be for your final research results (the answer to your research question); and

- a research plan and timeline.

Part of this exploration should be connecting your values, background, history, and experiences to the issue you are interested in, describing how you are invested in the issue. Another part of this exploration should be cross-analyzing your purpose in researching and writing along with the wants and needs of your intended audience. Finally, you will need to think about the specific context you are researching and writing in so that you construct a project that is doable within the constraints of your schedule.

Starting Your Research Proposal

To keep yourself interested and inspired in your research topic, be sure to select something that interests and engages you. In addition, you need to choose a topic that will interest and engage your readers. To complicate things further, if you are writing in the context of a class for which you have to complete an assignment, then you must choose a topic that will meet the criteria for the assignment.

No wonder it can be so difficult to choose a topic—writers have to balance the needs and interests of several different groups! Sometimes those needs and interests can compete with one another, too. Perhaps you can think of a time when you heard someone go on and on about a topic to the point of completely boring the people who were listening. It's very possible that the speaker was interested in the topic, but the audience wasn't. Or imagine taking a course on Ethics in Science and the instructor assigns a term paper having to do with one of the ethical issues discussed in class that semester. If you write a paper about the development of the designated hitter rule in baseball, then you probably won't meet the criteria for the assignment—even though you may be very interested in the topic.

What we suggest is that you start with your own interests and then think about what the purpose for your writing is and who your audience will be. Weighing each of these factors into your topic choice will help you find something to write about that you will be interested in, that your audience will enjoy reading, and that will fulfill your purpose in writing.

> **Activity**
> See "Write: What's Important to You?" on page 39 of Chapter 3.

Often when students are confronted with a research assignment where they need to choose a topic, the most difficult part is finding something to research and write about. Sometimes we are able to start with an idea of what we're interested in, and then we can go to the Internet or other research sources to find more information and focus our topics. Other times, we don't really know where to start and we need some help thinking of possible topics to focus on.

> **Activity**
> See "Techno Tip: Use Technology to Explore What You Already Know" on page 41 of Chapter 3.
>
> **Activity**
> See "Techno Tip: Use the Internet to Explore a Possible Topic" on page 42 of Chapter 3.

Once you have chosen a broad topic for your writing, it is important to focus your attention on a particular issue that you will research and write about. Topics are broad, general subject areas, and issues are specific conversations, and sometimes points of disagreement, within a topic. If you've had difficulty in the past with researching and writing about something for which you found too much information, then you might have been researching a topic instead of focusing on a specific issue within that topic. For example, let's say we're back in that Ethics in Science class. One of the students decides to write about the use of animals in laboratory testing. This topic is rather broad, and it doesn't tell us what the student is interested in within that topic. The student would need to think about what kinds of conversations people have about animal testing, and he or she might specifically brainstorm a list of the points on which people disagree. Each of these points is an issue, and the student could then choose one of them for extended research and writing.

> **Activity**
> See "Reflect: How Can I Make a Topic Manageable?" on page 43 of Chapter 3.
>
> **Activity**
> See "Write: Focus Your Research Topic" on page 44 of Chapter 3.

An important component of your research proposal will be a clear statement of your research question and a description and exploration of your investment and bias regarding the topic and issue you have chosen.

> **Activity**
> See "Write: Write a Research Question" on page 45 of Chapter 3.
>
> **Activity**
> See "Reflect: What Is the Writer's Place in the Rhetorical Situation?" on page 46 of Chapter 3.

Examples of Research Proposals

For more student samples, go to *Sample Essays* on the online resource center at www.cengage.com/english/Miller-Cochran/WGTR.

Example 1: Li Chen, Can I Have a Clone? Li Chen, an international student, chose to research and write about cloning. Her essay provides an example of a proposal written for an academic research paper on a controversial issue. She discusses her reasons for pursuing this topic and what she believes her focus will be in her research. Although we present this proposal as an example, keep in mind that there are strengths and opportunities for revision within the final proposal. We have included the instructor's comments on Li Chen's final proposal so that you can see the feedback that she received on this paper.

Li Chen

ENG 108

16th February 2008

Can I Have a Clone?

Have you ever watched the movie *Hammerhead*? It is a movie about a scientist, Dr. King, who has found a method to bring his son back from death after undertaking some stem cell research. He made him into a stronger creature – a man and shark hybrid!

I love science fiction movies. I am one of those people who could spend hours watching *National Geographic*. I enjoy watching how animals behave and especially the growth and development of human beings, and *The Human Body* is one of my favorite series. Needless to say, biology is my favorite subject. Probably that is why I am majoring in Pharmacy, because I like chemistry, too.

Cloning is a very interesting topic to me. When I was in kindergarten, I was simply told that "A man and a woman make babies." Later in elementary school, I learned that what the statement really means is that many living things reproduce by sexual reproduction, the sexual union of male and female gametes. In other words, giving rise to offspring requires the fertilization of an egg cell by a sperm cell. This idea was deep in my mind and it seemed like a law, a law of nature, just like $1 + 1 = 2$. When I took biology classes in high school, though, I was taught that some simple living organisms like amoeba reproduce by a process called asexual reproduction. I was shocked by the fact that something could duplicate itself – it could

I like how you're giving us background information on your interests. Make sure that you tie these interests into a discussion of your potential perspective and bias on this topic.

You might develop some stronger connections between the previous paragraph and between the sentences at the beginning of the paragraph.

I like how you transition from your own experience to discussing the field in more general terms here.

This definition section seemed like it should have come earlier in the proposal.

If any of these definitions came from outside sources, then you need to provide documentation.

Again, you need to cite sources if you received information from an outside source.

break the law. Even more amazingly, the teacher introduced the term "cloning" to us as the first sheep clone, Dolly, was born in 1996.

This was a gigantic leap in the science field. Thanks to the rapid increase in knowledge, the immense improvement in technology, and scientists' hard work, things that were thought of as impossible one hundred years ago are now possible. Until just recently, human cloning was merely a kind of "magic" that appeared in movies and novels, but now it is something that is becoming a real possibility. It is a hot issue that is widely discussed in newspapers, periodicals, journals, television programs, the Internet, and even textbooks. One of the most controversial issues that has evolved from human cloning is the ethical problem. Is human cloning morally right? Should scientists continue to invest in exploring this technique or should it be banned? As controversial as it is, I would like to make my own judgment on this issue.

Human cloning technology is a form of asexual reproduction in which an embryo is created by using biotechnology to replicate the genetic make-up of an individual, unlike the normal pathway of reproduction that involves the union of male and female gametes. Human cloning can be classified into two main types, productive cloning and therapeutic cloning. Productive cloning is the process in which a nucleus is injected into an enucleated oocyte and then put back to the reproductive track to grow after cell division. Therapeutic cloning is the same in the first step in the sense that a person's DNA is used to produce a cloned embryo. But the difference is in the second step. Instead of putting this embryo into a substitute mother after cell division, stem cells are taken out of the embryo to generate any type of tissue or organ like the heart, liver, and skin. This type of cloning does not involve replicating an entire human but creating a human repair kit. Scientists could clone our cells and fix genes that cause diseases. It is believed that embryonic stem-cell research could later develop skills to treat and cure incurable diseases. In fact, the British government passed some laws to permit cloning of human embryos to conquer diseases like Parkinson's and Alzheimer's.

However, many critics, including President Bush, oppose both productive and therapeutic cloning saying that many embryos, which might develop into human beings, would be dumped due to the high failure rates (the success rate is only about 3%) and that destroying them makes the practice equal to murder. In addition, cloning is a very dangerous thing that may create major problems in the replicates. For instance, there is a risk of premature aging in clones.

Nevertheless, others see cloning as a way to help a couple with infertility problems. Another option for cloning would be to bring a deceased family member back to life. Someone's great grandmother could be recreated if a piece of her DNA was available. This brings up many ethical problems. As a result, most fundamental Christians and Catholics, as well as socially conservative Republicans, say that all forms of cloning and related research should be banned. Yet, until now there have been no federal restrictions on privately funded embryo research in the US, although most Americans, 88% in 2004, opposed human cloning.

> According to whom? What about other groups?

> Where did this statistic come from?

In my opinion, human cloning is something against nature. There must be a reason for the fact that human beings reproduce sexually. To me, giving rise to offspring is a combination of a male and a female into a single person. The next generation also shows characteristics of both parents, instead of a replicate of one of them. So, if cloning can help a couple with infertility problems to make babies who possess only characteristics of one parent, is it losing the meaning of human reproduction? At this point, human cloning seems morally wrong, but perhaps it is acceptable if the practice really is for the good of mankind.

In the following months, I will be focusing my research on the benefit of therapeutic cloning as well as the moral problems that arise from both types of cloning. I am interested in finding out the reason for scientists to research cloning despite the high failure rate and huge costs. Can cloning really benefit human beings? Or is it just some group of mad scientists looking for recognition in the science field? If human cloning becomes legal, will we still be human beings or will we someday be a hybrid of ourselves and some other species?

Discussion Questions

1. Can you clearly tell what Li Chen's research question is? If you think it needs clarification, what suggestions would you make to the author?

2. What is the author's purpose in researching this topic? Where does the author discuss the purpose, and what recommendations would you make for clarifying the purpose?

3. Who does the author intend to address with the final research project? What suggestions would you make to clarify the intended audience?

For more information on documenta- tion styles, see Chapters 12–15.

4. Li Chen's teacher suggested that she include references for the information that she got from outside sources. If she were going to revise this proposal to incorporate those citations, what citation style should she use? ▢

Example 2: Megan Trevizo, Is Breast Always Best? Megan Trevizo chose a very personal topic for her research project—the choice a mother makes in whether or not to breastfeed a child. Her essay provides an example of a proposal written for an academic audience on a topic in which she is clearly invested. In this example as well, there are strengths and opportunities for revision of the proposal. No instructor comments are included in this example, however. Read the example and think of comments you would make if you were reading it in a peer review session. What suggestions could you make to Megan?

Always Best?   1

Is Breast Always Best?
Megan Trevizo
English 102
Section 2519
November 8, 2007

Is Breast Always Best?

In a perfect world, mothers would always nurse their babies for the first year of their lives. The reality, however, is that breastfeeding is not for everybody. The issue that I will be further researching is the long-standing debate of breastfeeding versus formula feeding. There is a great deal of unnecessary pressure put on mothers-to-be to nurse their baby. In fact, one of the most common questions a woman is asked while pregnant is, "Do you plan on breastfeeding?" Although none of them have ever said so directly, organizations such as La Leche League and many hospitals and doctors have given me the impression that breastfeeding is the only option for raising a healthy child. I believe this issue is not so simple, and that one option is not always better than the other.

This topic is controversial because mothers are judging each other on the way they feed their children. People have set ideas about what is right for their children, and what should be done to aid them in their development. When someone tells these parents, be it another parent or even a doctor, that they are not doing what is best for their children, then they will feel defensive.

My main reason for wanting to delve into this topic is because I recently had to choose how I wanted to feed my baby. When I found out I was pregnant, I knew right from the start that I wanted to nurse my son until he was at least six months old. After some intensive investigation by way of the Internet, books, and my doctor, I was confident I was making the optimal choice for my unborn son. On May 2, 2006 I welcomed a wrinkled baby boy named Jayden into this world. My first time nursing my son in the hospital was one that can only be described as frustrating. Neither of us were doing it right and the nurse who was in the room sighed, sounding annoyed. "Sit up straighter. And you're supposed to hold him like this," she showed me. That was the first time I experienced the pressure to breastfeed that many women are faced with after having a baby.

As trying as it was, I did not give up because this was something I felt strongly about continuing. As the days went by with both the baby and me struggling with this new concept, I realized that the breastfeeding I had so longed to master might possibly not work out. That was the first time I experienced the guilt associated with *not* breastfeeding. When my son was about three weeks old I developed a breast infection that caused me to be very ill. Feeling defeated, I began to offer my son formula. I was devastated and for the first few weeks felt like a horrible mother. I was, after all, made to feel like this other form of nutrition was comparable to poison. Fortunately, Jayden handled the switch much better than I did, and he took a liking to the new food instantly. My son is now six months old and weighs a whopping 20 pounds. I can not imagine him being any happier or healthier than he is right now.

My purpose in writing on this topic stems from my experiences with breastfeeding my son. It upsets me that parents are made to feel in the wrong for choosing to bottle feed their baby. I believe that instead of trying to influence mothers one way or the other, our society should let them decide what they prefer. While I can acknowledge that breast milk certainly holds more nutritional value than the makers of formula could ever replicate, I am positive that there are valid reasons many women choose formula, and I am even surer that they do not deserved to be judged.

For the final research project my audience will be myself, my instructor, and some of my classmates. In this project I expect to fulfill the wants of my audience by showing them a different perspective to the debate over breastfeeding versus bottle feeding. They will want to know both sides of the story, the mothers who choose to breastfeed and those who use formula. I will hopefully spark the interest of my audience and maintain it throughout my proposal. One of the issues I see as being my biggest challenge in this project is the task of getting my point across as I mean it. Because this is an online

Always Best?   4

class and I cannot truly *know* my audience, it might be challenging getting some classmates interested in this issue.

It is important to manage my time wisely in order to complete this project. I plan on first making an appointment to talk to a lactation consultant. I spoke to one when I was at the hospital having my baby but I could always use a refresher. Since the Internet is such a powerful tool, I plan on utilizing it as best as I can for my research. Blogs will play a key part in my exploration of this topic; there is nothing like hearing people's real experiences on what they went through when feeding their children.

Discussion Questions

1. What is the author's purpose in researching this topic? Where does the author discuss the purpose, and what recommendations would you make for clarifying the purpose?

2. Who does the author intend to address with the final research project? What suggestions would you make for clarifying the intended audience?

3. If you were writing a response to Megan Trevizo for a peer review, what would you suggest she consider in a revision? You might take another look at the criteria for research proposals presented earlier in this chapter, and also consider the topic and the author's investment in that topic.

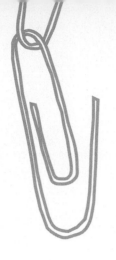

PART 2

□□□□□□□□□□□□

Conducting Research

↓ ↓ ↓

RESEARCH IN PROGRESS:
Writing a Review of Research

Finding Resources through Secondary Research

4

One of the most difficult things about conducting research is getting started. Many students are often paralyzed by the overwhelming number of options for answering a research question. Where should you start looking for information? What search terms should you use to locate resources? Should you gather information from other people and conduct field research? If so, who should you ask? What questions should you ask? Or, should you solely rely on published resources? The options can seem limitless.

Most students, however, already have experience coping with feelings of "Where do I go from here?" Have you ever pulled out your school bag on a Sunday evening, looked at your schedule and homework deadlines for the coming week, and then just felt dazed trying to figure out how you were going to get it all done? Perhaps nothing was due the next day, but >

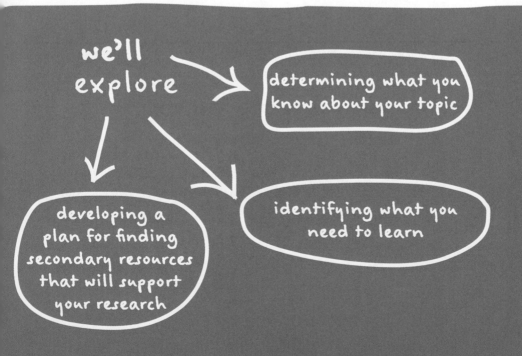

we'll explore → determining what you know about your topic

developing a plan for finding secondary resources that will support your research

identifying what you need to learn

Author: Ricardo needs to complete a project on a twentieth-century painter for an art history class. He is required to use outside resources, write at least a ten-page research paper, and then make a 5- to 10-minute presentation to the class about his research.

Topic: Ricardo knows that he really likes Picasso's work, especially his painting *Three Women*. He visited a Picasso exhibit at a local art museum two weeks ago, and he was inspired by it.

Audience: Ricardo's audience includes his art history instructor as well as his classmates.

Purpose: Ricardo needs to develop, conduct, and produce a research project in the five remaining weeks of the semester.

QUESTIONS

1. How will Ricardo get started with this project? How might he incorporate the Picasso exhibit into his research plan?

2. How will Ricardo know what types of information he will need?

3. How will Ricardo know where to look for information?

4. Have you ever had a project where you were responsible for locating large amounts of information? How did you know what you needed to find? How did you know where to look?

> you knew you needed to get started. And how did you handle it? You probably made some type of plan to get started working on all the projects so they were completed in time for their deadlines.

You can build on your experience dealing with these types of situations. The good news about conducting large research projects is that you can break the process down into manageable steps. If you completed a thorough rhetorical analysis of your writing situation and a critical self-evaluation of your perspectives, experiences, biases, and knowledge, you are already off to a good start. You have an idea of why you are interested in your topic and what information you need to balance the perspective you are developing on your issue. Chances are that you have already read a few things to begin thinking about the topic. And if you focused your research project on a few key research questions, you already have the beginnings of your search terms.

Conducting Research

You have information about nearly any topic available at your fingertips, so it is critical to carefully plan how you will conduct your research. An Internet search engine like Google is probably not the best place to begin. Searching for the key terms from your research question in Google will probably give you thousands (if not millions) of potential sources and Web sites that you will need to comb through, and that can be quite overwhelming (not to mention inefficient!).

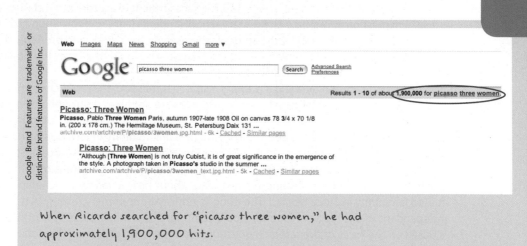

When Ricardo searched for "picasso three women," he had approximately 1,900,000 hits.

A better plan is to

- ⏏ reflect on what you already know about your topic,

- ⏏ decide what kind of information you need about your topic,

- ⏏ narrow your research results by developing specific search terms, and

- ⏏ plan where to look for that information.

2 Conducting Research

As you respond to the following writing activities, think about the rhetorical situation for your writing. Who is your audience, and what is your purpose for writing? Keep this in mind as you respond, and you will have the tools you need to develop a research plan that will give you useful results.

Identifying the Information You Need to Find

See "Reflect: Take an Inventory of What You Know" on page 47 in Chapter 3.

What kind of information do you need to find for your topic? The first step is to "take inventory" of your knowledge about your topic. Once you have determined what you already know, you can start developing specific lists of what you need to learn and what resources you need to find. By taking the time to develop a detailed list of the types of resources you hope to find, you will be able to check categories on your list as you find resources that fit into them. ◻

Primary and Secondary Research One big decision you will need to make is whether to conduct primary research or to rely solely on secondary resources. **Primary research** entails going straight to the source to answer your research question. There are two criteria for defining primary resources. First, the resource itself must be the primary object of study. Primary resources include the data collected from field research as well as from works of art when they are the primary object of the study. Therefore, if Ricardo's question is about the construction of femininity in Picasso's painting, *Three Women,* the painting itself would be a primary resource. If the Picasso exhibit at his local art museum happens to include *Three Women,* he could observe the painting himself and draw his own conclusions. Likewise, if a student in an education class had a research question about how elementary school students learn multiplication tables, her primary resources would be the students themselves, their work, and probably the teacher and his or her lesson plans. All of those materials would be part of the object, or the primary focus, of the research question.

The second criterion defining a primary resource is that you, the researcher, are the one collecting the data. The data from the resources are not filtered through any other person. For example, if Ricardo's research question was "How have art scholars in the past one hundred years discussed the construction of femininity in Picasso's painting, *Three Women*?", the painting itself would no longer be his primary resource. Instead, scholarly articles about femininity and the painting would be his group of primary resources. He would be collecting his own data about how a variety of scholars discussed femininity in *Three Women*. The thing to notice about primary resources is that, independent of the type of resource, book, painting, or person, the label of "primary" is based on the focus of the research question and the person collecting the data.

Secondary resources, on the other hand, are produced by someone else. In other words, your knowledge and experience of the primary resource to answer your research question is mediated through another author or authors. Therefore, journal articles about elementary education and elementary levels of math would probably make up the list of secondary resources for the research question about kids learning multiplication tables. And again, if Ricardo's research question is "How does Picasso construct femininity in *Three Women*?", articles about Picasso, his painting, and femininity are secondary resources that mediate Ricardo's understanding of the primary object of study, the painting itself. However, if Ricardo's research question is, "How have art scholars in the past fifty years discussed the construction of femininity in Picasso's painting, *Three*

Women?", those articles that were secondary resources for the first research question become primary resources for this second question.

Conducting Primary or Secondary Research To decide whether you will be conducting primary or secondary research, return to your rhetorical situation. The type of information you need will be partially determined by your research question, your perception of your audience, and your purpose for writing. Although it is critical that Ricardo conduct primary research for either research question about femininity in the *Three Women* project, it is advisable that he also see what scholars say because he is not an expert in art interpretation. However, if the initial *Three Women* project was just a journal prompt for his art history class, his instructor may not expect secondary research. In this case, it's important to consider the expectations of your audience (your instructor) and the requirements for the assignment.

Should You Conduct Primary or Secondary Research?

To help you determine what type of research will best answer your research question, fulfill your project's purpose, and appeal to your intended audience, you will want to make sure that you are gathering the right types of resources. Use the following chart to help you decide what types of resources you will need and what types of research you will conduct based on your rhetorical situation. You might not be able to think of both primary and secondary resources for every category—that's okay. If you are having trouble thinking of examples for one column or the other, try asking a classmate, a teacher, or a friend. If you are still having trouble thinking of possibilities, that might be a clue as to which type of research you should conduct.

	Primary	Secondary
Purpose: What do you want your readers to do after reading your paper? What types of resources will help you achieve that purpose and motivate your audience to action?		

>>>

>>>

	Primary	Secondary
Audience: What types of resources/data does your audience value— numbers and statistics? anecdotes and stories? case studies and ethnographies? expert testimonies? What will be most convincing?		
Topic/question: What type of information do you need to answer your question thoroughly?		
Author: What time frame do you have for completing this project? What types of resources do you have access to? Who can help you locate and gather information? What and who do you have access to for gathering information?		

If primary research is part of your plan, see Chapter 5, "Conducting Primary Research."

If you are still having difficulty determining where to start, you might want to begin with secondary research because it will give you a foundation in what others have said and written in response to your issue. Secondary research, in essence, helps you understand the rhetorical situation surrounding your issue, and it can give you a solid foundation before embarking on primary research. The remainder of this chapter focuses on strategies for conducting secondary research.

Locating Resources

If you have spent time and energy preparing to research, the process of locating resources will be much simpler than if you start with a blind Internet search. Use the following list to help you get started.

1. Find the resources you already know about.

2. Find the resources that emerged during your planning.

3. Ask a librarian to help with your search.

4. Systematically search through new resources.

Start with the obvious and then search out resources that you did not know about. Once you have tapped the resources that you, your friends, your family, your classmates, and your instructor(s) have suggested, then go to the librarian. Librarians are trained to find information; however, they cannot serve you well if you haven't prepared for meeting with them. Instead of thinking of the librarian as the starting point, think of him or her as a place to go for additional help once you have begun to determine the direction of your research. A good thing to prepare before you talk to the librarian is a list of search terms.

Specific Search Terms

When you begin to search for secondary resources, you need a list of specific terms that will help you locate those resources. Obviously, you will need to use specific terms to locate secondary resources in the library or on the Internet. However, have you considered that terms that seem like synonyms might return a different group of hits? For example, try searching for the terms "distance learning" and "distance education." Although there will probably be some overlap, the search will also yield a lot of different sources. Sources dealing with "distance learning" focus more on the actual teaching and learning activities in a "distance" class and sources discussing "distance education" focus more on institutional and programmatic concerns like how many courses to offer and how to train teachers. Therefore, you may want to use closely related terms to help you locate more resources during your research. Be aware, though, that subtle differences of meaning might impact your search results.

In the quest to identify search terms, you already have a key resource, your research question. Obviously, the key words in your research question will be your principal search terms. The key words are the descriptive nouns, verbs, and adjectives in your research question. If you can't easily identify key words in your research question, you may need to go back and continue narrowing and focusing your question. And if the key words seem a little vague or you find that you are collecting an abundance of data, again, you may need to continue narrowing and focusing your research question. Once you have that initial list of key words from your research question, developing a larger list of search terms is a relatively easy process.

Ricardo decided he was most interested in examining how art scholars have discussed the concept of femininity in Picasso's painting, *Three Women*. Ricardo circled the following key words in his research question:

How have art scholars

in the past fifty years

discussed the construction of femininity

in Picasso's painting, *Three Women*?

Although adding these extra key words to Ricardo's search did help diminish the number of hits, Google still returned approximately 5,260 hits.

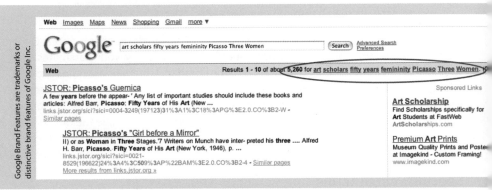

With a deadline in five weeks, Ricardo did not have enough time to search these 5,260 resources, as well as all the leads that his art history instructor gave him. Ricardo had a couple of options: he could try a search engine that would give him more focused results or he could focus his search terms further.

Internet Search Engines   One strategy Ricardo should try is to get away from the standard Google search. General search engines such as Google can return many different resources, but because they do not limit the kinds of resources returned they are not a helpful starting point for Ricardo. Because he is focusing his research on scholarly interpretations of femininity in Picasso's painting, he should start by using a search engine, or a database, that looks for academic articles and resources. By simply changing his search engine from Google to Google Scholar, but still using the same search terms, Ricardo would limit the number of resources returned from 5,260 to 3,820.

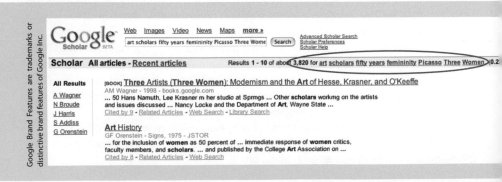

He could also try searching in an academic journal database, such as Gale's Academic File One. These types of academic databases would be available through his school's library. 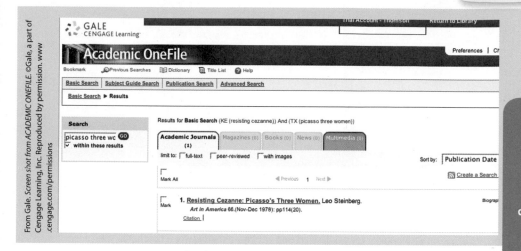 This search only returned one hit for the search terms "Picasso Three Women."

For more information on databases, see the "Periodicals" section later in this chapter.

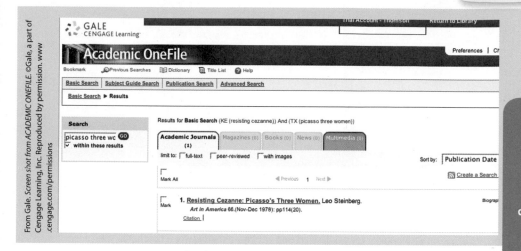

From Gale. Screen shot from ACADEMIC ONEFILE. ©Gale, a part of Cengage Learning, Inc. Reproduced by permission. www.cengage.com/permissions

2. Conducting Research

While the 3,820 resources Google Scholar yielded are slightly more manageable than 5,260, Ricardo might want to focus his Internet searching by narrowing his search terms further. However, with only one hit in the library database, he'll definitely need to use alternative search terms and speak with a librarian.

Expanding and Focusing Search Terms There are three primary methods to help identify, evaluate, and further focus key words.

1. Be sure to carefully acknowledge the literal differences between the words in your research question. Using a dictionary, look up the definitions for each key word from your research question as well as two or three alternative words. Notice the subtle distinctions between the definitions. Are any of those distinctions completely inappropriate to answer your research question? Will your intended audience heartily approve or disapprove of specific definitions? For example, Ricardo knows that his instructor will accept the ideas and perspectives of art "scholars" but not art "critics."

...write...

List Alternative Key Words

After you circle the key words in your research question, write them in the accompanying chart. Brainstorm alternative terms for each key word. After you've run out of ideas, ask your friends, family, classmates, and instructors to help you.

>>>

>>>

	Key Word 1	Key Word 2	Key Word 3
Brain-storming			
Friends & family			
Classmates & instructors			

For each original key word, select one or two alternative words that might work well. Why do you think they will work well? Did you check the dictionary definitions?

For each original key word, select one or two alternative words you know will not work. Why won't they?

2. Try adding modifying phrases to the key words in your research question. For example, if you are researching the differences between Chevy automobile models in the 1950s, you may find a lot of information. You might first focus on a specific model, like the Bel Air. You may decide you want to focus only on specific years, like the major differences between '55, '56, and '57. The further you focus, the more modifying words you add to your key search terms.

3. As you conduct your research, identify the alternative phrases people use when talking about your subject. Once you've identified some of those alternative phrases, carefully distinguish why one person refers to your topic using one phrase and another person uses a different phrase. As you did with the literal, or dictionary, definitions, search for subtle differences to help you further focus your research as well as to start processing your data.

...write...

Develop a List of Search Terms

Once you have your initial set of key words, based on your narrowed and focused research question, you can produce a list of viable search terms using the following activity. Once you have that list, be sure to talk to a librarian. The librarian will help add, and cull, terms from your list based on his or her experience as a researcher. The librarian should also be able to help you identify related Library of Congress classification terms that will help you find information in the library more readily. Keep your chart of search terms with you as you collect your data. While reading articles or listening to interview responses, other useful terms might emerge during your research process.

	Key Word 1	Key Word 2	Key Word 3
Librarians & the Library of Congress classification terms			
Terms you find during your research process			

You may have to remove some search terms from your list to keep your research manageable and focused. Many researchers find they have too much information and need to identify the resources that are most pertinent to their specific topic. In other words, after spending so much time narrowing and focusing your research question, developing a list of search terms broadens the possible field of resources. To keep yourself sane, try to keep your search terms narrowed and focused as well.

Search Engines and Web Directories Ricardo's searches in Google and Google Scholar provide one example of how a researcher's choice of search engine can make a difference in the resources he or she finds. Different search engines yield varied results because they are programmed to search differently. Depending on how the search engine has been programmed, it might rank returns differently as well. If you have not tried more than one search engine, you might try your search terms on a couple of different search engines to see what results you receive. A few of the most popular search engines are:

- Ask.com (http://ask.com)
- Google (http://www.google.com)
- MSN.com (http://www.msn.com)
- Yahoo! (http://www.yahoo.com)

You might also try a couple of metasearch engines that compile the results of multiple search engines for you. Several popular metasearch engines are:

- Dogpile (http://www.dogpile.com)

- Excite (http://www.excite.com)

- WebCrawler (http://www.webcrawler.com)

If you are having difficulty finding helpful sources on your topic, then a metasearch engine might be a useful tool.

In addition to search engines, Web directories can be useful starting points for locating online resources dealing with your research topic. The Open Directory Project (http://www.dmoz.org) is an example of a Web directory, a list of links to other useful resources on a multitude of topics. Web directories are different from search engines because they do not list links, or hits, based on key words. Instead, they list links by categories and subcategories. Web directories are edited by actual people who submit sites for inclusion in different categories and review the appropriateness of sites included in the directory. This is distinct from search engines, which use programmed Web "crawlers" that search available Web sites automatically.

techno_tip >

> Refine Your Search Results <

For an interactive tutorial about refining search results, go to *Student Resources* on the online resource center at www.cengage.com/english/Miller-Cochran/WGTR.

Most search engines now include an option to use advanced search functions to narrow a search.

Google includes an "Advanced Search" link, and Ask.com has a link that just says "Advanced." Advanced search options let you narrow the search to include all of the words in your search terms, only results from a specific date forward, or only results in a specific language, among other things.

Google Advanced Search

Advanced Search Tips | About Google

Use the form below and your advanced search will appear here

Find web pages that have...

all these words:

this exact wording or phrase:

one or more of these words: OR   OR

But don't show pages that have...

any of these unwanted words:

Need more tools?

Results per page:	10 results
Language:	any language
File type:	any format
Search within a site or domain:	

(e.g. youtube.com, .edu)

⊞ Date, usage rights, numeric range, and more

Advanced Search

Types of Resources

In this text we talk about different kinds of resources you might find through two different categorizations: how they change over time and how they are reviewed. Before discussing resources any further, it's important to understand these two distinct characteristics.

How Texts Change over Time

One of the defining characteristics of a resource is how it changes (or does not change) over time. When you begin to evaluate your resources and consider how you will interpret them and incorporate them into your writing, ◻ you first need to understand the nature of the resources that you find. Understanding the nature of the resource is also important when you need to determine how to cite the source. ◻ Resources can be categorized in these three ways:

- **Static**. Static resources are only "published" once and do not generally change. They may go into other editions, but those are considered separate entities. Examples include books, paintings, films, and basic html coded Web sites.

- **Syndicated**. Syndicated resources are released, or syndicated, over time under the same general title. Examples include periodicals (magazines and journals), television shows, blogs, and podcasts.

- **Dynamic**. Dynamic resources are never permanently published in a final form. If there are repeat *performances* or *publications,* they are different every time. Examples include plays and other live performances, wiki publications, and field research (observations, interviews, and surveys).

How Texts Are Reviewed

Another important characteristic of the resources you find is the process by which they are reviewed. Review generally takes place before publication, but with the technological capabilities that individuals now have for publishing material, review sometimes happens after the fact.

- **Edited**. Before the resource is published, someone with some type of authority or certification (besides the author) reviews the resources and provides suggestions for revision. Editors also act as a filter prior to publication.

- **Peer reviewed**. Before the resource is published, it must not only pass the editor's criteria but must also be approved by peers in the same profession as the author.

- **Self-published**. The author publishes the resource. There is no authoritative editor or other filter. Whoever provides the author with resources to help publish, however, may function as some form of filter.

Understanding the review process of your resources will also be helpful as you evaluate the usefulness and credibility of the resources that you find.

See Chapters 7 and 10 for more information on evaluating and incorporating resources.

For more information on documentation styles, see Chapters 12–15.

2. Conducting Research

Library Resources versus Internet Resources

In the past, you might have thought about resources as being either "in the library" or "on the Internet." This is an easy distinction, but it is not always accurate or applicable.

For more information on documentation styles, see Chapters 12–15.

Consider an article that you might find in the *New York Times,* a newspaper that can be read in print or online. You might find the same article in the print version of the paper and online. If it's the same article, does it matter where you found it? For the purposes of evaluating the credibility or usefulness of the resource, probably not. It's still a newspaper article. If you are determining how to cite the resource, however, the location of the resource does matter. 🗅

When you are reviewing and analyzing your resources, keep in mind that the library/Internet distinction is not quite as simple as it might seem at first. The Internet is where students often turn when they are having difficulty getting started. Many instructors warn students against using Internet resources because they are easily alterable and because anyone can construct and publish a Web site. These points are important to remember, but it is essential to use clear evaluative criteria when you are looking at *any* resource. Print resources can be self-published as well. Analyzing how easily a resource is changed, how often it is changed, who changed it, who reviews it, and who is responsible for the content will help you choose resources that are reliable and credible, wherever you might find them.

Some Internet resources, because of the nature of their publication and review processes and the ease with which they can be accessed, need to be scrutinized especially carefully, however. Many instructors warn students about using sources on *Wikipedia,* for example (http://www.wikipedia.org). *Wikipedia* is an online encyclopedia where any users can add, revise, and delete content. *Wikipedia* has an elaborate review system where various users take responsibility for reviewing and monitoring content, but it is not fool-proof. If you have never tried making a revision to an article in *Wikipedia,* you should—if for no other reason than to see how easy it is for any user to change the content of the reference. You might also notice whether or not someone else makes a change to the page you edited. How often is the information shifting?

An equally important point to remember is that *Wikipedia* is not just an online resource—it is the online equivalent of a reference book. References such as encyclopedias, like *Encyclopedia Britannica* and *Wikipedia,* can be good places to learn general information about a subject, but they are not the most authoritative resources to use as evidence in an argument. Reference books are compilations of the research done by others. In other words, they are not primary resources or even necessarily secondary resources—they are often, in essence, *tertiary* resources. They can be helpful at the beginning stage of a project, though, because they often include useful bibliographies that point you to other helpful resources. They might also help you identify potential search terms.

One of the best methods for finding the most reliable perspectives on a specific topic is to search through and compare a variety of types of resources. As we mentioned earlier, you should not limit your research to an online search of a few terms. Yes, you can find some very valid and useful resources on the Internet; however, you should also search more traditional resources found in your school or public library. Consider looking through and/or using the various media and digital resources described in the next sections to help you find resources on your topic. The resources listed are divided according to how they change over time: static, syndicated, and dynamic. They are also discussed in terms of the review processes that they might use, when appropriate.

techno_tip >

> Edit and Review the History of a Wikipedia Page <

For an interactive tutorial about editing and reviewing wikis, go to *Student Resources* on the online resource center at www.cengage.com/english/Miller-Cochran/WGTR.

Pages in *Wikipedia* can be edited by clicking on the "edit this page" tab located at the top of each entry. Readers can also look at a list of the edits made by clicking the "history" tab at the top of a

Wikipedia page. Looking at the history of a page will also give you a good idea of how often the information in *Wikipedia* changes. Of course, some topics are edited more often than other topics. The accompanying Web screen gives an example of the "history" page for the entry on "secondary research"; readers can click on any of the links to see previous versions of the page.

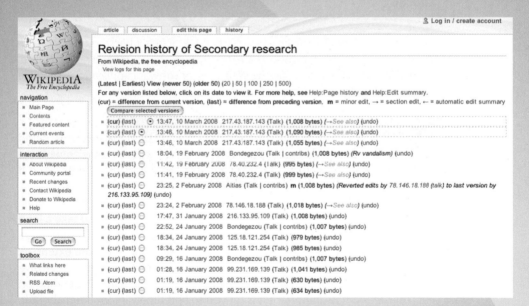

Pages for topics that are in the news frequently, however, are not open to public editing. See the page for the entry on "global warming" on the next page as an example. You can view the "history" of the page, but there is no option to "edit this page."

You'll also find that pages for major celebrities and political candidates are also closed to public editing. The "discussion" tab is always open for public comment, though, and that can provide access to insightful exchanges about the topic.   >>>

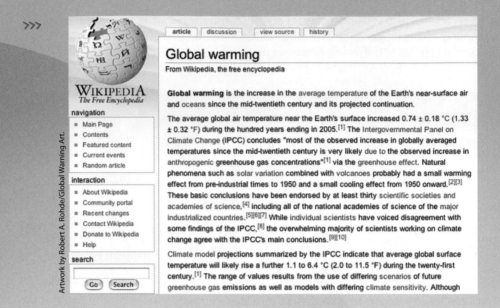

Static Resources

Static resources are often the ones that students think of first when they start to conduct secondary research. Static resources are usually published once and rarely revised. If they are revised, as in the case of books, Web sites, or software applications, they are usually released as a separate edition.

Books

Many students think of books as the most authoritative and desirable resource to find when completing a research project. After all, if someone took the time to write an entire book, then they must have a lot of useful information to share, right? And if someone took the effort and expense to publish the book, then it must be authoritative. Right? Well, sometimes . . . but not always. Books can be useful because they compile a great deal of information into one publication. However, books can also take a long time to publish, so they are not always the best place to start looking for cutting-edge research on a current issue. On the other hand, books are generally more extensive, in-depth treatments of a topic, so they often have excellent bibliographies and can give a researcher a good sense of the background and context of an issue. Depending on what your topic is and how important it is for you to find timely information about it, books might or might not be the best place to start.

If you look for books on your topic, you will want to scan several things that will help you quickly evaluate the usefulness of a book in answering your research question.

1. **Copyright.** The date of publication will give you a sense of how current the information in the book is.

2. **Publisher.** If the publisher is a reputable one (e.g., an academic press or a press that publishes a great deal in a particular area or field), then it could help you

determine how reliable the information in the book is. An academic press also probably has a peer review process, which means that other professionals in the field reviewed the information in the book and suggested revisions and corrections prior to publication. See what information you can find about the publisher's review process. You might also do a search for any reviews of the book. Be aware that the Internet has made it quite easy to self-publish books; in such cases, it will be of the utmost importance that you verify the author's credibility.

3. **Table of contents**. If you have been looking for information on this topic already, a quick scan of the table of contents will give you a sense of whether the book presents a balanced and thorough treatment of the subject.

4. **Bibliography**. The bibliography should provide evidence that the author(s) consulted a multitude of other resources in writing the book. Scanning the bibliography will give you a sense of how balanced and thorough the author's research was.

One of the best places to start looking for books is at a university or college library. Searching the online catalog will give you a sense of whether or not the school has any books that might be useful for answering your research questions.

Search the Library Catalog

...write...

You might start your search for resources by looking through your library's online catalog. As you search, take notes on what you find in response to the following tasks.

1. Enter your search terms into the keyword search in the library catalog. How many resources does the catalog return? Which ones look potentially useful to you? Make sure you note the call number of particularly promising resources so that you can find them on the library shelves.

2. Use variations on your search terms. You might try different combinations of terms, or you might try some variations on your key terms. What kinds of results did you find when you altered your search terms? Which key terms were most useful?

3. Your campus might have multiple libraries, or you might have access to libraries on other campuses through interlibrary loan. What resources could you request from other locations? If you request resources from other libraries or campuses, make sure that you leave enough time to receive the resources and look through them before an assignment or project is due.

4. Your library might also have access to electronic books, or ebooks. If you are doing your search remotely, ebooks can be an especially useful resource. Does the library catalog list any ebooks on your topic?

5. Go to the shelves and look for the resources that sound most promising to you. Once you find the section in the library shelves that has books on your topic, browse the shelf. You might be surprised at the useful resources you find by reading the spines of books surrounding yours on the library shelves. What titles do you see that look promising?

Web Sites

Well-chosen Web sites can provide some of the most up-to-date information on a subject. If your research question requires that you find the most current information available, you might want to search the Internet for appropriate and useful Web sites. As we mentioned earlier, though, the amount of information available (and the number of Web sites on some popular subjects) can be completely overwhelming. If you decide to surf the Web for information on your topic, you should carefully narrow your search to find resources that will be applicable and useful. To determine how reliable the information is on the Web site you have found, look for the following key pieces of information.

1. **Author**. Who wrote the information on the Web site? What are the author's credentials? If you cannot find an author, that is not always cause for alarm. In such a case, look for a sponsoring organization and see if that alleviates your concerns.

2. **Sponsoring organization**. Is there an organization sponsoring the information on the Web site? For example, is the Web site published by a government entity? Is it a corporate Web site? Sometimes you'll have to dig for information, but you should be able to find an author, sponsoring organization, or both. Sometimes the extension on the URL can give you a hint as to where the information came from as well. For example, .gov indicates a government-sponsored Web site, .edu is generally an educational institution, .org is a nonprofit organization, and .com is a commercial Web site, most often a corporate or personal Web site. If you cannot find either an author or a sponsoring organization, then you should be skeptical about the information you have found.

3. **Date of publication and/or last update**. When was the information on the site published? This might be important for your topic, depending on your rhetorical situation. You might also look at how recently the information was updated.

One of the biggest concerns about Internet resources is that there is not always a clearly stated review process. If a resource you have found is located in an online publication, you might be able to find specific details about their review and publication process. And if the Web site is published by a sponsoring organization, you could probably conclude that the organization approves of the content (unless a disclaimer is attached to the article/site).

Audio and Video Files

If audio and video clips would provide useful data for answering your research question, you might try looking for audio or video files in your school's library and on the Internet.

For more information, see the section "Syndicated Resources" later in this chapter.

Your library might even provide remote access to some audio and video files, if you have a password-protected connection to the library's collection. On the Internet, you can search iTunes for audio files, and some search engines (such as AltaVista) provide audio- and video-specific searches. If you are interested in video clips, try searching YouTube and Google Video. If you find a podcast that you find useful, it would be considered a syndicated resource because it is published periodically in installments.

Of course, the considerations that apply to Web sites also apply to resources that you find online, such as audio and video files. You'll want to ask similar kinds of questions as you consider the reliability of those resources, especially about who uploaded the information. Also, be certain to check that the person who uploaded the material did not violate copyright if you are going to use it in your research.

Microfilm and Microfiche

Many libraries provide access to older periodical information and rare pieces in their collection through microfilm and microfiche (also called microforms on some campuses). If you are researching a historical topic, microforms can be invaluable. Many libraries find it costly and space-prohibitive to maintain all of the possible older and historic documents that their collection could hold, so microfilm and microfiche provide ways to make these documents accessible. If you have never used a microform reader before, don't hesitate to give it a try. You just might find a treasure trove of useful information that you didn't realize was available to you.

Syndicated Resources

Syndicated resources are published in installments over time, usually under the same general title. For example, magazines and newspapers are syndicated resources because they publish issues periodically that include new articles and information. Likewise, blogs are syndicated resources because the authors publish new entries over time.

Periodicals

Periodicals include newspapers, magazines, academic and trade journals, and other publications that are released "periodically" under the same title. They can be found in print and online, and sometimes the same publication can be found in both places. Many newspapers, for example, have both print and online versions. If you choose to cite periodicals as references, it is important that you understand what kind of periodical you are reading.

- **Newspapers and magazines** tend to divide into two categories: consumer periodicals and trade/business periodicals. Each type is targeted to a different audience.

- **Journals** can be divided into at least two categories: trade journals and academic journals. They have various degrees of review before publication, and they also have different standards for research appropriate for their audiences.

Academic journals are often considered most authoritative because of their rigorous review process, but your topic might not be discussed in academic journals. As you choose resources for your project, think about who your audience is and what your purpose is in writing. What kind of publication will be most authoritative and convincing to your readers?

The most efficient and effective way of searching for periodicals is through the online databases available through your library. Most libraries have two kinds of online databases—general databases and subject-specific databases. General databases for academic journals include Gale's Academic File One or Academic Search Premier.

2. Conducting Research

Google Scholar is a search engine that is specifically focused on academic resources, and it is available to the public. Your school library probably also has databases for newspapers and magazines as well as subject-specific databases for academic journals.

...write...

Search for Resources in Periodicals

Try the following steps to find resources in periodicals that will help you answer your research question. As you complete each step, take careful notes on what you find so that you can locate the resources again later.

☐ Use an academic database through your school library. With the search terms that you have decided on, follow these steps:

   o Search for your terms in a general academic database.

   o Try a different set of terms in the same database to see if you get a different set of results.

   o Choose a subject-specific database, appropriate to your topic, and search for your terms again.

☐ Search for your terms in Google Scholar, an academic search engine. What resources do you find that are different from the journal databases?

☐ Enter your search terms into a newspaper database to see if you can find any news stories about your subject.

For more information about audio and video files, see the section "Static Resources" in this chapter.

Podcasts

Podcasts are audio files that are published in installments. They operate almost like an audio version of a magazine or blog. The difference between an individual audio file and a podcast is simply that podcasts have more than one episode, or installment. Podcasts and individual audio files can be evaluated similarly, but they are cited slightly differently. ▢

Blogs and RSS Feeds

A blog (which is a shortened version of the phrase "Web log") is a Web site where entries are published over time and usually organized chronologically. Many people keep blogs as a sort of public, online journal, while other blog sites are collectively written by a group of people. Some blogs focus on a particular subject while others are more general in scope.

Because blogs can be hosted on free public sites and started by anyone willing to take the time to set up an account, you need to be particularly careful when choosing blog entries as resources in your research. Be aware of who the author is. The blog should have an "About" tab that gives information about the author(s), and if you have difficulty finding such information, you might question the credibility of the site. Try to determine what makes the author a reputable source of information on the subject. If you choose to cite a blog entry in your research, give the resource an appropriate context. Explain where the information came from, and consider whether you need to defend the relevance of the blog entry in your argument.

If you are interested in looking for blogs that deal with your topic, try searching an online blog directory. Several directories of blogs exist, and you can find personal and professional blogs on a variety of topics. Try looking for blogs at:

- BlogCatalog: http://www.blogcatalog.com

- BlogHub: http://www.bloghub.com

- Blogarama: http://www.blogarama.com/

- Feedster: http://feedster.com/

- Technorati: http://www.technorati.com/

If you find a potentially interesting blog, you could follow it for a while and watch for new posts. An easy way to do this, without having to visit the blog on a regular basis, is by subscribing to an RSS (Really Simple Syndication) feed. An RSS feed will alert you when new blog entries or updates have been posted on Web sites that you are "watching," and all of the new information can be gathered in one place for you by using an RSS aggregator. RSS aggregators can save the time spent visiting multiple Web sites.

2 Conducting Research

techno_tip >

> Set up RSS Feeds <

For an interactive tutorial about RSS feeds, go to *Student Resources* on the online resource center at www.cengage.com/english/ Miller-Cochran/WGTR.

Several RSS aggregators are available online:

- Google Reader: http://www.google.com/ reader

- Bloglines: http://www.bloglines.com

- Gritwire: http://www.gritwire.com

- SharpReader: http://www.sharpreader .net

An easy, and free, RSS feed aggregator to start with is Google Reader. If you start at the Google homepage (http://www.google.com) and click the "more" link, you'll find "Reader" on the list of other options. Set up an account by clicking the link on the Google Reader homepage.

Once you have created your account and logged in, you can easily add blogs or Web sites that you would like to subscribe to by clicking the "Add Subscription" link. Google Reader will compile the blogs you are watching, and you can read new entries in the center of the screen.   >>>

>>> Reading an RSS Feed in Google Reader

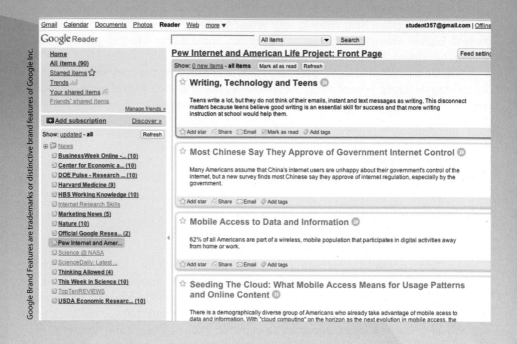

Google Brand Features are trademarks or distinctive brand features of Google Inc.

Dynamic Resources

Dynamic resources are meant to change. They are continuously changeable over time through repeated revisions or performances. Dynamic resources are often not edited or peer reviewed before publication, but they are usually reviewed (or perhaps just revised by a reviewer) after they are published. The reviews might be in the form of comments or suggestions. They might also take the form of discussion such as that found under the "discussion" tab in *Wikipedia*. In such cases, it is important to remember that the credibility and authority of the resource should be measured by looking at the entire context of the source—not just the original text but also its revisions and reviewers.

Email Lists and Newsgroups

Email lists and newsgroups are probably the least "changeable" of the dynamic resources. Individual email messages and postings to newsgroups often cannot be changed or altered, but other participants in the list or group can respond to the message by affirming, disagreeing, or revising. Depending on the topic of your research, you might find an email list or newsgroup dedicated to your issue or area of interest, and you might find it helpful to join the list or group and "listen" to the conversations in progress. Some lists will have an archive of past messages that can be searched as well. If you are interested in looking for email lists or newsgroups, check out Google Groups (http://groups.google.com), Yahoo Groups (http://groups.yahoo.com), and MSN Groups (http://groups.msn.com).

Social Networking Sites

Social networking sites, such as MySpace and Facebook, provide opportunities to connect with and communicate with other people in a Web-based environment. Many social networking sites have groups within them that are interested in specific subjects, and you might find a group that is discussing the issue that you are researching. You can also create your own social network through applications such as Ning (http://www.ning .com) if you'd like to invite people to talk who are interested in your research question.

Online Communities

While email lists, newsgroups, and social networking sites are all different types of online communities, they are all primarily *asynchronous* environments; that is, participants do not generally interact at the same time. In *synchronous* online communities, participants communicate at the same time and can instantly respond to one another. Instant messaging (IM), or chat, discussions are an example. Chats are usually between just two individuals; some IM technologies, however, like Google Talk, allow multi-user chat sessions. IM and chat technologies generally allow you to record a transcript of the live discussion, making it easier to use the chat as a resource later. MUDs (Multi-User Dungeon or Domain) and MOOs (MUD Object-Oriented) are text-based multi-user virtual environments. MUDs and MOOs have slowly been replaced by graphics-based virtual environments like SecondLife (http://secondlife.com/) and World of Warcraft (http://www.worldofwarcraft.com/index.xml). Depending on the software that runs the virtual environment, you may be able to record a live session.

Synchronous online communities can often be useful for conducting primary research, either by observing the environment or by meeting individuals in the environment to talk about your research topic. In either case, the strength of conducting research in an online synchronous community is the ability to get instant feedback. If you have a question, you can ask it; if you need clarification, you can get it immediately.

If you are using an online synchronous environment as a primary resource, you need to carefully consider the ethical concerns of working with human participants. ▢

See "Ethical Considerations" in Chapter 5.

Wikis

Wikis are software applications that allow users to create and edit pages easily, often in a collaborative environment. Wikis exist for all sorts of purposes, but they are often used for collaborative writing and development. *Wikipedia* is arguably the most famous wiki, but wikis exist for other purposes as well. Not all wikis are public, and not all wikis that can be viewed online are open to editing by the general public. If you are interested in searching for a wiki that focuses on your subject, try searching at WikiIndex (http://wikiindex.org). Several resources are available if you would like to try setting up your own wiki, which can be especially useful if you are working on your research project with one or more collaborators. Try one of the following applications to set up your own wiki space:

- PB Wiki (http://www.pbwiki.com)

- WetPaint (http://www.wetpaint.com)

- Google Docs (http://docs.google.com). Note: Google Docs works similarly to a wiki, and it also has elements of a word processor. It can be especially useful for collaborative writing.

2 Conducting Research

...write...

Search for a Variety of Resources

Once you have read about all of the different kinds of resources, take a few minutes to brainstorm some ideas about how you might use various resources to answer your research question. Write down your responses to the following questions.

1. What kinds of resources could you use in the invention stage of your research process? Could you look at blogs to help refine your research question? Could you browse news-related Web sites to search for ways to focus your research? Would browsing through recent periodicals help you think through your topic? Look through the different kinds of resources listed in this chapter and write down a few that might be useful as you plan your research and writing.

2. Where might you find the most authoritative, persuasive resources that will help you answer your research question? What kinds of static, syndicated, and dynamic resources might you search for?

3. How will you evaluate the credibility of the resources that you find? What criteria will you use to determine if they are persuasive, reliable resources? Consider your rhetorical situation and compare it with what you know about your resource: who wrote it and when; how and when it was updated or revised; how it was reviewed and by whom?

Developing a Research Plan

Finding useful resources is the heart of research—collecting information and data about your topic in general and your research question specifically. To be successful in this step, it is important to have a clearly defined research plan. Many students become easily overwhelmed at this step because of all of the possible resources they might access for information. For example, imagine a student in an English department who is doing a study on contemporary adaptations and representations of Charles Dickens's *Oliver Twist*. During the first step of her research, she would develop a focused research question: "How do historical representations of Charles Dickens's *Oliver Twist* impact interpretations and representations in the first part of the twenty-first century?"

During the next step she would develop a research plan that includes a detailed list of the types of information she needs to find. She might also keep a checklist or chart, like the accompanying one, of the various types of resources she should search to find information; she wouldn't want to miss something in her research process. In Table 4.1, notice the variety in changeable resources (static, syndicated, and dynamic) as well as the variety in who reviews the information, usually before it is published (edited, peer reviewed, and self-published).

Table 4.1.
Types of Resources on *Oliver Twist*

	STATIC Published once and does not generally change	SYNDICATED Released, or syndicated, over time under the same general title (e.g., magazines, newspapers, journals)	DYNAMIC Continuously changeable through repeat performances or revisions
EDITED Reviewed before publication by someone with authority or certification	Novel form of *Oliver Twist*; contemporary films and filmic adaptations of *Oliver Twist*	Original syndicated version of *Oliver Twist* published in *Bentley's Miscellany*	Video tape of a live theater production of *Oliver Twist*
PEER REVIEWED Reviewed by others in the same profession	Scholarly books about Dickens, *Oliver Twist*, the history of the novel, and popular culture	Articles from the following types of scholarly journals: *Dickens Quarterly*, *Dickens Studies Annual*, *Victorian Literature and Culture*, and *Sight and Sound* (for articles about film adaptation of *Oliver Twist*)	Wikipedia entries about Dickens and *Oliver Twist* that include comments and citations from noted Dickens scholars
SELF-PUBLISHED Published and revised by the author	A Dickens scholar's personal Web site	Blog publication of "*Oliver Twist* in 10 minutes": http://asgt.livejournal.com/36313.html	Observation of restaurant in Seattle called *Oliver's Twist*; video footage of a group of students reading *Oliver Twist* aloud

Now that you know what you need and have an idea of how and where to look for it, you need to develop a research plan. "But wait," you might ask, "I know what I want and how to get it, so why don't I just get started?" You can, but how will you know what you still need to find during the process if you don't first outline a research plan? Good research is a systematic study of a specific topic. Medical doctors don't just ask random patients about the results of a new surgical procedure; instead, the doctors carefully plan which patients will be asked to participate in the research, in what manner and how often they will be assessed, and what criteria will be used to evaluate the patient's progress under the new method.

The components, structure, and steps of your research plan will depend on your rhetorical situation. However, all research plans are based around the following key questions.

- What data do you need to collect?
- In what manner will you collect that data?
- On what timeline will you collect that data?

> If you are interested in considering primary research for your project, look at Chapter 5.

In other words, what, how, and when will you conduct your research project? If Ricardo decides to conduct both primary and secondary research for his project, his research plan might look like Table 4.2.

For now, consider the secondary resources that you will need to find for your project.

Table 4.2.
Ricardo's Research Plan

What types of resources does Ricardo need to find?	Where will Ricardo locate these resources?	When will Ricardo locate these resources?
Primary documents articles by art scholars that discuss femininity in Picasso's *Three Women* • Feminist art scholars	Ask his art instructor Ask other art instructors Ask librarian Search "Google Scholar"	Week 2: Monday Week 2: Tuesday Week 2: Wednesday Week 3: Monday Week 3: Tuesday
Secondary documents articles that discuss how art scholars have talked about femininity in Picasso's *Three Women* • Art scholars • Feminist scholars	Ask his art instructor Ask other art instructors Ask librarian Search "Google Scholar"	Week 2: Monday Week 2: Tuesday Week 2: Wednesday Week 3: Monday Week 3: Tuesday

What's Your Plan?

If you have already completed, and possibly reflected back upon and revised, the various activities in this chapter, you have a working draft of your research plan, without the timeline component. You can fully develop a research plan in three steps.

1. List the different types of data and resources you need to collect. If possible, break the types of data and resources into smaller pieces. For example, if you are searching for statistics that prove Earth has a population problem, you can break it into smaller groups of statistics about rising birth rates, rising life expectances, and rising population numbers based on continents or countries. Ask classmates and family members to help you break down your data and resource needs into the smallest possible groups.

2. For each piece of information, describe where and how you will locate and collect that data. Be specific about where you will be looking—list not only that you'll be using the school's library databases, for example, but which specific databases. If for some reason you have to stop searching in the middle of a session, you'll be able to refer back to which databases you wanted to search (and if you tracked your data collection well, which ones you already searched). Ask your instructors and librarians for help with ideas on where you might locate different types of resources.

3. Provide a timeline, preferably deadlines, for each task that you have to complete. Just think, the smaller each task is (the smaller each group of data to collect, the smaller each step of collecting it), the easier it will be to "fit" your research into your already busy schedule. If you leave your research plan in big pieces of work, you will only be able to work in big pieces of time. If you take the time to break your research up into smaller, more manageable pieces, you'll be able to fit it into smaller portions of your day; therefore, you'll work more consistently and chip away at your research project.

>>>

>>>

Types of Resources	Location of Resources	Deadlines

Conducting Primary Research

As you search for an answer to your research question, you need to determine what kind of research will best fit your rhetorical situation. Will you need to collect data on your own (primary research), will you need to read the research results of others (secondary research), or will you need to do both? Secondary research is likely more familiar to you, but you shouldn't avoid primary research just because you have never conducted an interview or designed a survey. Sometimes primary research is essential for answering a research question. If your question deals with a specific local situation, for instance, primary research might be the best way to answer it. For example, Kira's situation detailed on the next page requires primary research to answer her research question.

This chapter describes three common types of primary research: observations, interviews, and surveys. Each method provides distinct possibilities for the kinds of information you can gather and the ways in which you might answer a research question. Take a look at Table 5.1 on page 93 for descriptions of types of primary research. >

we'll explore

- when and how to conduct interviews, observations, and surveys
- what ethical considerations are important to keep in mind
- developing a research plan
- how to interpret and present the results of primary research

© Kharidehal Abhirama

Author: Kira, a student at a community college, is taking a biology class and her professor has asked the class to consider community practices that affect the environment. Her assignment includes writing an investigative report on one issue and its implications on the environment.

Topic: Kira has noticed that the students on her campus fail to use recycling bins for aluminum cans and plastic bottles, and she decides to investigate the reasons students don't recycle on campus.

Audience: Kira's primary audience is her biology professor, and her secondary audience is the staff on her campus who might be interested in recycling efforts.

Purpose: Kira's immediate purpose is to write a report to fulfill the requirement for her biology class. An additional purpose, though, is to raise awareness among students, faculty, and staff about the importance of recycling.

QUESTIONS

1. How would Kira gather information about the frequency of recycling on her campus?

2. How might Kira use the research that others have published to support her investigation?

3. If you were Kira, what would be your first step in working on this project?

Table 5.1.
Types of Primary Research

Type of Primary Research	Method of Data Collection
Observations	Gathering data through your own senses
Interviews	Asking questions of one or more people in person
Surveys	Asking questions of larger groups of people

2. Conducting Research

> As you read the descriptions of different methods of primary research in this chapter, keep in mind that researchers often use more than one method of gathering data in order to avoid inaccuracies in the research and to confirm findings. Validating the research results is the researcher's responsibility, and you could confirm your research conclusions by finding two or three reliable sources or methods that provide similar results. For example, as she prepares to investigate the question about recycling on campus, Kira realizes that she can't answer her question solely by reading the research that others have published. She might be able to gather some general information through secondary resources about why people don't recycle but she won't be able to determine reasons for lack of recycling on *her* campus. Instead, she plans to form a hypothesis about whether or not people recycle on her campus (based on the general information she gleans from her secondary resources), and then she will test that hypothesis by conducting a series of observations to determine the extent of the problem. She could also develop a hypothesis about why people don't recycle on campus and test it by conducting interviews with students on campus and designing and distributing a survey. Her secondary research will help her determine the extent of the problem (and might help her fine-tune her research question), but the results of her primary research will form the basis of her response to her research question. Such a combination of methods will help her interpret the data more accurately, especially if that analysis is paired with background investigation from secondary resources that help her understand the results of her primary research.

Observations

When researchers conduct observations, they use all of their senses to note everything they can about a subject and its environment. Observations can be a useful way to gather first-hand information about a subject by relying on senses and note-taking skills. Observing a subject directly is sometimes a useful way to narrow your research question down in the invention stage, to determine the extent of a problem or issue that your research question addresses, or to answer the question itself. Observations are often a central part of a research project, as the following research questions show.

- **How do bilingual speakers switch back and forth between English and Spanish in casual conversation?** In this case, a researcher would observe the conversation of bilingual speakers and note when they switch back and forth between languages.

- **At what times of day are voting locations most busy on election days?** To answer this question, a researcher might observe voting locations at various times of the day.

- **To what degree does "light pollution" obscure the view of the night sky in a particular metropolitan area?** Part of the response to this research question should include an observation of the night sky on various occasions.

Including Observation in Your Research Plan

Your rhetorical situation may or may not call for observation. Consider the following questions as you determine whether observation would be a useful data-gathering technique for your project.

- **Is there a person, place, activity, or ritual that you might watch, hear, or experience in order to answer your research question?** If so, you might want to directly observe your subject.

- **Would observing your subject over time provide data that would help you answer your research question?** In this case, you might schedule observations at certain intervals that would help you collect the appropriate data.

- **Would your presence as an observer influence the subject that you are observing?** This influence is often called the **observer's paradox**—the presence of the observer sometimes affects the environment being observed and, therefore, the data collected. Sometimes it cannot be avoided, but it is important for the researcher to be aware of his or her potential influence on the subject being observed. ▢

- **Could you participate in an event, ritual, or environment that would give you unique insight into the subject you are studying?** If so, you might consider being a **participant observer**, an ethnographic term for a person who is collecting data and researching a subject while participating in or with it. In such a case, you need to be clear about your relationship to the subject when

> Take a look at the activity in Chapter 3: "Reflect: What Is the Writer's Place in the Rhetorical Situation?" (page 46) to help you determine how your perspective, or even your presence, might influence your research.

you describe your data-collection method, and consider your perspective as a participant in your analysis of the data.

Conducting an Observation

Once you have decided to conduct an observation, what should you do? First, determine where and when you will observe and have a plan for taking clear notes about your subject as you observe. Some researchers keep notes in a journal, and many organize their journals as **double-entry journals** to keep their observation and analysis/response separate. In a double-entry journal, one side is generally reserved for the observations themselves (which might even be organized by senses or themes) and the other side is used for interpretation, response, or comment on the observations. For example, if someone were observing the coffee shop where one of the authors of this textbook likes to sit and write and were keeping notes in a double-entry journal, it might look something like Figure 5.1. The observations are listed on the left-hand side, and the observer wrote comments and interpretations about what he or she observed on the right-hand side. Such notes could be taken In either a journal notebook or on a laptop.

Observation	Response
Eleven customers present	
All are white, apparently middle-class	Specific clientele, could be influenced
Four appear to be under the age of 30	by the neighborhood
Only two are sitting together talking; everyone else is either reading or working on a computer	Shop is organized to cater to people who come here to work or get away, more than for socializing
Tables are small; could only accommodate two people comfortably	
Free wi-fi provided to customers	Could almost function as an "office
Extension cord with additional outlets is extended into the middle of the floor	away from work"
Microwave in the corner	
Conference room is being used by three people working individually on computers	Even the space that is designed for group gathering is being used by individuals who are working
Background music is classic jazz	
Temperature is slightly cool; around 65 degrees	

Figure 5.1 Example of a Double-Entry Journal

Careful note-taking is essential to completing a useful observation, especially if you are the sole person responsible for data collection. Ideally, you will conduct your observation and then have time to return to your notes later, when you will have a different perspective. You might write down some of your interpretations as you conduct the observation (or immediately after), but then you might add interpretations in the right-hand column when you read your notes later. As you read the notes, especially when you have some distance from the subject, patterns will emerge that might lead to interesting conclusions about your subject.

In addition to having a clear plan for taking notes during your observation, you should keep in mind that it is not possible to be entirely objective when you observe. Your experiences, beliefs, and perspective will influence you, drawing your attention to certain sights, sounds, and smells (among other things). You should strive to experience as much as possible, though, and to be aware of—and try to limit—the influences that could bias your observation. One way to do so is to have a method for conducting the observation. If you have never done an observation, try the following exercise to practice observation skills, and then consider using the strategy for collecting data to answer your research question as well.

...write...

Practice Observing Your Subject

Choose a space to observe for 10 minutes. It might be a location on your campus, at your place of work, or in your home. Make sure that you won't be interrupted for the 10 minutes that you are observing, and bring a double-entry journal with you to record your observations. Note: You might practice this method by observing a space with which you are familiar before beginning your observation for your research project.

1. Start by observing the space immediately surrounding you, only going out one or two feet from where you are sitting. First, observe what you see, then what you hear, then what you smell, touch, and taste.

2. Extend your observation out a few feet. Again, record what you observe with each of your five senses.

3. Again, extend your observation out about ten feet, recording what you observe through each of your five senses.

4. Finally, focus on each sense and write down everything you observe—as far as you can see, hear, smell, touch, or taste.

Once you have finished noting your observations, take a moment to write comments on your observations in the other column of your double-entry journal. What patterns do you see? What surprised you?

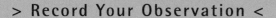

> Record Your Observation <

Taking notes in a double-entry journal can be a great way to collect data during an observation, but other kinds of technology can help facilitate your observation as well. Depending on the nature of your observation, you might choose to record your subject either through a video or audio recording. If you want a transcript of language use or of sound, an audio recording might be an ideal method of data collection, for example. ▢

Any recording of your subject should only be done with permission, though, so pay close attention to the "Ethical Considerations" section later in the chapter.

2 Conducting Research

Interviews

For some research projects, the researcher needs to ask questions of someone directly involved with an issue. Like observations, interviews might be used when you are trying to determine how to focus your research question, and they might also be used once you have defined your research question and want to answer it. Interviews are often integral to answering a research question, as in the following examples.

- **What are the writing practices of individuals in the software engineering field?** In this case, the researcher might interview one or more professionals in the field to find out what kinds of writing they do.

- **How do international students use social networking software to connect with friends and family?** A research question such as this might include an interview to hear the student's perspective, as well as an observation to learn how the student uses the application.

- **How might climate change influence the flora of the eastern coast of North Carolina, and how soon would that influence be evident?** For this project, the researcher might want to interview one or more experts on the subject. An observation wouldn't be feasible for a short-term research project since the research question is projecting into the future. If the researcher could conduct an extended project, though, observations might also help answer this question.

Including Interviews in Your Research Plan

You might notice from the preceding research questions that interviews can be used in a variety of ways. You might interview an expert in a specific field in order to gather data that will help you answer your research question. You might also interview people who are participants in or members of a community (such as a profession) that you would like to study. Depending on your research question, you will also need to determine how many people to interview. As you consider whether interviewing might be a good method for your research, consider the following questions.

- Would talking to experts in a particular field help you to answer your research question?

- Would speaking with participants in an activity or members of a specific community help you to answer your research question?

- What could you learn from speaking with someone that you can't learn from reading published information or from conducting an observation?

- Could you conduct an interview on the phone or online if it is not possible to conduct the interview in person?

Conducting an Interview

If, after answering the previous questions, you have determined that you should conduct an interview for your research project, then you will need to start planning your interview. First, you need to do three things:

- **Set the interview time and location with the person (or people) you will be interviewing.** Try to select a location that will make the interviewee feel comfortable but not distracted, and keep the length of the interview reasonable. Thirty minutes to an hour is a reasonable length of time. Keep in mind that your interviewee is doing you a favor by setting time aside for you, so be careful to schedule around the interviewee's commitments. If you realize you need more time, ask to schedule a follow-up interview. Sending a confirmation before the interview and a thank-you note afterward is a nice, courteous touch.

- **Write your interview questions.** If you are conducting an interview, you should come prepared with specific questions so that the interview is efficient and you get the information you need to answer your research question. Remember that the interviewee is giving you his or her time, so be prepared and professional. As you write your questions, avoid closed questions that elicit short "yes/no" responses (i.e., "Are professionals in your field expected to write much?"). Instead, write open-ended questions that will invite the interviewee to talk about a particular subject. Open-ended questions generally start with *who, what, when, where, why,* or *how,* such as "What kinds of writing are professionals in your field expected to write?" or "How much writing is expected of professionals in your field?" In addition, make sure that you keep the number of questions reasonable for the time allotted. You might have a few questions in reserve in case you have additional time, and you might want to order your questions based on importance in case you run out of time.

- **Decide how to record the interview.** You might want to digitally record the interview or you might take notes. When you choose your method, consider how important it will be to have the interviewee's exact words. Note-taking, as you would in an observation, could work if you can just paraphrase and summarize the responses of your interviewee. An audio recording will work if you need the exact words of your subject, and a video recording might be best if it is important for you to notice expressions or gestures. Keep in mind that each method of recording (note-taking, audio recording, and video recording) could be increasingly distracting to your interviewee, and that will likely affect his or her responses. If you don't need a video recording, for example, then opt for a less distracting method. And if you do need a video or audio recording, make sure that your recording device has enough memory to record the entire

Draft Interview Questions

Before you begin to write questions for your interview, write your response to the following prompts.

☐ What do you need to know from your interviewee? Why do you want to interview this particular person? Freewrite for 5 to 10 minutes.

☐ Once you have finished your freewrite, read your response. Look for patterns. Are there specific things that you need to know? Generate a list.

☐ Now go through your list and put the things you would like to know in order of priority.

☐ Finally, write a question for each item on your list; keep them open-ended. If you find you have several closed questions (questions that will elicit only a "yes/no" response), try putting "Why?" at the end of such questions.

Once you have finished a preliminary list of questions, consider how many questions you will have time to ask. Are there some questions you should combine? Are there some that should be separated? Then try your interview questions out on a friend. Revise as you ask them, looking for questions that are awkward or confusing.

interview. Of course, in order to do a video recording, you would need to interview the subject in person (or have the subject use a webcam if your subject is agreeable). ☐

Regardless of whether you audio or video record your interview, you might want to use a double-entry journal during the interview, too. The double-entry journal will work similarly to when you conduct an observation. You can record your questions on one side and your interviewee's responses on the other. You could include a third column for notes and analysis that you might add later, as shown in Table 5.2.

> Any recording of your subject can only be done with permission, so if you plan to record your interview, pay close attention to the "Ethical Considerations" section later in the chapter.

Table 5.2.
A Triple-Entry Journal for an Interview

Interview Questions	Responses	Comments/Analysis

If you are doing an audio or video recording, a double-entry journal could be used to take notes that will help you refer to specific parts of the interview when you review your recording. Even though you would not write comments as you are conducting the interview, you'll have the space to go back and insert your analysis later.

Conducting a successful interview takes a tremendous amount of practice. If you haven't had much experience in conducting an interview, preparing well is the best thing you can do. Also, you might consider "trying out" your interview questions and technique on a trusted friend before going to your official interview.

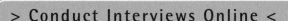

techno_tip >

> Conduct Interviews Online <

 For an interactive tutorial about conducting interviews online, go to *Student Resources* on the online resource center at www.cengage.com/english/ Miller-Cochran/WGTR.

Interviews can be conducted in person or on the phone, but they can also be conducted online. The most common ways to conduct interviews online are through email and instant messaging (IM). If you choose to conduct an interview in email, ask fewer questions than you would during an oral interview. It takes more time (and often more effort) for most people to respond to questions in writing than it does to talk about them. If you conduct an interview via IM, make sure that you save a transcript of the interview before you log out. If you conduct the interview using Google's IM client (among others), a transcript of the interview will be automatically saved for you.

Another possibility is to have a synchronous voice interview using an application such as Skype (http://www.skype.com), an online phone service that is free. Both you and your interviewee would need to create Skype accounts, and you would both need microphones in order to use such an application. You could also conduct an interview using a webcam or video conference, but stick to technologies that are easily accessible to both you and your interviewee and with which you are both familiar so they don't become distractions.

Surveys

Some research projects require asking questions of a large group of people and would not be manageable by doing individual interviews. In such cases, surveys are often the best option. Because a survey can take a considerable amount of time to design, distribute, and assess, it works best when the researcher has a well-defined research question that clearly calls for the kind of data a survey would produce—that is, data from a large group of people that could help to identify a widespread trend or phenomenon. Surveys can provide essential data for answering some research questions, as in the following examples.

- **How do American college students rate speakers of different dialects of American English on multiple characteristics such as intelligence, likeability, and friendliness?**

- How many citizens in my town generally vote on election days, and what reasons do they give?

- How well do graduating seniors from my college feel the required first-year writing class(es) prepared them for the writing they did in other college classes?

Including a Survey in Your Research Plan

To decide if a survey would fit the criteria for your rhetorical situation, consider not only the kind of data you would need to answer your research question but also how feasible it would be to conduct a survey. Surveys can take a tremendous amount of time to do well, and you would need access to the appropriate people who would be willing to complete your survey. As you determine whether or not you will conduct a survey, consider the following questions.

- **What can I learn from a survey that I can't learn from an interview or observation?** Surveys enable a researcher to ask questions of a large group of people and also have the advantage of providing the researcher with the exact responses of the participants in text form. (Of course, an email interview would do the latter, too.)

- **How many people would I like to poll in order to answer my research question?** If the number is larger than you could reasonably interview, a survey might be the way to go. The number for your research project must be small enough to be manageable but large enough so that you will have the interpretive power necessary to answer your research question. You might have noticed that all of the sample research questions just listed involve surveying large groups of people who have something in common (American college students, citizens in my town, graduating seniors in my college). In other words, one of the first challenges of conducting a survey is determining who you will survey.

  Many students who are designing surveys for the first time make the mistake of surveying an unrepresentative group. For example, in the recycling scenario at the beginning of the chapter, if Kira surveys twenty of her friends, she is not likely to get a representative sample (because they're all her friends, and twenty is a fairly small number if she's generalizing her results to the whole campus). If she surveys the students in a few different classes, however (especially if the classes are in different departments), she might come closer to getting a better representation of the student population on her campus.

- **Do I have the time to design a successful survey, distribute it, collect responses, and analyze the data?** Surveys can be quite time-consuming, and you will want to consider how much time you have to devote to your project as you design your survey.

Conducting a Survey

If you have determined that you should conduct a survey for your research project, in addition to choosing a representative group of participants, you need to pay close

2 Conducting Research

attention to two issues involved in design: (1) writing successful survey questions and (2) distributing and collecting your survey.

First, as you write the questions for your survey, think about how many responses you will be analyzing; keep your project manageable. It is also critical to consider the kinds of questions and responses that will help you answer your research question. Two kinds of questions are most common on surveys: closed, or fixed-response and open-ended. Take a look at the different kinds of questions in Table 5.3.

Table 5.3.
Types of Survey Question

Type of Question	Issues to Consider	Sample Questions

Closed Question
• Multiple choice
• True/false
• Yes/no
• Rating on a Likert scale
	Gives a certain set of possible responses, so they are easily comparable with the responses from other participants.	• Which item are you most likely to recycle?
		  a. Cans
		  b. Bottles
		  c. Paper
		  d. I don't recycle
		• I regularly place used soda cans in the recycling bin on campus.
		  ___ True ___ False
		• Do you have access to the Internet at home?
		  ___ Yes ___ No
		• How confident do you feel in anticipating the needs of different types of readers when you write?
		  1—Not confident
		  2—Somewhat confident
		  3—Confident
		  4—Highly confident

Open-Ended Question	Allows participants to give more information, but responses are not as easily compared as answers to closed questions.	• What technological support do you receive as a student? • What differences do you perceive between taking a course online and taking a course in person?

Many surveys incorporate both closed and open-ended questions so that the researcher has statistics that can be compared but participants can also explain their answers, giving the researcher interesting information that helps to interpret the results of the survey.

2 Conducting Research

...write...

Draft Survey Questions

Before you begin to write specific questions for your survey, write your response to the following prompts.

☐ Who will you survey? How and why did you choose this group of people?

☐ What do you need to know from your survey participants? Why do you want to survey them?

Read your responses to these questions. Look for patterns. Are there specific things that you need to know? Generate a list. Now go through your list and put the things you would like to know in order of priority. Next, consider the kind of data that would be most useful in responding to your research question. Should some questions be closed questions in order to collect quantitative data? Which ones should be open-ended? Finally, write a question for each item on your list.

> reflect <

Is the Survey Valid and Reliable?

Before using your survey with a large group of people, test it on a few friends. Look for points of confusion in the survey. Which questions should be revised for clarity?

As you test your survey, you'll also be determining whether the survey is *valid* and *reliable*. Ask the following questions as you revise the draft of your survey.

☐ Is it valid? Does the survey actually assess what it's supposed to assess? For example, in the recycling scenario, asking "Do you think recycling is important?" doesn't tell the researcher whether the person recycles. Also, if the questions are confusing, you might not be "testing" the same thing for everyone.

☐ Is it reliable? Is the survey conducted in a similar way and scored identically for all

participants? Your survey must be administered and scored consistently in order to be reliable. For example, participants should have a similar amount of time to respond, and if you are looking for patterns in open-ended responses, you should consider **inter-rater reliability**. ☐

This is discussed in more detail in the section "Analyzing Qualitative Data" later in the chapter.

Distributing Surveys and Collecting Responses

Once you have designed your survey, you will need to plan how to distribute and collect responses. One of the biggest challenges in conducting a survey is getting people to respond, so you might consider some strategies that would help increase your response rate. Some researchers offer incentives to survey participants (but the incentives shouldn't influence the data). For example, incentives could be food, a gift certificate, or something else that would be of value to the participants. Another strategy is to conduct the survey in a closed space, like a classroom (with the teacher's permission, of course). One of the disadvantages of this strategy is that it limits the group of participants, but it might increase the number of responses. All strategies should be disclosed when you report the results of your research.

techno_tip >

> Consider Online Survey Services <

One way to increase response rates on a survey is to make the survey easy and convenient to complete by putting it online. You might look at an online survey service such as Survey-Monkey (http://www.surveymonkey.com) to see if it would be a useful strategy for your research project. Many online survey services will help you analyze the data by displaying graphic representations of the results.

Ethical Considerations

If you are conducting research that will include other people (especially if you are asking questions of them), then you'll probably need approval from a group on campus that oversees research that involves **human subjects**. Such a group is usually called an **institutional review board** (**IRB**), and it exists to make sure that research on humans is conducted ethically and doesn't violate anyone's rights (especially privacy) or have adverse effects on health or well-being. Many institutions of higher education have IRBs, although schools that are less focused on research might not. Ask your instructor if your project would need to be reviewed by an IRB and if your school provides a process for gaining IRB approval for a project.

Even if you do not need IRB approval, you will need consent, or permission, from the people that you are interviewing or surveying. You might also ask consent for an observation, if you are observing in a closed space. An observation in a public space, like a restaurant, would not generally require consent. To ask for consent, you would disclose as much as you can about your project (without altering the data you are hoping to collect) and then ask for the participant's consent and signature. If you are collecting data electronically, you cannot collect a physical signature from the participant, so you might use an electronic signature or include an "I grant permission" button in the survey form. In either case, you'll want to phrase the letter differently. Figure 5.2 shows a letter of consent written for a research project that included completing online surveys. The goal of the study was to compare how well students believed they had achieved the objectives of a course in two learning environments, but notice that the letter of consent does not go into much detail (so as not to influence the students' responses).

ENG 101/102 STUDY

Dear Student:

I am a graduate student under the direction of Professor Jane Smith in the Department of English at XX University. I am conducting a research study to compare instructional environments for teaching ENG 101/102.

I am requesting your participation, which will involve completing two surveys that will ask about your perceptions of your experience in ENG 101/102, one at the beginning of the term and one at the end of the term. Your participation in this study is voluntary. If you choose not to participate or to withdraw from the study at any time, it will not affect your grade and you will not be penalized in any way. Although the survey will ask for your name, your name will only be used to identify your survey if you should choose to withdraw from the study. The results of the study may be published but your name will not be known.

If you have any questions concerning the research study, please call me at 480-555-4653 or Professor Jane Smith at 480-555-9427.

Sincerely,
Susana Rodriguez

Figure 5.2 A Letter of Consent

If you are working under an instructor's supervision, you could include the instructor's name in the letter of consent as your project advisor. Make sure that you show any research plans and your letter of consent to your instructor before starting your research project.

2 Conducting Research

techno_tip >

> Gather Data Online <

If you gather data in an online environment, you still need to get consent from your participants. The lines are somewhat blurry, though, in spaces such as online gaming environments, chat rooms, and virtual worlds such as Second Life. The best rule of thumb to follow is to obtain consent from anyone you are observing, interviewing, or surveying. A simple consent letter can be provided to participants that either collects their electronic consent through a signature or permission button, or that indicates that if they participate in the activity you are observing while you are observing it or complete the interview/survey you are conducting, their participation indicates their consent. It is also a good idea to check the documentation for any gaming environments, chat rooms, or virtual worlds in which you would like to conduct research to see if procedures for conducting research or limitations on research are stated.

Interpretation of Data

You might remember from the beginning of the chapter that it is best to collect data from a variety of sources and in a variety of manners to compare responses and interpret the results. Researchers call this **triangulation** of the data. Consider this scenario: imagine that you conduct a survey and receive several similar responses to one question. But one of your participants gives a response that is completely opposite to all the other responses. If the survey was not anonymous and you have the opportunity to do a follow-up interview with that participant, you could ask about his or her response to understand it better—instead of jumping to conclusions about that response or dismissing it without knowing the purpose or reasoning behind it.

As another example, think about the ways that you have seen your teachers evaluated. Most likely, you've had to fill out an evaluation survey for a teacher at the end of a course. You likely have also been in a classroom when a teacher was being observed by someone. When the teacher is evaluated, all of the data can be considered. For example, if the students' written evaluations note that the instructor is particularly good at leading class discussion, the observer might be able to elaborate on that evaluation by describing several specific things the teacher did in class that facilitated discussion. Likewise, two separate types of data can pick up different trends. For example, if the students note in their evaluations that the teacher is particularly helpful in office hours outside of class, the observer would not have observed that. In this case, it would be important to have both survey data and observation data in order to fairly assess the teacher's performance as a whole.

Once you collect your data, search for patterns that will help you draw conclusions. There are two major categories of data—quantitative and qualitative—and your analysis and interpretation will vary depending on which type of data you have collected.

Analyzing Quantitative Data

Quantitative data can be analyzed numerically. You can tally results and compare averages, look for statistical patterns, and determine whether a majority of respondents said the same thing. Of the types of research discussed in this chapter, only surveys can generally be used to collect quantitative data. Quantitative data are often valued because they are more generalizable; that is, they are collected from a large population.

Analyzing Qualitative Data

Qualitative data are not intended to be analyzed statistically, but they can provide insight into a subject. Interviews and observations provide qualitative data, as do the open-ended responses on surveys. When you analyze qualitative data, you look for patterns and trends. In some cases, you might be searching for the number of times you observed a certain phenomenon or the number of times a participant used a certain word or phrase, but because of the small number of participants you would not draw statistical conclusions about the significance of a phenomenon or generalize the results to a larger population. In this case, you would want to carefully aggregate the data and have a second person also aggregate the data, identifying the occurrences of a phenomenon. This process is called **coding**. The second coder would help to provide inter-rater reliability. In other words, the results are more powerful because the researcher is not the only one verifying the patterns in the data. You can check your interpretation of the data with another person.

Regardless of whether you collect quantitative or qualitative data, strive to phrase your conclusion in a way that is appropriate to what is called the **interpretive power** of your study. You'll want to provide your readers with a clear understanding of the limits of extending your results, based on the scope of your study and the way you defined your rhetorical situation. You could also use hedging terms to provide for the possibility that another researcher would find a different result since you will be unable to observe all situations or interview/survey all possible participants. Hedging terms include words like *generally, usually, often, might,* and *could.* For example, let's imagine that Kira, when conducting the recycling project, surveyed 75 students and found that 80 percent of the survey respondents mentioned that the recycling bins on campus were not conveniently located. She could write in her conclusion that "The location of the recycling bins is a *likely* reason that students do not recycle regularly." Using the term *likely* allows for the fact that she did not survey all students, and not everyone responded the same way on her survey. Yet, 80 percent is a strong response rate for such a large number of students.

Presenting the Results of Primary Research

When you present the results of primary research in many disciplines, especially those in the sciences and social sciences, your audience might expect you to follow what is often called **IMRAD** format. IMRAD is an acronym that stands for the following steps:

- **Introduction**—generally an introduction to the subject, an overview of the secondary research on the topic, and a clearly stated research question. This section should answer *What's the subject?*

- **Methodology**—a clear description of the methods used to conduct the research, including a description of the participants, how they were selected, what was observed, what questions were asked, how data were collected, and how they were analyzed (i.e., if you had a second coder look at the data, this is where you would explain your process). This section should answer *What did you do?*

◻ **Results**—a presentation of the data collected. This is generally separate from any analysis of those data, which comes in the next section. This section should answer *What did you find?*

◻ **Analysis**—conclusions you have drawn from the data you collected. This section should answer *What do the results mean?*

◻ **Discussion**—implications of the results of your research or suggestions you are making based on the results and analysis of your data. This section should answer *What are the implications of the results?*, or more informally, *So what?*

If you're not sure what format to use to present the results of your research, IMRAD provides a useful outline to follow.

Decide What Primary Data to Collect

If you have read this entire chapter, you might already have an idea of the kinds of primary data you should collect. If you're still having trouble deciding, though, try writing your responses to these questions, which were asked in the sections on observations, interviews, and surveys.

Observations

◻ Is there a person, place, activity, or ritual that you might watch, hear, or experience in order to answer your research question?

◻ Would observing your subject over time provide data that would help you answer your research question?

◻ Could you participate in an event, ritual, or environment that would give you a unique insight into the subject you are studying?

Interviews

◻ Would talking to experts in a particular field help you to answer your research question?

◻ Would speaking with participants in or members of a specific community help you to answer your research question?

◻ What could you learn from speaking with someone that you can't learn from reading already published information or from conducting an observation?

Surveys

◻ What can you learn from a survey that you can't learn from an interview or observation?

◻ How many people would you need to poll in order to answer your research question?

◻ Do you have the time to design a successful survey, distribute it, collect responses, and analyze the data?

What Does Your Research Plan Look Like Now?

At this point, take some time to plan the kinds of research you need to conduct. At the end of Chapter 4, you might have started a research plan that sorted through the different kinds of secondary resources for your project. If you are interested in conducting primary research, you can take that information and put it into a more comprehensive research plan, using the chart below.

You also need to decide when you are going to complete your research. Keep in mind that it will be of the utmost importance to manage your time well if you are conducting primary research; be sure to plan enough time to collect and analyze data.

Types of Resources	Location of Resources	Deadlines
Primary Resources		
Secondary Resources		

Reading Resources Rhetorically

This chapter's research situation involves someone who will be filtering through a huge amount of resources on cars and buying cars. She will have to filter through not only what individual people (i.e., friends, family, and maybe even some bloggers) say about different types of cars but also through the large amount of material published by the car manufacturers and materials distributed by more "objective" resources, such as independent research firms. The strategies presented in this chapter will give you, as well as Yoshi, methods to read resources effectively and pick out elements related to your specific rhetorical situation.   >

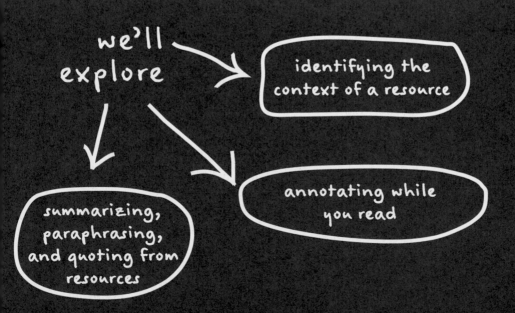

we'll explore → identifying the context of a resource

summarizing, paraphrasing, and quoting from resources

annotating while you read

© David McNew

Research in Action

Author: Yoshi just graduated from college last year and works for social services in her hometown. Although she loves her job, she has to budget very carefully—especially for large purchases—because the pay is rather low.

Topic: Yoshi needs to research her options in purchasing a new car.

Audience: Yoshi's research is primarily for herself.

Purpose: Yoshi would like to find the least expensive but reliable car. She is also concerned about related costs, such as insurance and gas, and she would like a car that would be appropriate for a longer trip so that she can visit friends and family who live far away.

QUESTIONS

1. What are the various elements of the rhetorical situation in this research scenario? How do they affect one another?

2. What types of resources might Yoshi seek out for her research?

3. When was the last time you had to make a large purchase? What did you buy? What criteria did you consider for your purchase? What elements of your rhetorical situation affected your selection of criteria? Your purchase choice?

4. Do you have a big purchase to make in the near future? What do you need to buy? What criteria will you need to consider? What elements in the rhetorical situation will affect your choice of criteria and ultimate purchase?

› Rhetorical Reading

You've been reading for a long time. And not only have you been reading, but you've been reading to learn and to gather information. You may have also been doing what we are calling **purposeful reading**. Simply defined, purposeful reading is reading with a purpose and a goal. It is paying attention when you read. For example, before voting in an election, you might closely read the candidates' statements to decide if your ideals and goals align with theirs. You purposefully read their statements with the goal of helping you decide which candidate will receive your vote, and as you read you are choosing which statements most closely align with your values and beliefs.

To get the best results from resources you consult for any research question, it is wise to go one step further and **read rhetorically**. To read a source rhetorically, you not only read for a purpose but also pay attention to the context of the document you are reading, closely analyzing its rhetorical situation. Let's say you are watching a movie. If you just watch the movie and zone out, you will probably laugh when everyone else at the theater is laughing and not remember much of it the next morning. In this case, you are just passively "reading" the movie. If you go to the movie to be entertained, you will be purposefully reading the film as you watch it. The next morning you would be able to explain to someone whether you liked the movie, whether you found it entertaining, and why. However, if you were to read the movie rhetorically, you would be paying attention to how certain things are depicted (e.g., women and characters of color), considering the historical context in which it was made, or comparing it to other films by the same director, screenwriter, or editor.

Let's consider an example from a different research situation. Imagine you're conducting research on gun control laws and you come across a Web site titled, simply, "Gun Control." The Web site begins with a quote from Thomas Jefferson and includes sections on "The Second Amendment" and "Gun Control: A Statistical Perspective."

2. Conducting Research

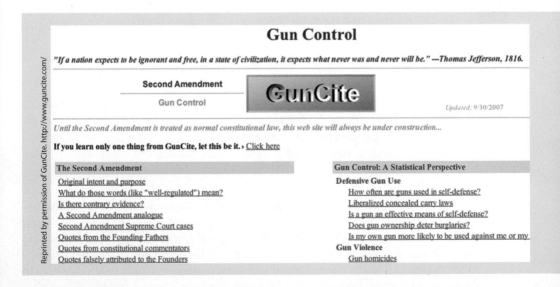

Reprinted by permission of GunCite. http://www.guncite.com/

The Web site asks and responds to many of the questions you have been considering in revising your research question:

- How often are guns used in self-defense?

- Does gun ownership deter burglaries?

- What does the Second Amendment mean and how should it be interpreted?

On the surface, this Web site might seem like a perfect match for your research. If you were reading the site purposefully, looking for information on your research topic, the site provides a wealth of responses to relevant questions. A careful *rhetorical reading* of the Web site, however, reveals that the site has a clear bias toward an interpretation of the Second Amendment that protects gun owners and limits gun control. The Web site gives very limited attention to other perspectives on the issue. Additionally, you would have difficulty establishing the credibility of the source because the authors are not clearly identified. The site refers to "GunCite" as the sponsoring organization but offers no specific information about that organization or the authors of the site. Reading your resources rhetorically will help you to evaluate them for usefulness in your research project.

For more information, see Chapter 7, "Tracking and Evaluating Data."

> reflect

Are You Reading Purposefully or Rhetorically?

To help distinguish between a *purposeful* and a *rhetorical* reading, list the various texts that you have read during the past couple of days. Then label each reading experience as either purposeful or rhetorical. Ask yourself the following questions to help categorize your reading experiences.

- What was the goal in reading the material?
- Did I consciously have this goal in mind before reading the material?
- Did I pay attention to the rhetorical elements of the material (the text's author, purpose, audience, and topic)?
- Did understanding the rhetorical elements of the material affect my goal for reading the material?

In your list, circle the reading experience that you are most confident was purposeful, circle another experience that you are most confident was rhetorical, and circle a third that you had the most difficult time labeling as either purposeful or rhetorical. Discuss these three experiences with a friend or classmate. Does your friend or classmate agree with your labeling? Why or why not?

Like all the activities related to writing that are described in this book, rhetorically reading requires paying attention to the rhetorical situation. To be successful in reading something rhetorically you need to be aware of your purpose for reading the material. You will use your purpose as the criterion for deciding what material is important and worth remembering and what material is worth only skimming. In many cases, when you read rhetorically you end up reading a document more than once. With something like a new car, you might not read the directions at all when you first get the car (you already know how to drive, right?). However, once you've decided you are tired of the stereo's clock flickering the wrong time at you, you purposefully read the manufacturer's car manual to change the time on the clock. However, if you had lost the manual, you might go online to find the instructions for setting the time. You would read rhetorically, considering who was writing and publishing the Internet resource before following the instructions. You wouldn't want to break the clock in your new car!

When you rhetorically read documents in an academic setting, you generally have to read them more than once to obtain all the information you need. While reading resources for a research project, you probably want to read through them at least three times:

1. Read (or perhaps even skim) for the main point or claim of the resource so that you can decide whether it is worth your time and energy to read the material closely.

2. Read to identify the rhetorical situation of the resource so that you can understand the context as well as figure out how it will fit into your research project's specific rhetorical situation.

3. Do a closer reading for details. In this reading you will probably annotate the resource and take notes paraphrasing the claim, reasons, and evidence presented in the resource.

One thing to keep in mind is that in order to argue a particular claim effectively and to influence people who believe differently from you, you must demonstrate that you understand their perspectives. People will not be willing to listen to your reasons for believing differently unless they feel you understand their beliefs and their perspectives. To help understand those who might think or feel differently about your topic, and to make better connections with that same group later, it is important that you rhetorically read materials from their perspective. While doing research on your topic, especially secondary research, seek out a variety of materials and perspectives. To help understand the different perspectives, as well as prepare for your writing, be especially careful to read rhetorically and take notes on the resources. Much of the rest of this chapter is devoted to helping you develop these reading strategies for your own research.

2. Conducting Research

Choose Resources to Read

...write...

As you conduct your secondary research, you will find a large number of possible resources. Knowing that you can't possibly read them all, you need to quickly assess whether a resource is worth your time to read more closely. Practice choosing relevant resources to read by using an Internet search engine to do a search with one of the key terms of your research question. After reading only the introduction, conclusion, and subject headings, answer the following questions about the first four hits.

>>>

>>> ☐ Are you able to quickly identify who wrote the resource, on what subject the resource is focused, when it was published, where it was published, and what the purpose of the resource is?

☐ How does the material in the resource directly respond to your specific research question, not just your research topic?

If the resource is organized enough to answer the first question and is specifically addressing your research question, it is probably worth your time to read it more closely. Reading rhetorically is the first step in choosing and evaluating resources, but to determine whether you'll use a resource in your project requires more intense reading and evaluation.

Considering Context

As a piece of communication in its own right, every resource you read has its own rhetorical situation, or context. Just like everything that you write, each resource you read has a purpose, an audience, a topic, and an author that help to define the context in which it was produced and distributed. Rhetorically reading a resource means carefully understanding not only what it says but also its purpose in saying so. You really need to know the rhetorical situation of a piece of writing in order to "understand" what it says.

Let's go back to the car stereo example. What if you had an after-market stereo installed in the car and lost the manual that shows how to change the clock? You might search the Internet for help and find multiple resources: one by the stereo manufacturer and another by a car stereo enthusiast. You might read them an extra time to figure out which resource is more appropriate for changing the clock. After skimming the resources again, you realize that although the stereo manufacturer's Web site provides the directions for changing the clock, the car stereo enthusiast's site includes that information and also discusses putting alternative resources into the stereo system. And it seems clear from the enthusiast's page that he or she has spent a lot of time playing around with the stereo and knows how to use it. Since you also knew you wanted to figure out how to play your iPod in the car, you print the instructions from the car stereo enthusiast's site. Although the manufacturer's Web site may have been more authoritative at first glance, the car enthusiast's Web site may better fit your specific needs.

...write...

Situate a Resource Rhetorically

Select one of the resources you have found that could help you answer your initial research question. Respond to the following questions about that resource.

- [ ] Who is the author of the resource, and what are his/her/their credentials?

- [ ] With whom is the author affiliated (employer, organization, or other group)?

- [ ] For what purpose(s) did the author write the resource? In other words, is the author trying to provide information? persuade readers? entertain? What clues help you to identify the piece's purpose?

- [ ] Who is the audience? How do you know? How might the audience have affected the way that the resource is written?

Once you have responded to all of these questions, consider the resource as a whole. How might the answers to these questions have influenced the writing of this resource?

Annotating Resources

Simply put, annotating is writing on or about something. You can annotate a resource in a variety of manners. Usually, the method in which you annotate your resource is based on your purpose for reading the resource. For example, if you are enrolled in a literature class that is currently discussing tone and rhythm, and you are reading the *Odyssey*, you will probably mark sections and take notes about language choice. However, if you were reading the *Odyssey* in an ancient world history class, you might mark sections and take notes about passages that refer to specific historical events. In both cases you are reading the same text; however, the method in which you annotate is based on the information you need from that text.

The annotation method you use is directed not only by your reading purpose but also by the materiality of the text itself. The best way to annotate resources is to physically write on them. However, if you borrowed the book from someone or from a library, it is better to use sticky notes or extra notebook paper for annotations instead of writing on the pages. If you are reading a Web site, you might use software that allows you to takes notes onscreen, but many people take notes from the Internet on paper.

While reading resources for larger, more complex research projects, spend some time identifying and annotating the resource's claim, reasons, and evidence. The **claim** is the overall point that the resource is making, or its thesis. Whereas identifying the claim in a scholarly, academic resource is fairly easy (it is usually located somewhere within the first few paragraphs), identifying the claim of a more informal resource—a blog, a newspaper editorial, a song, a movie—may be more difficult. For example, all commercials claim that some specific product is good, and furthermore, that you should spend money purchasing it. A primary claim might be explicit, but it is often implicit, and you might need to read the resource multiple times to identify a claim.

After identifying the claim that the resource is making, you will want to identify the **reasons** that the author is using to support his or her claim. The overall claim of car commercials is that a specific car is better than all others and that you want or need that car. However, different commercials provide different reasons for claiming that a car is good. Engine size and speed are often the primary reasons given in commercials for sports cars, but secondary reasons might include that the car would make you more popular, attractive, or envied by your neighbors. On the other hand, fuel efficiency and safety are often the primary reasons in commercials for more family-oriented vehicles.

These reasons support the argument, or claim, in an advertisement that a specific car is good enough to spend thousands of dollars on it.

Finally, resources need to provide **evidence** to support their reasons and claims. Evidence is material provided about the object being discussed as support for the reasons and claims. Car companies might cite how quickly a car can go from zero to sixty miles per hour as evidence of a specific sports car's speed. They might also cite how many cylinders the engine has, or how much horsepower it puts out, as evidence of its engine size. Commercials for family cars might cite the number of air bags in the vehicle as evidence of the car's safety, or they might cite independent researchers who agree that the car gets more than forty miles to the gallon as evidence of fuel efficiency.

As you annotate a resource, make notes about how you think it might help you to answer your research question. When you read rhetorically, consider not only the rhetorical context of the resource but also your research context. How might this resource fit into your research plan? Does it provide a perspective that is lacking in the resources you have found so far?

In this example of the Honda Fit, Honda is clearly addressing a younger audience. First, the advertisement uses bright colors and video game iconography, and it suggests that the retail price for the car is relatively low (for individuals at the start of their careers in lower paying jobs). The option to click on either "Which Fit Fits?" or "Build Your Fit" is clearly enticing the audience into further engaging with the Web site as a method to keep potential customers linked to the site so that they learn about the car. As with any advertisement, the Web site suggests that this is the car to buy, and although the text gives the "logical" reasons for purchasing the car, the design of the Web site provides the reason that this is a "trendy" vehicle. And with an intended audience of young adults, "trendy" might be more important than issues such as "space" and "safety." And the layout, colors, and fonts of the advertisement provide the evidence for "trendy" reasoning.

Annotate a Resource

Once you have chosen at least one resource to help you answer your research question, use the following strategies to practice annotating it.

☐ **Print source:** Write on the pages directly if you printed it yourself or "mark" it with sticky notes if it's a borrowed book.

☐ **Electronic source:** Take notes onscreen or paper, or print sections so that you can mark them and keep track of your thoughts.

Annotate your source by responding to the following questions.

1. Who is the **author** of the text and what are his/her/their credentials?

2. What is the **purpose** of the text and who is its intended **audience**?

3. What is the major **claim** made in the resource?

4. What are the **reasons** given for supporting that claim?

5. What **evidence** is provided to support those reasons?

6. How useful will this resource be in your own research? How does it fit with the other resources that you have found?

techno_tip >

> Search Electronic Documents <

For an interactive tutorial about searching electronic documents, go to *Student Resources* on the online resource center at www.cengage.com/english/Miller-Cochran/WGTR.

Have you ever been confident that a book has the information that you need in it but you can't find the information? Perhaps the title seemed promising but the chapter titles and index didn't help you navigate the book. Or perhaps you had read something interesting at first glance but then couldn't find that information on a second reading. If you are lucky, the introduction or preface has detailed chapter descriptions that help you identify what chapter to read; if not, you just have to dig into the book. However, with electronic documents, everything has changed. Whether you have a word-processed document, a Web page, or a PDF file (Portable Document Format, which was developed by Adobe Systems and requires the free Adobe Acrobat Reader), you will be able to electronically search the document, word by word.

To try this feature, select an electronic resource that you aren't positive that you will want to use in your research. Then locate your extended list of search terms that you developed in Chapter 4. Electronically search your document for all of your terms. For every "hit," be sure to read the   ›››

>>> surrounding sentences, and consider skimming the entire paragraph. After you have searched your terms, decide whether you need to read the document more carefully.

Pull up another electronic document that has been giving you difficulty in identifying the claim and reasons. Reread the introduction to the text (probably the first couple of paragraphs). Are there any words in the introduction that you think are key to the argument's reasoning? If so, search for those words or phrases that you think will lead you to the reasons developed in the argument.

Summarizing

After you read one of your resources, you should be able to summarize it briefly. Summarizing the resource is important to do for two reasons. First, you need to be sure that you understand the main point of the resource. What is it trying to say? What does the author want the reader to do or think after reading the resource? Although you will want to read it again more closely to accumulate details about the information and arguments presented in the resource, it is important that you initially understand what the resource is doing. At minimum, summarizing the resource will help you to understand whether it applies to your specific research project.

Also, you will want to summarize the resource for a more practical reason—keeping your research organized. A short summary of the resource will be a reminder of what is in the document when you start organizing, and reorganizing, your resources. With summaries of various documents, you will be able to quickly assess whether you have enough information in one area of your project and if you need more in another.

The easiest way to summarize a document is to briefly answer the standard journalists' questions. In other words, you will want to know the *who, what, when, where, why,* and *how* of the resource. A summary, by definition, is a brief document that gives the main points but not all the discussion and is briefer than the original source. A helpful guideline is to remember that your summary should be no more than 10 percent as long as the original resource. In many cases, you can summarize a source in one or two sentences. Your summary will also probably reflect what you found most interesting in the resource.

> reflect <

How Do You Write a Summary?

Remember, while constructing a summary of a resource, you are not trying to include all the details, just enough information for easy comparison with other resources.

Pretend you are Yoshi, who needs to purchase an affordable new car. What might your summary look like for this blog entry?

Reprinted by permission of Rebecca Lueckenotte and LiveJournal (www.livejournal.com).

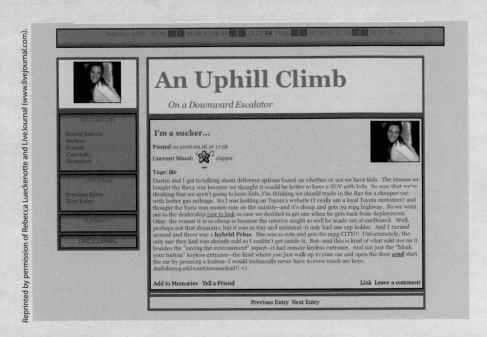

An Uphill Climb

On a Downward Escalator

I'm a sucker...

Posted on 2006.09.18 at 17:56

Current Mood: chipper

Tags: life

Dustin and I got to talking about different options based on whether or not we have kids. The reason we bought the Rav4 was because we thought it would be better to have a SUV with kids. So now that we're thinking that we aren't going to have kids, I'm thinking we should trade in the Rav for a cheaper car with better gas mileage. So I was looking on Toyota's website (I really am a loyal Toyota customer) and thought the Yaris was sooooo cute on the outside--and it's cheap and gets 39 mpg highway. So we went out to the dealership just to look in case we decided to get one when he gets back from deployment. Okay, the reason it is so cheap is because the interior might as well be made out of cardboard. Well, perhaps not that dramatic, but it was so tiny and minimal--it only had one cup holder. And I turned around and there was a **hybrid Prius**. She was so cute and gets 60 mpg CITY!!! Unfortunately, the only one they had was already sold so I couldn't get inside it. But--and this is kind of what sold me on it besides the "saving the environment" aspect--it had remote keyless entrance. And not just the "blink your button" keyless entrance--the kind where you just walk up to your car and open the door ***and*** start the car by pressing a button--I would technically never have to even touch my keys. Andohmygoshlwantitsooooobad!! =)

Add to Memories   Tell a Friend   Link Leave a comment

Previous Entry Next Entry

Summaries not only answer the journalist's questions but also often hint at the reader's purpose for using them as resources.

2. Conducting Research

Summarize One of Your Resources

...write...

Now, choose one of your own resources that you plan to use in your research project. Do a first reading of the resource (which you may have already done when you chose the resource in the first place) and summarize the main point of the resource. Keep the journalists' questions in mind as you summarize, and also try to maintain a balance between keeping your summary concise and thorough enough to be helpful as you work on your research later.

Swap your summary with someone in your class, or a friend or family member. Ask him or her to read the summary. Did you provide enough information? If you have time, ask the person to skim the resource and recheck your summary. What information might he or she include in the summary? What information should be cut out? Why?

Paraphrasing

For more information on **when** to cite resources to avoid plagiarism, see Chapter 8 "Understanding Plagiarism and Integrating Resources." For more information on **how** to cite resources, see Chapters 12-15.

Another way to take notes on your resources is to paraphrase them. When you paraphrase a resource, or a part of a resource, you put the author's argument or ideas into your own words. Such a strategy might be helpful if you don't want to quote the resource or idea in its entirety but you also don't want to condense the ideas that were interesting and useful to you. For example, if you found a long passage in a print resource that had some great information in it but the resource was written for a very scientific audience (and your research is not), you might paraphrase the ideas to use in your writing later. In this case, you don't want to condense, and possibly lose, some of the ideas in the resource, but you'll need to use different language when you share the information with your audience. Of course, when you paraphrase in this way, you need to provide a citation to tell where the ideas came from. ▢

One other guideline to keep in mind when paraphrasing is that you need to put the ideas in *your own* words—not just change a word or two here and there. If you find yourself keeping the same basic sentence structure as the resource but changing just a few words, it might be best to just quote the resource.

Edmunds.com offers independent detailed reviews of different makes and models of automobiles. In this review of a Toyota Yaris, a car Yoshi might consider purchasing, the reviewer discusses "driving impressions" of the Yaris.

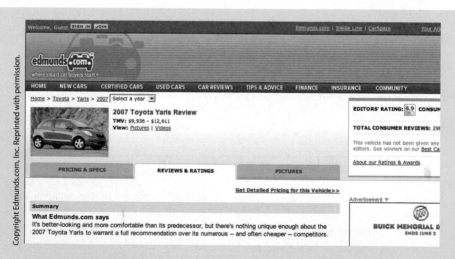

Driving Impressions

With the suspension stiffened by 47 percent over the Echo, the Toyota Yaris feels buttoned-down and, dare we say, fun on curvy roads. The suspension design is nothing earth-shattering—tried-and-true MacPherson struts up front and a torsion beam out back. But with redesigned bushings, a single upper mounting point for the front struts (rather than three as in the Echo), firmer calibrations and a lower center of gravity, the Yaris doesn't even feel related to its wallowing forebear. The 106-hp engine is surprisingly peppy, with a smooth delivery even when revved to high rpm. Off-the-line acceleration can be sluggish with the automatic transmission, but all models have enough midrange pull for easy merging and passing at highway speeds.[1]

When paraphrasing, be certain to use your own words and sentence structure—don't simply copy the syntax of the original and change a word here and there. If you find yourself doing that, it's best to just quote.

Inappropriate paraphrase of the first sentence: The Toyota Yaris is fun to drive on windy roads because the suspension has been stiffened by 47 percent over the Echo (Edmunds.com).

This paraphrase uses much of the original phrasing of the first sentence and has just changed the order of the clauses. Even though a citation is included at the end of the paraphrase, it is inappropriate because too many of the original words and phrases are used without quotations marks.

Appropriate paraphrase: According to Edmunds.com, the Yaris has tighter suspension over the Echo and is fun to drive. The suspension is normal for the type of car; however, it has improved bushings, struts, calibrations, and a lower center of gravity compared to the Echo. The engine has a lot of pick-up, especially at highway speeds, even though acceleration can be slow in the model with automatic transmission (Edmunds.com).

Notice that there still is a citation at the end of the paraphrase to indicate the source of the information being paraphrased. The reference to the Web site at the beginning of the paraphrase indicates that all of the information between the introductory statement and the citation came from the same source. ▢

For more information about integrating resources into your writing, see Chapter 8.

2. Conducting Research

Paraphrase One of Your Resources

...write....

Now, choose one of the resources that you plan to use in your research project. Skim through the resource to find a passage that is particularly interesting or that you think you might use in your research project. Try paraphrasing the passage, putting it into your own words. Once you have paraphrased the passage, reread the original passage and decide whether it would be best to use your paraphrase (with reference to the source) or to quote the resource.

---

1 Copyright Edmunds.com, Inc. Reprinted with permission.

Selecting Potential Quotations

Sometimes you might decide that it is best to quote directly from a resource. You might choose to quote, instead of summarizing or paraphrasing, for several reasons:

- You are doing direct analysis of a written text and need to provide the specific examples you are analyzing.

- The section of text that you would like to use is short and could easily be incorporated into your larger text.

- The author(s) of the resource used language that you believe to be particularly powerful and/or persuasive for your intended audience, and you would lose meaning or emphasis if you paraphrased it.

- The text is well known and your audience might be familiar with the quotation you have chosen.

- You know you will want to comment directly on the author's ideas and/or language.

As you are reading your resources, take note of quotations that you think might be particularly powerful to use in your research project. As your research project develops, you might find that some of those quotations are more useful than others. ▢

See Chapters 9 and 10 on using quotations as you begin putting your research together in the form of a developed argument.

...write...

Take Detailed Notes on a Resource

As you choose resources for your research, you might subconsciously be thinking that some of the resources are particularly useful. Often, in the first stages of a research project, we mentally categorize the resources we are finding into *resources I'll definitely use* and *resources I might use*. If you did this as you were doing your preliminary research, pick one of the resources that you think you would *definitely use* for this activity.

Now try using several of the strategies discussed in this chapter to rhetorically read your resource. Note: If you are completing the writing assignment in the "Research in Progress: Writing a Review of Research" section, you will

want to complete this activity for each resource you include in your review.

As you read your resource, take the following steps.

1. Physically annotate your resource. Use a method that you are comfortable with—write on the document itself (if it is yours, you have printed it, or it is a copy), use sticky notes to keep track of ideas as you read, or keep notes on a separate piece of paper or on your computer as you read.

2. Summarize the claim or main point of the resource.

3. Paraphrase the reasons given in the resource for its claim or main point.

4. Make note of the evidence used to support the claim and reasons for the claim in the resource.

5. Contextualize the resource by noting its purpose, intended audience, author, and topic.

6. Project how and why this resource might help you answer your research question.

7. Finally, note sections that include evidence or reasons that you would want to quote directly. Carefully note specific phrases and sentences you might want to quote.

Starting to Evaluate Your Resources

The rhetorical reading strategies described in this chapter will help you read through, understand, take notes on, and comprehend the resources you have chosen during your preliminary research. By completing these tasks, you are beginning to evaluate the usefulness of the resources you have collected. You can narrow your list of resources based on these rhetorical reading and note-taking strategies, but this discussion will continue as your research progresses. Once the focus of your research project is clearer, you will also be able to evaluate your resources based on the construction of your argument and the final product of your research project.

At this point, you are identifying potential evidence for your final research project. As we move along with your research project, you'll begin to consider which evidence is most appropriate for the argument that you want to develop.

Tracking and Evaluating Data

As we mentioned in Chapters 4 and 5, good research is done in a systematic manner—it is carefully planned and even more carefully documented. You need to keep track of the information that you collect during your research process, and we encourage you to do more than just pile it up in a shoebox or computer file. It is much more efficient, and will better prepare you for the final presentation of your research, if you systematically track the data you collect.

Keeping track of a few resources is not a difficult task; however, chances are that a lack of resources will not be your problem. Instead, with the proliferation of information on the Internet, you are more likely to have too much information. As you read the "Research in Action" scenario for this chapter, imagine the different kinds of data that Amy might collect while completing her research project: information from companies who use different file-sharing programs, descriptions and documentation about the programs from their Web sites, and suggestions and feedback from her colleagues. Likewise, imagine a first-year writing student who has chosen to research water conservation efforts and legislation in her city. She >

we'll explore

finding the resources that you need

keeping track of the resources you've found

filling any gaps in your research to build a strong argument

responding to the resources that you plan to use

© Harry Sieplinga/Getty

Author: Amy is a technical writer who needs to be able to collaborate on writing projects with coworkers around the world.

Topic: Amy's supervisor wants her to look at collaborative writing/document-sharing software that will allow more than one person to work on a project at the same time instead of sending files back and forth through email.

Audience: Amy's audience includes her coworkers, her boss, and herself. Amy's boss explicitly said he wants her to compare systems by checking with companies who already use them. Amy knows her coworkers will not be open to change unless they are included in the process.

Purpose: She needs to find an application that will simplify the process of working on written projects together. She has to conduct the research and write a proposal that will meet the needs of different audiences.

QUESTIONS

1. How will Amy get started with this project? How will she know what types of information she will need?

2. How will Amy keep track of the information she has collected? How will she know when she has collected enough?

3. Have you ever had a project where you were responsible for keeping track of, even organizing, large amounts of information? What did you do to make sure you did not lose material? How did you organize it in a meaningful manner?

> might collect general information about water conservation, documentation about water conservation in her community, minutes from city council meetings, interviews with city council members, and perhaps observations or interviews with people in her community. To keep her resources organized in a meaningful way, she will probably want to track her data in four ways:

- **Verify**. She should verify that she has collected everything that she needs.

- **Copy**. She should keep copies of the actual data collected.

- **Respond**. She should reflect on and respond to her data, considering how the data answer her research question, compare to other resources, and might affect her intended audience.

- **Fill gaps**. She should use the results from her consistent verifying and responding to identify gaps in her research that she still needs to fill.

Each of these methods includes an evaluation phase that would help her to determine whether she has collected useful, credible, and valid data. These strategies will help you to track and organize your resources as well.

Verify

The downfall of many novice researchers is that they get stuck in the "data collection" mode. By not developing a well thought-out research plan, they just continue to collect data because they do not know when they have enough. To help keep you organized and consistently moving forward in your research project, you need to compare what you have found with what you actually needed according to your research plan. In other words, use your research plan as an initial data-tracking checklist.

As you start collecting resources, both primary and secondary, be sure to quickly check them against your research plan. For example, while Amy was searching for secondary resources, she found a wonderful article that compares time management software programs. Although she knows it is important to manage time when working on team projects, the article did not directly connect to her project. Since she didn't have that type of resource listed in her research plan, she marked the article for personal future reference and moved forward. Evaluating your resources at this stage means making sure that they actually focus on your research question.

An important criterion to keep in mind as you verify the importance of resources is their potential usefulness to your project. For example, finding the article about time management software helps Amy realize that it could be useful to have a time management tool in the project management software. She adds time management assistance as a criterion for comparing project management tools to her research plan.

As you find and verify the importance of your resources, you may have to make changes to your original plan based on what you have found. If you do have to make changes (and who doesn't?), be sure to take note of them. Instead of writing the changes in a separate document, handwrite them or type them as bold or italic notes in your original research plan.

See the final activity in Chapter 5 for an example of a research plan.

Use the "Write: Choose Resources to Read" activity in Chapter 6 to verify and evaluate your resources.

2 Conducting Research

Copy

Once you've verified that a resource is worth keeping, it is critical that you copy it carefully or take detailed notes from it. If you are doing secondary research, we suggest that you obtain a complete copy of the secondary text. At some point, you might need to refer to the larger context of the piece, and documenting your resources will also be much easier if you have complete copies of them. Therefore, if you find a journal article in the library or in the library databases, photocopy or print it. If you find a blog posting on the Internet, print or bookmark it.

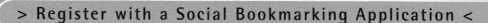

techno_tip >

> Register with a Social Bookmarking Application <

> For an interactive tutorial about registering with a social bookmarking application, go to *Student Resources* on the online resource center at www.cengage.com/english/Miller-Cochran/WGTR.

Many researchers have begun using various free social bookmarking service like Furl (http://www.furl.net), Del.icio.us (http://del.icio.us), and Diigo (http://www.diigo.com) to keep track of electronic resources they find on the Internet. Like your Internet browser, a social bookmarking service saves the URL of Web pages you want to visit again. If you've used "My Favorites" in Internet Explorer, or bookmarks in Firefox, you already know the usefulness of bookmarks; however,

bookmarks saved on your computer cannot travel to other computers or be shared with anyone. Since the social bookmarking services are Web-based, you can access your list of resources from any computer connected to the Internet. The services also track the date you located your resource, which is one of the many pieces of information required for bibliographic citations. Finally, most social bookmarking services allow you to tag, categorize, rate, and comment on resources you find.

One of the authors of this book tracks her research in del.icio.us, and you can see her bookmarks with the tag "web 2.0" in the accompanying screen shot.

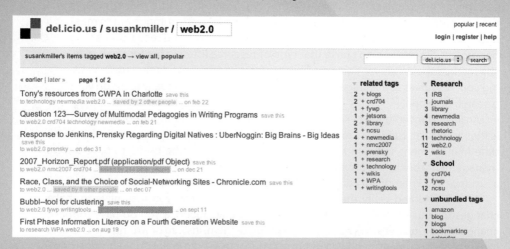

These bookmarks are Web sites that the author found that relate to her research and teaching. Notice the different categories and bundles of tags listed on the right side of the screen. These are categories that the author has created to find resouces that might be helpful for a variety of projects. You might also notice that the resources listed on the screen usually have more than one tag associated with them, so there are multiple ways to find the resource. Social bookmarking accounts can be infinitely customized to your interests and research.

2 Conducting Research

If you are conducting primary research, you will want to carefully store your original texts (questionnaire results, interview tapes, highlighted literary work, etc.). You may even want to make copies of your primary data to work with and put your originals someplace safe. Whether your primary data are in hard copy or electronic format, it is always advisable to make a backup copy. For example, Amy conducted observations of her coworkers while they were working on a collaborative project. She videotaped them as well as asked that they install screen capture software on their computers so she could record what they were doing on the computer. Having the information in several formats (observation notes, video files, and screen capture files) will give Amy back-up information if any of her data are lost.

If for some reason you can not obtain a complete copy of your secondary, or even primary, resource, be sure to take careful, thorough, well-organized notes that focus on the content of the text (exactly what is in it), not your reaction to it. For example, if your library holds a book in its special collections that includes information you need and photocopying the pages isn't allowed because it will damage the book, consider directly hand copying the parts of the text that are important to you. Be sure to write careful summaries and paraphrases before returning the primary document. □

As a part of copying, be sure to capture as much bibliographic data as possible to prepare for writing your bibliographic citations. If you are able to photocopy or print your resource, you probably have most of the information you need; however, it is good to be overly cautious and take note of more, rather than less, of the bibliographic information.

To help take detailed notes from your resources, use the "Write: Annotate a Resource" activity in Chapter 6.

Track Bibliographic Information

...write...

The easiest way to take note of the various types of bibliographic information you will need for a resource is to use the journalists' questions. Select one resource that you know you will use in your research project and answer all of the following questions.

- ☐ **Who** is the author? editor? publisher? owner/webmaster?

- ☐ **What** is the name of the article? journal (page number, volume number)? Web page? Web site? chapter? book? blog entry? blog title?

- ☐ **When** was it published? posted to the Web? When did you find it? (Be as detailed as possible, day/month/year.)

- ☐ **Where** did you find it? What is the name of the library? name of database? name of search engine? URL/Web address? (If a book, what city was it published in?)

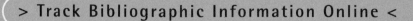

techno_tip >

> Track Bibliographic Information Online <

 For an interactive tutorial about tracking bibliographic information online, go to *Student Resources* on the online resource center at www .cengage.com/english/Miller-Cochran/WGTR.

Several Web-based software applications will help you track bibliographic information online. Your school might give you access to a program, such as RefWorks, that will help you track bibliographic information and generate a references or works cited list when you are ready to do so. If your school does not give you access to such a program, you could use Zotero for free (http://www .zotero.org). Zotero is an online project management package that will capture bibliographic information from the sources that you are looking at online. It will recognize and capture bibliographic information from Web sites and also from articles you find in library databases. You can take notes on the source in a Zotero page.

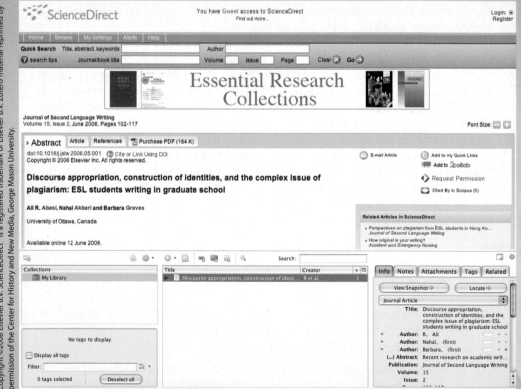

This screenshot shows an article in Science-Direct in the top half of the screen and a Zotero note card on the bottom half of the screen. There is space to take notes and organize information within the Zotero program. It works as an extension in Firefox.

Another part of the copying step in your tracking process is to write a brief summary for every secondary source you collect. These summaries will help you to keep your secondary sources organized as the pile of resources grows. The summaries will also allow you to group like sources together as you start working with your data. ▱

If Amy tests a variety of document-sharing technologies, she could collect copies of her secondary sources through screen captures of similar pages in the program. If she is thorough about her summary of each page (each piece of primary data), she will have an easier time working with them later. She will be able to group the images in a variety of ways, via type of technology, brand of technology, and type of tool within the technology.

To help develop a summary for every resource, use the "Write: Summarize One of Your Resources" activity in Chapter 6.

Evaluating Credibility

As part of your note-taking during the copying phase, remember you should also carefully note the purpose and audience of the resource. To help prepare for your analysis of the resource, you need to know who produced it as well as their purpose in producing it. For example, if you were doing research on breast cancer, you might find legitimate information from accounts of survivors as well as articles reporting the research of doctors working with patients. However, to adequately assess how and why you might use each resource in the answer to your research question, you need to understand the credibility and authority of its author. ▱

Respond

A common mistake many students make is simply to combine several quotations and summaries from different resources and call it a paper. They miss the opportunity to make the project their own. In the first project described in this book ("Research in Progress: Writing a Research Proposal," pp. 49–59), you made the research question your own by reflecting on how and why you are invested in the topic. While conducting the research, you need to make research your own by making personal connections to your resources. In other words, you need to spend time with your data—to know the information that you have collected—and respond to it.

Use the "Write: Situate a Resource Rhetorically" activity in Chapter 6 to evaluate a resource's credibility and authority.

Responding to your data goes beyond just "taking notes" on it. Notes are reminders of the original information documented—the who, what, when, where, why, and how of the original resource. Responding to your data goes beyond reminding yourself of the content of the resource; it includes analyzing the resource in relation to your research question. When responding to your resources, consider the following questions.

▱ How does the resource answer your research question?

   o Does it provide an answer? What evidence does it provide for support?

   o Does it introduce more questions? If so, what questions? How do these new questions affect your understanding of your original research question?

◻ How does the resource compare with other resources?

    o Does it say the same thing as some of your other resources? If so, which ones? How are they related?

    o Does it say something different from some of your resources? If so, which ones?

    o Does it use similar language and ideas?

    o Does it refer to similar people, places, and other resources?

Evaluating Validity

When discussing primary experimental research, "validity" means something very specific. It refers to the logical appropriateness of the methods for a specific study. Evaluating the validity of a resource in your own research is somewhat similar; you are assessing the content of the resource itself. This step differs from evaluating credibility, when you are looking at who conducted the research and wrote the document you might use as a resource. When evaluating validity, you will need to look at two areas:

◻ **Internal structure**. Look at whether the argument or presentation of information follows coherent lines of reasoning with easily identified claims and reasons and logically connected evidence.

◻ **External comparison**. Look at how the types of information or conclusions being presented compare with other resources that present or use similar types of information and draw similar conclusions.

See Chapter 5, "Conducting Primary Research," for more information about carefully developing and conducting primary research.

Therefore, when you are evaluating the validity of your primary research, pay close attention to your methods for inspecting and collecting data from your primary resources. If you are interviewing people, you should document how you chose your interviewees, what questions you asked and why, and the rate of reply. You can then compare your methods, and your results, to similar studies that you found in your secondary research. ◻

When evaluating the validity of secondary resources, you are critically assessing the information in the text. You might assess how current the information is that is cited in the source (if currency is important to your topic), how authoritative the sources are that your resource relies upon, and how well developed the claims, reasons, and evidence presented in the source are.

Although we are suggesting that you compare your resources as a test for validity, do not automatically throw out a resource that radically stands out from the rest. Sometimes when new ideas emerge, they are shockingly different from everything that has come before them. Some of the most groundbreaking work throughout history was questioned in terms of its validity in the beginning—consider the work of people such as Galileo and Albert Einstein. If you have a resource that fits into the "radically different" category, then it will be of the utmost importance to evaluate its validity by critically examining its internal structure to make sure that it contains a logical and well-supported argument. Also, be aware that if you are using such work as support for your argument, your audience (depending on who they are and what they value)

Evaluate Validity

Select one of the scholarly secondary resources that you will be using in your research project. Ask yourself the following questions about the resource.

1. Can you easily identify the claim, reasons, and evidence provided in the resource?

2. Do the evidence and reasons logically support the claim? Why or why not?

3. Do you have a similar resource that either argues the same perspective or conducts a similar study?

4. If so, did the two resources use similar methods for gathering and presenting data for their argument? How are they similar and different?

might question such a resource, so you might need to defend its validity in order to use it effectively as a reference.

Fill the Gaps

Do not wait until you've collected all of your data to start verifying, copying, and responding to it. First, you'll want to carefully copy everything as soon as possible so you do not lose information. Second, you will need to know what you've collected so that you do not waste time collecting too much of the same information. Amy may have lots of secondary resources comparing the various document-sharing technologies she is considering; however, if she still hasn't piloted one of the major programs in her own work context, then she needs to stop collecting secondary resources and get going on her primary research. Third, the trends and themes you begin to identify as you respond to and reflect upon the data might identify gaps in your original research plan. You may find that you need to collect other types of data to answer your research question effectively.

For example, since the original problem for Amy and her company was keeping track of a specific document, who was working on it, who needed to make specific changes, and who would work on it next, Amy did not instantly think of security as an issue. However, once she started researching various technologies, she noticed that they all had sections in their advertising that discussed security measures. The prevalence of security measures in these software programs helped her to realize that she had overlooked an important area in her research. Security was a "gap" in her research that she needed to fill. Identifying the research gaps, and filling them in, is the final step in tracking your research process.

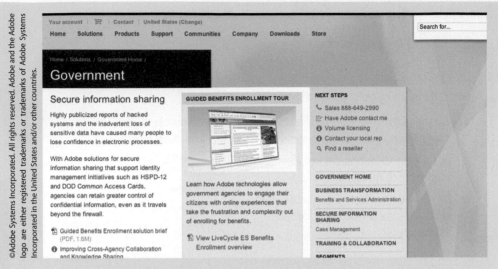

Amy found that many Web sites discussed security in file sharing.

One way to fill some gaps in your research is to trace the resources referred to in one of your most useful, credible, and valid resources. Sometimes while you are conducting secondary research, you will find a "gold mine" that covers everything that you think is important. Both proficient and efficient researchers take advantage of the work others have already done. When a researcher finds that type of resource, he or she carefully checks the resource's reference lists or works cited page to search for more "veins of gold." For example, when Amy found the accompanying comparison chart early in her research process, it provided not only the name of other technologies to look at but also a list of criteria that she could use to start building her own evaluation criteria for the various programs.

Amy found this chart to help her compare file-sharing software.

Although tracing research and information this way will not always lead to other important resources that you should read for yourself, it might lead you to one or two cornerstone pieces on the topic. You may also find an author's name repeated throughout numerous reference lists—that is a sign that you should probably look into that author's work yourself. And if you see a particular resource referred to across different reference lists, you should definitely search it out. Sometimes you'll see the names of one or two popular periodicals in the field. If you get those names, you may want to find the older issues in your library's stacks (or a list of the table of contents on the Internet) to see if the periodical has other articles that might work for your topic.

...write...

Trace a Line of Research

Once you've started collecting a pile of resources, pick out two or three that you think are your strongest. Carefully read through, and compare, the reference lists to look for common sources, authors, and periodical titles. If you do not find any overlap, consider looking at the reference lists of other resources. Finding overlapping references can point to a specific conversation in the field that might be of interest, and you'll want to be sure to follow those threads. Write down one or two points of overlap that you should follow up on, and then do a search using those terms (or names). What did you find?

2 Conducting Research

...write...

Make Cover Sheets

Consider using the following cover sheet for each resource you collect (especially secondary resources).

Bibliographic Information
- ☐ Date you found the resource: _____
- ☐ Name of the resource/article/book chapter/Web page/blog entry: _____
- ☐ Journal (page no., volume no., issue no.):_____
- ☐ Book: _____
- ☐ Web site/blog title: _____
- ☐ Author: _____
- ☐ Editor:_____
- ☐ Publisher and place of publication (city): _____
- ☐ Owner/webmaster of the Web site: _____
- ☐ Date of publication/copyright/posting to the Web (day/month/year):_____
- ☐ Medium of publication: _____
- ☐ Name of library: _____
- ☐ Name of database/search engine: _____
- ☐ URL (Web address), if needed: _____

>>>

>>> **Summary**
_____
_____
_____

Verification
____ Checked off on your research plan

Usefulness
How does the material in the resource directly respond to your specific research question, not just your research topic? _____
_____
_____

Copies
____ Photocopy or printed copy attached to this worksheet
____ Detailed notes attached to this worksheet

Credibility

❑ Who is the author of the resource, and what are his/her/their credentials? With whom is the author affiliated? _____
_____

❑ For what purpose(s) did the author write the resource you have chosen? In other words, is the author trying to provide information? persuade readers? entertain? What clues help you to identify the piece's purpose? _____
_____
_____

❑ Who is the audience for the resource? How do you know? How might the audience have affected the way that the resource is constructed? _____
_____
_____

Response

❑ How does the resource answer your research question? _____
_____
_____

❑ How does the resource compare with other resources? _____
_____
_____

Validity

❑ Is the resource internally consistent and logical? If not, what problems do you see? _____
_____
_____

❑ Are the resource's content and methods similar to other resources you have collected? If not, is that a concern? _____
_____
_____

Understanding Plagiarism and Integrating Resources

8

Following the conventions of documentation and avoiding plagiarism are key responsibilities of researchers. As a researcher, you must document how and where you locate your resources for three primary reasons:

- ✐ to give credit to the original author/artist/speaker,

- ✐ to help your audience find the same resource,

- ✐ and to build your credibility as a researcher.

Documentation is your ethical responsibility to the individuals who produced the resources from which you are drawing your information, and you demonstrate good will to your audience by providing them the information they need to find the original source in a manner that they can easily understand. By understanding and abiding by the principles of copyright and by documenting how and where you locate information or ideas that are not your own, you are following legal guidelines and demonstrating your high ethical standards. >

we'll explore →

principles of copyright and fair use

ways to effectively integrate resources into research-based writing

how to avoid plagiarism by accurately documenting resources

Research in Action

Author: Jeff is a graduate student in clinical psychology, and he would like to work as a school counselor when he is finished with his graduate degree. He is particularly interested in working at a two-year college.

Topic: Jeff is conducting research on first-year, first-generation college students. He wants to be prepared to work with students dealing with depression, and he realizes that the pressures and demands of college are often overwhelming to first-year students, especially those who have no college graduates in their immediate families to act as mentors and role models.

Audience: Because of Jeff's career goals and the topic of his research, he could publish the results of his research in several places. Other scholars in the field of psychology might be interested in his research, so he could publish his work in an academic journal. He might also look at a less research-oriented magazine geared toward teachers and school administrators. In addition, Jeff might think about sharing his work with parents of first-year students in a newsletter or other publication marketed to parents of college students.

Purpose: Jeff wants to share the results of his research with others who can help first-year students deal with the pressures of academic life, and he also wants to contribute to the ongoing research in this field.

QUESTIONS

1. Where might Jeff look for research that has already been done on this topic?

2. Can you find appropriate publications that Jeff could consider as venues for sharing the results of his research?

3. Looking more carefully at one of those publications, what documentation conventions do you see? Are sources cited carefully in the text? Are reference lists provided at the end of articles? Why do you think the authors follow the conventions they do in this publication?

4. What citation style is being used in the publication? Why do you think that style is used?

› Copyright

One of the reasons we document resources is to uphold the copyright laws that protect the information that we use. Copyright laws regulate the use of a particular expression of an idea. Ideas that are considered "common knowledge" are not protected by copyright, but many people disagree about what constitutes common knowledge. Therefore, if an idea you include in your writing is not your own, you must cite it as someone else's work and give that person the credit.

Copyright laws protect the author, or producer, of any given text (written, audio, visual, performance, etc.) from people who might reproduce that text without permission. The entertainment industry, both in music and movies, fights to keep very strict copyright regulations on their texts so that they will continue to earn money for the work and resources that went into the production of those texts. Similarly, scholars, and the publishing houses that publish their work, also want to retain control over their materials. You should be aware that even though you might not see a copyright symbol, ©, or the statement "all rights reserved" on a text, copyright is automatically granted to the author or producer of a work once it is published in a tangible form. For example, you own the copyright to all of the papers you write for various purposes.

Copyright does not last forever, however. The length of any text's coverage under copyright law depends on when and how the text was published, among other things. Copyright coverage can expire after a certain length of time. But remember, the ethics of documentation are not only about following copyright but also about giving credit where credit is due and being responsible to your audience by providing pertinent information about the resource so they can find it themselves.

Fair Use

What should you do if you want to refer to something in a resource that is still protected by copyright? Fair use allows individuals to copy small portions of texts to use them in other contexts, especially research and education. If you are doing a critical analysis of a book that has been written in the past fifty years, you may quote a few small excerpts from it under the fair-use doctrine. Even though fair use gives you this right, you still need to document how and where you found the information. This gives credit to the copyright holder while providing your audience with the information needed to find the original sources.

Ideas versus Words

Copyright technically protects the expression of an idea, not the idea itself. And fair use allows individuals who are researching or critiquing that text to copy small portions of the text to make specific points. However, in academic research is it expected that you will also document where and how you found specific ideas. For example, imagine that a doctor who specializes in hip replacements has conducted research into a new method for connecting the replacement hip to the patient's thighbone. When writing his article about the new method, he needs to briefly discuss the methods currently in use to demonstrate why his new method is better. When referring to the other methods, he is not reprinting the exact details of them; however, he still must cite the resources that originally presented the other methods. If the audience wants, or needs, to read more specific or detailed material about the other hip replacement methods, the documentation will provide the way.

Plagiarism

Remember, documentation and plagiarism are ultimately about ethics. Therefore, if you plagiarize by copying the work of others without documenting, you are being unethical in two ways:

1. you are most likely breaking copyright law, and

2. you are not acknowledging the work of others.

When we are talking about plagiarism in an academic setting, most instructors are highly concerned about the second issue. The production of original ideas is valued in academic settings, and it is important to give credit to the original author(s). Writing assignments are one of many methods that instructors use to evaluate how much you have learned in the course. If you copy someone's work without documenting it, you have committed plagiarism: you have stolen someone's ideas and you are not demonstrating your own learning.

Part of the difficulty in talking about plagiarism, however, is that it can be difficult to define. Plagiarism includes many kinds of academic violations, including the following:

-   turning in an entire work composed by someone else and claiming it as your own

-   using someone else's exact words in your writing without acknowledging the source

-   paraphrasing someone else's work or using someone else's ideas in your writing without acknowledging the source

In addition, some professors classify turning in work that you have completed for another class as a form of academic dishonesty. To complicate matters, plagiarism (as it is defined in academic settings) happens in other settings as normal practice. In some contexts, copying parts of a text into a new document is considered normal, accepted practice (in the writing of contracts, for example). Furthermore, in different cultures and settings, the "rules" of documentation and plagiarism shift. Simply put, plagiarism is a complex issue, and the rules of plagiarism are shaped by rhetorical context, just like everything else that we have discussed in this text.

Two kinds of plagiarism are commonly viewed as academic violations, however. In academic contexts, students who plagiarize often fall into one of two categories:

1. **Blatant plagiarism**. Someone knowingly copied sections of other resources and submitted them as his or her own work.

2. **Careless plagiarism**. Someone knowingly used information from an outside resource but thought that it was considered common knowledge or did

not adequately provide in-text and full bibliographic documentation within the paper.

Both kinds of plagiarism have serious academic consequences, and it is important to understand the conventions of citing sources in order to avoid them.

Blatant Plagiarism

Is there a difference between copying a whole paper and copying and pasting text from several sources into a paper? For the purposes of following an academic code of conduct, not really! In either case, the writer is knowingly copying another resource and presenting that work as his or her own. Obviously, if you submit an entire paper that was written by another individual, you are plagiarizing. However, if you copy and paste small sections from another resource, shouldn't that count as fair use? Yes, if you document where and how you found that resource both within the paper (through the use of quotation marks or block quotations and in-text citations, explained later in this chapter) and in the bibliographic citations at the end of the paper. If you do not properly cite those copied and pasted sections, you are plagiarizing.

Why would a student do something that is so readily characterized as plagiarism? There are a few common reasons, and at least two of them are completely avoidable with proper planning:

1. The student didn't understand the assignment or the material and relied on someone else's work instead.

2. The student ran out of time to work on the assignment and copied someone else's work out of desperation.

In the first instance, the student who doesn't understand the assignment or material should seek help from the instructor, or perhaps from someone else in the class or in an academic support center, to understand the requirements of the assignment. Planning ahead and seeking help early can avoid this situation. Planning ahead will also help you avoid the second circumstance, running out of time and plagiarizing from desperation. The assignments laid out in this text will also help you avoid that circumstance; a carefully written research plan, for example, will help you plan the time to find all of the information you need to complete your own work.

Careless Plagiarism

Many cases of plagiarism are what we call "careless plagiarism"—plagiarism that could have been avoided by an understanding of the rules of citation and careful documentation of outside sources. The first step in avoiding this type of plagiarism is learning to identify appropriate and inappropriate uses of secondary sources and understanding when to use in-text citations. Learn how to correctly paraphrase and summarize so that you avoid plagiarism.

A vast majority of the time, careless plagiarism could have been easily avoided if the student had left enough time to double- and triple-check the documentation. Understanding the conventions of documentation will go a long way toward helping you avoid plagiarism due to carelessness. ▢ Make sure to give yourself enough time to carefully document and double-check your research before turning it in for a grade or sharing it with someone else.

For standard conventions of documentation, see Chapters 12–15.

2 Conducting Research

Integration of Resources into Your Argument

Once you have developed your argument and know what resources, data, and evidence you will incorporate into the final published product, you should start thinking about how to incorporate those resources into your writing. For every outside piece of information that you present in your writing, whether it is from primary research or from a secondary resource, make sure to do the following four things.

1. Introduce the resource.

2. Incorporate the resource as a summary, paraphrase, or quotation into your writing.

3. Interpret the resource, connecting it to your argument.

4. Document the location of the resource.

If you follow these four steps when incorporating resources into your writing, you will be sure to avoid plagiarism as well as provide your readers with the information they need.

Introduction of the Resource

One of the common challenges students face in research-based writing is figuring out how to elegantly incorporate resources into their own argument. What often happens is that a student ends up "plopping" a quotation in a paragraph, or stringing several quotations together, or just putting a quotation in a paragraph by itself. Introducing a resource that you are citing gives your audience a context for why the resource is important and also retains your voice in the argument you are constructing. The introduction of your resource functions in two ways. First, it acts as a transition from what you were previously discussing in your argument. Second, and more importantly, it introduces the resource itself—what it is, and if needed, where it comes from. In the following example (in APA format, used by the American Psychological Association), the authors (Marini et al., 2007) introduce the summaries of multiple articles with a brief introduction about why they are important—they are recent studies.

> The cardioprotective effects of exercise training are well known and out of any dispute. Recent studies have clearly shown that training at >60% VO2max increases myocardial tolerance to ischemia-reperfusion (I-R) (Strøm et al., 2005), improves cardiac performance and ameliorates the cell defence capacity against stress (Powers et al., 2002; Freimann et al., 2005). (p. 503)

The emphasis on this example is the date of the studies and what the studies demonstrate. The authors of the studies are not the main point here; the resource is supporting the statement that the studies are recent; therefore, the authors' names do not need to be introduced into the actual text of the manuscript—the names appear only in the in-text citation. However, in the next example, the author's name is incorporated into the sentence. Yan Le Espiritu is a well-known Asian American scholar; therefore, by building Espiritu's name into the sentence, the writer (Han, 2006) is not only making the point about Asian American identity formation but is also backing the point by showing that it came from a well-known scholar.

> However, as Espiritu (1992) points out, identity formation for Asian Americans in the United States is more a reflection of common experiences they found within Western borders than the discrepant histories and cultures of their homelands. (p. 9)

To put this in a completely different context, think about how you might use a movie review in a conversation. If you quote a reviewer about a particular movie, you might just emphasize what the reviewer said. However, if you were trying to convince a friend that this movie is worth going to you might say, "Ebert gave it a thumbs up." Not only would you be quoting the source on the quality of the movie, you would also be working the well-known reviewer's name into your reference to give it more weight and authority in your argument.

If you are doing primary research, like Jeff at the beginning of the chapter, you will also need to introduce the primary data. In Jeff's example, he might give pieces of background information about specific students to help his audience understand how to interpret the information he is giving them. For example, he might describe how old they are and if they have children before he incorporates a quote about the stress of balancing a personal and home life with attending college.

2 Conducting Research

...write...

Introduce Secondary Resources

Find a specific section of a resource that you are fairly certain that you will use in your final research paper. Answer the following questions about this specific information or piece of evidence.

1. Why might this resource be helpful in the development of your argument? What might be important to point out to your audience about the information so that they pay attention to this resource in your argument?

2. Who is the author? Is the author well known in the field? Will the audience know the author's name? Does the author have very strong credentials related to this topic? (If so, you might consider incorporating the author's name, and maybe even his or her credentials, when introducing the resource.)

Now try writing an introduction to the information from that resource that you could include in your final paper. Include the relevant information that will help your audience interpret the resource you are presenting to them. Here are two examples.

> Leading researchers in child psychology agree that spanking can be damaging to a small child . . .

> According to Glenn, a respected researcher in child psychology . . .

Incorporation of the Data

Once you've introduced the information from your resource, you then need to incorporate the actual data you are using into the sentence. You can directly quote the resource or more casually refer to it by summarizing or paraphrasing the information provided in the resource.

For guidelines on when to quote a source directly, see Chapter 6.

Quotations from Resources   Many beginning researchers make the two common mistakes of incorporating lots of direct quotes and incorporating very long quotes into their papers. To avoid committing these common errors, make sure that you are directly quoting for the right reasons. □ Generally, you only need to quote a resource directly for one of the following reasons.

- You are doing direct analysis of a written text and need to provide the specific examples you are analyzing.

- The section of text that you would like to use is short and could easily be incorporated into your larger text.

- The author(s) of the resource used language that you believe to be particularly powerful and/or persuasive for your intended audience, and you would lose meaning or emphasis if you paraphrased it.

- The text is well known, and your audience might already be familiar with the quotation.

- You want to comment directly on the author's ideas and/or language.

If you can articulate why you chose to quote directly instead of paraphrase a resource, you generally are doing it for the right reasons. If you are only directly quoting a resource because you have the resource and want to include it in your argument, you probably should summarize or paraphrase instead.

Many scholars examine texts and language and are interested in the specific phrasing that someone might use in an expression. While analyzing any text, they must refer to the specific words on the page as well as the specific utterances of individuals. In this case, the scholars are focusing on the choice, order, and style of words, among other things. They must include detailed quotations from the texts that they then continue to analyze in their papers. Obviously, this type of scholarship requires writers to include direct quotations from resources into their papers.

Although other scholars may not be specifically studying language and texts, they are sensitive to highly expressive moments where someone wrote or said just the right thing. For example, in 1964 when the U.S. Supreme Court ruled in the case *Jacobellis v. Ohio* on whether a specific film was pornographic, a portion of Justice Potter Stewart's concurring opinion attempted to define pornography and included these words: "I shall not today attempt further to define the kinds of material I understand to be embraced. . . [b]ut I know it when I see it." Since then, many arts and humanities scholars who have written about the difficulty of defining pornography quote Stewart when referring to his attempt at a definition. The exact language is striking ("I know it when I see it.") and the sense of ambiguity would be lost if someone paraphrased it.

Many arguments that revolve around definitions use direct quotes to distinguish specific ideas, concepts, and perspectives from one another. As Jeff, from the beginning of the chapter, starts to write about his research about depression in first-generation college students, he will need to define both "depression" and "first-generation college student." Especially in the case of depression, Jeff will have to clearly explain how and why he defines depression in a certain way. To articulate his definition, he will need to refer to different psychologists' definitions. He will probably quote some he agrees with, focusing on expressive and "perfectly stated" language. Jeff might also quote psychologists' definitions that he disagrees with, and he could use direct quotes to emphasize the difference between his definition and theirs.

Ultimately, it is important to remember that you do not always need to directly quote individuals who support your opinion, perspective, or argument. Unless the specific language is essential to your argument, you should try to summarize or paraphrase your resources. ▢

Summarizing and Paraphrasing Revisited   Unless you need to directly quote for one of the reasons listed, you should either summarize or paraphrase the resources you are incorporating into your argument. Summarizing might be useful if you want to condense some of the ideas of a particular resource to support your argument. If you don't want to condense the ideas but you don't have a reason to directly quote the original author, you might paraphrase the source. This could be a useful strategy if the original language of the source might be inaccessible to your audience, for example. ▢

Interpreting the Resource

Another important step when incorporating resources into your writing successfully is to interpret the resource for your audience. Many novice researchers tend to "dump" quotations or statistics into their writing, without making explicit connections to their arguments. When a writer does this, he or she is expecting the audience to make the connections themselves. A better approach is to provide the connection for your reader, which prevents him or her from making the wrong connection or interpreting the resource in a manner that does not support the argument. By interpreting your resources for your audience, you are also ensuring that your voice, not someone else's, remains the dominant one in your research.

This final connection can take place in either the sentence that includes the information from the resource (as well as the introduction and in-text citation) or in a separate sentence. Sometimes getting everything (introduction, resource, interpretation, and in-text citation) into one sentence is overwhelming and it is easier on both the writer and the reader if you interpret your resource in the following sentence. If you choose to do the latter, always interpret the resource immediately following the sentence in which you included the resource.

Some resources might not need interpretation, however. If you have found a particularly effective quotation, for example, you might want to have it stand alone without interpreting for your reader. Such cases should be conscious choices, though. In other words, if you choose not to interpret a resource you have included, you should have a clearly understood reason for not doing so.

For more information on how to use quotations, including activities to help you quote accurately and effectively, see Chapter 6.

2. Conducting Research

For more information about summarizing and paraphrasing resources, including activities to write summaries and paraphrases, see Chapter 6.

Good interpretations can be challenging to write. Try to avoid the trap of just writing, "This quotation means that. . ." Instead, think about how to use your interpretation to point the reader back to the argument that you are developing. Consider the earlier example about Justice Stewart's language for defining pornography. A student writing about the difficulty of regulating pornography on the Internet might write the following passage:

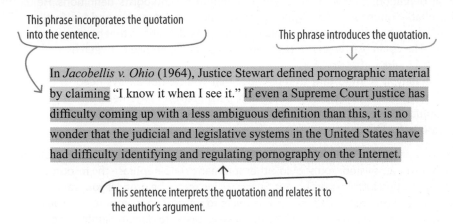

This phrase incorporates the quotation into the sentence.

This phrase introduces the quotation.

In *Jacobellis v. Ohio* (1964), Justice Stewart defined pornographic material by claiming "I know it when I see it." If even a Supreme Court justice has difficulty coming up with a less ambiguous definition than this, it is no wonder that the judicial and legislative systems in the United States have had difficulty identifying and regulating pornography on the Internet.

This sentence interprets the quotation and relates it to the author's argument.

Documenting the Resource

After introducing and incorporating information from the resource, documentation is the next step. You must document the resource in the same sentence as you refer to it in your argument. Most guidelines require a two-step documentation process for previously published resources:

1. **In-text citation**. In-text citations give the reader just enough information to locate the correct full bibliographic citation elsewhere in the document. In-text citations are brief so that readers are not disrupted by them and can continue to read with the flow of the text.

2. **Full bibliographic citation**. Full bibliographic citations provide detailed information on how and where to locate the resource. Since full bibliographic citations are bulky and do not fit well within the flow of the text, most are found in either footnotes (at the bottom of the page) or endnotes (at the end of the paper).

What to Cite You should cite any information that you locate from an outside resource. The only exception is if the information is considered common knowledge within the context in which you are writing the document. (In other words, is this common knowledge to your audience?) Your citations should be included in *every sentence* that incorporates information from an outside resource.

How to Cite Before figuring out how to construct your in-text and full bibliographic citations, you need to determine which citation style you will follow. This book contains guidelines for four of the most popular citation styles, which have been developed by professional organizations for academic writing.

- **Modern Language Association (MLA)**. Scholars who study literature, languages, and other humanities generally follow MLA documentation style.

- **American Psychological Association (APA)**. Scholars who study psychology, sociology, and other social sciences usually follow APA documentation style.

- **The Chicago Manual of Style (CMS)**. CMS includes two types of citation styles, one designed for the humanities and one designed for the social sciences. History scholars tend to follow CMS documentation style.

- **Council of Science Editors (CSE)**. CSE is a good example of a citation style in the sciences; however, engineers, chemists, and doctors often have discipline-specific citation style guidelines as well.

As with any other decision you make during your research process, your selection of citation style should be based on your rhetorical situation.

2 Conducting Research

Decide Which Citation Style to Use

...write...

As you consider which citation style to use, answer the following questions.

1. What is your topic? What style guides are specifically associated with your topic?

2. Look at the resources you've collected thus far. What style guides do many of those resources use?

3. What citation style will your audience be expecting?

4. Where will you be publishing or sharing your work? Do the publishers have their own style guidelines?

In-Text Citations   One of the challenges in citing resources accurately is figuring out what the in-text citations should look like. A second challenge is figuring out where and when to include citations in the text. The rules for when and where to include in-text citations are fairly consistent across citation styles. In-text citations should be included for every idea, quotation, and piece of information that you take from another resource. When in doubt, cite.

Descriptions of in-text citations for the four citation styles mentioned are included in Chapters 12–15.

Take a look at the following paragraph, noting where in-text citations have been included—and where they have not. The annotations explain why citations were or were not included. This example is in MLA format.

No citation is listed after the first sentence because this could be considered common knowledge.

A citation is included for the quoted resource. No page number is listed because it is from an Internet-based article in the *Chronicle of Higher Education*.

Many students have difficulty figuring out how to define plagiarism and don't understand when to include citations in their work. According to a study of Internet-based plagiarism in student writing, students may have ". . . an attitude that anything on the Internet is public domain, and they're not seeing copying it as cheating" (Kellogg). But students need to understand that in academic writing, attribution is expected—not just of exact words but also of ideas. Many students also don't realize that borrowing the word choice or phrasing of the original author is also considered plagiarism if it's not put in quotation marks (Howard 799); changing a word or two does not create an appropriate paraphrase.

The in-text citation is included in the middle of the sentence, just after the information that came from the resource. The reader can assume that the rest of the information in the sentence is the author's own ideas or interpretation.

Practice In-Text Citations

...write...

Open a research-based document you wrote before—perhaps a paper you finished for a different class. Save it as a new file and delete all of the in-text citations (if it is a long paper, you might just copy and paste a small portion of it for this activity). If you are in a class, switch documents with a partner and mark all of the places in your partner's document where you think an in-text citation should go. Then switch back and see if you agree with what your partner marked in your document. Compare the marked sections with your original paper—did you include all of the in-text citations that you should have included? Where do you and your partner disagree?

Full Bibliographic Citations   Compiling a full list of references at the end of your research is an important part of the research process. Your bibliography, list of references, or works cited list will provide further information and resources for your readers in case they would like to follow up and discover more information about your topic for themselves. For example, a works cited list (MLA format) for the paragraph excerpt included in the preceding section would look like this:

Works Cited

Howard, Rebecca Moore. "Plagiarisms, Authorships, and the Academic Death Penalty." *College English* 57.3 (1995): 788–806. Print.

Kellogg, Alex P. "Students Plagiarize Less Than Many Think, a New Study Finds." *The Chronicle of Higher Education*. 1 Feb. 2002. Web. 25 Nov. 2007.

Full guidelines for writing MLA citations are included in Chapter 12.

As you compile your list, keep in mind that you are providing a trail for your audience to find the same resources that you used in conducting your research. So, even though you might be able to find the same article in several places (online and in a print-based newspaper, for example), you should provide the correct information for your audience to find the version of the article you read.

As you think about the different places that you might be able to find the same resource, consider this example from a student's research for a biology class. Tawnee is a college student in New York City. Her biology class has gotten her to think a lot about sustainability. On December 10, 2006, while sitting at a local coffee shop, she picked up the *New York Times* and read an article about eco-tourism and being carbon neutral. If she were to write a full bibliographic citation in APA format for that article, based on the one she read in the physical newspaper, it would look like this: □

Higgins, M. (2006, December 10). Carbon neutral: Raising the

ante on eco-tourism. *New York Times*, section 5, p. 12.

Once Tawnee started the spring semester, she emailed a couple of her friends about the article. She just gave them the name of the article, the name of the author, and that it was in a December issue of the *New York Times*.

Sarah, one of Tawnee's friends, looked for it on the *New York Times* Web site and decided she might use it in a paper as well. Sarah's full bibliographic citation in APA format would look like this:

Full guidelines for writing APA citations are included in Chapter 13.

Higgins, M. (2006, December 10). Carbon neutral: Raising the ante on eco-

tourism. *New York Times*. Retrieved February 13, 2007, from http://

www.nytimes.com/

Notice that Sarah does not have the section and page number; this is because that information is not provided on the Web site. However, if the section and page number had been provided, she should include it in the citation.

Teresa, another one of Tawnee's friends, looked in one of her library's databases for the article. Her citation in APA format would look like this:

Higgins, M. (2006, December 10). Carbon neutral: Raising the ante on eco-tourism.

New York Times, section 5, p. 12. Retrieved February 13, 2007, from Lexis-

Nexis.

Notice, Teresa did include the original print page numbers because that information was included with the electronic copy in LexisNexis.

Each of the citations has distinct features that would help a reader find that exact version of the article. While this might seem inconsequential at first (they're all the same article after all, right?), consider this: in an online version of a periodical, many publishers provide a space where readers can comment on an article similar to a blog. Such additional commentary might have been helpful to you in interpreting the content of the article, and you might want to point your readers to that discussion. In addition, some periodicals only include portions of the full article in the online version, and readers might not be able to find the section you are quoting if you read the print version and then reference the online version.

As you put together your full list of resources at the end of your research, follow the guidelines for the citation style you have chosen. Each style has its own unique details, but you'll see commonalities among them. We've found that students encounter some common problems, regardless of the style they are following. Try to avoid these common pitfalls.

1. **Incorrect formatting of authors' names**. Check the formatting guidelines for the citation style you are using to make sure you are listing the authors' names and capitalizing the title of the work correctly. For example, in MLA format, you include the author's full first name, but in APA format, you include only the initial of the author's first name.

2. **No author listed**. If you cannot find an author for your resource, consider the following steps:

   o *Really* search for the author. On Web sites, the author's name may be listed on a different page. Take some time and really search.

   o Government agencies, organizations, and corporations can be authors.

   o If you really can't find an author, do not start your citation with the date. Use the title of the work in the place of the author. □

See Chapters 12–15 for examples of citations with no author listed.

3. **Incorrect use of italics**. Titles of major works (books, films, television shows) and periodicals (magazines, newspapers, and journals) are italicized. Specific articles, chapters, and television episode titles are not italicized. In some citation styles, they are put in quotation marks—see the specific guidelines for your citation style for more guidance. Keep in mind that italicizing and underlining serve the same purpose—underlining actually is used to indicate a place where the text should be italicized for programs, printers, or fonts that cannot italicize. (The Modern Language Association (MLA), in their current guidelines, endorse the use of italics in place of underlining.)

4. **Incorrect punctuation**. Follow the exact punctuation guidelines for your citation style for every period, comma, semicolon, and quotation mark. Each style has its specific rules, and they are important to follow. For example, in APA you should not include periods at the end of a full bibliographic citation with a URL.

5. **Inaccurate listing of URLs for digital resources**. If your source is a Web site, provide the full URL (Web site address). If it is from a database, give only the

database name. If it is from a very large Web site with a good search engine, like a newspaper Web site, provide the general URL. Styles differ in the specifics for listing URLs. See the detailed examples included with your citation style's guidelines.

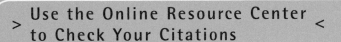

> Use the Online Resource Center to Check Your Citations <

The online resource center for *The Wadsworth Guide to Research* offers a citation guide that includes examples of different types of citations in MLA, APA, CMS, and CSE styles. If you cannot find an example of the kind of citation you need in this book, check out the resource center at www .cengage.com/english/Miller-Cochran/WGTR.

2 Conducting Research

RESEARCH IN PROGRESS:
Writing a Review of Research

At some point during the process of gathering information for a project, a researcher needs to compile the notes on various resources in one location. By doing so, she is able to get a broader perspective on what information she has, what she still needs, and what themes, trends, and connections she is starting to see. Most researchers are good about seeking information that supports their initial position on the research topic. However, good researchers know that in order to understand the entire rhetorical situation, they need to be sure to search for not only resources that agree with them, but also the opinions and perspectives of other groups invested in the issue.

Compiling a review of research can be a helpful step in the research process. Writing a literature review or annotated bibliography can help shape the final research project, and it can also help you save time. Many researchers find that what they write in their research review ends up in their final research project, either in full or in part.

In this section, we offer guidelines and an assignment for writing a review of research in either the form of an annotated bibliography or a literature review. Either genre will provide a framework for you to organize and present the information you have gathered on your topic. The elements of the review assignment included in this book are designed to help you draw on the principles discussed and practiced in Chapters 4 through 8, as well as the work you have done in Chapters 1 through 3. Specifically, this assignment is designed to encourage you to look at multiple perspectives on the issue you are researching. You can adapt the assignment to fit your rhetorical situation.

The Assignment

The goal of this assignment is to discover how your issue might be depicted differently by people who see the issue from various perspectives. You might be surprised at how much you can learn about your issue by considering how diverse people represent the debate. As you read and write about the perspectives that you have found, consider the biases of the authors, the interests they represent, and the reasons they might have for vocalizing their opinions. One way to do this is to consider the rhetorical situation of the piece that you are reading. Think about the audience the author was writing to and his or her purpose for writing. ▢

> Use the strategies from Chapter 6, "Reading Resources Rhetorically," to guide your reading.

As you search for resources, keep in mind that researching alternative perspectives is not restricted to seeking out the "pros and cons" of an issue. Most research questions can be answered with something other than a simple "yes" or "no." And even if the research question is a yes/no question, a variety of perspectives might be represented on both sides. For example, the manager of a fast-food restaurant may decide that the tomatoes the restaurant is currently purchasing are costing too much. Recognizing that cost is not everything, the manager may assign you to research whether the restaurant should continue purchasing tomatoes from the current vendor. Although this is a simple yes/no question, there are a variety of perspectives to consider. The owner and manager may not like the current vendor because the tomatoes cost too much; however, the manager realizes that the current vendor is very responsible and has never missed a delivery date. While testing out tomatoes from other vendors, the kitchen staff decides that they prefer the tomatoes from the current vendor because they are consistently fresher and therefore easier to work with. In this example, two groups (manager and staff) represent different perspectives on agreeing that the answer to the yes/no research question should be yes, but they agree for different reasons. The rhetorical situation of each group, especially how and why they are invested in the topic, impacts how they interpret the research question and go about answering it. Issues are usually much more complex than they first appear, even issues as seemingly simple as choosing a tomato vendor.

During your research process, you should make an effort to find numerous perspectives on your issue. By compiling all of your data in one location, you will be able to map out the perspectives you have researched, as well as the perspectives you are missing. Annotated bibliographies are a method of gathering information in one location so that it can be shared with others during the research process, and they read like a works cited or reference list with short paragraphs of information about each resource. Literature reviews serve a purpose similar to that of annotated bibliographies, but they are generally written in the form of an essay.

Your annotated bibliography or literature review will list the resources you have found, providing information about each one in the form of short summaries and descriptions of the rhetorical situation of the resource. In addition, you might include a brief discussion about how each resource might help you answer your research question. You could discuss the usefulness of each source, and you might discuss connections between the sources, demonstrating how they provide a complex picture of the issue you are researching. As you write, think of an audience that is also interested in learning about what has been written on this topic.

Features of Reviews of Research

The format of your final written review of research will depend on whether you are writing an annotated bibliography or a literature review. The basic process of writing both types is similar, however. Reviews of research should contain a list of resources with a description and a summary of each one. If you are writing an annotated bibliography, each annotation will include a citation following a consistent documentation style and a paragraph of description about the source. The example on the top of the next page is in MLA format, but your project should follow the most appropriate citation style for your rhetorical situation.

The description of each source usually summarizes its main points and expands the understanding of how its author perceives the issue. In addition, you might evaluate the various positions taken by people who are concerned with the issue. As you write an annotated bibliography, you may wish to list key themes that appear in the source, and you might want to speculate as to why the author holds the position he or she does. Consider including a context for the source to help understand the author's claim

Include a citation following a standard documentation style.

Include information about the authors and their motives.

Halstead, Ted, and Michael Lind. "Double Jeopardy: Can It Be a Crime to Seek Treatment for a Deadly Disease? Congress Seems to Think So." *Washington Post* 5 May 2002: B4. Print.

As the president and a senior fellow of the New America Foundation, the authors of this article are advocates of therapeutic cloning due to its potential to treat various debilitating illnesses. Halstead and Lind assertively argue that therapeutic cloning should not be banned because it would be hard to enforce such a ban, and the scientific breakthrough might have significant social benefits. Instead, they argue that therapeutic cloning in America should be legalized with regulation, as in other advanced democracies. In contrast, Halstead and Lind do urge a ban on reproductive cloning, not only because it is unsafe, but also because there is no contribution to either the medical or social sector. The authors provide a complex understanding of the distinctions among different kinds of cloning, instead of resorting to a simple yes/no answer.

Conclude by showing what makes this source unique or useful.

The bulk of the annotation provides summary.

and position. A useful annotated bibliography illustrates the complexity of an issue by mapping out the positions and reflecting on their parties' investment in them.

A literature review includes basically the same information as an annotated bibliography, but it is written in the form of an essay. Instead of breaking the writing into chunks of annotation, the literature review provides a picture of the issue by drawing relationships among the sources found on the issue. Many researchers find it helpful to write the basic summaries of the sources first and then look for connections among them before drafting the literature review. You must include a list of sources at the end of your literature review since the full citations will not be included in the text of the review.

Traditionally, scholars construct bibliographies or literature reviews on a specific topic. Normally primary research, especially qualitative and quantitative data, is not included in an annotated bibliography. However, you, or your instructor, may want to include descriptions of your primary data so that your annotated bibliography or literature review provides a complete picture of your research process. Most citation styles do not provide guidelines for citing full bibliographic entries of primary research (the data are usually just presented in the research report). If your instructor wants you to include annotations on your primary research, you will need to work out how to construct a bibliographic entry based on the citation guidelines provided in Chapters 12 through 15.

At a minimum, your annotated bibliography or literature review should provide

- an overview of the research already conducted on your topic (in other words, a picture of the conversation that is in progress on this issue);

- summaries of what those sources have concluded about your topic, including differing perspectives;

- some information about the rhetorical situation surrounding those various perspectives;

- information about where to find the original sources (included in the citations in the text of an annotated bibliography or in the references/works cited list at the end of the literature review);

- a sense of how the resources will help you respond to your research question.

Starting Your Review of Research

If you are using this text in a writing class, your instructor might ask you to complete the following assignment. If so, one of the first things that you should do is to read the assignment carefully and be sure you understand its requirements. After the description of the assignment, we have included some activities to help you get started.

In this assignment, you are asked to research an issue in order to

- discover how that issue is depicted by people interested in it;

- understand the different perspectives that people have on that issue;

- begin to formulate a response to your research question.

To do this, you will write an annotated bibliography or literature review of multiple resources on your issue. Your instructor might give you a specific number of resources to include in your review of research; if not, we recommend including at least seven resources so that you will get a balanced perspective on your issue.

The purpose of this assignment is to discover how your issue is discussed by people who hold different positions on it. While researching the perspectives on your issue, you will start finding the resources that will help answer your research question and support your position. If you already have a clear position on your issue, be sure to find both resources/evidence that support your position and resources/evidence that argue against your opinion.

In addition, your review of research should include an introductory paragraph that identifies the issue you are researching and some of the controversy surrounding it as well as a concluding paragraph that describes what you have learned by looking at different perspectives on that issue. This conclusion might discuss the connections among the resources and/or your growing understanding of the issue. You may also include a discussion of the research you realize you still need to conduct.

See Chapters 12–15 for documentation guidelines.

You should follow a consistent documentation style throughout your review of research. ☐ If you are writing an annotated bibliography, resources should be listed in alphabetical order unless you choose another organization (by topic, for example). Before you choose an alternate organizing structure for your annotated bibliography, you might want to discuss it with your instructor.

To help you get started, try responding to one or more of the following activities.

Activities to do as you start your research:

☐ Write: Develop a List of Search Terms, on page 72 of Chapter 4

☐ Reflect: What's Your Plan? on page 89 of Chapter 4

☐ Reflect: What Does Your Research Plan Look Like Now? on page 109 of Chapter 5

Activities to do as you read and summarize your resources:

☐ Write: Choose Resources to Read, on page 115 of Chapter 6

☐ Write: Situate a Resource Rhetorically, on page 116 of Chapter 6

☐ Write: Take Detailed Notes on a Resource, on page 124 of Chapter 6

Activities to do as you draft your review of research:

☐ Write: Summarize One of Your Resources, on page 121 of Chapter 6

☐ Write: Decide Which Citation Style to Use, on page 149 of Chapter 8

Examples of Reviews of Research

For more student samples, go to *Sample Essays* on the online resource center at www.cengage.com/english/Miller-Cochran/WGTR.

Example 1: Li Chen, Should All Forms of Human Cloning Be Banned? Li Chen has continued her research on cloning. She wrote an annotated bibliography of her sources, and she included introductory and concluding paragraphs to give basic information about her topic and what she found. As with all examples, keep in mind that there are strengths and opportunities for revision of this annotated bibliography. We have included the instructor's comments on Li Chen's final paper so that you can see the feedback that she received. Her annotated bibliography is written in MLA format.

Chen 1

Li Chen

Dr. Susan Miller-Cochran

ENG 108

March 9, 2008

Should All Forms of Human Cloning Be Banned?

Since the birth of the world's first mammal clone, Dolly, scientists have been attempting to clone humans in a similar manner. The controversy that arises from human cloning includes whether or not it should be banned. Human cloning consists of reproductive cloning, in which a genetically identical replicate can be created, and therapeutic cloning, which is to harvest stem cells from cloned embryos for medical research. While most critics oppose reproductive cloning, arguing that the practice diminishes the uniqueness and dignity of humankind, some advocates view it as a hope for infertile couples to have their own children. Since the potential benefits of therapeutic cloning have become apparent, the number of its supporters has been growing for the reason that it helps scientists to gain insights into treating incurable diseases. Yet, some critics reject both types of human cloning, saying that the practices as well as those of related research are grossly unethical.

"The Ethics of Cloning." Editorial. *Washington Post* 9 Jan. 2003: A24.
    Print.

This editorial presents the views of two authorities who have written individually to oppose Richard Cohen's argument in favor of human cloning. One of them is Bill Rebeck, an associate professor of neuroscience, who disagrees with Cohen's idea that "reproductive cloning would not be unethical if proven safe." He points out that DNA that has accumulated mutations could be passed on to the replicate when it is used in reproductive cloning. Therefore, it is unethical since it puts the clone at risk of fatality. William L. Saunders, Jr., is a Senior Fellow in Bioethics. He claims that neither therapeutic nor reproductive cloning is ethical according to the Nuremberg Code. To support his argument, he quoted Principles 5 and 7, which state, respectively, "No experiment should be conducted where there is an a priori reason to believe that death or disabling injury will occur"

Margin annotations:

Your title states a clear research question.

The phrasing of this sentence is somewhat awkward. Could you make a connection between this sentence and the one that follows?

You provide a clear picture of the controversy surrounding the issue.

Who is Richard Cohen? We don't have any context for understanding this summary.

Refer to what authors have written in the present tense: "he quotes."

Chen 2

and "Proper preparations should be made and adequate facilities provided to protect the experimental subject against even remote possibilities of injury, disability or death."

Two authorities discuss the ethical problems that arise from human cloning. They declare their claims in reference to their knowledge and the Nuremberg Code, making the arguments more sound and reliable than the very last article written by Scott and Savori, who support both types of human cloning without any related credible references.

Halstead, Ted, and Michael Lind. "Double Jeopardy: Can It Be
    a Crime to Seek Treatment for a Deadly Disease? Congress
    Seems to Think So." *Washington Post* 5 May 2002: B4. Print.

As the president of the New America Foundation and a senior fellow, the authors of this article are advocates of therapeutic cloning due to its potential to treat various debilitating illnesses. Halstead and Lind seem excessively assertive when they describe therapeutic cloning as a "safe and reliable treatment," but I agree with them that criminalizing therapeutic cloning has more drawbacks than advantages. Halstead and Lind argued that therapeutic cloning should not be banned due to the reason that it would be hard to enforce such a ban, and the scientific breakthrough has significant potential social benefits. Instead, therapeutic cloning in America should be legalized with regulation, as in other advanced democracies. The authors explain that the US, which is a leader in pursuing advanced technology, would lose competitiveness to those countries causing damage to science and business. The ban would also be a precedent for restricting other scientific research in the future. In contrast, Halstead and Lind do urge a ban on reproductive cloning, not only because it is unsafe, but also because there is no contribution to either the medical or social sector.

Hansen, Brian. "Cloning Debate." *CQ Press* 14.37 22 Oct. 2004.
    Web. 23 Feb. 2006.

This comparison might make more sense when you summarize Scott and Savori. You could remind us of this first annotation and then point out the contract.

I like how you have embedded information about the authors' rhetorical situation here.

So, is this article basically a review of the literature itself?

Chen 3

The author of this article presents an overall picture of human cloning. He has gathered opinions mostly from scientists and researchers. The majority of them support therapeutic cloning and stem cell research, saying that it would potentially cure diseases by using stem cells extracted from cloned embryos. Yet, those scientists oppose reproductive cloning since it is unethical to put the lives of clones in danger due to the high failure rate of cloning and the practice undermines the uniqueness of humankind. However, advocates of reproductive cloning view it as an effective way to help infertile couples to have their own children. Hansen also reports the views of some critics, who are, on the other hand, skeptical of the feasibility of stem cell therapy, as evidence has shown that rejection would still occur even using genetically identical stem cells for transplantation. Moreover, it is immoral to create and then destroy human embryos merely for scientific experiments. Other critics also argue that therapeutic cloning would inevitably lead to reproductive cloning; therefore, it is crucial that both types of cloning should be banned.

Hayes, Richard. "Break the Cloning Deadlock." *Christian Science*
        Monitor. 10 June 2002: 9. Print.

Richard Hayes holds a position similar to the one that Halstead and Lind hold. Hayes asserts, "People intuitively understand that creating a child by cloning would be an affront to human dignity and individuality, would serve no good purpose, and should be banned." On the other hand, therapeutic cloning enables biomedical scientists to do research on using embryonic stem cells for treatments; he believes that it would be a better idea to consider tough rules and regulations to monitor the practice instead of a ban on such potentially beneficial research. He also suggests some requirements to be included in the rules if therapeutic cloning is legalized.

Compared to the other authors, Hayes did not explicitly express his opinions, but he focused on the importance of imposing regulations to control and monitor the practice of therapeutic cloning. This is one of the main points I want to include in my final paper.

Chen 4

Scott, Thomas R., and Ron Savori. "Human Cloning." *Truthtree.com.*
    31 Oct. 2002. Web. 23 Feb. 2006.

The authors of this article advocate both reproductive and
therapeutic cloning, as opposed to the other sources. Scott and Savori
believe that there should be no laws to ban any kind of human cloning or related research, as human cloning does more good than harm.
They contend that it is perfectly fine to clone reproductively simply
because creating a human clone is just like having an identical twin
on purpose. Scott and Savori assert that it is very hard to foresee
the benefits of new scientific advances unless efforts are made to
research into them. The idea that extracting stem cells from embryos
equals killing a become human being is rejected by the authors, since
they contend that embryos are not conscious.

This article was written by two software engineers who are not
experts in the science field. They declare their claims without scientific evidence but just based on their own justification. Although they
are not as credible as other authors, they express some distinctively
different arguments in supporting both types of human cloning. It
is also very interesting that the opinions of Scott and Savori are
completely opposite to that which Rebeck and Saunders hold.

After comparing and contrasting perspectives from different
sources, I have a clearer picture of the issue, which has allowed
me to draw a conclusion. Obviously, the vast majority agrees that
reproductive cloning, which can only help a small group, is immoral
and unsafe and it should be outlawed. Therapeutic cloning, however,
is more acceptable as it is a medical breakthrough that can potentially treat a wide range of currently incurable illnesses suffered by
millions of Americans. Proponents of therapeutic cloning believe that
under careful regulation, related researches are more beneficial than
harmful and it should not be criminalized.

> You provide a bal-
> anced assessment
> here, acknowledging
> both the strengths
> and weaknesses of
> their argument.

Discussion Questions

1. Li Chen's annotated bibliography includes both an introduction and a conclusion. Although these are not always required features of an annotated bibliography, do you think they are helpful additions? Do you have any suggestions for revisions of either section to offer the author?

2. The author chose MLA format for this paper. Why do you think she chose this citation style? What choice would you make for this annotated bibliography?

3. How well do you think the author develops the annotations in the piece? What suggestions would you make for revising the annotations themselves?

4. Do the sources in the annotated bibliography represent a variety of opinions on the issue? Do you think any perspectives are missing?

Example 2: John Lewis, Will Distance Learning Replace Traditional Instruction? The following literature review was written by a student interested in exploring the development of distance learning in universities and colleges. The student chose to write a literature review that described some of the origins of distance learning to respond to the question of whether distance learning would replace other kinds of instruction. The literature review is in APA format, more common in the field of education than MLA format.

Distance Learning   1

Will Distance Learning Replace Traditional Instruction?

John Lewis

October 28, 2002

Distance Learning   2

The increasing popularity of distance learning in higher education is placing pressure on universities to develop distance learning
classes. Yet this development often occurs rapidly with little research
concerning distance delivery in the context of individual courses.
There also seems to be a prevailing fear in higher education that
distance learning classes will replace other forms of instruction and
that students might be the ones to suffer. Many of these fears can be
relieved by looking closely at the development of distance learning
historically and understanding the premises on which it was first
implemented.

It is difficult to pinpoint precisely when distance learning was
first introduced in the United States, possibly because it is so difficult
to define distance learning itself. While the advent of computer
technology and the Internet have given distance learning increased
popularity and viability, the concept of education at a distance is
not new. The term "distance education" was first popularized in
the United States in 1987 by Bjorn Holmberg and Michael Moore
(Verduin & Clark, 1991) at a time when computer technology was
just beginning to expand the possibilities for distance learning, but
courses had been offered "at a distance" in America for nearly a
century already. Several researchers place the first distance courses at
the Pennsylvania State University, the University of Chicago, and the
University of Wisconsin in the late 1800s (McIsaac & Gunawardena,
1996; Pfefferle, 1999; Verduin & Clark, 1991). These courses were
offered by correspondence, and later courses were offered using a
variety of media such as radio, television, telephone, and video.

Despite the relatively long history of distance learning in the
United States, distance learning options have always remained on the
margins of higher education until recently. The growth of distance
learning was slow until the late 1980s when computers and network
technology began to change the face of distance learning. In 1987
fewer than ten states promoted distance learning, but nearly all of the

fifty states actively promoted distance learning just two years later (McIsaac & Gunawardena, 1996).

While distance learning has recently been popularized in the United States, Europe has historically led the way in the development and use of distance learning technology. The Open University of the United Kingdom opened in 1969 with the purpose of providing educational opportunities to students regardless of educational qualification, recently focusing on improving access to students with disabilities. The Open University has provided educational access to over two million students (The Open University, 2002). In 1992 the twelve members of the European Association for Distance Teaching Universities proposed to open a European Open University, based on the British Open University model (McIsaac & Gunawardena, 1996). This model also influences the development of distance learning in the United States, especially with the recent development of the Western Governors University, one of the first online universities in the United States (Western Governors University, 2002). Courses at the Open University use various types of multimedia and include many varieties of distance learning, focusing on offering educational opportunities to students who might not otherwise have access to higher education.

Regardless of the type of media used, however, Garrison (1989) claims that educational researchers agree that distance learning is only one of many educational media options, and *education*, not the distance between the teacher and the students, must remain the focus. The literature published in this area seems to agree that distance learning will not replace other forms of instruction but that it offers an alternative to students who might otherwise not be able to pursue higher education.

Distance Learning   4

References

Garrison, D. R. (1989). *Understanding distance education: A framework for the future*. New York: Routledge.

McIsaac, M. S., & Gunawardena, C. N. (1996). Distance education. In D. H. Jonassen (Ed.), *Handbook of research for educational communications and technology: A project of the Association for Educational Communications and Technology* (pp. 403–437). New York: Simon & Schuster Macmillan.

The Open University. (2002). Media relations: Factsheets. *The Open University*. Retrieved July 13, 2002, from http://www3.open .ac.uk/media/factsheets

Pfefferle, W. T. (1999). *Writing that matters: A rhetoric for the new classroom*. Upper Saddle River, NJ: Prentice Hall.

Verduin, J. R., & Clark, T. A. (1991). *Distance education: The foundations of effective practice*. San Francisco: Jossey-Bass.

Western Governors University. (2002). About WGU. *Western Governors University*. Retrieved July 13, 2002, from http://www .wgu.edu/wgu/about

Discussion Questions

1. How do the forms of a literature review and an annotated bibliography differ? What are some of the key similarities? What are some of the primary differences (other than the format)?

2. Do you think an annotated bibliography or a literature review would be the best choice for your project? Why?

3. How well does the author of this essay explain the controversy he is exploring? Is his research question clear to you?

4. What suggestions would you make to the author in terms of the resources included in the literature review? Would you recommend he look at any other perspectives?

PART 3

Reporting on Research

[
　　　RESEARCH IN PROGRESS:
Writing a Researched Argument
]

9

Constructing an Argument

The research scenario described on the next page might be similar to assignments you have had or will have in college. Sam knows that there are a number of issues related to political science that he could write about for his college class. Likewise, there are a variety of ways he could approach an argument on the subject he chooses, a Supreme Court case. Sam will have to consider the rhetorical situation of his project while researching and writing, and he will also have to consider elements of how to construct a convincing argument based on the data he finds. As you read the research scenario, consider how Sam's rhetorical situation might shape his research and writing. How would you go about developing a researched argument in response to this assignment? ›

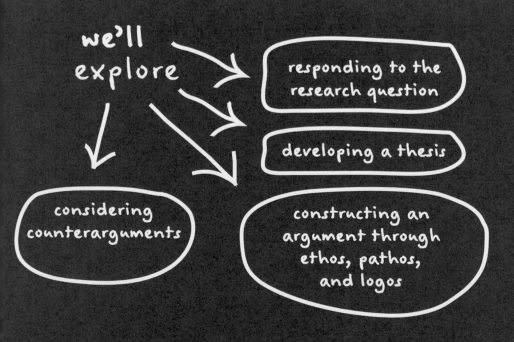

we'll explore

responding to the research question

developing a thesis

considering counterarguments

constructing an argument through ethos, pathos, and logos

Research in Action

Author: Sam is a college student, taking his first class for his political science major. Sam wants to go to law school when he finishes his undergraduate degree.

Topic: Sam's professor for the course has assigned an end-of-semester paper that must present an argument about a legal issue that has been discussed in class and has been heard by the courts. The only guideline is that the topic should deal with something controversial and current, an issue that has been in the news within the last 10 years. Students must take a position on the court's decision and argue for their position using their knowledge of legal precedence.

Audience: Sam's audience is his professor.

Purpose: Sam decides to write a report on a court case that is of particular interest to him, but he's in the awkward position of reporting on a topic to someone who already knows quite a bit about it. In his textbook, he read about a Supreme Court case from 2005 that dealt with whether or not college campuses could ban military recruiters. He thought he might be interested in learning more about it because he had two connections to the case: he is of legal draft age and the controversy took place on a law school campus.

QUESTIONS

1. What are the various elements of the rhetorical situation in this research scenario? How do they impact one another?

2. Where could Sam look for specific information about the case he is researching, and where might he look for information on related court cases?

3. In what ways could Sam develop his argument, and where should he start?

4. What kinds of strategies might help Sam organize the ideas and information he has gathered?

5. Have you ever been assigned a paper and you felt you had lots of information but didn't quite know how to organize it all and where to start writing a draft? What did you do?

› Reporting versus Arguing

Sam faces another challenge—when he first sits down to write a draft, he finds himself primarily summarizing the background information for the case and the things that different people have said about the case and the decision. He writes about three pages when he decides to visit the campus writing center to see if he is on the right track. At the writing center, a tutor reads what he wrote, and she points out that he wasn't really "arguing" for a position on the case but was "reporting" what others had said. Sam needed to figure out one legal issue to focus on, his position on it, and how to defend it. He was spending too much time summarizing his research instead of using it to defend his position. The tutor suggested he reconsider his goal in writing the paper to make sure that he was actually accomplishing it.

Table 9.1 gives some examples of activities that generally fall into either the reporting or the arguing category.

Sam realized that he was probably writing a lot of summary because he was learning about the case himself, but he probably didn't need to include all of the summary in his final draft because his audience (his professor) was already familiar with the specifics of the case. He needed to refocus his writing on the purpose of the assignment, but the writing he had already finished was helping him understand some of the controversial issues surrounding the case. The tutor suggested that Sam consider some of this writing to be part of his invention; he should keep all of it for later reference, but he might not include it all in his final draft.

Many of us need to revisit the rhetorical situation of our writing when we begin interpreting our research and drafting. Sam realized that the preliminary writing and summarizing he had done was useful because it helped him to identify and understand the controversy surrounding his issue. At that point in his writing, though, he needed to refocus and pick one aspect of the controversy to defend in an argument. Sam should also realize, though (as you might realize when you complete the "Reflect: Is It Reporting or Arguing?" activity), that when summarizing and reporting on a topic, he was presenting a version (or an interpretation) of what he had read and learned; therefore,

Table 9.1.
Reporting versus Arguing

Reporting	Arguing
Summarizing	Interpreting
Paraphrasing	Analyzing
Quoting	Concluding
Describing	Claiming
Telling	Persuading

3 Reporting on Research

he was starting to present a kind of argument. In other words, he was implicitly arguing what he thought was important about the topic (what he included) and what did not matter (what he excluded). Sam was pretty certain that this type of argument wasn't what his professor was looking for in this paper, though; he needed to refocus his draft on a more explicit claim about the Supreme Court case he was researching. After conducting in-depth research on an issue and looking at so many people's perspectives, it can be easy to lose the original focus of the writing task. One of the best things to do as you sit down to write is to remind yourself of the rhetorical situation.

> reflect <

Is It Reporting or Arguing?

To help distinguish between texts that report and texts that argue, list the various pieces of writing you have completed in the past 6 months or so. Then label each of them as either something you reported (such as an email with show times for a movie at the local theater) or something you argued (for example, an email claiming that you should watch one film instead of another on the upcoming Friday night). In other words, was the primary goal to provide information to your audience (reporting) or to persuade your audience (argument)? Ask yourself the following questions to help create your list and identify your writing as either reporting or arguing.

☐ What pieces of writing have you done for school? your job? in your personal and home life? in your civic or community life?

☐ What was the purpose for the piece of writing? What was its goal?

☐ Who was your audience for the piece of writing? What did you want your audience to do after reading your text?

In your list, circle the writing experience that you are most confident was reporting, circle another experience that you are most confident was arguing, and circle a third that you had the most difficult time labeling as either reporting or arguing. Discuss these three experiences with a friend or classmate. Does your friend or classmate agree with your labeling? Why or why not?

...write...

Define the Rhetorical Situation

Before you start to dig into drafting, take a moment to remind yourself of your rhetorical situation. This activity will help to focus your thoughts as you begin to write. It will also give you the chance to rethink some elements of the rhetorical situation that might have shifted as you conducted your research. For example,

you might have come across some resources that suggested a specific, different audience than you had originally imagined. Use this as an opportunity to fine-tune your focus before developing a direction for your argument and a complete draft. Write down your answers to the following questions.

- What is the research question you are trying to answer? If you need to rephrase or refocus the research question, this is a good time to do so.

- What is your purpose for researching and writing about this issue? Consider multiple purposes that you might have, and try to list them in order of priority.

- Who is the audience you are addressing? Be specific and describe as much as you can. Also consider the possibility that you might be addressing direct and implicit audiences in your research and writing.

- How do you fit into the context? In other words, how might your beliefs and understanding affect what you write and how you interpret your resources?

- Where do your answers to these four questions overlap? How might those overlapping questions further focus your research topic?

Once you have written responses to these questions and/or completed the Venn diagram below, consider sharing them with a classmate, friend, parent, or co-worker. Encourage the person to ask you questions that will help to refine your focus.

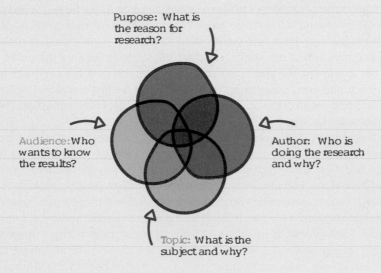

Purpose: What is the reason for research?

Audience: Who wants to know the results?

Author: Who is doing the research and why?

Topic: What is the subject and why?

Responding to the Research Question

Arguments are often, at their cores, responses to questions. Sometimes the questions are asked directly and sometimes they are implied. In the case of the research that Sam is doing, and in the research that you are completing, the argument is developed in response to the original research question. As you plan how you will respond to your research question, consider what the answers might be, what responses might work best for your purpose and audience, and what you can support with the evidence and resources you have found. This is the point in the research process where all of your work starts to come together.

A clear focus on your research question and rhetorical situation, along with an understanding of the resources you have gathered on your topic, will help you generate a list of possible responses to your research question. Sam wants to focus his research question on the Supreme Court decision in *Rumsfeld v. Forum for Academic and Institutional Rights, Inc.* As he began his research, however, he quickly discovered that the Court had been unanimous in its opinion, so perhaps it wouldn't make sense for him to develop an argument for or against the Court's decision. The Court had ruled that institutions of higher education who receive federal funding must allow military recruiting on campus. Sam began to wonder if there were any circumstances in which military recruiting could be banned, so he drafted the following research question:

> Under what circumstances could an institution of higher education ban military recruiting on campus?

By looking through resources dealing with earlier courts' decisions on the case, as well as reading the Court's final decision, Sam was able to begin drafting a list of possible responses to his research question.

Generating possible responses to a research question is important in other kinds of research as well. For example, imagine someone who is looking for her first apartment to rent. Her research question might be very simple ("Which apartment should I rent?"), but her list of possible responses to that research question might be very long because there would be several factors to consider. For example, in narrowing her list down to the "supportable" responses, she would need to consider factors such as the cost of the apartment in view of her monthly budget, the safety of the area, the possibility of sharing the apartment, the apartment complex's policy on pets, her commute to work and/or school, and many other issues that would affect her final decision. Her first step, though, is to find out all of the options, or possible responses to the question. Then she can narrow down her list.

The first step in developing your argument is to consider all of the possible responses to your research question. Then you must decide which answers fit your rhetorical situation and which ones you can support with the evidence you have gathered. Part of the difficulty with this step in the research process, though, is that it is not always easy to determine which answer is best. Sometimes a particular answer to a research question might be difficult to argue to a specific audience, but it's not impossible. For example, it might be difficult to argue for a nightly curfew to students on a college campus (more difficult than, say, making the argument to their parents), but it's not necessarily impossible. The effectiveness of the argument will depend on the evidence you provide, how appropriate and convincing it is to your audience, and how you develop your argument. Once you have generated a list of possible responses that is narrowed down to those that are *reasonable, supportable,* and *feasible* for your rhetorical situation, the next step is to choose one response and develop it into an effective thesis.

Create a Cluster Map

…write…

To focus on thinking of the possible ways to respond to your research question and then generate a position that you could support, we suggest putting your responses in a cluster map, like the one in Figure 9.1. In order to complete this activity, you will need access to your gathered resources, along with your previous writing and brainstorming about your rhetorical situation. Write your answers to the following prompts, working through them in order.

1. What is your research question? Write it down. Make this the central bubble in your cluster map.

2. Think of all of the *possible* answers to your research question. Start by responding with what you know and have learned from researching the issue. Take a look at some of your resources to see how others have responded to this issue and if there are possible answers you should add to the cluster map. There's no need to put specific details about how you would support the answers at this point; just generate all of the responses you can. You might also share your research question with someone else—a classmate, friend, or other person interested in this issue. Ask them to help you generate responses that are not already on your map. Make these responses the branches that generate from the central bubble on your cluster map.

3. Now start to narrow down the list. Start by considering the *purpose* of your research—why are you completing this research? Take a look at your possible answers (the branches) and cross off all that do not accomplish this purpose.

4. Consider the *resources* you have gathered on your topic. At this point, consider which responses you could actually defend and support with meaningful, reliable evidence. Try listing resources as branches of responses to the research question on the cluster map. Cross off all responses that you think you would have difficulty supporting.

5. Consider the *audience* for your research. Which responses to your research question would be most feasible to that audience? Who will read or hear your research? What do they already know and think about the topic? Which responses to your research question could you support and defend to your audience? Consider the research you have gathered on your issue, and think about what evidence your audience might find convincing. ⬚ Cross off all responses that you do not think you could effectively argue to your audience.

For more information, see Chapter 10, "Selecting and Integrating Evidence."

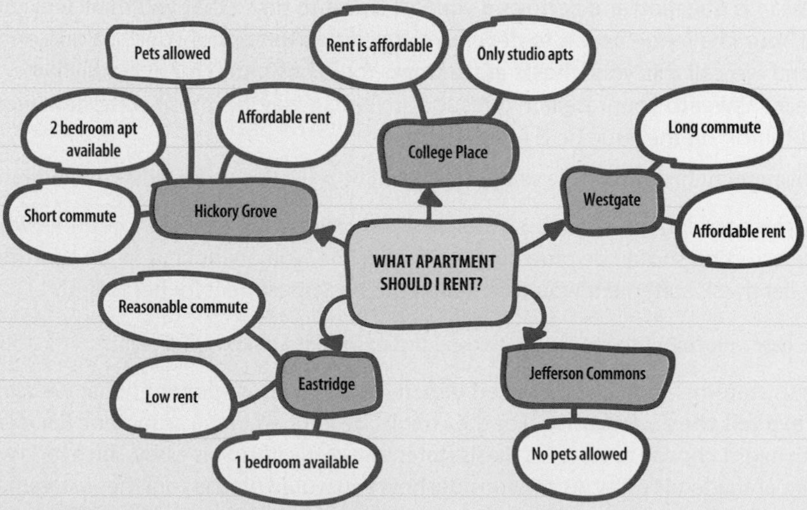

3 Reporting on Research

Figure 9.1   Cluster Map of Apartment Options ⬚

See the appendix for more information on cluster mapping.

>>>

>>>   Your cluster map probably resembles the one in Figure 9.2 at this point, showing fewer possible answers, and maybe even the one answer you want to pursue.

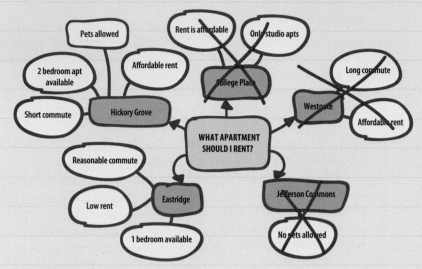

Figure 9.2   Narrowing down the Possibilities

Developing a Thesis

At this point in your research, you have considered different possible responses to your research question and narrowed your list down to those that you think you could defend. Your challenge now is to develop a specific statement of your position on the issue, and we call this your **thesis statement**. Your thesis statement simply needs to be a clear answer to your research question. In Sam's essay, his thesis statement would take a position on the issue he is researching.

Military recruiting on college campuses should be protected under most circumstances.

His introduction, and the rest of his paper, would develop the circumstances under which military recruiting should be protected by law. For the woman looking for an apartment to rent, her thesis statement would center on the best apartment for her to rent.

The best apartment to rent is the two-bedroom unit at Hickory Grove.

Thesis statements might be stated directly in a written argument (what we would call an **explicit thesis statement**) or they might be implied in the argument. For example, Sam might choose to state his thesis statement explicitly in his essay, since he is writing a formal academic essay. As you consider how you would phrase your thesis statement, keep the following guidelines in mind. A thesis statement for an argument should

- be a statement and not a question.

- make a precise claim and not merely be a statement of fact or observation.

- be clear, avoiding unspecific language.

Depending on your rhetorical situation, your thesis statement most likely should also

- be a complex statement, not simply a "yes" or "no" answer to your research question.

- give your audience an idea of what to expect in your argument.

Sam's thesis statement is somewhat vague, so he should either clarify the circumstances he is talking about in the introduction or revise his thesis statement to be clearer. As you draft your thesis statement, you might think of it as containing two parts: the precise claim itself and the reasons for your claim. You might not include the reasons in an explicit thesis statement in your argument, but for now it will be helpful in thinking about how to defend your claim to consider and write down your reasons for that claim.

Example Thesis Statement 1

Precise Claim: The best apartment to rent is the two-bedroom unit at Hickory Grove.
- Reason: It has the shortest commute to my office.
- Reason: The apartment complex welcomes pets.
- Reason: The rent is reasonable for my monthly budget.

Example Thesis Statement 2

Precise Claim: ABC University should enforce a nightly curfew for students.
- Reason: Violent crime on campus has escalated after 1 A.M. in recent years.
- Reason: Students would study more for classes.
- Reason: Students would sleep more.

A thesis statement can also do more than simply answer the original research question.

- It could identify areas that will be developed in the argument, providing a basic outline for the argument itself. This might be the case for Example 1 if the three reasons are listed as a "because" statement after the claim:

  The best apartment to rent is the two-bedroom unit at Hickory Grove because it has the shortest commute to my office, the apartment complex welcomes pets, and the rent is reasonable for my monthly budget.

- It could invite the audience to take action on the thesis statement or to be part of a solution to a problem. This might be the case for Example 2 if the argument is directed toward administrators at the university.

The way you choose to write your thesis statement, of course, depends on your specific rhetorical situation.

3 Reporting on Research

...write...

Draft a Thesis Statement

As you work on this activity, keep your original research question in front of you along with your list (or cluster map) of possible responses. Use these steps to draft the two parts of your thesis statement (your claim and your reasons). Keep in mind that your claim is the answer to your research question, and the reasons could be thought of as "because" statements that support the claim. Read the example, and use it as a guide to write your own thesis statement.

Sample research question: Should a law be passed to make English the official language of the United States?

Precise claim: Congress should pass a law making English the official language of the United States.

Reasons/blueprint

☐ A common language would encourage unity among citizens.

☐ Learning English is empowering to people because of its status in global communication.

Complete thesis statement: Congress should pass a law making English the official language of the United States because it would encourage unity among citizens and empower people to participate in global communication.

Now it's your turn. Write your responses to the following prompts for your research project.

Research question:

_____

_____

Precise claim:

_____

_____

Reasons/blueprint:

_____

_____

_____

Complete thesis statement:

_____

_____

_____

Note: Even if you choose not to use both the claim and the reasons in your thesis statement, you have begun supporting your argument by developing the complete thesis statement.

Using Qualifiers

As you develop your argument, you will realize that there are often exceptions to any claim and line of reasoning. One way to address a potential exception is to offer a **qualifier**, a word or phrase that "hedges" or limits the claim. Consider Sam's thesis statement again:

Military recruiting on college campuses should be protected under most circumstances.

Sam used the qualifier "most" to allow for circumstances where military recruiting is not, or should not be, protected. In the case of Example 2 in the previous section, the thesis might be written in any of the following ways:

ABC University should suggest a nightly curfew for students.

ABC University should enforce a nightly curfew for freshmen and sophomores.

ABC University might consider a nightly curfew for students.

Each of these thesis statements has a slightly different meaning based on the qualifiers.

Sometimes qualifiers are simply words that are included in a claim or reason in order to allow for an exception. Such qualifiers include words like *often, generally, usually, most,* and *many* (instead of definitive words such as *always* and *all*). For example, in the first sentence of this section, we used the word *often* to qualify our claim that there are exceptions to any claim and line of reasoning. It would probably (another qualifier) be too strong a statement to say that there is *always* an exception to a claim or line of reasoning. On other occasions, it might be more appropriate to include a phrase or sentence as a qualifier for a claim or even an entire section of the paper as a qualifier for the argument. For example, someone arguing that parents should spank their children might offer a qualifier that spanking should only be used under certain circumstances or done in a certain way.

Using qualifiers in the development of an argument can be tricky, however. You don't want to discredit the argument that you have developed by qualifying it too much or in a way that makes it less persuasive. You might even consider trying different versions of your claim and reasons—with qualifiers, without qualifiers, and with different kinds of qualifiers—on a willing listener to see how he or she responds.

> reflect <

Can You Recognize Qualifiers?

Although candy companies would love to proclaim that all kids like their products, they recognize that there are probably exceptions to this claim. Therefore, they can be sure to keep from alienating their audience members by leaving a space for dissent; instead, they say something like "Nine out of ten kids like XXXX."

Practice identifying qualifiers by looking at this advertisement from the smoking industry as it appeared in the *New York Times* and over 400 other newspapers on January 4, 1954. How do they qualify their claims? What terms do they use to allow for exceptions and dissent?

3 Reporting on Research

A Frank Statement to Cigarette Smokers[1]

Recent reports on experiments with mice have given wide publicity to a theory that cigarette smoking is in some way linked with lung cancer in human beings.

Although conducted by doctors of professional standing, these experiments are not regarded as conclusive in the field of cancer research. However, we do not believe that any serious medical research, even though its results are inconclusive, should be disregarded or lightly dismissed.

At the same time, we feel it is in the public interest to call attention to the fact that eminent doctors and research scientists have publicly questioned the claimed significance of these experiments.

Distinguished authorities point out:

1. That medical research of recent years indicates many possible causes of lung cancer.
2. That there is no agreement among the authorities regarding what the cause is.
3. That there is no proof that cigarette smoking is one of the causes.
4. That statistics purporting to link cigarette smoking with the disease could apply with equal force to any one of many other aspects of modern life. Indeed the validity of the statistics themselves is questioned by numerous scientists.

>>>

---

1. "A Frank Statement to Cigarette Smokers" from *The New York Times*, January 4, 1954.

>>> We accept an interest in people's health as a basic responsibility, paramount to every other consideration in our business.

We believe the products we make are not injurious to health.

We always have and always will cooperate closely with those whose task it is to safeguard the public health. For more than 300 years tobacco has given solace, relaxation, and enjoyment to mankind. At one time or another during those years critics have held it responsible for practically every disease of the human body. One by one these charges have been abandoned for lack of evidence.

Regardless for [sic] the record of the past, the fact that cigarette smoking today should even be suspected as a cause of a serious disease is a matter of deep concern to us.

Many people have asked us what we are doing to meet the public's concern aroused by the recent reports. Here is the answer:

1. We are pledging aid and assistance to the research effort into all phases of tobacco use and health. This joint financial aid will of course be in addition to what is already being contributed by individual companies.

2. For this purpose we are establishing a joint industry group consisting initially of the undersigned. This group will be known as TOBACCO INDUSTRY RESEARCH COMMITTEE.

3. In charge of the research activities of the Committee will be a scientist of unimpeachable integrity and national repute. In addition, there will be an Advisory Board of scientists disinterested in the cigarette industry. A group of distinguished men from medicine, science, and education will be invited to serve on this Board. These scientists will advise the Committee on its research activities.

This statement is being issued because we believe the people are entitled to know where we stand on this matter and what we intend to do about it.

SPONSORS

THE AMERICAN TOBACCO COMPANY, INC.
Paul M, Hahn, President

BURLEY TOBACCO GROWERS COOPERATIVE ASSOCIATION
John W. Jones, President

PHILLIP MORRIS & CO. LTD., INC.
O. Parker McComas, President

BENSON & HEDGES
Joseph F. Cullman, Jr., President

LARUS & BROTHER COMPANY, INC.
W. T. Reed, Jr., President

R. J. REYNOLDS TOBACCO COMPANY
E. A. Darr, President

BRIGHT BELT WAREHOUSE ASSOCIATION
F. S. Royster, President

P. LORILLARD COMPANY
Herbert A. Kent, Chairman

STEPHANO BROTHERS, INC.
C. S. Stephano, D'Sc., Director of Research

BROWN & WILLIAMSON TOBACCO CORPORATION
Timothy V. Hartnett, President

MARYLAND TOBACCO GROWERS ASSOCIATION
Samuel C. Linton, General Manager

TOBACCO ASSOCIATES, INC.
(An organization of free-owned tobacco growers)
J. B. Hutson, President

BURLEY AUCTION WAREHOUSE ASSOCIATION
Albert Clay, President

UNITED STATES TOBACCO COMPANY
J. W. Peterson, President

Supporting an Argument

Once you have defined the claim that you are going to make in your argument, you need to support it with reasons and evidence. As with the other research-based writing discussed in this book, supporting an argument is rhetorically situated. You could choose from numerous methods for developing, supporting, and organizing your argument, and you could reason with your audience in many ways, based on your purpose and goal. In this chapter we will present a variety of reasoning methods you might use to support your argument.

Ethos, Pathos, and Logos

One way to support an argument is to develop specific appeals to your audience. As mentioned in Chapter 2, Aristotle defined rhetoric as searching for "the available means of persuasion." He divided what he saw as the various kinds of persuasive appeals that a speaker could make to an audience into three categories:

- **ethos**—appeals to credibility and authority

- **pathos**—appeals to emotions

- **logos**—appeals to reason and logic

You can find examples of each of these appeals all around you. If you observe a classroom immediately after a teacher has handed back a graded test, you might find several varieties of appeals (with varying degrees of persuasive success) if students are unhappy about their grades on the exam. For example, one student might appeal to ethos by pointing out a passage in the textbook that disagrees with the answer marked as correct on the exam. Relying on the passage in the textbook would be an appeal to a credible authority. Another student might appeal to logos by reasoning through the different answers to a question and showing how the answer marked as correct doesn't make logical sense if interpreted in a certain way. And yet another student might appeal to pathos (probably unsuccessfully) by explaining to the teacher that he or she must get a high grade in the class to keep a scholarship. While these are somewhat flippant examples of rhetorical appeals, they illustrate different approaches that one might take in constructing an argument. Depending on the rhetorical situation, of course, some kinds of appeals may be more effective than others.

Let's consider another example. Imagine a boxing enthusiast who wants to develop an argument that Muhammad Ali was the greatest boxer of all time. She first might appeal to ethos by quoting an authority on boxing who says that Ali was the greatest boxer of all time. If she wanted to appeal to logos, she might use statistics from Ali's career record or cite and analyze an example of a specific boxing match, such as his legendary fight against George Foreman in 1974. And finally, she might appeal to pathos by describing the way that Ali overcame adversity to reestablish his career after being out of boxing for several years. Depending on the person's audience and purpose for writing, one of these appeals might be more persuasive than the others, or it might be best to include a combination of different kinds of appeals.

Ethos Arguments based on ethos refer to the credibility and authority of an individual or a group of individuals. When providing evidence from expert or personal testimony, you are making an argument based on ethos. You, as the author of a researched argument, also need to develop your own ethos as a credible and authoritative researcher and writer. If you do not provide evidence that you have done your research carefully and systematically, your audience will not trust your results.

Much of the time *expert* credibility and authority are demonstrated through education and training. Experts usually have degrees and high positions in the field of their expertise. Sometimes, however, experts are also certified by their vast amount of experience. Degrees and highly ranked positions usually imply experience; however, some fields do not necessarily have degree programs. For example, although a water purification expert may only have an associate's degree, there are not yet many educational programs for that field. Most of the experts in water purification gain their ethos from years of experience.

Individuals who provide evidence based on *personal testimony* also have to demonstrate the ethos of the personal experience. For example, if a pre-med student were doing research on diabetes, she might find personal testimony of people diagnosed with diabetes as well as people who live with diabetics. Both groups have a certain amount of credibility and authority to discuss the topic with personal anecdotes. Obviously, a doctor who specializes in diabetes would have the ethos of an expert. Personal testimony, though, often needs to be qualified when it is used to support an argument to avoid overgeneralization.

When using arguments based on ethos, it is critically important to provide evidence of the individual's credibility and authority. The easiest way to do that is to introduce the source (e.g., an expert or an established agency), as well as its qualifications, before quoting or paraphrasing it in an argument. For example, the pre-med student writing about diabetes might include the following statement in her argument about developing an elementary school support program for diabetes:

> Both the U.S. Department of Health and Human Services (2003) and the Centers for Disease Control (2001) emphasize that schools need to take responsibility in teaching students, especially those with diabetes, about healthy eating habits.

The pre-med student would also need to develop her own ethos in researching and writing about diabetes. Her student status would give her some credibility because the audience would assume she has taken some classes that would give her more information on the topic. By providing a well thought-out, researched, developed, and organized argument about diabetes, she would provide evidence of being a careful and systematic researcher and writer.

...write...

Develop Your Authorial Ethos

As you begin to develop and support your argument, consider how you could construct your own ethos in the argument.

☐ What is your experience with this topic? Do you have first-hand or detailed knowledge about the topic that gives you authority to research and discuss it?

☐ What is your experience with your audience members? Do you have first-hand or detailed knowledge about them that will allow you to make explicit connections to their wants and needs?

☐ What resources have you located that demonstrate authority and credibility? Do you have resources by experts on the topic? Do you have research studies or experiments conducted by qualified researchers?

☐ And finally, what would be most persuasive to your audience? Which members of your audience would be most persuaded by an appeal based on credibility?

Pathos Arguments based on pathos appeal to an audience's emotions, attempting to persuade through the power of emotional response. Personal testimony can also be a way to develop pathos. If you have ever watched the president of the United States give the State of the Union address, you have most likely seen a compelling use of personal testimony as pathos because the president always has at least one special guest in attendance whose story he can tell to underscore one of his initiatives that year. A personal testimony might be an effective way to open an argument (or even to frame an argument). If the story is used to encourage an emotional response from the audience, it is an example of pathos. If it is used to develop the credibility of a source or of the argument's author, it is an example of ethos. Sometimes, of course, personal testimony can be used to do both at the same time. For example, when the president refers to the experience of a special guest in the audience at the State of the Union address, he appeals to pathos because he is drawing on the audience's emotions, and he also appeals to ethos because the guest has had personal experience with the issue at hand.

Many authors use pathos to motivate their audiences to action. For example, many of us admit that although the reward would be nice, we would not do something with extreme physical risk just to "win" a lot of money. However, many parents will put themselves into extremely risky situations to save their children from harm. Whereas the "logical" argument of earning more money does not motivate an individual, saving a family member might.

In Western culture, pathos is generally not the sole foundation of a persuasive argument. Audiences often want to be convinced based on reason (logos). However, we do see pathos used frequently in introductions and conclusions as a way to motivate audiences to read or listen to the argument and then act on it.

...write...

3 Reporting on Research

Develop Emotional Arguments

Now consider how you could incorporate appeals based on pathos into your argument. Write down your answers to the following questions.

☐ How and why are you invested in this topic? What motivates you to continue researching and writing about this topic when you are tired and worn out?

☐ How and why are your audience members invested in this topic? How does this topic affect

    o your audience members' finances?

o your audience members' living situations?

o your audience's families or close circles of friends?

o your audience members' employment or employment processes?

Logos Most academic arguments are primarily based on reasoning and logic, categorized by Aristotle as logos. Many include four major elements: claims, reasons, evidence, and warrants.

- The **claim** is a precise statement about your topic, usually an answer to your research question.

- **Reasons** are statements that demonstrate *why* your claim is valid.

- **Evidence** is provided to demonstrate that each reason you provide is valid. The evidence supports your claim.

- **Warrants** are the assumptions that the audience must accept in order to believe your reasons and evidence. Warrants are ideas, concepts, and beliefs that connect the reasons to the claim, as well as the evidence to the reasons.

Many presentations of arguments do not explicitly include all four elements; however, these elements are usually present implicitly. Because we discussed claims and reasons earlier in the section on developing your thesis, we'll jump right into talking about evidence and warrants.

Offering Evidence

Evidence can take many forms, but one thing remains consistent—evidence is an essential part of developing and supporting an argument. Evidence is the key component that persuades your audience to accept your claim. While reasons answer the audience's implied question "Why?" evidence responds to an audience that challenges you to "Prove it!" Evidence might include any of the following kinds of information (and you might be able to think of others to add to this list, based on your research topic).

- **Statistical data.** Although statistical data provide concrete numbers that people like to rely on in an argument, it is critical that researchers carefully check the method used to collect, interpret, and report the statistics. If the collection method is not valid, the numbers are meaningless.

- **Experimental results.** Like statistical data, many people place high credibility on the results of an experiment. And, again like statistical data, it is important for the researcher to carefully examine the methods of conducting the experiment, as well as collecting and reporting the results.

- **Expert opinions.** Relying on expert testimony is useful as long as you clearly outline how and why the individual is considered an expert in that field. Be sure that your audience values those criteria of expertise. In other words, if the audience doesn't think the person is an expert, then the testimony doesn't matter.

- **Personal experience and/or testimony.** Sometimes research questions require feedback from people who have some experience with the topic; however, they might not necessarily be considered experts. As you would with expert opinions, carefully identify how and why a person's experience is relevant to your topic.

- **Observations.** Although personal observation of a person, place, or thing can be a powerful form of evidence, you have to carefully describe what you observed (who and what), the circumstances in which you observed (when and where), and your method of observation (why and how).

Just like every other choice you will make in writing and research, the selection of effective, persuasive evidence depends on the rhetorical situation. Especially consider your audience as you select which evidence to include in your argument: What would this audience find persuasive? What resources would your audience find authoritative? For example, an advertisement for a specific product might rely on one person's endorsement about how well that product works to convince potential customers to buy the product. If the product is a new type of testing kit for diabetics, then the advertisement might have someone sharing his or her personal experience that the testing kit is more reliable and hurts less (diabetic testing kits must have a sample of blood to read the person's blood sugar level) than other testing kits. It will most likely be persuasive to the target audience (diabetics) if the person in the commercial is also a diabetic (ethos). However, what if the advertisement were targeting diabetics who are children? The advertisement appeals to both logos (reliability) that the parent might find attractive and pathos (less pain!) that the child having her fingers pricked would appreciate. In this case, both types of appeal arise from one type of evidence, testimony.

Researchers should select a good balance of different kinds of evidence to make an argument more persuasive to their audiences. For example, we mentioned personal testimonies as an example of ethos and pathos. Personal testimony could be used to convince your audience, but it generally won't be effective as the only piece of evidence in an argument. Even multiple personal testimonies might be insufficient. Instead, an effective argument will generally incorporate a variety of kinds of evidence from a variety of sources. For example, Sam's paper on the court case might include the following types of evidence:

- precise language from the ruling

- interpretations of the ruling by experts in the field

- comparisons to similar court cases

As another example, a person researching health care providers for her company might include different types of evidence in her report, such as:

- survey results from employees about their health care wants and needs

- statistics on how many other companies use a particular health care provider

- comparisons to similar companies who use a particular health care provider

- referrals from Human Resource specialists and other employees from companies who use a particular health care provider

Finally, the most persuasive arguments generally include a similar amount of evidence for the different reasons given in the argument. Of course, every argument

See Chapter 11, "Sharing the Results," for further discussion on patterns of organization.

Chapter 10 goes into more detail about selecting and incorporating evidence into your argument, and also includes a discussion of the various kinds of evidence.

has weaker and stronger points, and the stronger points can be emphasized based on the pattern of organization you choose. ▢ A researcher should seek some balance in the argument, though. If you have three or four good pieces of evidence for one reason and only one piece of evidence for another reason (and not a very convincing piece of evidence at that), consider looking for more evidence to support that point or think about taking it out of your argument. As you seek this kind of balance in your argument, also look for a balance among elements of ethos, logos, and pathos—the most convincing arguments do not solely rely on one type of persuasion. ▢

Determining Warrants

Warrants are the connections between the claim and the reason in your argument and between a specific reason and its evidence. They are the assumptions that the audience must accept in order for a claim to seem plausible, and therefore, persuasive. Sometimes the warrant, or assumption, is one that you can assume your audience will readily accept because it is not controversial (see Example 1). If this is the case, then you could develop your argument based on that warrant without explicitly stating it or defending it. If the warrant itself is controversial, however (see Example 3), then you will need to defend the warrant before you can assume that the audience will accept and agree with your reason and/or evidence.

In the examples below, we have identified the specific claim, a reason for that claim, and the warrant, or assumption, that the audience must accept in order for the reason to support the claim.

Example 1

Claim: You should not drive while intoxicated.

Reason: Intoxicated drivers can cause serious, and often fatal, accidents.

Warrant: Situations that cause serious accidents should be avoided.

Most people would agree that serious accidents should be avoided; therefore, this warrant does not need further support in the argument.

Example 2

Claim: Cell phones should not be allowed in restaurants.

Reason: I think it's annoying to listen to people's conversations in restaurants.

Warrant: What I don't like should be eliminated.

Although many people might find use of cell phones in public somewhat annoying, most realize that one individual not liking them is not a valid reason to disallow them entirely. However, if the reason were that a large number of people do not think cell phones in restaurants are appropriate, the warrant might have more sustainability (what a lot of people do not like should be abolished).

Example 3

Claim: My father should be elected town mayor.

Reason: Our family has lived in this town for five generations.

Warrant: A candidate with a long family history in the town will make a better mayor.

In this third example, the audience may or may not agree with the warrant about family history and suitability to lead the town. This writer may need to provide some evidence to support the warrant. For example, perhaps members in this person's family have historically participated in key junctions of the town's development. As a member of this family, this person has grown up knowing detailed history of the town as well as being surrounded by family members with a civic commitment to the town's well-being. Such an explanation would help to connect the reason to the claim.

While deciding whether a warrant needs further support, be sure to think about your audience. You might think the warrant is solid, but your audience might have different ideas.

Example 4

Claim: I should purchase the new iPod with larger memory.

Reason: A newer technology with larger capacity is better than an older technology with less capacity.

Warrant: Bigger and newer are worth purchasing.

Are bigger and newer always better? Do people have to always have the newest thing to get the job done? If the person already has a fairly new iPod with a medium-range memory capacity, does she really need a new one? What if the audience is the parents paying for the new iPod? Would they agree with this warrant? Always double-check your warrants with your audience's specific beliefs.

Remember that these descriptions of claims, reasons, evidence, and warrants are guidelines and not a formula to follow. Each argument is different and might not follow this pattern exactly. Just use the principles to get started and develop your argument as it fits your rhetorical situation.

3 Reporting on Research

...write...

Understand Your Warrants

Revisit the complete thesis statement you have developed, the one that includes your claim and reasons. Focus on one of the reasons. As you might notice from the preceding examples, all warrants have two parts, one explicitly connected to the claim and one explicitly connected to the reason. State the warrant connecting your claim to your reason and decide whether you need to further support your warrant. Use the following questions to help articulate your warrant.

1. Does your warrant include one section for your claim and one for your reason?

2. Does your warrant sufficiently connect your reason to your claim?

3. Will your intended audience undeniably agree with your warrant? Why or why not?

If your answer is "yes" to the third question, you probably do not need to support your warrant any further. However, if your answer is no, be sure to develop reasons and evidence to support your warrant.

After you have explicitly stated your warrant and decided whether it needs to be supported further, talk to a classmate, friend, or colleague about your claim, reason, and warrant. Do they agree that you have identified the correct warrant? Do they agree that you do or do not need to further support your warrant?

Providing Counterarguments

Sound reasoning to support your claim is key to developing your argument. However, it is often necessary to acknowledge alternative perspectives and provide counterarguments. For example, if Sam claims that military recruiting could be banned on college campuses in some circumstances, he realizes that there are many who would disagree with his opinion. If he does not acknowledge that he has accounted for these differing perspectives, readers who understand the issue might think he has not done his research well. To bolster his own ethos, it is important that Sam acknowledge alternative perspectives and then provide counterarguments that demonstrate why his perspective is better.

Sam can provide counterarguments using two methods: rebuttals and qualifiers. He could openly acknowledge an alternative perspective and offer his rebuttal. Or he could qualify his claim about military recruiting on college campuses by clarifying the circumstances under which it might be banned.

Including Rebuttals

Once you acknowledge your research topic is part of a larger conversation, you usually recognize that there are multiple perspectives on the issue. If there are very popular and well-supported perspectives that differ from your own, address them. You might also have to provide rebuttals if any of your warrants is debatable. Finally, be sure to have a classmate, friend, or family member carefully read a draft of your argument. If they come up with serious questions or concerns, you need to refute those issues as well.

...write....

Develop Counterarguments

Start identifying possible counterarguments. Look back over your research and identify perspectives that are different from your claim. Rank the differing perspectives from strongest (has the most validity, legitimacy, and credibility) to the weakest (is incomprehensible, unbelievable, and dismissible). Construct a rebuttal against the two strongest alternative perspectives on your list.

Once you've constructed your rebuttals, have a classmate, friend, or colleague look them over. You may also want to ask that person if they think any of the other alternative perspectives on your list require refutation.

...write....

Construct an Argument

This guide can help you construct your argument, and you can add and subtract elements as needed. Many writers find templates or guidelines like this helpful to start planning their written project; however, they will break away from it as the project's rhetorical situation demands.

Research question: *Is tech. in education hindering learning is subje such as Math.*

Answer/thesis/claim: *Tech. in the classroom is distracting students from learning + understanding ~~the~~ the information needed.*

Ethos: Many ~~People~~ Professors, such as ~~a~~ Paul Printzler at Penn State,
believe technology is being used the wrong way in education
Would your audience find appeals based on ethos to be persuasive? Where and how will you demonstrate your credibility and authority as an author? Yes, ~~as~~ their credibility as
professors make the topic more persuasive.

Pathos: If people can't see how education needs to be changed, our children +
future generations will be more mislead than we are in learning
Would your audience find appeals based on pathos to be persuasive? Where and how will you
include appeals to the audience's emotions? I think so, but not by itself. ~~❀~~

Logos: Even with the fancy new tech, present, ~~schools~~ higher education itself
is outdated and doesn't fit with current time
Would your audience find appeals based on logos to be persuasive? Where and how will you appeal
to your audience through logic and reasoning? Yes, it's the cold hard facts of
education

Reason 1 _____
    Warrant connecting reason 1 to claim _____
    Evidence 1 _____
    Warrant connecting evidence 1 to reason 1 _____
    Evidence 2 _____
    Warrant connecting evidence 2 to reason 1 _____
    Evidence 3 _____
    Warrant connecting evidence 3 to reason 1 _____
Reason 2 _____
    Warrant connecting reason to claim _____
    Evidence 4 _____
    Warrant connecting evidence 4 to reason 2 _____
    Evidence 5 _____
    Warrant connecting evidence 5 to reason 2 _____
    Evidence 6 _____
    Warrant connecting evidence 6 to reason 2 _____
Reason 3 _____
    Warrant connecting reason 3 to claim _____
    Evidence 7 _____
    Warrant connecting evidence 7 to reason 3 _____
    Evidence 8 _____
    Warrant connecting evidence 8 to reason 3 _____   >>>

>>>   Evidence 9 _____

    Warrant connecting evidence 9 to reason 3 _____

Reason 4 _____

    Warrant connecting reason 4 to claim _____

    Evidence 10 _____

    Warrant connecting evidence 10 to reason 4 _____

    Evidence 11 _____

    Warrant connecting evidence 11 to reason 4 _____

    Evidence 12 _____

    Warrant connecting evidence 12 to reason 4 _____

Objections your audience might have:

    Objection 1 _____

        Refutation 1 _____

    Objection 2 _____

        Refutation 2 _____

    Objection 3 _____

        Refutation 3 _____

Qualifiers: Which claims, reasons, or refutations might you need to qualify? _____

_____

_____

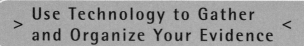

techno_tip >

> Use Technology to Gather and Organize Your Evidence <

 For an interactive tutorial about using technology to gather and organize your evidence, go to *Student Resources* on the online resource center at www .cengage.com/english/Miller-Cochran/WGTR.

See "Techno Tips: Track Bibliographic Information Online" in Chapter 7.

You can use project management software designed for research such as Zotero (http://www.zotero.org/) or RefWorks (your institution might have a license for this application) to gather your evidence and to begin organizing it. In Chapter 7, you read about how to use project management software to track your data. ☐ Most project management software applications that are designed for research will also help your organize your data so that you can begin structuring the evidence that you will use in your argument.

Selecting and Integrating Evidence

In order to develop an effective and persuasive argument, a writer must select evidence that will be convincing to the audience and relevant to the context. Each writing situation is unique, and there may be specific circumstances that a writer must consider in choosing evidence and developing reasons for his or her argument. As you constructed your argument in the previous chapter, you developed specific reasons for your position that establish your claim. For each reason, you need to provide evidence to convince your audience that the reason is valid, and the evidence will be most convincing if it comes from sources the audience values and respects.

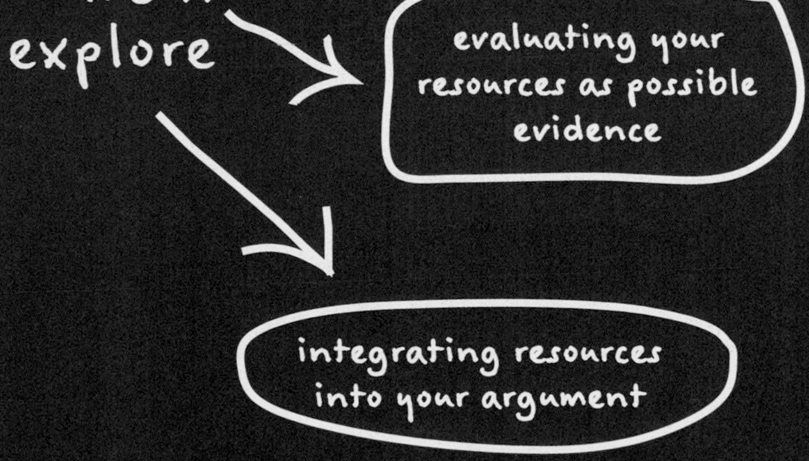

>

we'll
explore

evaluating your
resources as possible
evidence

integrating resources
into your argument

© Ken Hurst/Shutterstock

Research in Action

Author: Raj specializes in developing mass transit systems, and he has been working at a civil engineering firm for one year.

Topic: His firm would like to bid on a project to develop a light rail system for commuters, and he has been charged with the task of leading the team that will develop and submit the proposal.

Audience: Raj has at least two primary audiences: the city government, who would award the project, and his supervisors at the engineering firm, who will be interested in his performance in leading a project team and his success in the proposal process.

Purpose: Raj must write a successful bid that will carefully balance the needs of commuters, the desires of city planners, and the requirements of a structurally sound and efficient light rail system.

QUESTIONS

1. What types of resources and evidence does Raj need to find for each audience?

2. How will Raj decide what evidence is appropriate for each audience?

3. Have you ever needed to meet the needs of different audiences within one writing project?

4. If so, how did you identify the resources and evidence you needed for the different audiences?

5. Were there types of evidence that members of your audience absolutely had to have? Were there types of evidence that members of your audience absolutely would not accept?

> Developing Project-Specific Evaluation Criteria

To choose the evidence you will incorporate into your argument, you need to evaluate the resources you have found and select the ones that are most appropriate to your rhetorical situation. Because each writing and research situation is distinct, you need to develop evaluation criteria that are specific to your project. You must consider what evidence your audience will find most convincing and what is most appropriate to the topic and argument you are making. You must also consider issues such as audience and purpose, but you might also consider timeliness and relevance, as well as other criteria applicable to your project.

Audience and Purpose

Raj is addressing multiple audiences in his proposal. The primary audience, of course, is the city government and the authorities who will be selecting the firm to build a light rail system. Raj also has at least two other audiences: the citizens of the city (who might be paying for the light rail system through their taxes) and his supervisors at work (who might consider him for a promotion and/or raise if his bid is well written and successful). He realizes that he might need to include a variety of evidence and different kinds of resources to address these multiple audiences.

Consider the audience for your argument. Do you have one, explicit audience? Is there also an implied audience (or audiences) that you need to consider? What kinds of evidence will be most convincing to your audience(s)? In order to answer this last question, you might think about what your audience values. Understanding the audience's values will help you choose evidence that will be persuasive to them, and it will also help you determine the best way to construct and phrase your argument and reasons. In addition, consider what your audience already knows about your topic. What do you know that they already believe about your topic?

As you consider the way your audience shapes the kind of evidence you choose, also consider your purpose. What do you want your argument to accomplish? What are you hoping your audience will do in response to your argument? Will the evidence you have found persuade your audience to accomplish your purpose? In Raj's case, he needs to choose evidence that will be persuasive to all three of his audiences, and he needs to consider his purpose in addressing each of these audiences. He needs evidence that will persuade the city authorities to adopt his proposal over others, and he also needs evidence that will persuade the citizens that funding his light rail system is a good use of public resources. Finally, he needs to choose evidence that will be respected by his supervisors at work. He knows, however, that if he wins the bid, then that will be the most convincing evidence of all to his supervisors.

3 Reporting on Research

> reflect <

Are You Addressing Your Audience's Wants and Needs?

As you begin to think about which evidence to include in your argument, start by reflecting on your audience. Try responding to the following questions to help you determine which evidence might be most useful and persuasive to include in your argument.

1. Who is/are your audience(s)? Think about who your primary audience is, and then consider whether there are other audiences that you are also addressing. You might have an explicit audience that is more defined and also an implicit audience. For example, if you are writing a paper for a class, you might address an explicit audience that would be appropriate for your topic, but then you always have the implied audience of your instructor to consider as well.

Now answer each of the following questions for each audience that you identified in item 1.

2. What does your audience value? What is important to them?

3. What will your audience be expecting in terms of evidence? What types of evidence are you required to include (if any)? Have you found evidence that would be undoubtedly convincing to your audience?

4. What does your audience think about your issue? Do they already have well-formed opinions in response to your research question? Do you know whether they already agree or disagree with you? Your response to this question will help you determine not only *which* evidence to include but also *how much*. If your audience disagrees with you, then you may need to include more evidence. If your audience is open to different ideas or already agrees with parts of your argument, then you might use less evidence in certain parts of your argument.

Timeliness, Relevance, and Other Criteria

Several additional criteria might help you determine which evidence to choose. First of all, consider the timeliness of the evidence that you are considering. Does this matter for persuasive effect in your argument? For example, doctors doing cutting-edge research on how to replace worn-out hip joints need to know what other doctors are doing. How will a research doctor's paper on a "new" method for hip replacement be received if the readers (other orthopedic doctors) realize he did not know about a successful method that was published in the past two years? What will lack of knowledge, or lack of acknowledgement, do to the research doctor's credibility? To sustain her credibility, the research doctor must know the most up-to-date information. Similarly, eco-friendly arguments about recycling and global warming often depend on the most current research both to set the stage for the crisis and to provide evidence that the proposed solution will help.

However, research projects about literature or a historical topic may not require the most "timely" research. Instead, such research usually requires that the writer demonstrate an extensive knowledge about what has already been written on the topic. For example, if an undergraduate English major is writing about Shakespeare's play *Romeo* and Juliet, his professor will probably not expect him to focus on the most recent research, nor will he expect him to read everything ever written about the play. Instead, his professor will expect that the student read enough scholarship on Romeo and Juliet, and incorporate it into the course paper, to demonstrate a broad understanding of the play and how other scholarship fits into the paper's argument.

While some research may require the most current information and other research may not rely as much on timeliness, certain research projects may require research from a specific time. Instead of defining "timeliness" simply as "current," "timeliness" may refer to specific historical information. If a movie reviewer wanted to comment on the reception of the sixth Rocky film, Rocky Balboa (2006), she may have to do research comparing the reception of each of the other five Rocky films (1976, 1979, 1982, 1985, 1990). Since the six films cover a thirty-year span, the reviewer may need to know not only how the different films were received but also what was going on historically when each film was released.

Relevance is just as important as timeliness. How relevant is the evidence you have found to the purpose and scope of your argument? For example, Raj may have found great resources and evidence from an ongoing light rail project in another city; however, many of his primary audience members recognize that the other city might be in a radically different setting. If Raj is to incorporate this evidence into his argument, he will need to carefully acknowledge the differences in the situations of the two cities. Similarly, the student doing research on Shakespeare's Romeo and Juliet may have found a recent article about dialogue between the female characters in the play, but if he is writing about symbolism in the play, the article is probably outside of the purpose and scope of the project.

What other criteria should you consider for your topic/project? Look to elements of your rhetorical situation to develop more criteria. For example, Raj might have to consider how his plan will affect the environment because the city council might also be considering various types of environmental legislation. Similarly, a child care agency that is researching methods to help parents get involved in reading to their young children might have to consider evidence that takes into account the radically different socioeconomic backgrounds of the children and their families.

3 Reporting on Research

...write....

Develop Evaluative Criteria

To help develop criteria to use while constructing arguments and selecting evidence, write your answers to the following questions.

1. Who is/are the audience/s for this research project? What do they want to know? What do they need to know?

2. What is the purpose of this research project? What must be conveyed for that purpose to be achieved?

3. How timely is this research project? What types of contemporary information must you address? What types of historical

information must you address? How recent must information be to be relevant and persuasive?

4. How did you continue to narrow and focus your research question? What type of information must you find to fit within that scope? What information may be only tangentially relevant?

>>>

>>>   5. What other elements or issues about your topic must be covered?

6. What elements or issues about your topic might be interesting but not useful since they do not fit the purpose or scope of your project?

Use these criteria to start reevaluating your research. Based on these criteria, divide the results of your research into three piles.

☐ information you *must* include in your project

☐ information you *might* include because it is tangentially relevant

☐ information that you *will not* include because it is not useful or relevant

Put the information that is not relevant in an envelope or shoe box. Tuck it safely away somewhere. Although you will probably not use it and do not want to be distracted by it any longer, do not throw it away yet. Depending on the direction your project takes, the information might be useful later.

Resources as Evidence

Evidence can emerge from any type of resource; however, different types of resources often need to be evaluated in different manners. For example, you may find expert testimony in a variety of resources: individually published blogs, edited trade publications, or peer reviewed journals. However, since these three types of publications have different processes of editorial review, a researcher needs to evaluate appropriately. We're not claiming that a researcher shouldn't evaluate a peer reviewed journal article, but he or she knows that other scholars in the same field evaluated the article before it was published. Similarly, an article in a trade publication was reviewed by an editor who likely knows a lot about the particular industry the publication represents. However, the researcher may need to do a little bit of extra research to check the validity of the blog posting. Unless it is noted on the blog, it is highly unlikely that anyone edits an individually published blog; therefore, the researcher must verify the blog author's identity and credentials for publishing on the subject. This means that it is important to evaluate some of your evidence based on where you locate it.

With the invention of the Internet and the resulting relative ease with which individuals could publish their ideas, opinions, histories, and other information on the Web, many scholars started to distinguish between paper or hard-copy resources and electronic or soft-copy resources. In other words, secondary resources could suddenly be found outside the library; however, many times these resources were less authoritative and trustworthy. To be more specific, scholars were worried that much of the information found on the Internet did not have an editorial review process. For example, although popular books, magazines, and newspapers do not necessarily have resident experts on all subjects, they do have knowledgeable editors that help to filter the information that goes into print. What made scholars wary of electronic resources is that so many people could publish to the Internet without any form of editorial evaluation or review. As we mentioned in Chapter 4, many writing textbooks distinguish between library and Internet resources, often stating that the Internet resources are not to be trusted without a critical and thorough evaluation.

However, with the turn of the century and the proliferation of Internet-based electronic resources of originally printed materials, we can no longer easily dismiss electronic, soft-copy, or Internet-based resources. For example, many school libraries no longer subscribe to the paper copies of many scholarly journals; instead, they subscribe to various databases that provide electronic copies of those journals. And students access these databases through Web browsers on the Internet. Likewise, new types of solely electronic resources, such as blogs, wikis, and listservs, can be scholarly, authoritative, edited, and even peer reviewed. Similarly, the technologies that have helped proliferate numerous self-published electronic resources have also contributed to a larger number of authors self-publishing in hard copy media as well, especially books.

In Chapter 4 we classified resources by how easily and how frequently they change (static, syndicated, and dynamic) and by who filters the information before it is published (edited, peer reviewed, and self-published) on pages 75–86. Table 10.1 provides definitions and examples of each type of resource in the context of Raj's project.

Table 10.1.
A Resource Evaluation Matrix

	Static	Syndicated	Dynamic
Edited	State and local legislation and other government documents about public transit issues for the city and comparable metropolitan areas	State and local newspaper articles from the city and comparable metropolitan areas	
Peer Reviewed	Books by engineers about metropolitan public transit	Scholarly journal articles about metropolitan public transit and eco-criticism of public transit systems	Wikis of similar projects by other groups of engineers
Self-published	A Web site published by a special interest group about the light rail system's role in reducing air pollution in a major city	Blogs about local public transit and "green" issues in the city and comparable metropolitan areas	observations of public legislation sessions in the city

3 Reporting on Research

Your audience will want to know that you critically evaluated your evidence in an appropriate manner, regardless of where you found it. It is important to carefully evaluate Internet-based resources because of the fluidity of the Internet and because of the ease with which information can be changed, especially when that information is self-published. To evaluate a self-published resource, it is helpful to answer the following types of questions.

- What is the purpose of the self-published resource? How can you tell? How might its purpose bias the information being presented? Who is the primary audience? How can you tell?

- How detailed and thorough is the information being presented? Is there documentation of the information? What other methods can you use to evaluate the credibility of the information presented? How does the information in the self-published resource cross-reference with information in edited or peer reviewed resources?

- Who has the authority to publish or update the self-published resource? Who is paying for or hosting the publication? If it is an Internet-based resource, what is the suffix on the end URL (universal resource locator, which is the Web address)? Where does the site link from? Where does the site link to? Are there advertisements on the site? If it is a hard-copy resource, who is the publisher? What other types of resources does that publisher produce?

- When was the self-published resource last printed or updated? How can you tell? Can you contact the author or the webmaster?

The criteria and scrutiny we apply to self-published resources isn't so different from what we apply to edited and peer reviewed resources:

- Critically evaluate the resource based on its rhetorical situation.

- Know when the resource was published and if it has ever been updated.

- Evaluate the credibility of the information it contains by checking its documentation and cross-referencing it with other resources.

On some level, evaluating the credibility of the information in a self-published resource and an edited or peer reviewed published resource is identical, but we often trust the editorial and peer review processes to weed out "bad" information for us.

Generally, it is much easier to locate the information needed to evaluate your resources in static and syndicated resources than in dynamic resources. Most static and syndicated resources imply some desire for longevity; static resources remain permanent and syndicated resources continue syndicating material. Therefore, the authors of a static resource (e.g., a new book, film, or song) generally want credit for their publication so that they gain notoriety and can make, publish, and sell more static resources. And the producers of syndicated materials (e.g., periodicals, television shows, and podcasts) generally want audience members to know where the information comes from so that the audience will come back, and possibly pay for, more. Dynamic resources, on the other hand, may be a little more difficult to evaluate.

Obviously, you cannot evaluate the results from your own experiment or originally collected field research in the same way; however, you can explicitly describe how you designed the experiment and collected the data. For example, scientists always give explicit details about how they construct their experiments and collect their data so that other scientists can duplicate their experiments. A social scientist would be sure to include copies of interview questions or survey instruments as a part of the publication process. Duplicating original research is one way that researchers evaluate one another's work. Other dynamic resources, like live play performances, would similarly require detailed descriptions of the methods in which the researcher documented the resource as well as careful documentation of the specific time and date of the performance. And although it is possible to quote a dynamic resource, such as lines from an audience participatory play or an entry in a wiki, the line from the play or the wiki entry may change the next day. It is critical that you, the researcher gathering and evaluating this dynamic resource, carefully document the date and location of the resource you quoted. That way the readers of the paper based on your research can verify your dynamic resources by checking with others who saw the play that same day or use a program like Wayback Machine (http://www.archive.org/) or the wiki's version tracker to evaluate an Internet-based wiki page.

...write...

Evaluate Types of Resources

Select one of the resources you categorized as something you *must* include based on the previous activity. Categorize it as static, syndicated, or dynamic. Also categorize it as self-published, edited, or peer reviewed. Answer the following questions based on your categorization of the resource.

☐ How would your audience react to this type of resource? Would they find this to be a reliable source? Why or why not? If not, what information do you need to provide to persuade them? For example, could you emphasize the credentials of the author or perhaps the timeliness of the information?

☐ What types of information would your audience need to know about this resource? Is that information already included in the full bibliographic citation? What information do you need to provide for them to locate the *exact* resource you looked at or worked with?

☐ How critical is this resource to your research? Does your rhetorical situation demand that you incorporate this resource into your project?

3 Reporting on Research

Matching Reasons with Evidence

At this point in your research process, you have been thinking about your research topic, your resources, and your position for a while. You know what your motivation is for researching, and you've identified a potential audience that would be interested in what you have discovered. Now is the time to pull everything together and match specific resources and pieces of evidence with your reasons. Because you have gathered so much information about your topic, and you have begun to construct the reasoning for your argument, it is time to think about what resources and pieces of evidence will best support your claim, purpose, and audience and how you will structure your argument and include that evidence.

Instead of just starting to write, or drafting blindly, we suggest that you spend some time thinking about the natural grouping or clustering of the materials you collected and the lines of reasoning you have developed.

You may consider doing clustering activities at a variety of points during your research process; however, we definitely suggest you do them at one, or both, of the following points:

- after you've collected all of your data and are trying to make meaning of it.

- after you've drafted a thesis statement with reasons and are trying to make connections to your research to organize everything.

...write...

Draw a Cluster Map

Depending on how focused your argument is at this point in time, complete one of the following clustering activities. After you develop the cluster, try sharing it with someone who knows something about your topic and someone who knows nothing about your topic. Both people can give you insightful ideas about the connections you have made.

☐ **You have collected a lot of information and are still trying to process and organize it to develop a thesis and reasons for your argument.** Start with your research question written in the middle of the page. What are the major issues explicitly connected to your research question? What are the major "answers" to your research question? Either the major issues or the major answers, and possibly both, will be your first round of satellite clusters. Write those in a circle spaced around the research question and connect them to the middle with lines. Now, start filtering through your research notes. Add subtopics and/or notes from specific resources as satellites to their relevant research-related issue or answer. If you have research notes or resources that do not fit in your initial cluster, think about whether you need to add a satellite point from the research question. And if you have large groups of information or notes around one of the satellites, try grouping them into further levels of satellites.

☐ **You have already developed a tentative thesis and reasons for your argument, but you are still figuring out how your research fits together and how it should all be arranged.** Start with your thesis statement or argumentative claim in the center of the page. Put your reasons as the first round of satellites in the cluster map and connect them back to the center. Now filter through your research and connect specific resources, notes, and evidence to each reason. If you have a large number of resources or evidence linked to a specific reason, see if you can group them into like categories. If you only have one or two resources or pieces of evidence associated with a reason, you may need to rethink your line of reasoning or conduct a little more research.

Once you have completed your cluster map, try transferring it to the form of an outline. What information would you put first? second? third? Begin to consider how you would prioritize information in your argument. ▢

For more information on outlining, see the appendix.

techno_tip >

> Create Clusters on the Computer <

For an interactive tutorial about creating cluster maps on the computer, go to *Student Resources* on the online resource center at www.cengage.com/english/Miller-Cochran/WGTR.

If you would like to construct your cluster on the computer instead of on paper, there are a variety of clustering, or mind/idea mapping, types of applications. Microsoft Word® has a simple diagram or organizational chart tool embedded in the program. Go to "Insert" and then "Diagram" to insert one of the visuals into your document. MS Word allows you to "switch" the type of diagram being used without changing the text you have entered. Switching the diagrams with your information might give you different ideas about how to cluster, or organize, your ideas and materials.

Three other tools are also worth checking out, listed in order of complexity:

1. Bubbl is a free online clustering tool that will make a cluster map for you and allow you to export the map as a separate file. (http://www.bubbl.us)

2. Gliffy, a free online diagramming tool (http://www.gliffy.com/), allows you to make more complex cluster maps and diagrams. Gliffy also allows you to export your cluster map as a jpeg image file so that you can easily import it into a document or Web page. With the variety of shapes, colors, and fonts, Gliffy allows you to construct rich visual layers to your cluster map. With Gliffy you can assign different shapes and colors to different types of evidence (for example, testimonies, numbers/statistics). It would then allow you analyze the amount of evidence you have associated with each reason as well as the balance in the types of resources.

3. Cmap Tools is a more robust mapping program that you can download for free (http://cmap.ihmc.us/download/). However, it is both more difficult to use and more difficult to export your cluster/concept map into a usable format.

3 Reporting on Research

...write....

Find Additional Resources

Based on the claim, reasons, and evidence you have brought together so far, what holes still exist in your argument? Where is your audience most likely to disagree with your argument? Identify two areas in your argument cluster that you are concerned about. For each area of concern, take the following steps.

1. List specific types of information, resources, and pieces of evidence that you would like to find to support your areas of concern. Talk to an instructor, mentor, or librarian to help you identify where you might find the items on your list.

2. Share your cluster map or an outline of your argument with a classmate, family member, or friend. Ask them to identify your two weakest spots.

3. Share your cluster map or an outline of your argument with a different classmate, family member, or friend. Specifically identify your areas of concern; ask them if they agree with your concerns. Ask for suggestions on strengthening your argument.

Based on this feedback, produce a new cluster map, outline, or draft of your argument.

Sharing the Results

Now is the time to pull everything together, to share the results of your research with your audience in a way that will interest them and accomplish your initial goals. Because you have gathered so much information about your topic, and you have begun to construct the reasoning for your argument, it is time to think about how to arrange your argument and how to present it to your audience. You'll want to consider your rhetorical situation once again, choosing an organizational structure and medium of presentation that will communicate your research results in a way that will suit your purpose and persuade your audience. In the research scenario on the following page, Kristi has several possibilities for how she could present the results of her research. As you read, consider what presentation format you would choose for such an assignment.

we'll explore

arranging your final project

designing your final project to share the results of your research

writing introductions and conclusions

Author: Kristi, a senior in college, is taking a history course.

Topic: Kristi's history professor has assigned a family history project and asked students to think of a unique approach that they might take to writing their families' histories. Kristi is also engaged to be married, and she has asked her professor if she could write a combined history of her two families (her birth family and her in-laws), looking at the intersections between them.

© Gazimal/Getty Images

Audience: The audience consists of Kristi's professor, but she also plans to share her project with both families.

Purpose: Kristi needs to investigate the histories of both families to find points of intersection. She would like to develop a visual representation of the history to accompany her written research report; she thinks that looking at family photographs would be a good starting point for identifying patterns of intersection between the two families. She needs to talk to members of both families and also find photographs that will demonstrate connections.

QUESTIONS

1. How could Kristi present the "results" of her research visually?

2. How might she organize the photographs, and what form do you think the presentation might take?

3. How might she connect the visual representation with her essay?

4. Can you imagine another way Kristi might approach this research project, given the purpose and audience for the research?

Arrangement of Your Argument

As you consider possible patterns of organization for your research project, you will want to choose the organizational strategy that will best support your claim, purpose, and audience. The pattern of arrangement you choose depends on a balance between the reasoning of your argument and your rhetorical situation (your purpose, audience, and topic). Since you have already been constructing the reasoning for your argument in terms of your rhetorical situation, you now need to do two things:

1. Decide on a pattern of argument (evaluation, definition, proposal, cause and effect).

2. Determine how to organize the argument that you are constructing (most important to least important, least important to most important, or chronological).

In Kristi's case, she decides to start her research by asking that members of both families pull out old photo albums and other "boxes" of memorabilia. After going through and picking out the photos and other documents that were sturdy enough to withstand being scanned, she starts trying to group them into like piles. She looks for connections between them and tries a number of arrangements. First she tries making piles based on the family members in the photos (Figure 11.1). Then she tries organizing the photos based on theme (Figure 11.2). Then she considers a chronological organization. By just spending time with the photos, the "evidence" of her family history, she gets to know the "data" better and she starts to construct an arrangement pattern for her project.

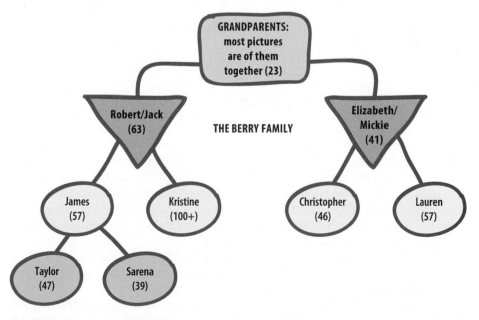

Figure 11.1   Cluster Map of the Pictures Kristi Found Based on Family Member (includes number of photos per person)

3 Reporting on Research

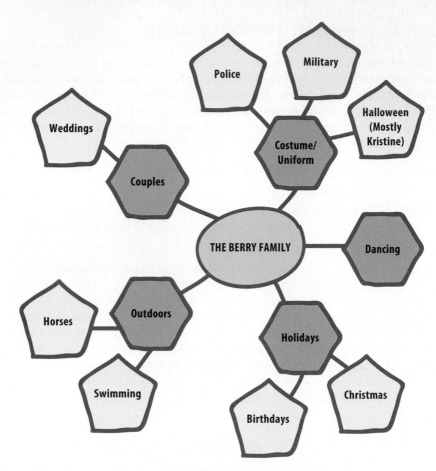

Figure 11.2   Cluster Map of the Pictures Kristi Found Based on Theme/Topic of the Pictures

Clustering her photos helps Kristi understand the types of photos she has accumulated and gives her some ideas about the visual arrangement of her project (which she decides to construct in Microsoft PowerPoint®). Once she starts clustering based on the theme/topic, she sees that the two families have several shared experiences, traditions, and values. Based on this finding, she writes a few interview questions and wonders if this might provide an organization for her final project. She could compare and contrast some of the families' shared experiences, but she would need to find out more information to determine if this pattern of argument would work for her research. Then she would need to determine how to arrange the various details in her argument as she compares and contrasts shared experiences.

Once you've identified your thesis and reasons, consider doing some of the listing and clustering activities found in the appendix to help with this process. Once you have grouped the information and evidence associated with each reason in your argument, you will need to start thinking about the order in which you will present the information you found during your research. There are a variety of common argument patterns associated with specific types of arguments and lines of reasoning. You might choose one of these common argument patterns for your researched argument, or you could just start with one and then adapt it to fit your argument and rhetorical situation.

Common Argument Patterns

Although there are a variety of types of arguments, the vast majority of them fall into the following four categories: evaluations, definitions, proposals, and cause-and-effect arguments. More sophisticated or complex arguments, usually associated with more complex research questions and issues, often include more than one of these types of argument. As you read through the following descriptions, first think about your thesis or argumentative claim. Does it appear to clearly fit into one of these categories? If yes, you might want to follow the argument pattern outlined. If not, focus on each line of reasoning: does it fit into one of these categories? If yes, you might want that section of your argument to follow the argument pattern outlined.

Evaluation   In evaluations people judge an object against a specific set of criteria. For example, movie reviews evaluate a movie based on the criteria provided by the reviewer. However, if you don't agree with the reviewer's criteria of "what makes a good movie," you might not agree with the evaluation. Therefore, evaluation arguments become two-layered arguments: the first layer argues for a specific set of criteria, and the second layer argues for how a specific object meets that set of criteria. Here's an outline of what an evaluative argument might look like.

Claim: A specific object is a good/bad example of a specific group.

Section 1: Describe the first evaluative criterion (justify the criterion if needed) and apply the criterion to the specific object.

Section 2: Describe the second evaluative criterion (justify the criterion if needed) and apply the criterion to the specific object.

Section 3: Describe the third evaluative criterion (justify the criterion if needed) and apply the criterion to the specific object.

Repeat this pattern as often as needed, depending on the number of evaluative criteria in your argument.

Comparison and Contrast   Sometimes arguments pit one specific object against another, or group of others, by comparing and contrasting them. For example, a film reviewer might compare *Pirates of the Caribbean: Dead Man's Chest* (2006) to the first *Pirates of the Caribbean: The Curse of the Black Pearl* (2003). Or, instead, the reviewer might compare *Dead Man's Chest* with a variety of pirate movies that came before it. In either case, the comparison and contrast requires a set of criteria, or categories, on which to base the comparison, so it is also a type of evaluation. A comparison and contrast argument can be structured in two ways, the first arranged based on the criteria and the second arranged according to the objects being compared or contrasted.

Claim: A claim compares or contrasts one specific object in relation to another (or others).

Section 1: Describe the first evaluative criterion (justify the criterion if needed) and apply the criterion to all the objects being compared/contrasted.

Section 2: Describe the second evaluative criterion (justify the criterion if needed) and apply the criterion to all the objects being compared/contrasted.

Section 3: Describe the third evaluative criterion (justify the criterion if needed) and apply the criterion to all the objects being compared/contrasted.

OR

Claim: A claim compares or contrasts one specific object in relation to another (or others).

Section 1: Establish and argue for the set of criteria.

Section 2: Describe one of the objects in terms of all the evaluative criteria.

Section 3: Describe another object in terms of all the evaluative criteria.

Section 4 (if needed): Describe another object in terms of all the evaluative criteria.

Depending on the goal of your argument, one of these patterns might fit better than the others. You can decide which pattern might work best by considering which section of your argument will need the most development.

Definition   In an argument of definition, the author makes a claim about how a specific object fits in a category (an evaluation of what a specific object is) or how a group of specific objects fit together to make a specific category (comparison of multiple objects to develop common criteria). Therefore, the argument might be arranged in two different structures. For example, in the first instance, an author might claim that a specific object, an electronic book, still remains a "book" based on the definition of "book." The argument is then arranged around the specific elements of the definition, in other words, the criteria for "book."

Claim: A specific object is (or is not) a part of group based on the definition of the group.

Section 1: State the first criterion for definition of the group and specific evidence for the object demonstrating that criterion.

Section 2: State the second criterion for a definition of the group and specific evidence for the object demonstrating that criterion.

Section 3: State the third criterion for a definition of the group and specific evidence for the object demonstrating that criterion.

In the second type of definitional argument, the author has a group of objects that he or she then compares, and possibly contrasts, to identify a common group of elements the objects share that make a definition for the group. For example, an author might make a claim to define the concept of a "book" by looking at the common elements of different types of texts that could be considered "books," to include ebooks and printed books.

Claim: The common elements of a group of objects form the definition of the category of objects.

Section 1: Describe the first common element and provide evidence from all the objects in the group.

Section 2: Describe the second common element and provide evidence from all the objects in the group.

Section 3: Describe the third common element and provide evidence from all the objects in the group.

For either of these patterns, you would include as many sections as you needed, based on the number of criteria or common elements you need to include in your argument.

Proposal   In some arguments, it is appropriate to propose a plan for action that will solve a problem identified in the argument. Such arguments generally contain two primary parts: a section identifying the problem and a section describing the solution. If we use the terms often used in formal debate, the argument proposes a "case" (the establishment of the problem) and a "plan" (the solution). If you would like to offer a proposal as part of your argument, you will likely include one of the other organizational patterns in this section to develop the case section, establishing the problem that you are identifying.

Proposals usually follow an organizational plan such as the following.

Claim: A specific problem needs to be solved and your solution is the best option.

Section 1:   Establish the problem or dilemma that needs to be solved (the case).

Section 2:   Describe your proposed solution to the problem, and show how this solution is the best for addressing the problem (the plan).

Depending on the emphasis of your argument and the nature of the issue you are researching, you might spend more time on either of the two main sections. Think about what you need to convince your audience of the most, and spend more time developing that section. You will also need to consider how much space you should devote to convincing your audience that your solution solves the identified problem.

Cause and Effect   If the purpose of an argument is to demonstrate why something has happened, then a cause-and-effect argument might provide the best pattern to follow. In an argument of cause and effect, the author describes the causes of a situation and connects those causes with the result, showing how certain circumstances, actions, or other instigators contributed to creating the existing situation. Cause-and-effect arguments can be particularly useful in conjunction with proposals to structure the first part of the proposal argument (establishing the problem). If the author can demonstrate what caused a particular circumstance or situation, then the author could show how a specific solution would solve the problem.

Cause-and-effect arguments are often structured in one of two ways: establishing the causes and then their effect(s), or describing the effect and then showing what caused it. The organizational structures might look something like this.

Claim: A specific set of circumstances caused a situation.

Section 1:   Describe the circumstances.

Section 2:   Demonstrate the relationship between those circumstances and the situation, showing that they caused the situation to occur.

OR

Claim: A specific set of circumstances caused a situation.

Section 1:   Establish the nature of the situation.

Section 2:   Describe the circumstances that caused it.

As with the previous argument structures, the option you choose might depend on what you would like to emphasize in your argument.

Common Presentational Patterns

No matter which argument pattern (or set of patterns) you might select, you also need to think about the order in which you present reasons and evidence. Generally, you base this organizational decision on the relative strength and weakness of your reasons and pieces of evidence. Depending on the subject, the pieces of evidence might be presented chronologically as well.

Least Important to Most Important Sometimes an author chooses to start with the least important reason and build toward the most important. Such an organizational structure leaves the audience with the most important, or most convincing, reason and pieces of evidence in mind as he or she finishes reading the argument. This strategy is especially effective for a long argument because audience members tend to "tune out" during the middle of the argument. This strategy might not be as effective if an audience is resistant to the argument from the beginning. In other words, if already resistant readers think it is a weak argument from the start, then they'll stop reading.

Most Important to Least Important If the author really needs to keep the audience engaged and convinced from the beginning of the argument, he or she might begin with the most important reason and then present the remaining reasons that further support the one main, most important reason. If an author goes with this organizational strategy, he or she will re-emphasize that first, and most important, reason during the conclusion section to motivate and persuade the audience to agree with the argument.

In both of these organizational structures, an author might use a variation in order to place strong reasons both at the beginning and at the end. For example, an author addressing a somewhat resistant audience might put the strongest argument at the end, but he or she might put the second most compelling argument at the beginning to convince the audience to continue reading.

Chronological Organization Depending on your topic, it might make sense to present your evidence and reasons chronologically. If Kristi is making an argument that her two families share certain values and experiences, for example, she might want to present the evidence of her argument by chronologically describing events in the families' histories. Kristi could use an argument pattern of comparison and contrast (comparing the two families) but then present the evidence for the argument chronologically.

...write...

Develop an Outline

Using the various structures presented here, develop an outline for your argument. Start with your claim and list your reasons and evidence. After you have produced the outline, describe what structural patterns you used and why you used them.

> See the appendix for examples of the three types of outlines.

You can develop your outline as a formal outline, sentence outline, or scratch outline. ☐

If you're not certain in your choice of argument pattern or organization, try using another set of structures and develop a second outline for your argument. Describe what structural patterns you used for this second outline and discuss why you used them.

Share your outline(s) with a classmate or a friend. If you developed more than one, ask which argument or organizational pattern he or she preferred and why.

Introductions and Conclusions

Although introductions and conclusions are sometimes considered the most important parts of your argument (i.e., you can't persuade people to change their minds if you can't even persuade them to read the argument), many authors write, or at least revise, these sections of the argument last. Generally, both introductions and conclusions carry a large amount of responsibility for the effectiveness of arguments. People tend to use ethos (arguments developed from personal authority) and pathos (emotion-based arguments) more blatantly in introductions and conclusions. The introduction needs to motivate the audience to continue to read, or listen to, the argument. Similarly, the conclusion needs to motivate the audience to go out and do something with the information. Both introductions and conclusions have other work to do as well, however, and it's important to keep these multiple responsibilities in mind as you write.

> reflect >

Are You Grabbing Your Audience's Attention and Motivating Them to Action?

Good writers know they need to motivate their audience, both to read the document and to take action on the argument. By this point in the process, you have narrowed your audience enough that you have a very good idea about who they are and what they care about. To help construct introductions and conclusions that motivate your readers, answer the following questions about your primary audience.

- ☐ Why is your audience invested in this topic in general? Why are they invested in the answer to your specific research question?

- ☐ What interests your audience about this topic? What could change from the status quo that would greatly satisfy your audience?

- ☐ What scares your audience about this topic? What could change from the status quo that would concern your audience even more?

3 Reporting on Research

Ancient rhetors claimed there were three possible sections for an introduction and, based on the rhetorical situation, you could include any one, or all, of the three parts. First, authors need to prepare the audience for receiving the message. In other words, the author needs to make sure the audience is sincerely engaged in hearing the argument. The second section includes a brief introduction to or history of the topic, and the third section outlines the argument. Depending on your rhetorical situation, you might include one or more of these sections in your introduction. Regardless of which sections are included, you need to carefully understand the purpose and audience of the argument to develop a powerful introduction.

Many contemporary scholarly writers start with showing how their research identifies a gap in what is known about an issue. In other words, they demonstrate that no one else has asked a specific research question (or answered it sufficiently). By identifying the research gap, the author implies that his or her answer to the question will fill the gap. Introducing the gap, or problem, that your research is going to fill is one way to get your readers' attention and motivate them to continue reading. For example, Kristi could explain that looking at the histories of the two families together provides insight that isn't possible if their histories are written in isolation. Indeed, she might be able to make connections with her families' shared histories and larger historical events or trends. She can introduce her family history, and her method of looking at both histories together, as filling a gap in the knowledge of either family's individual history. Her research will enrich the families' understanding of their individual and shared histories.

Draft an Effective Introduction

...write...

As you draft your introduction, keep your rhetorical situation in mind—especially the purpose of your argument and the audience you are addressing. Freewrite in response to the following questions to help draft your introduction.

☐ Why is this topic important? How does it affect the audience? the community? the world?

☐ What is the audience's stand on the issue? How does it differ from yours? If their perspective is different from yours, how might you show respect for their perspective so that they might read yours?

☐ What is your authority on this topic? Who are other major "players" that write or talk about this topic? What are their strengths and points of authority? their weaknesses?

☐ Does your audience know the topic, or its history, well? What do they already know? What do they need to know to understand your perspective?

☐ How long will your paper be? How complex will your argument be? Do you need to give the audience a road map to prepare them for your argument?

Once you have drafted your responses to these questions, look for the most compelling point in what you wrote. Copy and paste that below what you wrote (or even highlight it or circle it if you're writing in a notebook), and then freewrite about that idea for another 5 minutes. Is this something you could develop into an introduction for your argument? You could try this looping activity a couple of times until you find something that you think you could develop into your introduction.

An important thing to remember is that you do not have to start writing your draft with the introduction. Although it might help you to start with the introduction, most likely you will revise it radically before completing the final version. Similarly, you do not have to wait to write your conclusion until after you've written the entire paper. Sometimes it helps to write a draft of your conclusion earlier to continue reminding yourself of the main point or purpose of your research project. In other words, the main goal of the conclusion is to motivate your readers to action. However, also like the introduction, conclusions can do much more.

A common mistake many student writers make is to simply summarize their argument in the conclusion. While argument summary is one possible function of the conclusion, a summary, like everything else, needs to be rhetorically situated. If your argument is a twenty-page proposal for making your college campus sustainable and "green," the reader might need a summary to remind him or her of the most important information in the last twenty pages. However, if the argument is much shorter, the reader might be able to remember the argument without requiring a summary in the conclusion.

Instead of ending the paper with a summary, try returning to the purpose of your writing. Why is it important that the audience read the results of your research? What do you want them to do with the information you give them? Keep in mind that suggesting change and motivating someone to change are two different things. Both logical arguments and emotional arguments can be effective motivators for change. Ancient rhetors had a list of what might be included in conclusions as well as introductions. If the argument is long and complex, you may need to summarize it at the end of the paper. However, ancient rhetors also realized that people are more likely to leave an argument energized if the author appeals to their emotions, whether through excitement, anger, or fear. Is there a consequence to your argument that you should highlight in your conclusion? Or is there a memorable point that you want to remind your audience of as they finish reading your argument?

...write...

Develop Closure

Continue to keep your rhetorical situation in mind as you work on a conclusion for your argument. Remember that you are trying to bring a sense of closure to your argument, and consider what you want your audience to be thinking or feeling when they are finished. Freewrite in response to the following questions to begin drafting your conclusion.

☐ What issues raised in your argument need to be repeated for your audience? Is there any support offered in your argument that bears repeating?

☐ What will happen if the current situation continues as it is? What effects might impact your audience, and what effects might impact others that your audience will be concerned about? How could you demonstrate the importance of these effects?

☐ How could you demonstrate that the current problem violates the shared values of a community?

☐ Is this present issue parallel in any way to a previous situation? Are there circumstances or effects from a previous parallel situation that might spur your audience to action (perhaps because they want to avoid those effects or because a previous situation was resolved well and you'd like to see a similar resolution)?

>>>

3 Reporting on Research

>>> ☐ To which person, or group of people, should your readers address their concerns? How might you encourage them to share those concerns?

☐ Will this situation continue if nothing is done? If so, how will the audience be impacted?

Once you have drafted your responses to these questions, look for the most compelling point in what you wrote. Copy and paste it below what you wrote (or even highlight it or circle it if you're writing in a notebook), and then freewrite about that idea for another 5 minutes. Is this something you could develop into a conclusion for your argument? You could try this looping activity a couple of times until you find something that you think you could develop for your conclusion.

Once you have drafted an introduction and conclusion, you might even try switching them in the order of your paper. Sometimes authors find that what they originally wrote as a conclusion actually works well as an introduction, or vice versa. In either case, you'll get a better sense of the impact on your audience, and the effectiveness of what you have written, if you try changing the order of your introduction and conclusion when you read through your draft one time.

Another strategy you might consider as you draft is to provide a similar image, quotation, or reference in both the introduction and conclusion. This technique is called **framing**, and it can be an effective way to bring closure to a piece if you feel that an image or reference you have used in the introduction is particularly compelling. Writers often engage ethos or pathos in both their introductions and conclusions, and repeating a meaningful image, or reminding your audience of what interested them in reading your argument in the first place, can be an effective way to bring closure to your argument. Often the same things that grab the attention of readers are the things that motivate them to action. If the frame is too heavy-handed, however, it might not be effective.

Identify Possible Frames

...write...

Reread the draft of your introduction and highlight the most effective, or persuasive, image, quotation, or reference. If you are reading a digital version of your paper, copy that section of your introduction. Then read (or scroll down to) your conclusion. Reread what you have written, looking for a location where you could effectively insert the reference from your introduction. Then copy (or paste) the image into your conclusion, and write effective sentences to contextualize that reference in your conclusion. You might look toward the beginning or the end of your conclusion for an opening point, and keep in mind that repeating that reference will signal to your audience that you are wrapping things up in your argument.

Putting Everything Together

At this point in the process you have spent a lot of time thinking about what you are going to say, why you are going to say it, and even in what order you will say it. You may have written small portions of your argument, or you may have large sections drafted. Regardless of where you are in the process, this is the time to write. Start with compiling all of the pieces that you have started drafting for your final argument, and begin putting everything together.

...write...

Draft Your Final Argument

Open a new document in your word processor and either type in or cut and paste your outline. Select one of the sections that you think you can write about without needing to check your resources. Even if that section is in the middle of the outline, it's okay to start writing there. Once you have completed all that you can, without help from your resources, stop. Now go and find the resources that will help you develop that section. Once you have completed the section you worked on first, move on to the next one. Before you know it, you'll have a complete draft.

As you write, or once you have completed several successive sections, look at how you can make effective connections between those sections. Even though you may draft in chunks, moving back and forth to different sections in the paper, you need to make connections between the sections and even out the prose so that the final version reads as one, fluid argument.

3. Reporting on Research

---

techno_tip >

> Use Document-Sharing Technologies <

For interactive tutorials about document-sharing technologies, go to *Student Resources* on the online resource center at www.cengage.com/english/Miller-Cochran/WGTR.

As you draft, you may want to have others read and comment on your work. Depending on your writing preferences, you might share your work along the way or wait until you have a complete draft. If you are sharing your work electronically, consider using a document-sharing application to have readers look at, comment on, and even make changes in your document. Document-sharing applications are Web-based spaces where people can go to your document, instead of your having to send it to them as an email attachment. Two advantages to using such applications are that you avoid the virus risks of sending file attachments back and forth, and you avoid the confusion of having multiple versions of your draft existing in different places. The following Web-based applications are free and easy to use:

☐ Zoho writer (http://writer.zoho.com)

☐ Google Docs (http://docs.google.com)

☐ Foldera (http://www.foldera.com)

☐ Various storage spaces, such as Box.net (http://box.net) and Stixy (http://stixy.com)

Methods of Delivery

A final consideration as you write your research paper is how to present your research. If you are researching and writing for a class, you might be required to write an academic essay for the final presentation of your research. But research presentations can take other forms, and the same research can be presented in more than one way. For example, a researcher might develop an oral presentation to deliver to a live audience and then write an essay-based version as well. Or a research project might be delivered through several different media, creating a multimodal presentation. In the example that opened this chapter, Kristi will write an academic essay for her history professor, but she also plans to design a visual presentation to accompany it. She might even design a print-based pamphlet or guide to give to family members.

The most important consideration is your rhetorical situation, matching the presentation of your research to your audience, purpose, and topic. The first step is to know your rhetorical situation (which you do), and then to know your options for presentation. Then think about which presentation method will reach your audience most effectively.

For specific information about citation styles, see Chapters 12–15.

Academic Essays

Most research projects assigned in school take the form of academic essays. When writing an academic essay, it is important to follow the formatting requirements of the citation style you are using for the essay, and the citation style should be chosen according to the requirements of your rhetorical situation. □

Depending on your rhetorical situation, you might need to follow specific organizational patterns in the reporting of your research as well. For example, if you conducted a primary research study in the sciences or social sciences, you might be expected to follow what is often called the **IMRAD** format in the organization of your essay:

I = introduction

> The introduction usually provides a review of relevant literature related to the study, demonstrates why the study is important, and presents the research question and/or hypothesis.

M = methodology

> The methodology section describes the research methods used to investigate the research question or test the hypothesis. This section includes information about the participants involved in the study, the method of data collection, and the method of analysis.

R = results

> The results section provides the data collected during the study.

A = analysis

The analysis section provides an interpretation of the data collected.

D = discussion

The discussion section, or conclusion, generally demonstrates how the data answer the research question, what the implications of the study are, and often what future research is recommended to follow up on the study.

Not all academic essays follow such a prescribed format, but you should investigate the expectations of your audience and the disciplinary community in which you are conducting your research. If you are not to follow a format such as IMRAD, then you will want to include analysis throughout your essay instead of relegating it to one section of the paper. Find out the conventions of your audience and discipline, and also ask specific questions of your instructor if you are writing for a class, or of another faculty member or professional who works and writes in that field. At the very least, academic audiences expect a clear introduction, a thorough analysis and discussion in the body of the essay, and a conclusion that brings closure to the research and/or argument.

Alternative Modes of Delivery

Depending on the nature of your research project, you might find that a presentation mode other than an academic essay would reach your audience most effectively. Many factors can influence your choice of presentation mode, and you might want to remind yourself of the rhetorical situation you outlined back in Chapter 1, shown again in Figure 11.3, as you consider the options available to you.

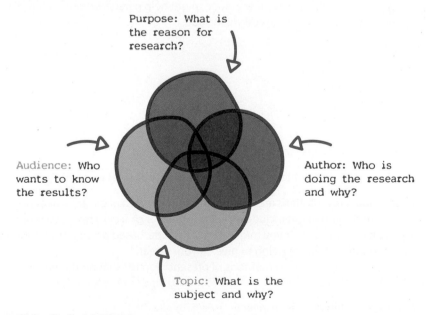

Purpose: What is the reason for research?

Audience: Who wants to know the results?

Author: Who is doing the research and why?

Topic: What is the subject and why?

Figure 11.3   The Rhetorical Situation

3 Reporting on Research

Also keep in mind the multiple audiences and purposes that you might be addressing in this project. For example, a student writing about solutions to parking problems on campus might address her research to specific administrators on campus, but she might also be conducting the research for a class where she is addressing an audience of her teachers and classmates. One purpose of her research is to propose a solution for campus parking, but she has an additional purpose of completing the assignment for class credit. Each of these influences is a factor in her choice of how she presents her research.

The following sections describe some of the presentation modes you might consider as you complete your research. Keep in mind that this list of presentation modes is not exhaustive. The categories outlined here might help you think of other possibilities, too; the important thing is to find the method that will reach your audience most effectively. The activity that closes this chapter will help you choose an appropriate presentation mode. (You might even want to look over the questions in that activity before you read through these options.)

In addition to academic essays, other kinds of text-based presentations might be best suited to your audience. You might consider presenting your research as:

- a newspaper article, or a piece in a periodical

- a blog entry

- a wiki

- a contribution to an online resource, such as Wikipedia

You might find that a visual presentation will best meet the needs of your rhetorical situation. For instance, if you are explaining a concept that is complex or difficult to understand in text, a graphic representation might help persuade your audience more effectively. Visual representations might include:

- flyers

- posters

- pictures

- graphs or charts

- slides (such as those made in PowerPoint)

- video broadcasts (which also combine elements of aural presentations)

Often, visual presentations are used in combination with another form of presentation. For example, you might include a picture, graph, or chart in a text-based presentation to emphasize a point. Or you might develop a slide-based presentation to support an oral presentation you are going to give on your research.

There are several *oral/aural* methods of presentation for sharing the results of your research. You might consider some of the following kinds of presentations:

- oral presentation, talk or speech

- audio file uploaded to a Web site

◎ podcast (if the research is something you would like to incorporate into a serial, or syndicated, broadcast)

Many research projects are best shared through a *multimodal* presentation that combines elements of several formats. For example, a blog entry might include a link to a video clip to emphasize a point. Or a slide presentation (such as one designed with PowerPoint) might include links to Web pages, pictures or other static images, animation, audio, and/or video. You could combine elements of any of the previously mentioned types of presentation to reach your audience. You might consider some of the various types of formats:

◎ pamphlet, brochure, or poster (if the project combines visual and text-based elements)

◎ interactive Web site

◎ film/video presentation

techno_tip >

> Develop Your Presentation <

For interactive tutorials about methods to develop your presentation, go to *Student Resources* on the online resource center at www.cengage.com/english/Miller-Cochran/WGTR.

As you design the presentation of your research, one principle is to *keep it simple*. Presentations don't have to be complex to be effective! In addition, you should locate tools that will help you present the results of your research most effectively and efficiently. There are many free applications you can choose from. You might find that one of these programs will provide you with the tools to try a different presentation format that will reach your audience.

☐ **Blog software**. Each of the following applications provides easy-to-use, free blogging software. The applications are very similar, with the exception that Edublogs is generally used for blogging related to teaching and learning. Blogs may be syndicated through an RSS feed so that readers can receive updates when new postings are available, and many can also receive comments from readers. More advanced blog

programs, content management systems, can construct entire Web sites.

- o Edublogs
  http://www.edublogs.org

- o Live Journal
  http://www.livejournal.com

- o Blogger
  http://www.blogger.com

☐ **Wiki applications**. Wikis are quickly and easily revised and updated Web sites that are collaboratively constructed by more than one person. Wikis are generally public, although they can be restricted to certain people and only revisable by them. Revisions are tracked as in document-sharing applications, and they invite open discourse and collaboration. The following applications are similar, although WetPaint requires less knowledge of coding in a wiki and can be made ad-free if the wiki is used for educational purposes.

3 Reporting on Research

>>>

>>>

- o WetPaint
  http://www.wetpaint.com

- o PB Wiki
  http://pbwiki.com

- o Wikispaces
  http://www.wikispaces.com

☐ **Graphic design**. The following applications provide various levels of sophistication for working with graphics.

- o Gliffy
  http://www.gliffy.com—best for constructing diagrams

- o GIMP
  http://www.gimp.org—provides photo editing and graphic design capability

- o OpenOffice Draw
  http://www.openoffice.org—a robust program that imports, edits, and manipulates graphics and diagrams

☐ **Audio files/podcasting**. If you would like to work on a spoken presentation of your research that is recorded, you might try developing an audio file. If you'd like to do a syndicated presentation of your research (dividing it into sections or posting a new file on a regular basis), you might try a podcast. The following applications provide audio file capabilities, with Gabcast allowing you to record an audio file from your cell phone (which could be useful if you don't have a microphone).

- o Audacity
  http://audacity.sourceforge.net

- o GarageBand
  http://www.apple.com/ilife/garageband—only for Mac platforms

- o GabCast
  http://www.gabcast.com

☐ **Video editing**. The following applications allow you to edit and process video files. Jumpcut and Eyespot also provide video-sharing capabilities.

- o VirtualDub
  http://www.virtualdub.org—video capture and processing application for Windows

- o Jumpcut
  http://jumpcut.com

- o Eyespot
  http://www.eyespot.com

...write...

Decide Which Presentation Mode Is Appropriate

As you consider the ways you might present the results of your research, take a few minutes to write your responses to the following questions. Use your responses to choose the best presentation mode for your research.

Purpose

☐ Are there requirements you must consider regarding the presentation of your research? If so, what are they?

☐ What will your presentation need to do in order to fulfill the original purpose of your research? Is there a presentation mode that will best meet those needs?

Audience

☐ What expectations does your audience have for the presentation of your research?

☐ What media will your audience have access to?

☐ What presentation form will reach your audience? What will they be most receptive to, and where would they be looking for your argument?

☐ When would your audience be interested in and/or open to hearing about your research? How would you reach your audience at that time?

☐ Who might be interested in your research that might not yet know about it? How would you reach that potential audience?

Topic

☐ What presentation format is most appropriate for your topic?

☐ What presentation format is most appropriate for the argument you are making about your topic?

☐ Are there aspects of your research that might be difficult to understand in an exclusively text-based presentation? How might you explain those parts of your research in a different way?

Author

☐ What media are you most familiar with? Is there a presentation format that you are unfamiliar with that you would like to learn more about?

☐ Would a combination of media present your research most effectively? Do you already know how to use them or could you enlist someone to help you use them?

3 Reporting on Research

RESEARCH IN PROGRESS:
Writing a Researched Argument

Your research does not benefit anyone unless you share your results, especially with those who are willing and able to act on them. The goal of the final "Research in Progress" section is to help you think through how to present the results of your research to your intended audience. In this section, you will work through an assignment that is focused on sharing your answer to your research question. Keep in mind that your research might be presented in a variety of formats or media, depending on the most appropriate way to reach your audience with your message.

The assignment in this chapter asks you to develop a clearly defined argument within a set of guidelines to include suggestions about the number of sources you might use and the length of the argument. Your instructor might ask you to follow these guidelines specifically, or you might have different criteria for writing. Be certain to pay close attention to the rhetorical situation of your writing, and follow the guidelines that are most appropriate to your writing task.

The Assignment

This final research assignment asks you to synthesize all of the writing and research you have accomplished thus far. Your goal is to determine a defensible position on your issue, an answer to your research question, and convince a specific audience of that position. If you have followed the assignment sequence outlined in this book, you have developed a focused research question in your project proposal, and you have identified the audience you would like to address in your final argument. In addition, Chapter 11 asked you to think about the most appropriate presentation format for your audience. Depending on the requirements of your rhetorical situation, you might choose to write an essay in print format, or you might choose to present your argument in another way. The guidelines provided in this section focus primarily on the form of an academic essay, but keep in mind that these guidelines could easily be adapted for various types of media.

The goal of this assignment is to present a well-defined position on your issue, provide compelling support for your position in the form of reasons and evidence, and consider competing positions that you might need to address. Direct your response to a specific audience whose thinking you want to influence. Your credibility will be very important in persuading this audience to adopt your evaluation of the issue or position, so you should present yourself as someone who is well-informed about the issue you are researching. Consider the sections on ethos, pathos, and logos in Chapter 9 as you think about ways to develop your polished argument.

In essence, this is your chance to present your argument and persuade others of your position.

Features of a Researched Argument

A researched argument should address a well-defined issue with a compelling argument. Your response to this assignment should:

- identify the issue you are writing about and why it is controversial.

- state (either implicitly or explicitly) your position on the issue, action, or policy.

- provide compelling reasons and evidence that support your position.

- state competing positions that are relevant to the situation and provide counterarguments, if necessary.

You might even propose a solution to the problem, if that would be relevant to your audience and issue.

You should include a variety of outside resources to support your argument, and that was a major part of your research-gathering task in the second "Research in Progress" section. Use those varied arguments to anticipate the challenges to your position, and develop an argument that answers those challenges.

Your Researched Argument

Working through the first two "Research in Progress" sections gave you a jumpstart on this assignment. As you think about how to construct your argument, you might try several of the activities in the textbook to get you started. Start by reviewing your rhetorical situation:

Activity

To remind yourself of your rhetorical situation, see "Write: Define the Rhetorical Situation." on page 174 of Chapter 9.

Activity

To define your position on the issue, see "Write: Create a Cluster Map" on page 176 of Chapter 9 and "Write: Draft a Thesis Statement" on page 180 of Chapter 9.

As you construct your argument, you might consider various ways of developing reasons for your position.

Activity

Try some of the writing activities in Chapter 9, if you haven't already, and then complete "Write: Construct an Argument" on page 190 of Chapter 9.

As you develop your argument, consider the order in which you want to introduce different arguments and evidence.

Activity

Refer to the activities in Chapter 10 for selecting and incorporating evidence, and then take a look at the "Write: Develop an Outline" activity on page 212 of Chapter 11 for help in organizing your argument.

There are different types of outlines, and various degrees of detail can be included in those outlines. Instead of trying to produce your outline in one sitting, try building continuous layers of the outline.

- Begin with an outline that has your claim (the answer to your research question) at the top of the page, and simply list the reasons for supporting that claim.

- Next, list the pieces of evidence (individual units of information) that support your reasons. Be sure to include the basic citation information with each outside source.

- Revise your outline by explaining how each reason connects to the claim (the logic of the reason).

- Finally, explain how each piece of evidence connects to each reason (the logic of the evidence). ▢

For more information on outlining and examples of outlines, see the appendix.

You will also want to include a compelling introduction that grabs your audience's attention and an effective conclusion that compels your audience to action. As you develop your introduction and conclusion, try the "Write" activities in Chapter 11.

Activity
"Write: Draft an Effective Introduction" on page 214 of Chapter 11.

Activity
"Write: Develop Closure" on page 215 of Chapter 11.

Throughout this process, you should be considering what presentation mode will best reach your audience. Although the following suggested activity is the last one listed in Chapter 11, it might be a good idea to work through the activity toward the beginning of your drafting and outlining process.

Activity
"Reflect: Decide Which Presentation Mode Is Appropriate" on page 223 of Chapter 11.

Examples of Researched Arguments

Example 1: Li Chen, Therapeutic Cloning: A Significant Promise for Future Success in the United States Li Chen has continued to work on her research regarding cloning. After completing her proposal and annotated bibliography, she constructed a researched argument. Because of her rhetorical situation, she chose to write an academic essay. Her essay is an example of a researched argument on a controversial issue written for an academic audience. As with all student examples, keep in mind that this essay has strengths and opportunities for revision. As you read, think about revisions you might suggest to the author. She has continued to use the MLA citation style in her researched essay. Would you have used MLA or would you choose a different style? Her instructor's comments are included so that you can see one response to this argument.

Chen 1

Li Chen

Dr. Susan Miller-Cochran

ENG 108

April 25, 2006

These definitions are very helpful, but is this the best place for them? Think about continuity of thought in your introduction.

Therapeutic Cloning: A Significant Promise

for Future Success in the United States

Human cloning technology has been a gigantic leap in the field of science. Human cloning includes reproductive cloning, in which a genetically identical replicate can be created, and therapeutic cloning, in which stem cells are harvested from cloned embryos for medical research. The controversial issue of human cloning has created a public storm. Is it morally correct? Is it harmful or beneficial to human beings? All these topics have been widely discussed and debated for the past few years. Nevertheless, there is still no definite answer.

The incident of a South Korean scientist, Dr. Hwang Woo-Suk, which happened a few months ago, reminded a U.S. Senate committee that it is time again to decide whether all forms of human cloning should be banned. Hwang, of Seoul National University, was suspected of intentionally giving false information about the progress of his team. It was reported that he had fabricated experimental data to support his claim that he had successfully extracted stem cells from cloned human embryos ("Hwang Woo-Suk"). Members of the Senate committee might argue that it again proves the infeasibility of therapeutic cloning and that both types of human cloning should be outlawed. Regardless of the outcome, however, this case calls into question the scientific competitiveness of the United States compared with other countries that permit human cloning for medical research. "The Korean study underlines the urgency for us to get moving if we're going to be part of the game," says Zach Hall of the California Institute for Regenerative Medicine (CIRM) (Kalb 8). While I believe that the federal government should continue to outlaw reproductive cloning because it is unethical and unsafe, therapeutic cloning should be legalized with strict regulations due to the potential to help research cures for deadly diseases and the importance of maintaining competitiveness in the medical field.

You have a clearly stated thesis that sets parameters on the argument you are developing.

Chen 2

Reproductive cloning is the process by which a nucleus is injected into an enucleated oocyte and then put back to the reproductive track to grow after cell division, so a genetically identical clone can be created. Although it seems fairly reasonable when proponents of reproductive cloning, such as Brigitte Boisselier, claim that the process is to benefit couples with infertility problems in terms of helping them to reproduce, the number of couples who can only rely on this method to have genetically related children is comparatively negligible. It is also undeniable that the procedure is against nature. The executive director of the Center for Genetics and Society, Richard Hayes, asserts, "People intuitively understand that creating a child by cloning would be an affront to human dignity and individuality, would serve no good purpose, and should be banned" (9).

Reproductive cloning should not be allowed due to a very important reason that the practice is grossly unethical. William L. Saunders, Jr., is a senior fellow in bioethics, and he draws a parallel to the Nuremberg Code in evaluating the ethical standard of human cloning ("The Ethics of Cloning"). According to the Nuremberg Code, reproductive cloning violates both Principles 5 and 7, which state respectively, "No experiment should be conducted where there is an a priori reason to believe that death or disabling injury will occur. Proper preparations should be made and adequate facilities provided to protect the experimental subject against even remote possibilities of injury, disability or death" ("The Ethics of Cloning"). Similarly, Bill Rebeck, an associate professor of neuroscience at Georgetown University, points out that DNA that has accumulated mutations could be passed on to the replicate when it is used in reproductive cloning, putting the clone at risk of serious injury or death ("The Ethics of Cloning").

Undeniably, there are grave risks to the clone, which account for the unsafe aspect of reproductive cloning. Efforts to clone animals have shown a high failure rate of 95 percent, and premature death due to organ abnormalities is not uncommon. Many experts and ethicists noted "only about 5 percent of all mammalian cloning attempts result in live births, which often exhibit severe genetic abnormalities" (Hansen). One can easily refer to the case of the

---

Is this something you already knew, or did this definition come from an outside source? Be certain to cite outside sources.

Where does she claim this? Can you provide a citation?

Where did this figure come from? You need to provide a source.

Chen 3

world's first mammal clone, Dolly, which was euthanized after being diagnosed with progressive lung disease at the age of 6, as compared to the normal life span of 11 or 12 years for sheep ("First Cloned Sheep Dolly Dies at 6"). Similar consequences could be anticipated with cloned humans.

All of these considerations justify a ban on reproductive cloning. In addition, the procedure has no remarkable contribution to society. Economically, both the process and the premature clone are unproductive. In the medical field, reproductive cloning serves no purpose in terms of reducing suffering and saving lives. On the social level, it is imaginable that possible confusion will be created in identifying suspects of a crime since a clone would have the same genetic makeup as the original DNA donor.

In short, reproductive cloning is unacceptable not only because it is unethical and unsafe but also because there is no contribution to the economy or the medical and social sectors. On the contrary, therapeutic cloning bears notable potential medical and economical advantage. It could be very beneficial to the United States and should not be prohibited.

Although a person's DNA is used to produce a cloned embryo in therapeutic cloning, which is similar to the first step of reproductive cloning, there is a noticeable contrast in the second step. Instead of putting the embryo into a substitute mother after cell division, the cloned embryo is allowed to develop in a laboratory petri dish until stem cells can be taken out of the embryo to generate other types of tissue or organ. "There is no implantation; there is no pregnancy," says Daniel Perry, head of the Coalition for the Advancement of Medical Research (Kalb 8). "This is a technique to develop tailor-made stem cells for patients in a glass dish" (Kalb, "A New Cloning Debate" 50). The intention is crystal clear. Therapeutic cloning exists for medical research, as opposed to being used for reproductive purposes. This type of cloning does not involve replicating an entire carbon copy of a human but creating a human repair kit. Scientists could clone our cells and fix genes that cause diseases. It is believed

This is an interesting tactic. I like how you included the arguments against reproductive cloning first, drawing in your audience who might agree with a ban on cloning. But once they have read this far, they might be willing to read your explanation about the benefits of therapeutic cloning.

Chen 4

that therapeutic cloning and embryonic stem cell research could later
develop skills to conquer diseases like Parkinson's, Alzheimer's,
cancers, type 1 diabetes, and AIDS.

Embryonic stem cells are unspecialized blank slates capable of
developing into specific specialized cells of any type of human tissue
or organ like the heart, liver, and skin. Because stem cells are bio-
logically flexible, scientists believe they could someday be used, in a
process known as stem-cell therapy, to regenerate lost organs, repair
damaged cells, and replace diseased tissues damaged by different
kinds of currently incurable diseases. Indeed, experiments have been
done on mice at the National Institutes of Health (NIH) in Bethesda,
Md., in which the rats were partially healed after receiving stem-cell
therapy. "It's a major medical milestone. It offers hope to millions
of patients suffering from a long list of diseases" said Robert Lanza,
vice president of medical and scientific development at Advanced
Cell Technology (Hansen).

Could you provide a citation for this study?

Furthermore, advocates of therapeutic cloning have proposed the
medical advantage of using embryonic stem cells through cloning over
normal cells. During the cloning process, DNA from the patient's cell
is inserted into an enucleated egg; as a result, the new stem cells are
genetically a 98 percent match to the patients' cells. If the recipient's
egg is used, the genetic makeup of the stem cells being transplanted
will be identical to the rest of the body cells. Thus, the procedure could
considerably reduce the risk of immunological rejection (Hansen).

In addition, therapeutic cloning enables scientists to understand
causes of various diseases. Embryonic stem cells extracted from
cloned embryos are used to search for potential treatments. Researchers could invent new drugs to treat fatal disorders by examining
activities of diseased cells in a petri dish and studying their behavior.
Pioneering researcher Doug Melton, co-director of the Harvard Stem
Cell Institute explained, "Now, instead of waiting until a patient gets
one of these diseases, we can try to figure out how these cells go
wrong" (Kalb 8). Even the disgraced scientist, Dr. Hwang Woo-Suk,

This is an important counterargument to address.

After a quotation, especially a long quotation like this one, it would be best if you interpreted the information and explained why it is relevant to your argument.

explained that "Our goal is not to clone humans, but to understand the causes of diseases" (Hansen).

Some of the members from the Senate committee and fundamental religious groups who oppose therapeutic cloning affirm that it is immoral because lots of human embryos, which they believe are destined to become human beings, would be discarded due to the high failure rates. Arthur Caplan, director of the Center for Bioethics at the University of Pennsylvania in Philadelphia, explains why this concern is not justified:

It is true that every human life begins with an embryo, but it is not at all true that every embryo begins a human life . . . Scientifically, it is not correct to say that every embryo has the potential to become a person, because many embryos are simply miswired and do not develop into anything at all. And philosophically, it's a terrible mistake to mix up potential people with real people. That's like saying acorns are the same as oak trees.

(Hansen)

Moreover, opponents of therapeutic cloning assert that mining for stem cells ruins human embryos and that the practice is equivalent to murder. President George W. Bush has mentioned he would veto any legislation that "destroys life in order to save life" (Kalb 8). However, cloned embryos can develop into humans only if they are implanted into a womb. It should be clearly understood that therapeutic cloning involves no implantation and no pregnancy. Why, then, should we destroy those embryos that will not happen to develop into human beings if the research has great potential to treat and eventually cure a wide range of debilitating diseases that are affecting millions of patients at this moment? "It is a weighing of morals," says Blackburn, of the University of California. "[Nobody] is hurt by therapeutic cloning or embryonic stem-cell research, but . . . a great many people could be harmed by banning them" (Hansen). Furthermore, would it be acceptable and ethical to criminalize the scientific invention that intends to combine new technologies with available knowledge in order to reduce suffering of millions of American patients? "Denying them the potential of life-saving remedies by criminalizing this

Chen 6

exceptionally promising area of research would itself be a crime"
(Halstead and Lind B4).

> But could it also set a precedent for allowing potentially harmful kinds of research? Always keep in mind the arguments your audience might be thinking of.

Criminalizing therapeutic cloning would be a "considerable
setback to our status as the world's leading scientific and technological nation" and would also "create an immediate competitive disad-
vantage for our economy, our biotech and pharmaceutical sectors,
and our scientific community" (Halstead and Lind B4). Scientists
will be hampered in pursuing advanced medical and pharmaceutical
knowledge. The ban would also set a precedent for restricting other
beneficial areas of scientific research in the future. It is irrefutable
that the United States will become a bystander to medical innovation because other developed and developing countries, such as
Britain, South Korea, and China, have already permitted and legalized
therapeutic cloning. It is only a matter of when and which country
will first announce another breakthrough. However, that country will
never be the United States if the government insists on outlawing all
forms of human cloning and related research. Undoubtedly, it would
be an irreversible loss.

> This sounds like an "everyone's doing it" argument. I'm not convinced it's one of your stronger arguments, and you might think about how to rephrase it.

All of the countries that participate in this research have been
careful to draw a clear line between reproductive and therapeutic
cloning. While reproductive cloning is prohibited, therapeutic cloning
is legalized and cautiously regulated. Similar laws should be enacted
in the United States. If therapeutic cloning is to be legalized, it should
be done under restrictions strong enough to prevent misuse and adhere
to strict safety standards. Research should only be performed by a
limited number of groups such as universities and hospitals. Labo-
ratories and researchers would be required to obtain licenses subject
to revocation before applying to begin embryo cloning. Policies
should be formulated to address researchers' responsibilities. Most
important, a special review board should be established to monitor
all cloning operations and research work on a regular basis and to
ensure that all the guidelines are properly followed. Also, the review
committee would be authorized to conduct inspections as needed.
Under the law, violators would have to face severe penalties, for

> This is the clarification of your "everyone's doing it" argument—good! How could you incorporate this clarification earlier?

Chen 7

instance, long-term prison sentence and be forced out of academic posts (Hayes 9; Normile and Mann 664).

Britain is the first nation that authorized therapeutic cloning for medical research. It has formed the Human Fertilization and Embryology Authority (HFEA) License Committee to issue licenses to qualified research groups. For monitoring purposes, they follow similar rules and regulations as those mentioned above. "This is an important area of research and a responsible use of technology. The HFEA is there to make sure any research involving human embryos is scrutinized and properly regulated" (Ross).

It would be to the benefit of millions of Americans if the Senate could clearly delineate the differences between reproductive and therapeutic cloning and pass legislation accordingly. I support legislation making the creation of humans by reproductive cloning a severe crime. There is overwhelming support for banning this unethical and unsafe practice, and the fact that it makes no remarkable contribution to medicine justifies the decision. On the contrary, therapeutic cloning exhibits significant promise for curing a wide range of devastating diseases, for reducing suffering and saving lives. It could be very beneficial to the United States in terms of maintaining competitiveness in the medical field. There is no denying the fact that therapeutic cloning holds great potential in contributing to the world. It is imperative that it should be legalized so that rules can be formulated to regulate the current situation. It is believed that under strict regulatory regimes, therapeutic cloning would be a noble practice to promote health and to express love and care for our neighbors.

Did these sources provide just this last idea, or did they provide most of the guidelines mentioned in this paragraph? Be sure to carefully give credit to where each idea came from.

I have highlighted several instances of sentences started by a "dummy subject" such as "there is" or "it is." Try rephrasing your sentences so that you are making the subject clearer.

Chen 8

Works Cited

"The Ethics of Cloning." Editorial. *Washington Post* 9 Jan. 2003:
    A24. Print.

"First Cloned Sheep Dolly Dies at 6." *CNN.com* 14 Feb 2003. Cable
    News Network. Web. 20 Apr. 2006.

Halstead, Ted, and Michael Lind. "Double Jeopardy: Can It Be
    a Crime to Seek Treatment for a Deadly Disease? Congress
    Seems to Think So." *Washington Post* 5 May 2002: B4. Print.

Hansen, Brian. "Cloning Debate." *The CQ Researcher Online* 14.37
    (2004). Web. 23 Feb. 2006.

Hayes, Richard. "Break the Cloning Deadlock." *Christian Science
    Monitor* 10 June 2002: 9. Print.

"Hwang Woo-Suk." *Wikipedia*. 18 Apr. 2006. The Wikimedia Foun-
    dation. Web. 20 Apr. 2006.

Kalb, Claudia. "Big Step for a Controversial Science." *Newsweek* 30
    May 2005: 8. Print.

---. "A New Cloning Debate." *Newsweek* 23 Feb. 2004: 50. Print.

Normile, Dennis, and Charles C. Mann. "Asian Countries Permit
    Research, with Safeguards." *American Association for the
    Advancement of Science* 307.5710 (2005): 664. Print.

Ross, Emma. "U.K. Issues First Cloning License." *CBS News* 11
    Aug 2004. CBS Broadcasting. 20 Apr. 2006. Television.

Discussion Questions

1. What is the author's position on the issue? Does she provide appropriate qualifiers to explain her position clearly? What suggestions would you make to the author?

2. What reasons does the author provide to support her position? Are these reasons sufficient? Are they clearly developed? What suggestions would you make?

3. What evidence does the author use to support her reasons? Are there pieces of evidence that are unclear? What missing evidence would you like to see

her provide? In other words, are claims or reasons given that have insufficient evidence? What suggestions would you make?

4. The author makes an effort to discuss and offer rebuttals to potential counterarguments. How successful do you think she is?

Example 2: Kelesia Bomar, Lowering the Voting Age in Arizona Kelesia Bomar wanted to tackle the topic of the voting age in her research. She was interested in movements to involve younger citizens in the democratic process, and she focused her research on the possibility of lowering the voting age in Arizona. Like Li Chen, she was writing for an academic audience, so she chose to write an academic essay. Her essay also demonstrates some strengths and opportunities for revision. As you read, think about what you might suggest to the author for a revision. Kelesia chose to use the APA citation style in her essay. Why do you think she might have made that choice?

Lowering the Voting Age   1

Running Head: Lowering the Voting Age in Arizona

Kelesia Bomar
ENG102/Section 3952
July 28, 2007
Writing Project 3 Final

Lowering the Voting Age   2

Lowering the Voting Age in Arizona

There have been several attempts across the nation to lower the voting age in America, including the state of Arizona. The controversy surrounding the issue to lower the voting age is whether teenagers, over the age of 16, are mature and knowledgeable enough to make well-informed decisions. They are allowed to drive vehicles at the age of 15—that requires constant 'good' decision making; obtain a job at the age of 16—which requires paying taxes; receive permission from parents to get married at the age of 17—that requires demonstration of adult responsibility and if convicted of a serious crime be tried as an adult in a court of law prior to turning the age of 18. Teenagers with adult responsibilities and expectations are currently not allowed to vote like an adult as the current age to vote in America is 18 according to the XXVI Amendment, which reads "The right of citizens of the United States, who are eighteen years of age or older, to vote shall not be denied or abridged by the United States or by any State on account of age" (NARA, 2007). A few reasons why the state of Arizona should reconsider lowering the voting age to 16 is stronger communities, increase in voter turnout rates, and educational opportunities.

Today's teenagers are actively participating in and strengthening their communities by showing they are capable of making 'good' choices and decisions. For instance, teenagers in New York put together an exhibit that highlighted the 'good' things they were accomplishing within their community. After taking a tour of the exhibit, a news reporter for *The New York Amsterdam News*, Linda Armstrong writes, "Many people believe a lot of negative things about teenagers. Today's teen is often seen as disrespectful, lazy, self-centered, and destructive" (2006). However, Armstrong further writes about how the exhibition called "Through Our Eyes: The Life of a Teen Activist in New York" demonstrates that many teens are actively participating in their communities with positive results. Michelle Victor, a St. Michael Academy student, who participated in the exhibit said, "A lot of the issues we have could be prevented if adults communicated with us regarding issues like sex and HIV, instead of trying to scare us, teach us about it. We need support in general, not a condescending view. That broadens that communication gap" (Armstrong, 2006). In addition, in Arizona, teenagers will be able to participate actively in strengthening their communities by assisting at the polls on election day(s) due to new legislation (Boggan, 2006).

Furthermore, teenagers will continue their education about civics 'hands on' while working at the polling booths helping adults to vote. In another state, Florida is taking steps to motivate their youth population by pre-registering teenagers to vote as a way to engage teenagers to participate in the civic process (Broward, 2007). Florida teenagers will also be able to assist their communities 'hands on' at the polling booths furthering their education on civics. Additionally, students in California are lobbying to ensure high schools are not penalized on election days when students volunteer to work at the polling booths (Nardi, 2006). California currently charges schools $35 per student that is absent per day. This figure totaled for one county district $1300 in 2005. Teenagers are not only aware of what is happening in their communities; they are also taking steps to improve and strengthen their communities further demonstrating their ability to make 'good' decisions.

Since 1982, the electoral participation across the nation has declined among 18 to 29 year olds (Kirby, Lopez, & Marcelo, 2007). However, disrupted for the past two elections, the pattern saw an increase from 22 percent to 25 percent. In Arizona, this trend ranged from 21 percent in 1994, dipping to 14 percent in 2002, then increased to 23 percent in 2006. In a report that examined KVUSA and its impact on Arizona, according to Bruce D. Merrill, PhD: "Kids Voting program continues to increase voter turnout in Arizona elections . . . Kids Voting helped bring an additional 50,000 registered voters to the polls on election day in 2000" (Merrill, 2000). Can you imagine what this figure would be if teenagers age 16 to 17 could

Lowering the Voting Age   4

vote? How many more parents would be responsive and motivated to vote? Youth voting turnout is on the rise in Arizona, opening further opportunities to increase this percentage for the upcoming elections by focusing on today's youth.

My experience with Arizona voting, just six years prior to 1994, was nonexistent because I was scared to vote when I turned 18. I did not know how or what I was supposed to do. Unfortunately, I dropped out of high school two years before I was to graduate. It is possible I missed the opportunity to receive formal training regarding voting and its processes. I felt awkward in asking my family and friends for fear of being viewed as incompetent. Finally, in my late 20s, I gained the courage I needed to ask questions. I overcame my fear by realizing numerous people died to ensure I had the freedom and the right to vote. If I had learned, voting was not as complicated as I thought it was earlier, I could have affected changes regarding important issues throughout my life. If the voting age limit had been 16, I may have had a different voting experience. Through educational exposure or experience, some politicians and organizations have assisted youths on their quest to lowering the voting age and receiving education they may otherwise not have had the opportunity. For example, providing an educational experience, Councilwoman Valerie Ervin demonstrated her belief in youths by hiring two teenagers to run her campaign (Aratani, 2006). Ervin gave two high school students an opportunity to experience first hand what is required in getting voters to the polls. Another example, Senator John Vasconcellos, surrounded by teenage supporters, introduced the concept of lowering the voting age to 14 in California during a news conference, supplying an educational exposure to the legislation process. According to Senator John Vasconcellos: "To not let them have a say in what affects their lives seems to me to be not very typically American" (Bailey, 2004). Granted, the proposal encountered with opposition by Senator Ross Johnson (R-Irvine) who stated, "To waste taxpayer money having children cast votes would be ridiculous

at any time . . ." (Bailey, 2004) Also, disagreeing with lowering
the voting age in California because the proposal called for counting
teenager votes in quarter or half measures, is the president of the
Center for Governmental Studies in Los Angeles, Bob Stern who
said, "So you're a quarter person? Or a half? Either you give the vote
to them or you do not. I just wonder how big an outcry there is for
this" (Bailey, 2004).

In addition, organizations such as Kids Voting USA (KVUSA,
2007) and National Youth Rights Association (NYRA, 2007) have
contributed immensely to the current awareness on educational
importance and youth activism in Arizona, as well as across the
nation. KVUSA and NYRA promote awareness, education, and
information on how to become a better citizen by being involved in
civics. For instance, KVUSA develops curriculum used currently in
schools across the nation to educate students on civics and encourages
parents to participate by interacting with their children on political
issues (KVUSA, 2007). Also, NYRA recently assisted in defeating
a Washington, DC, emergency legislation proposing to implement
an earlier curfew for teenagers (Clark, 2007). Although this does not
directly relate to teenage voting, it does show that NYRA (a youth-
based organization) is actively participating in communities and
educating youths on their rights.

Furthermore, as politicians and organizations promote awareness
with voting and actively participating within communities, that the
state of Arizona could take advantage of even more educational
opportunities. One of these beneficial opportunities is to promote
further education for students to begin creating a 'good' habit—voting.
Engaging students while they are in the "still learning" process will
initiate a habit that can be nurtured. According to KVUSA, "This
ongoing education [opportunity] develops strong skills and habits for
living in a democracy (2007). Preparing teenagers is less challenging
than trying to connect with most 18 year olds, who may be more
focused on graduating, starting college and possibly moving away
from home. This could also be one of the main causes that voter turnout
for the age group 18-24 has been very low. Establishing an early

Lowering the Voting Age   6

voting habit could potentially lead to voting consistency, thereby, increasing voter turnout. Another beneficial opportunity is encouraging parents to discuss politics with students who participate in the Kids Voting USA program. Students study civics in school and will continue learning by discussing at home with parents what they know. Therefore, the voter turnout rate would increase as parents become more responsive and motivated to act upon their civic duty to vote.

Additionally, for certain types of elections, several countries, such as Brazil, Cuba, East Timor, Germany, Israel, Isle of Man, Nicaragua, and Slovenia have lowered their voting age to 16 or 17 ("Voting Age," 2007). Recently, joining these countries in lowering their voting age to 16 is Austria, acknowledged with understanding regarding teenager responsibility in a letter written to NYRA. Austrian ambassador Eva Nowotny writes: "We demand so much responsibility from the younger generation and load so many burdens on their shoulders that we feel it was the right thing to do" (NYRA, 2007).

Many teenagers of America are serious about lowering the voting age. They have taken steps to lobby Councilwomen and Senators to introduce bills in several states, organized exhibits and assist at the election polls. Admittedly, there is skepticism that teenagers are not ready and legislation has proven difficult to pass for lowering the voting age. However, in the state of Arizona legislatures have the ability to enable Arizona and its communities to become the first state to lower the voting age in America. Teachers have the opportunity to engage Arizona's youth by promoting further educational standards within our schools and help bridge the gap between youth and politicians. The communities of Arizona would strengthen with legislation that allows families to truly encourage the youth to be more active with civic participation. Arizona should lower the voting age and become the first state of America to advocate democracy for all. The voting age in Arizona should be lowered from 18 to 16 because youths have better opportunities to learn about voting, establish early voting habit(s) increasing voter turnout, and strengthen the communities they live in.

Lowering the Voting Age   7

References

Aratani, L. (2006, November 4). Teens too young to vote blaze
a campaign trail; Ervin applauds students' political acumen.
The Washington Post. Retrieved July 15, 2007, from ProQuest
database.

Armstrong, L. (2006, June 1–7). Youth exhibit activist spirit. *New
York Amsterdam News*. Retrieved July 16, 2007, from ProQuest
database.

Bailey, E. (2004, March 9). The state; giving new meaning to 'youth
vote.' *Los Angeles Times*. Retrieved on July 16, 2007, from
ProQuest database.

Boggan, S. (2006, November 6). New law lets teens serve at voting
sites: Kids under legal age get civics lesson. *The Tribune.*
Retrieved July 16, 2007, from Access My Library database.

Broward: Sign up to vote when you sign up to drive. (11 June 2007).
CBS News. Retrieved July 7, 2007, from http://cbs4.com/local/
local_story_162160313.html

Clark, A. (2007, June 22). Emergency legislation, D.C. council rejects
earlier youth curfew. [Electronic version]. *The Washington Post*,
B04. Retrieved July 11, 2007, from http://www.washingtonpost
.com/wp-dyn/content/article/2007/06/21/AR2007062101356.html

Kirby, E., Lopez, M., & Marcelo, K. (2007, June). Youth voter
turnout increases in 2006. *CIRCLE*. Retrieved July 23, 2007,
from http://www.civicyouth.org/PopUps/FactSheets/FS07_
2006Mid termCPS.pdf

Kids Voting USA (KVUSA). (2007). *About Us*. Retrieved on July 10,
2007, from http://www.kidsvotingusa.org/page9592.cfm

Merrill, B. (2000, November). Evaluation of the Kids Voting program in Arizona. Retrieved on July 23, 2007, from http://www
.kidsvotingaz.org/new_research.cfm

NARA: The U.S. National Archives & Records Administration.
(2007). Retrieved July 27, 2007, from http://www.archives.gov/
national-archives-experience/charters/constitution_amendments_
11-27.html

Lowering the Voting Age   8

Nardi, E. (2006, September 27). Students lobby for bill aiding poll
    work: LAFAYETTE: Teens say schools shouldn't lose money if
    they miss classes to work at voting places. *Contra Costa Times*.
    Retrieved July 16, 2007, from Access My Library database.

NYRA. (2007). Lowering the voting age. National Youth Rights
    Association. Retrieved July 10, 2007, from http://www
    .youthrights.org/votingage.php

Voting Age. (2007, July 22). In *Wikipedia*, The Free Encyclopedia.
    Retrieved July 24, 2007, from http://en.wikipedia.org/w/index
    .php?title=Voting_age&oldid=146353874

Discussion Questions

1. How well did you understand the controversy surrounding this issue after reading the essay?

2. What is the author's position on the issue? Does she provide appropriate qualifiers to explain her position clearly? What suggestions would you make to the author?

3. What reasons does the author provide to support her position? Are these reasons sufficient? Are they clearly developed? What suggestions would you make?

4. What evidence does the author use to support her reasons? Are there pieces of evidence that are unclear? What missing evidence would you like to have seen her provide? In other words, are claims or reasons given that have insufficient evidence? What suggestions would you make?

PART 4

Formatting Your Research

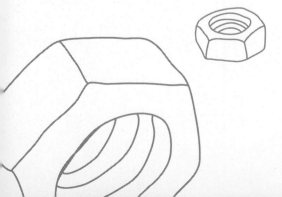

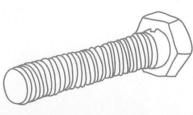

MLA Citation Style Guidelines

The *MLA Handbook for Writers of Research Papers* is the official style guide of the Modern Language Association of America, from whom the style takes its name. The Modern Language Association of America supports scholars who study the literature and culture of English and other languages. The MLA documentation style is generally used by language, literature, and other humanities scholars, and it would be most appropriate to use when writing about topics related to these disciplines, such as literature, language usage, art, and various types of media.

Since scholars who use MLA style can be working from texts that are centuries old and are published in a variety of editions, the MLA citation style privileges the names of the author and the text; therefore, the last name of the author of the text is given in the in-text citations, but not the publication year. And on the works cited page, MLA's name for the bibliography at the end of the paper, the author's name and the title of the text come before any of the publication information.

Because many texts can be found in a variety of locations, it is important to record all of the bibliographic information while researching and taking notes, including the medium of publication, such as Print, Web, etc. When you are including a direct quotation from a text, people will want to find that particular passage; therefore, it is important to include the specific publication information with the copyright year and any other relevant unique identifiers in your works cited. (How many different editions of Shakespeare's work have you seen in your academic studies?) Because the Internet is a dynamic medium and changes can occur so quickly, it is wise to print copies of your source documents.

For more information on in-text citations and tracking resources for a works cited list, regardless of citation style, see Chapter 7.

Note that MLA no longer recommends the inclusion of URLs (Web addresses) in your works cited unless the reader *probably cannot find the source without them or if your instructor requires them*. Include the date the page was posted and the date you accessed it. When used, type the URL after the medium of publication and a period, enclose the URL in angle brackets, and end the citation with a period.

For example, if you found a copy of Shakespeare's *Taming of the Shrew* on the Internet, the full bibliographic citation according to MLA style would look like this: ▢

MLA-1 Book Found on Internet (static) ∗ Citation Elements: book, single author, editor, digital, Web (medium of publication), URL

Author's name and the title of the text.

Name of the editor.

Shakespeare, William. *The Taming of the Shrew*. Ed. Amanda Ballard.
1999-2003. Web. 15 Oct. 2007. <http://www.shakespeare-online
.com/plays/tamingscenes.html>.

The date the researcher accessed the Web site.

Copyright years as listed by the Web site.

Medium of publication.

MLA recommends that you note the URL to the specific Web site for easy access within brackets.

Paper Formatting

MLA simplifies paper formatting so that students do not have to know how to use every tool in their word-processing programs.

Title Page

MLA style does not require a separate title page. Instead, in the upper left corner, on the first page of the paper, include the following information:

- your name
- instructor's name
- course title
- date

Spacing and Margins

MLA style requires that you double-space the entire document, including title page information (see Figure 12.1), quotations, and the list of works cited. You do not need to include extra spaces (i.e., quadruple space) anywhere in the text. Set your top, left, and bottom margins for one inch. All paragraphs should be indented by one-half inch.

Headers and Page Numbers

In the upper right corner of each page, include a header with your last name and the page number (Figure 12.1). All pages in the paper should be consecutively numbered. The header is placed one-half inch from the top of the page and one inch from the right side of the page. Include the header on the first page and all subsequent pages.

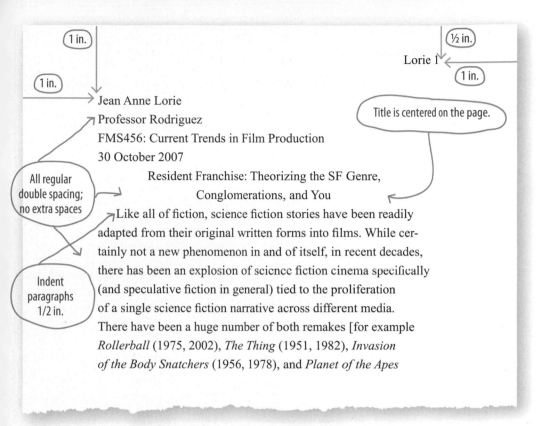

Figure 12.1   Title Page Information in MLA Style.

Section Headings

If your paper is long enough and it includes coherent sections, and even subsections, you might consider including section headings in your paper. MLA does not prescribe specific guidelines for section headings. For each section use an Arabic numeral with a relevant title. Make sure that all of your section titles are syntactically parallel. In other words, if you start your first section title with a noun, start all of your section titles with nouns. For example, the following outline could represent section headings from a paper in MLA style. Ultimately, MLA emphasizes that section headings be concise, well-organized, and above all, consistent.

1. Technological Advancements
    a. Advancements in Visual Technologies
    b. Advancements in Production and Distribution
    c. Advancements in Interactive Technologies
2. Narrative Structure
3. Ideological Differences

4. Hollywood's Enterprises
   a. Vertical Integration
   b. Further Economic Trends
5. Conclusions

Visuals

MLA style divides visuals into two categories: tables and figures. Whenever you place visuals into your text, you must place them as close as possible to the paragraph referring to them.

Tables

If you are presenting numerical data in a table format, label the table with the word *Table* (not italicized), an Arabic numeral, and a title. The label and title are placed on top of the table as it appears in your text. If you are reprinting the table from an outside source, you must include the full bibliographic citation for the table directly under the table (not at the end of your paper in the works cited list).

Table 12.1

A Table in MLA Style with Appropriate Captions

Kairos in the Rhetorical Situation	Purpose	Audience	Author
Time	What has happened in the past or is happening in the present that motivates research and communication? What will happen in the future that will require research and communication?	What has happened in the past or is happening in the present that motivates this audience to care about the topic? What does the audience need to do in the future that motivates their reading/learning about the topic?	What has happened in the author's past or is happening in the present or may happen in the author's future that motivates him or her to research and write?

Space	What persons, places, or things will be affected by the outcomes of this research?	What real-world things can the audience do to impact this issue based on the research and writing?	What resources does the author have to facilitate research, writing, and publishing on this topic?

MLA-2 Textbook (static) * Citation Elements: two authors, book, section from a book

Miller-Cochran, Susan K., and Rochelle L. Rodrigo. "Kairos in
the Rhetorical Situation." *The Wadsworth Guide to Research*.
Boston: Wadsworth-Cengage Learning, 2009. 250-51. Print.

Figures   MLA style refers to all other types of visuals such as charts, graphs, maps, and images as figures. Label each figure with the abbreviated word *Fig.* (not italicized), an Arabic numeral, and a title. The label and title of a figure are placed below the visual as it appears in your text, along with a reference to the source of the figure if it came from an outside resource (see Figure 12.2).

© Warner Bros./The Kobal Collection

Fig. 12.2. Image of Bullet Time from *The Matrix* (1999).

MLA-2

4 Formatting Your Research

Using the image in Figure 12.2 in a text that discusses bullet time technology and its impact on the meaning of a film would be similar to including a long quotation that describes the image. The image itself, in this instance, is a better representation of "bullet time." It would probably be better to directly "quote" by including the figure than to try to describe what the image would look like on the screen.

For more information on when to cite resources in-text, what to include in a works cited list, and documentation-related questions that are not specific to MLA format, see Chapter 7.

Citation Guidelines

In this section, you will find explanations and examples of how to cite resources that you use in your research, both in the text of your work (in-text citations) and at the end of your research (works cited list). ▢

In-Text Citations

You must include an in-text citation after every sentence that includes information from an outside resource. Even if you are only summarizing or paraphrasing the resource, you still must include an in-text citation in the same sentence in which you present the material. MLA in-text citations only require the author's name and, if you are including a paraphrase or direct quote, a page number.

Quotations and Paraphrases   Standard in-text citations in MLA format include the author's name and the page number in the citation, as the following example demonstrates:

> Science fiction films "self-consciously foreground their own radicality" of special effects (Freedman 307).

Since the in-text citation is considered a part of the sentence, the end-of-sentence punctuation is included after the in-text citation. If the source was written by more than one author, your in-text citation will include the names of both authors, like this:

> (Miller-Cochran and Rodrigo 252).

When incorporating short quotations or paraphrases, you can include some of the bibliographic information in the sentence itself. This strategy can be a way to emphasize the name of the author you are citing, or it can simply be a way to vary the sentence structure in your writing. If the author's name is already mentioned in the sentence, you only need to include the page number from which the information or quotation came in the in-text citation. The next example uses the same short quotation from Freedman's work and only needs to provide the page where the quotation was found because Freedman's name is included in the sentence itself:

> Carl Freedman criticizes science fiction films for "self-consciously foreground[ing] their own radicality" of special effects (307).

Long Quotations   In MLA style, text quotations that will be longer than four lines in your paper need to be presented in a block quote. Instead of using quotation marks to identify the text being directly quoted, block quotes indent the material so that it stands out on the page. Quotations that are longer than four lines of your paper must be formatted as block quotations, which are indented one inch from the left margin. Because they are direct quotations, block quotes need an in-text citation that includes the author's name and the page number of the quotation.

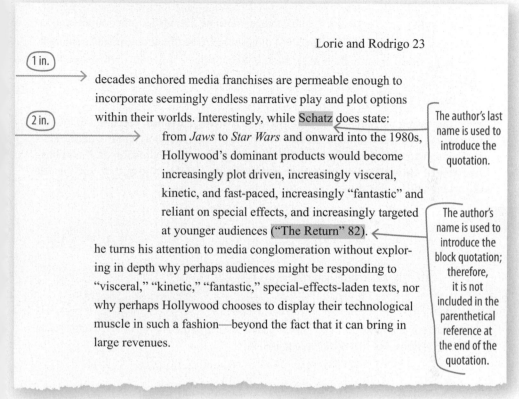

Lorie and Rodrigo 23

1 in.

decades anchored media franchises are permeable enough to incorporate seemingly endless narrative play and plot options within their worlds. Interestingly, while Schatz does state:

2 in.

> from *Jaws* to *Star Wars* and onward into the 1980s, Hollywood's dominant products would become increasingly plot driven, increasingly visceral, kinetic, and fast-paced, increasingly "fantastic" and reliant on special effects, and increasingly targeted at younger audiences ("The Return" 82).

he turns his attention to media conglomeration without exploring in depth why perhaps audiences might be responding to "visceral," "kinetic," "fantastic," special-effects-laden texts, nor why perhaps Hollywood chooses to display their technological muscle in such a fashion—beyond the fact that it can bring in large revenues.

The author's last name is used to introduce the quotation.

The author's name is used to introduce the block quotation; therefore, it is not included in the parenthetical reference at the end of the quotation.

Figure 12.3 An Extended Quotation in MLA Style.

Figure 12.3 shows a long quotation that includes the author's name in the introduction to the quote; however, at the end of the quote the in-text citation not only includes the page number but also an abbreviated title of the resource that gives enough information to find the resource on the works cited list. In this particular paper, the author uses more than one source by Schatz; therefore, to lead the reader to the correct bibliographic citation in the works cited list, the in-text reference also needs to include a portion of the resource's title. If only one resource by Schatz had been included in the paper, the in-text citation would have only included the page number, since Schatz's name is used to introduce the quote. Likewise, if no author had been listed for this resource, only the abbreviated version of the title would be used in the in-text citation (see the example below in "Summaries and Multiple Resources").

Summaries and Multiple Resources   If you are summarizing the main point of a resource and not referencing one particular part of the source, MLA style only requires that you provide enough information in an in-text citation to get the reader to the full bibliographic citation in the works cited list. In the following text example, the writer briefly refers to multiple texts within the same sentence. Notice, however, that these texts do not have authors; therefore, the writer's in-text citation includes the article title as the little bit of information that gets the reader to the correct section in the works cited list.

> Interestingly, even a mediocre film can open revenue streams for other outlets and media tie-ins, like *Van Helsing* (2004) did. Although the film only earned a reported $120 million domestic, short of its $160 million budget ("Top 250"; "Business Data"), its video game made *Electronic Gaming Monthly*'s Top 10 list for April 2004 ("Top 10. . . April 2004").

When discussing films in papers that follow MLA style guidelines, you need to include the year the film was first released after the first time you mention it in the paper. Electronic resources are cited in text in the same way as hard copy resources. If you have the name of the author, you include that information. If there is no author, you include a shortened title.

> reflect >

MLA: In-Text Citation Nuts and Bolts

In MLA format, typical in-text citations look like this:

> (Author Page number)

If no author is available (e.g., a government-published pamphlet), use an abbreviated version of the title of the source. The citation would look like this:

> (Title Page number)

If no page number is available (e.g., a digital resource), don't include anything in the place of the page number. The citation would simply look like this:

> (Author)

Or it might look like this:
> (Title)

...write...

Practice In-Text Citations

Use the following sample paragraph and its works cited list to practice inserting in-text citations. First, identify where you need to include in-text citations; the sample paragraph contains direct quotes, paraphrases, and summaries. Second, insert the in-text citations where they are required. Be sure to include the appropriate information for each type of in-text citation.

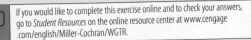
If you would like to complete this exercise online and to check your answers, go to *Student Resources* on the online resource center at www.cengage .com/english/Miller-Cochran/WGTR.

Strauss concludes that "the moral is that unless we show faculty members how technology can meet their needs, they won't consider using it." While studying what community college faculty needed to incorporate technology into their instruction, Quick and Davies found faculty needed time, money, software, classroom computers (professor podium), department computer lab, and faculty technical support and training. In discussing how to prepare college faculty for the incoming 'Net-generation of students, Clayton-Pedersen and O'Neill claim that "much of the learning technology innovation in higher education has been focused on K-12 teacher preparation and development" and that "more focus needs to be placed on preparing existing faculty for the future 'Net Generation students who will populate the twenty-first century classroom." They continue that call for action in claiming that "faculty's understanding of the teaching and learning power of technology needs to be increased" and "tools need to be developed to help faculty integrate technology into the curriculum." Strauss, Quick and Davies, and Clayton-Pedersen and O'Neill demonstrate that faculty first needs blatant introductions to the new technologies themselves: what they are and what they can do.[1]

Works Cited

MLA-3 Ebook (static) * Citation Elements: two authors, editors, online, book, digital, anthology/edited collection, section from a book

MLA-3

Clayton-Pedersen, Alma R., and Nancy O'Neill. "Curricula Designed to Meet 21st-Century Expectations." *Educating the Net Generation*. Ed. Diana G. Oblinger and James L. Oblinger. Washington: Educause, 2005. Web. 22 Aug. 2005.

MLA-4 Journal Numbered with Continued Pagination and Journal Numbered Separately * Citation Elements: two authors, journal (pages)

MLA-4

Quick, Don, and Timothy Gray Davies. "Community College Faculty Development: Bringing Technology into Instruction." *Community College Journal of Research and Practice* 23.4 (1999): 641-53. Print.

---

1. Reproduced by permission of Rochelle Rodrigo.

MLA-5 Online Weekly Trade Magazine (syndicated) ∗ Citation Elements: single author, online, digital, magazine (weekly or biweekly)

Strauss, Howard. "Why Many Faculty Members Aren't Excited about Technology." *The Chronicle of Higher Education* 24 June 2005. Web. 31 Dec. 2005.

Full Bibliographic Citations

MLA format requires a list of resources used in the paper, and this list is referred to as the "works cited." This list includes only the names of resources cited in the paper, not resources that you found and read during your research process but did not refer to in the paper. The works cited page should start at the top of a new page in your essay; however, it will need to be included in your continuous page numbering. Subsequent works cited pages do not have a special heading but simply include MLA-formatted page numbers. Entries in works cited lists are presented in alphabetical order by the author's last name. If you have more than one text by the same author, alphabetize within those author entries by title of the text. If you have texts with no authors, incorporate them into the alphabetical list based on title.

Entries in a works cited list are formatted with a hanging indent, a format that looks a bit like an upside-down paragraph. The first line of the citation is left-justified, with no indent. Then all subsequent lines have a half-inch indentation. The examples in Figure 12.4 demonstrate how the hanging indent looks on the page.

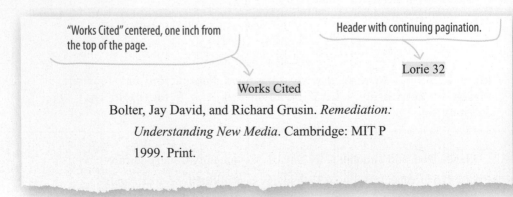

"Works Cited" centered, one inch from the top of the page.

Header with continuing pagination.

Lorie 32

Works Cited

Bolter, Jay David, and Richard Grusin. *Remediation: Understanding New Media*. Cambridge: MIT P 1999. Print.

Figure 12.4 Example of the First Page of the Works Cited.

MLA-6 Internet Page with No Author (static) * Citation Elements: no author, online, digital, Web page within a Web site

No URL needed to find correct source.

"Business Data for *Van Helsing* (2004)." 1990-2005. *The Internet Movie Database*. IMDb.com. Web. 28 Oct. 2005.

Since "Business Data for Van Helsing (2004)" has no author, it is alphabetized based on title of the text.

All citations are double-spaced with hanging indent.

Carpenter, Cassie. "Hollywood Players." *BackStage .com*. 21 Oct. 2004. *LexisNexis Academic*. Web. 3 Oct. 2005.

MLA-7 Online Trade Magazine (syndicated) * Citation Elements: two authors, magazine (weekly or biweekly), online, digital

Cohen, David S., and Ben Fritz. "Spielberg Gets in on Vidgame Action: Initial Work Has Already Begun on First Title." *Variety* 14 Oct. 2005. Web. 16 Oct. 2005.

MLA-6

MLA-7

Figure 12.4 Example of the First Page of the Works Cited. *(continued)*

---

techno_tip >

> Format a Document in MLA Style <

If you are using a standard word-processing program to write your paper, you can use its features to write your paper with minimal formatting difficulty. Use the formatting choices to set the following options for your paper.

☐ Double-space your paper throughout. Set this option before you type any text so that your entire paper is double-spaced.

☐ Set your header to include the appropriate heading with your last name and page number. Word-processing programs can automatically insert the page number for you after your name.

☐ On the works cited page, use the ruler at the top of the screen to set a hanging indent for your citations so that you don't have to hit "Enter" and "Tab" at the end of each line.

4 Formatting Your Research

MLA full bibliographic citation style generally provides information in the following order:

1. Name of author

2. Title of text

3. Publication information (usually publisher's name, place [city] of publication, copyright date)

4. Medium of publication: Print, Web, CD, DVD, etc. (Additional information on resource may *follow* the medium of publication for certain resources.)

Periods are included after each major section of information. For example, a period is included after the name of the author(s), after the text's title, and after the complete publication information. If there is *no author* for the text, start with the text's title; however, remember that government agencies and corporations can function as an author. With various online resources, you may have to look on other pages to find the author's name.

Similarly, you may have to search online resources for the last updated date as well (like the "history" page in wikis). If you cannot find a date, or other publication information, you may use the following abbreviations:

For more explanation about static, syndicated, and dynamic resources, see Chapter 4.

- n.p. No place of publication given

- n.p. No publisher given

- n.d. No date of publication given

The citation rules for static, syndicated, and dynamic resources all follow this general pattern, but each category has some unique characteristics.

MLA Citation Examples

 For more examples of MLA citations, go to the online resource center at www.cengage.com/english/Miller-Cochran/WGTR.

4 Formatting Your Research

Static Resources

Static resources (e.g., books, films, and pieces of art) are generally easy to cite using MLA style. These citations usually have an author, title, and publication information.

MLA-8 Book with Two Authors (static) * Citation Elements: two authors, book

Name of author: Notice that the first author's name is listed last name first and the second author's name is first name first.

Title of text: Be sure to include any subtitles; sometimes they are not found on the cover of the book but instead on the title page inside the book. Titles should be italicized. Do not italicize the punctuation following them.

Bolter, Jay David, and Richard Grusin. *Remediation: Understanding New Media*. Cambridge: MIT P, 1999. Print.

Publication information: Include the city where the publication company resides, followed by a colon, then the name of the publisher, followed by a comma, and the copyright year. MLA shortens the publisher's name by turning Press into P.

Medium of publication: The medium of publication, *Print* (not italicized), applies to any printed documents, such as a book, magazine, dissertation, or pamphlet.

If there had been three authors, the first author's surname (last name) would be first, followed by the first name, then the coauthors with their first names followed by their last names; for example, "Story, Jonelle, Anne Kroening, and James Anderson."

The following examples indicate how to cite various types of static sources.

MLA-9 Article from an Edited Collection with an Author, Translator, and Editor ∗ Citation Elements: anthology or edited
collection, section from a book, single author, translator,
editor, republished

Author, title, and original
publication date of the essay.

Translator's name. (Translated the
essay, not the entire book.)

Heilig, Morton. "The Cinema of the Future." 1955. Trans. Uri Feldman.

Name of the
anthology.

Multimedia: From Wagner to Virtual Reality. Ed. Randall Packer

and Ken Jordan. New York: Norton, 2001. 239-51. Print.

Editors.

City of publisher, publisher, and
copyright year of the anthology.

Page numbers
of the resource
in the anthology
and medium of
publication.

MLA style calls for the abbreviation of publisher's names. Therefore, if the publishing
company is based on the name of an individual, like W. W. Norton and Company above
in MLA-9, then you may just shorten the publisher's name to the person's surname.
Similarly, many publishing companies are presses associated with universities; if the
publisher is a university press, as in MLA-10, shorten the phrase "University Press" to
"UP." If you are unsure, either check the most recent edition of the *MLA Handbook for
Writers of Research Papers* or spell out the entire name.

MLA-10 Introduction to a Republished Book with a Translator ∗
Citation Elements: single author, book, republished, translator, foreword

This is the author of the
introduction. The book only
listed the author's initials;
therefore, there is no first
name in the citation.

If the introduction had a title
different from "Introduction," you
would first put the title of the
introduction in quotation marks
with a period. You would then
include the word "Introduction"
with another period (as seen here).

The title of the book.

The author
of the
book.

Baynes, W. E. C. Introduction. *The Prince*. By Niccolo Machiavelli.

Trans. Rufus Goodwin. Wellesley: Dante UP, 2003. 13-25. Print.

The translator of the book.

Publisher's
city, name, and
copyright year.

The page numbers of the introduction
and medium of publication.

The citation styles for introductions, prefaces, forewords, and afterwords are basically the same. If you are using one of these types of ancillary materials as a resource, start your citation with the author of the ancillary material, next include the title of the ancillary material (if it has one) in quotation marks, then include the word that represents it before the remainder of the book's citation. Therefore, if the introduction to *The Prince* in MLA-10 had a title, the title would be listed within quotation marks prior to the word "Introduction."

MLA-11 Book in a Series * Citation Elements: two authors, book, book in a series

Two authors and title of the book.

Sullivan, Patricia, and James E. Porter. *Opening Spaces: Writing*

   Technologies and Critical Research Practices. Greenwich: Ablex,

   1997. Print. New Directions in Computers and Composition Studies.

Publication information.

Name of the series.

MLA-12 Book with a Title within the Title and a Publisher's Imprint * Citation Elements: single author, book, a title in the title, publisher's imprint

The title of the film within the title of the book is neither italicized nor enclosed in quotation marks.

Sammon, Paul M. *Future Noir: The Making of* Blade Runner.

New York: Harper Paperbacks-HarperCollins, 1996. Print.

With a publisher's imprint, put the name of the imprint first, then a hyphen, and then the name of the publishing house.

MLA-13

MLA-13 Online Annotated Sacred Text ∗ Citation Elements: online, digital, sacred text, no author

| | If the title does not indicate the version, place the name of the version after the title. | |
| Name of the sacred text. | | The Web site did not list a copyright date. |

Cascading Bible. King James Version. n.d. Web. 21 Jan. 2008. <http://www .verselink.org/>.

Web address needed to ensure that reader finds the correct source.

Medium of publication (Web) and date of accessing the information on the Internet.

MLA-14, MLA-15

MLA-14 Entry from a Dictionary ∗ Citation Elements: reference, no author

MLA-15 Entry from an Online Dictionary ∗ Citation Elements: reference, online, digital, no author

The title of the entry in the reference work.

"Eclecticism." *Webster's Third New International Dictionary of the English Language Unabridged*. 1993. Print.

Copyright year of the reference work.

"Eclecticism." *Merriam-Webster OnLine*. 2008. Web. 21 Jan. 2008.

Title of the reference resource.

Medium of publication (Web) and access date for the online resource.

You only need minimal publication information if the reference resource (dictionary, thesaurus, encyclopedia, etc.) is well known. If the reference is not well known, include all bibliographic and publication information as in a book or other online resource.

MLA-16, MLA-17

MLA-16 Conference Proceedings * Citation Elements: conference proceedings, subscription database, digital, editor, two authors

MLA-17 Paper Published in Conference Proceedings * Citation Elements: conference proceedings, section from a book, subscription database, digital, editor, single author

Editors of the proceedings.

Title of the proceedings.

VanTassel-Baska, Joyce, and Tamra Stambaugh, eds. *Overlooked Gems: A National Perspective on Low-Income Promising Learners. Proceedings of the National Leadership Conference on Low-Income Promising Learners,* Apr. 2006, Washington, DC. Williamsburg, VA: Natl. Assn. for Gifted Children and Center for Gifted Educ., Coll. of William & Mary, 2007. *ERIC.* Web. 21 Jan. 2008.

Baldwin, Alexinia Y. "Untapped Potential for Excellence." *Overlooked Gems: A National Perspective on Low-Income Promising Learners. Proceedings of the National Leadership Conference on Low-Income Promising Learners,* Apr. 2006, Washington, D.C. Ed. Joyce VanTassel-Baska and Tamra Stambaugh. Williamsburg, VA: Natl. Assn. for Gifted Children and Center for Gifted Educ., Coll. of William & Mary, 2007. 23-25. *ERIC.* Web. 21 Jan. 2008.

Editors of the proceedings.

Database citation information: name of the database, publisher/producer of the database, medium of publication, and access date.

Information about the essay from within the proceedings: author's name, title, and page numbers.

When the information about the conference is included in the title of the proceedings, it is listed as part of the title (see MLA-16 and MLA-17); if the information about the conference is not included in the title, list it directly after the title without formatting it in italics.

MLA-18 Published Dissertation ∗ Citation Elements: dissertation or thesis, single author

MLA-19 Abstract of a Dissertation ∗ Citation Elements: dissertation or thesis, abstract of a dissertation or thesis, single author, subscription database, digital

Title of the dissertation; notice in the abstract reference the title is in quotation marks.

Author's name.

Degree-granting information: type of document, name of institution, and year of graduation.

Todorovska, Viktorija. *E-mail as an Emerging Rhetorical Space in the Workplace.* Diss. Arizona State U, 2000. Ann Arbor: UMI, 2000. Print.

Todorovska, Viktorija. "E-mail as an Emerging Rhetorical Space in the Workplace." Diss. Arizona State U, 2000. *ProQuest Dissertations and Theses.* Web. 21 Jan. 2008.

Title of the database, medium of publication, and date of access.

To cite an unpublished dissertation, include all of the information from the published dissertation up through the degree-granting institution and the year the dissertation was defended. In other words, everything but the publication information.

MLA-20 White Paper * Citation Elements: single author, white
paper

Author of the white paper.

Title of the white paper. The title
includes the quotation marks.

Bleed, Ron. "Keeping Up with Technology" Strategic Conversation.
Maricopa Community College District, Tempe, AZ. 8 June 2004. Print.

Location where the white
paper was presented.

Date the white paper was
presented or published.

MLA-21 Government Web site * Citation Elements: government publication, online, Web page on a Web site, digital

Name of the government agency
authoring and publishing the
resources.

Name of the resource.

Federal Communications Commission. *History of Communications.*
21 Nov. 2005. Web. 16 Oct. 2007.

Copyright year.

Medium of publication
and access date.

Like government agencies, corporations can also author resources. Similarly to MLA-21,
you can put the corporation's name as the author of a resource (see MLA-49).

MLA-22 Online Scholarly Project * Citation Elements: online scholarly project, online, two authors, editors, digital

Title of the project.

Names of those organizing or managing the project.

CompPile: 1939-current. Ed. Rich Haswell and Glenn Blalock. 2007. Texas A&M U-Corpus Christi. Web. 21 Jan. 2008

Last date the project was updated.

Name of the educational institution hosting the project.

Medium of publication and access date.

When projects are hosted on educational servers, be sure to include the name of the institution hosting the project.

MLA-23 Film in DVD Format * Citation Elements: film, DVD/video, edition, digital

Title of the film. Notice that *Moulin Rouge!* has an exclamation point as a part of its title. Normally you would just put a period after the title.

The director.

The names of the top handful of prominent performers (main characters in the film).

Moulin Rouge! Dir. Baz Luhrmann. Perf. Nicole Kidman, Ewan McGregor, John Leguizamo, and Jim Broadbent. 2001. Two-disc collector's ed. 20th Century Fox, 2003. DVD.

Year that the film was originally released.

The name of the specific edition of the DVD release. Other options sometimes include "widescreen" and "extended cut."

Distribution company and copyright year of the DVD.

Medium that the recording is published in (DVD, videocassette, HD, etc.).

Consider using the Internet Movie Database (http://www.imdb.com/) to find the names of directors, performers, and distribution companies.

MLA-24

MLA-24 Screenplay * Citation Elements: screenplay, single author

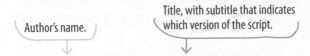

Author's name.

Title, with subtitle that indicates which version of the script.

Anderson, Paul Thomas. *Magnolia: The Shooting Script.* New York:

Newmarket P, 2000. Print.

Publication information: city, publisher, and year.

MLA-25

MLA-25 Film in a Language Other Than English * Citation Elements: film, DVD/video, edition, digital, foreign language

Name of the film in its original language. If you desire, you may include a translation of the title in brackets.

Director and performer information.

Sin Dejar Huella [Without a Trace]. Dir. María Novaro. Perf.

Aitana Sánchez-Gijón, Tiaré Scanda, Jesús Ochoa,

and Martín Altomaro. 2000. Alta Films, 2001. DVD.

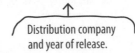

Distribution company and year of release.

If you are citing a resource that is in a language other than English, cite the original title (in its original language) and then, if you desire, provide the translation of the resource's title in brackets.

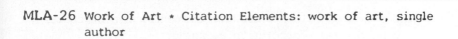

MLA-26 Work of Art * Citation Elements: work of art, single author

Name of the artist, in this case the architect.

Name of the work, followed by the years it was produced.

Wright, Frank Lloyd. *Fallingwater*. 1936-1939. Building. Western Pennsylvania Conservancy, Mill Run.

Medium of composition.

The name of the institution or individual that owns the work and the city in which it is housed.

MLA-27 Reprinted Work of Art in a Book with Numerous Editions * Citation Elements: work of art, book, edition, section from a book, single author, editor

The same as the initial entry, except in this case the book refers to the work by two titles.

Authors of the book.

Wright, Frank Lloyd. *Kaufmann House (Fallingwater)*. 1936-1939. Western Pennsylvania Conservancy, Mill Run. *Gardner's Art through the Ages*. 12th ed. By Fred S. Kleiner and Christin J. Mamiya. Belmont: Thomson-Wadsworth, 2005. 1017. Print.

Title of the book, with the edition listed after it.

City of publication, publisher, and copyright year.

Page that the work is reprinted on.

When referring to books in multiple editions, use the language you find on the title page of the book. Therefore, if it says second or third edition, put the numbers in your citation. If it says "Revised" or "Abridged" put "Rev. ed." or "Abr. ed." in the citation. Similarly, if your book is the fifth in a multivolume work, just include "Vol. 5."

MLA-28 Map Found on Flickr ∗ Citation Elements: map or chart, online, digital, corporation as author

MLA style does not list an author for maps; however, if you know the company who made the map, give them credit.

Name of the map in quotations and the name of the Web site where you found the map in italics.

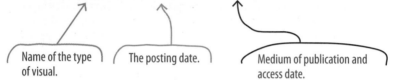

GISuser. "LIDAR Map of New Orleans Flooding from Hurricane Katrina."

Flickr. Map. 22 Jan. 2008. Web. 22 Jan. 2008.

Name of the type of visual.

The posting date.

Medium of publication and access date.

MLA-29 A Song from an Album ∗ Citation Elements: sound recording, four or more authors, musical composition, digital

Authors of the lyrics. Notice, you do not use the name of the band, in this case, *Deep Purple*.

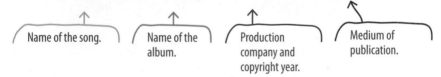

Gillan, Ian, Ritchie Blackmore, Roger Glover, Jon Lord, and Ian Paice.

"Space Truckin." *Machine Head*. Warner Bros., 1972. CD.

Name of the song.

Name of the album.

Production company and copyright year.

Medium of publication.

Practice Full Bibliographic Citations for Static Resources

What if you downloaded a song from iTunes or listened to it as it streamed from XM radio? Using the song in MLA-29, construct two citations with the following information. One citation will indicate that the song was downloaded from iTunes, the other will indicate that it was streamed from XM Satellite radio.

Citation 1

☐ Access date: October 3, 2007

☐ iTunes Store: http://www.apple.com/itunes/store/

Citation 2

☐ XM Radio: http://www.xmradio.com/

☐ XM station 41, The Bone Yard

To view the answers to this exercise along with a discussion of how the citations are constructed, go to *Student Resources* on the online resource center at www.cengage.com/english/Miller-Cochran/WGTR.

MLA-30 Published Interview from a Web Site ∗ Citation Elements: published interview, online, Web page in a Web site, digital, single author

MLA-30

Name of person being interviewed.

Title of the published interview.

Pelecanos, George P. "Hard-Boiled Heaven: Bob Cornwell in Conversation with George P. Pelecanos." *Tangled Web UK*. 2001. Web. 18 Oct. 2007.

The Web site that published the interview.

Date of publication of the original interview.

Medium of publication and access date.

Syndicated Resources

Syndicated resources are a little more complicated because there are usually multiple titles involved. Since many syndicated resources are now in digital format, their citations are also complicated because they generally include layers of publication information as well.

MLA-31, MLA-32

MLA-31 Newspaper Article Found in a Library Database (syndicated) * Citation Elements: single author, newspaper, subscription database, digital

MLA-32 Editorial Found at Newspaper's Web Site * Citation Elements: newspaper, digital, online, no author, editorial

Syndicated resources usually have two titles, the title of the individual text and the title of the syndication. In MLA style the title of the actual text is differentiated from the title of the syndication with quotation marks.

When citing from a library database, MLA requires that you include the name of the database.

Dutka, Elaine. "Hollywood Caught up in the Game: Better Technology and a Hot Video-Game Market Give Studios and Stars a Lucrative Movie Tie-In." *Los Angeles Times*. 10 May 2005. *LexisNexis Academic*. Web. 2 Oct. 2005.

"Swirl, Sniff, Sip, Check the Price." Editorial. *Los Angeles Times*. 19 Jan. 2008. Web. 22 Jan. 2008. <http://www.latimes.com/news/opinion/editorials/la-ed-wine19jan19,0,2045726.story?coll=la-news-comment-editors>.

The copyright date; the actual date the individual text was published in the syndication.

Medium of publication and access date.

If there is *no author* listed you just start with the name of the text you are citing. With editorials you include the term "Editorial" after the title.

Notice that *October* is abbreviated to "Oct." and *January* to "Jan." In MLA style, abbreviate names of months except May, June, and July.

MLA-33 Journal Article with Continuous Pagination across the Volume ∗ Citation Elements: journal, pages via volume or issue, single author, two or more works by the same author

MLA-34 Article by the Same Author with Separate Pagination in Each Issue ∗ Citation Elements: journal, pages via volume or issue, single author, two or more works by the same author

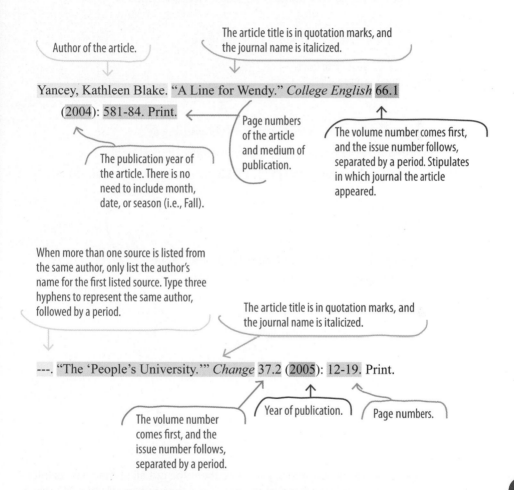

Author of the article.

The article title is in quotation marks, and the journal name is italicized.

Yancey, Kathleen Blake. "A Line for Wendy." *College English* 66.1 (2004): 581-84. Print.

The publication year of the article. There is no need to include month, date, or season (i.e., Fall).

Page numbers of the article and medium of publication.

The volume number comes first, and the issue number follows, separated by a period. Stipulates in which journal the article appeared.

When more than one source is listed from the same author, only list the author's name for the first listed source. Type three hyphens to represent the same author, followed by a period.

The article title is in quotation marks, and the journal name is italicized.

---. "The 'People's University.'" *Change* 37.2 (2005): 12-19. Print.

The volume number comes first, and the issue number follows, separated by a period.

Year of publication.

Page numbers.

Note in MLA-33 and MLA-34 that current MLA guidelines no longer make a distinction between journals that are numbered continuously (e.g., Vol. 1 ends on page 208, Vol. 2 starts on page 209) or numbered separately; that is, each volume starts on page 1. No matter how the journal is paginated, all of them must contain volume *and* issue numbers if they are available. One exception are journals with issue numbers only; simply cite the issue numbers alone as though they are volume numbers.

If your works cited list includes more than one entry by an author, you do not need to write the name of the author again (MLA-34). You will need to order the resources based on the alphabetical order of the titles.

MLA-35 Article in a Monthly or Bimonthly Magazine Found Online ∗ Citation Elements: monthly or bimonthly magazine, online, digital, four or more authors

MLA-36 Article in a Weekly or Biweekly Magazine Found in a Database ∗ Citation Elements: weekly or biweekly magazine, subscription database, digital, single author

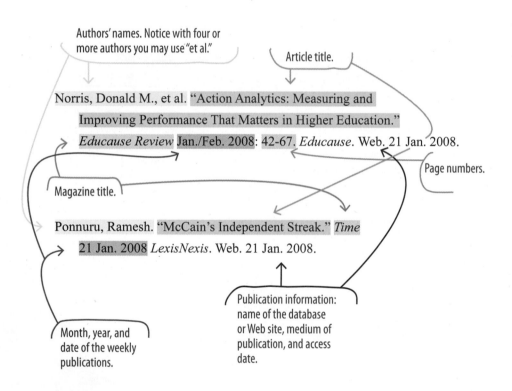

When you have four or more authors, you can either type out all of their names (MLA-29), or you can include only the first author's name and then put "et al." (MLA-35), which is Latin for "and others." Be careful not to put a period after "et" because it is an entire Latin word. The Latin abbreviation "al." (with a period) is an abbreviation for "alii" or "alia," which means "others."

MLA-37 Article That Skips Pages in a Monthly or Bimonthly Magazine ∗ Citation Elements: single author, monthly or bimonthly magazine, skipped pages

Author's name.   Title of the article.   Initial page number with the plus symbol.

Gale, Doug. "Biometrics Revisited." *Campus Technology* Jan. 2008: 28+. Print.

Title of the magazine.   Publication month and year.

When citing an article that skips pages, you may include the inclusive page numbers if they all run together (13-21, 46-63); however, if they bounce all over the periodical, just include the first page number and the plus symbol, +.

MLA-38 Article with a Quotation in the Title ∗ Citation Elements: two authors, quotation in title, pages

Authors' names.   Title of the article.

Kahne, Joseph, and Kim Bailey. "The Role of Social Capital in Youth Development: The Case of 'I Have a Dream' Programs." *Educational Evaluation and Policy Analysis* 21.2 (1999): 321-43. Print.

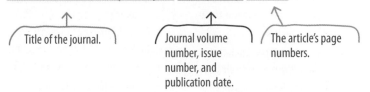

Title of the journal.   Journal volume number, issue number, and publication date.   The article's page numbers.

MLA-39 Review of a Book in an Online Journal ∗ Citation Elements: single author, review, journal, online, digital

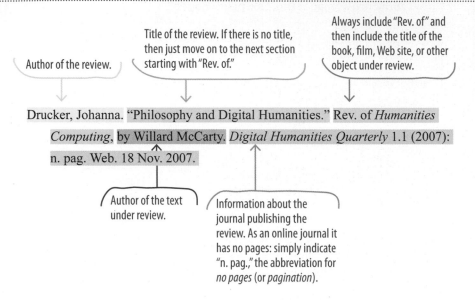

Author of the review.

Title of the review. If there is no title, then just move on to the next section starting with "Rev. of."

Always include "Rev. of" and then include the title of the book, film, Web site, or other object under review.

Drucker, Johanna. "Philosophy and Digital Humanities." Rev. of *Humanities Computing*, by Willard McCarty. *Digital Humanities Quarterly* 1.1 (2007): n. pag. Web. 18 Nov. 2007.

Author of the text under review.

Information about the journal publishing the review. As an online journal it has no pages: simply indicate "n. pag.," the abbreviation for *no pages* (or *pagination*).

You can adapt the various journal and magazine article citations for online publications of the journals by just adding the medium of publication (Web) and an access date. Follow with a URL if your instructor requires one.

Practice Full Bibliographic Citations for Syndicated Resources

...write...

Using the following information, write a full bibliographic citation for a journal article found in a library's subscription database.

- ☐ Title: The Relationships among Perceived Physician Accommodation, Perceived Outgroup Typicality, and Patient Inclinations toward Compliance

- ☐ Authors: Christopher Hajek, Melinda Villagran, and Elaine Wittenberg-Lyles

- ☐ Journal information: Communication Research Reports, September 2007, Volume 24, Issue 4, pages 293-302, 10 pgs, 2 charts

- ☐ Database information: Communication & Mass Media Complete (EbscoHost Research Databases), DOI: 10.1080/08824090701624189; (*AN 27009633*), http://www.ebscohost.com/thisTopic.php?topicID=56&marketID=1

- ☐ Access date: January 29, 2008

 To view the answers to this exercise along with a discussion of how the citations are constructed, go to *Student Resources* on the online resource center at www.cengage.com/english/Miller-Cochran/WGTR.

The following set of citations offers another example to help understand the conventions of MLA formatting. The examples are all of the same text, an episode of the television show *Bones*, accessed in three different locations. All three examples have the same basic information about the text and then each has the specific information about when, where, and how it was accessed.

MLA-40 Broadcast of Television Episode (syndicated) * Citation Elements: television, broadcast

MLA-41 Television Episode Downloaded from iTunes (syndicated) * Citation Elements: television, subscription database, digital

MLA-42 Episode from a DVD Season Box Set (static) * Citation Elements: television, DVD/video, digital

Notice that the core information about the individual episode remains the same.

Although the production company is the same (as these are all citations for the same episode of a show), the name is formatted differently on each source. Be sure to pay close attention to how names are formatted in/on the sources themselves.

Since television broadcasts , Web pages, and database entries can be easily changed (material added or edited out), they require the exact date of viewing or access.

"Superhero in the Alley." *Bones*. Dir. James Whitmore Jr. Perf. Emily Deschanel and David Boreanaz. Fox. FOX10, Phoenix, 8 Feb. 2006. Television.

"Superhero in the Alley." *Bones*. Dir. James Whitmore Jr. Perf. Emily Deschanel and David Boreanaz. 20th Century Fox, 2006. iTunes. Web. 30 Aug. 2007.

Medium of publication.

"Superhero in the Alley." *Bones*. Dir. James Whitmore Jr. Perf. Emily Deschanel and David Boreanaz. 2006. 20th Century Fox, 2006. DVD.

Downloading from iTunes is similar to retrieving an article from a library database. You need the name of the database, medium of publication (Web), and access date.

Copyright date. In the DVD you have the copyright of the original episode as well as the DVD box set.

As stated earlier in this chapter, MLA includes the following basic information in citations:

1. Name of author

2. Title of text

3. Publication information (including publisher's name, place [city] of publication, and copyright date)

4. Medium of publication: Print, Web, CD, DVD, etc. (Additional information on resource may follow the medium of publication for certain resources.)

As you look at the MLA-40, MLA-41, and MLA-42 examples, notice the following form of the information for the television episode.

1. A television show doesn't specifically list an "author," so the first category you should recognize is the director and performers; however, instead of coming first, this information is listed after the "title."

2. The title includes the episode and the show.

3. The second category of information is the publication information, including the production company, the date of publication, and the medium of publication.

MLA does not provide a method for citing a resource downloaded from iTunes, but if you understand the patterns of MLA formatting, you can piece together a citation for that resource as well. The citation would need to include the access date and the URL (if needed), just like other electronic resources found in subscription databases (e.g., in the library).

Practice a Full Bibliographic Citation for Streamed Resources

…write….

Now many of the broadcast television stations are streaming episodes of television shows on their Internet Web sites. Fox is streaming *Bones* and has posted the "Superhero in the Alley" episode. With the information from the three citations in MLA-40, MLA-41, and MLA-42 and the following information, construct the MLA citation.

☐ Access date: January 24, 2008

☐ Web site name: Fox On Demand

☐ URL: http://www.fox.com/fod/player .htm?show=bones

 To view the answers to this exercise along with a discussion of how the citations are constructed, go to *Student Resources* on the online resource center at www.cengage.com/english/Miller-Cochran/WGTR.

MLA-43 Blog * Citation Elements: two or more works by the same author, blog, online, digital, single author

MLA-44 Specific Posting in a Blog * Citation Elements: two or more works by the same author, blog, online, digital, single author, entry or post

MLA-45 Comment on a Specific Posting in a Blog * Citation Elements: blog, online, digital, comment or reply, single author

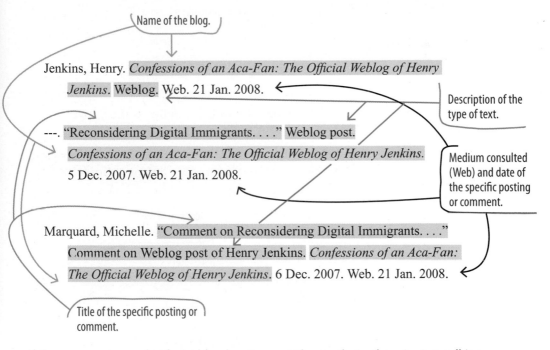

Name of the blog.

Jenkins, Henry. *Confessions of an Aca-Fan: The Official Weblog of Henry Jenkins*. Weblog. Web. 21 Jan. 2008.

Description of the type of text.

---. "Reconsidering Digital Immigrants. . . ." Weblog post. *Confessions of an Aca-Fan: The Official Weblog of Henry Jenkins*. 5 Dec. 2007. Web. 21 Jan. 2008.

Medium consulted (Web) and date of the specific posting or comment.

Marquard, Michelle. "Comment on Reconsidering Digital Immigrants. . . ." Comment on Weblog post of Henry Jenkins. *Confessions of an Aca-Fan: The Official Weblog of Henry Jenkins*. 6 Dec. 2007. Web. 21 Jan. 2008.

Title of the specific posting or comment.

If the comment or reply of a weblog has its own title, use that; otherwise just call it a "comment on" or "reply to" the title of the original blog posting.

MLA-46 Podcast * Citation Elements: podcast, online, electronic, single author, sound recording, digital

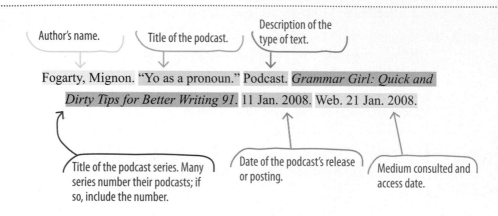

Author's name.

Title of the podcast.

Description of the type of text.

Fogarty, Mignon. "Yo as a pronoun." Podcast. *Grammar Girl: Quick and Dirty Tips for Better Writing 91*. 11 Jan. 2008. Web. 21 Jan. 2008.

Title of the podcast series. Many series number their podcasts; if so, include the number.

Date of the podcast's release or posting.

Medium consulted and access date.

MLA-47 Online Video * Citation Elements: single author, DVD/video, online, digital

MLA-48 Video Reply to an Online Video * Citation Elements: single author, DVD/video, comment or reply, online, digital

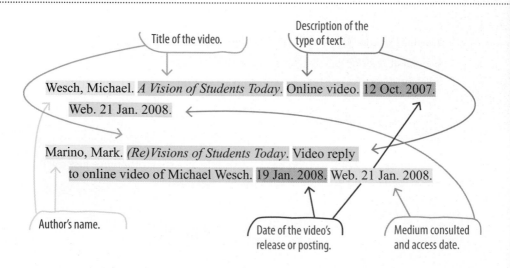

Title of the video.

Description of the type of text.

Wesch, Michael. *A Vision of Students Today*. Online video. 12 Oct. 2007. Web. 21 Jan. 2008.

Marino, Mark. *(Re)Visions of Students Today*. Video reply to online video of Michael Wesch. 19 Jan. 2008. Web. 21 Jan. 2008.

Author's name.

Date of the video's release or posting.

Medium consulted and access date.

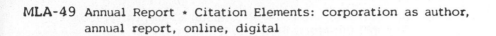

MLA-49 Annual Report * Citation Elements: corporation as author,
        annual report, online, digital

Company's name.   Name of the report.

Payless Shoe Source. *Inspiring Possibilities: 06 Annual Report.* 3 Apr. 2007.

    Web. 21 Jan. 2008. <http://www.annualreports/Click/6964>.

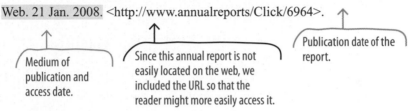

Medium of
publication and
access date.

Since this annual report is not
easily located on the web, we
included the URL so that the
reader might more easily access it.

Publication date of the
report.

Dynamic Resources

Since dynamic resources change regularly, it is very important to include the exact date
that you found, read, or interacted with the resource.

MLA-50 Page from a Wiki (dynamic) * Citation Elements: no
        author, Web page in a Web site, wiki, digital, online

The title of the page
within the wiki site.

The name of the wiki
Web site.

Last date the Web
page was updated.

"Tools and Platforms." *Handbook 700.* 19 Aug. 2007. Web. 18 Nov. 2007.

    <http://handbook700.wikispaces.com/Tools+and+Platforms>.

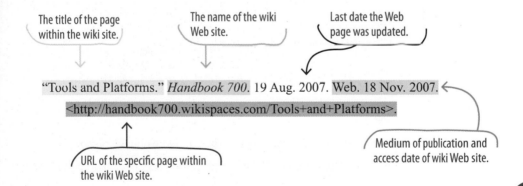

URL of the specific page within
the wiki Web site.

Medium of publication and
access date of wiki Web site.

For a resource that lists no author, start with the title. Most wiki pages have a "history" or "page history" link or tab that will allow you to see the last time the page was
updated.

MLA-51 Live Personal Interview * Citation Elements: personal interview, single author

Name of person you are interviewing.

Kind of interview (Personal interview, Telephone interview, etc.)

Saunders, Barry. Personal interview. 19 Oct. 2007.

Date of the interview.

Although a personal interview is considered primary research, MLA requires that you include an in-text and a full bibliographic citation to give readers the details of where and when you conducted the interview.

MLA-52 Public Address * Citation Elements: single author, lecture or public address, live performance

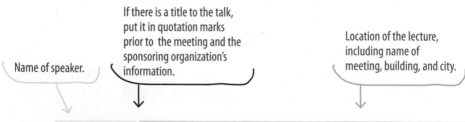

If there is a title to the talk, put it in quotation marks prior to the meeting and the sponsoring organization's information.

Name of speaker.

Location of the lecture, including name of meeting, building, and city.

Gilyard, Keith. National Council of Teachers of English Annual Convention. Marriott Marquis Times Square Hotel, New York. 16 Nov. 2007. Keynote speech.

Be sure to include an appropriate descriptive label (Address, Lecture, Keynote speech, Reading, etc.).

Date of address.

MLA-53 Lecture Notes * Citation Elements: single author, lecture notes

Author of the notes (not necessarily the person who delivered the lecture).

Title of the lecture.

Type of text.

Hellner, Nancy. "Three Waves of Feminism." Lecture notes. WST209: Women and Film. Mesa Community College, Mesa, AZ. 29 Aug. 2007. Print.

Name of the course that the lecture is from.

Date the notes were published (not necessarily the day of the lecture).

MLA-54 Dramatic Performance * Citation Elements: live performance

Title of the performance.

Playwright.

Director's and performers' names, like citation of a film or television show.

Vagina Monologues. By Eve Ensler. Dir. Felicia Davis. Perf. Malinda Williams, Nicole Ari Parker and Vanessa Williams. Herberger Theater, Phoenix. 26 April 2008. Performance.

Date of the performance and type of publication.

The site of performance (the name of the theater and the city it is located in).

MLA-55 Personal Letter ∗ Citation Elements: letter, single author

MLA-56 Email ∗ Citation Elements: online, digital, email, single author

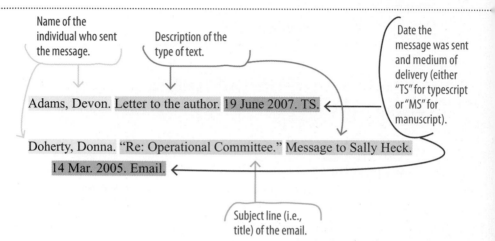

Name of the individual who sent the message.

Description of the type of text.

Date the message was sent and medium of delivery (either "TS" for typescript or "MS" for manuscript).

Adams, Devon. Letter to the author. 19 June 2007. TS.

Doherty, Donna. "Re: Operational Committee." Message to Sally Heck. 14 Mar. 2005. Email.

Subject line (i.e., title) of the email.

If the letter or email is published as a part of a larger work, then treat it like a section from a book.

MLA-57 Message Posted to a Discussion Group ∗ Citation Elements: discussion post, online, digital, single author

MLA-58 Wall Message on Facebook ∗ Citation Elements: discussion post, online, digital, single author

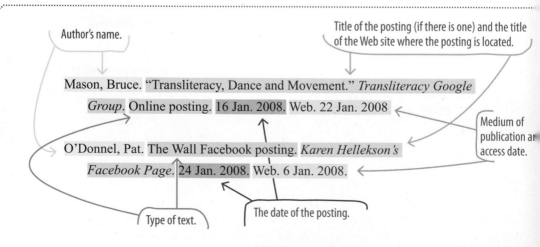

Author's name.

Title of the posting (if there is one) and the title of the Web site where the posting is located.

Mason, Bruce. "Transliteracy, Dance and Movement." *Transliteracy Google Group*. Online posting. 16 Jan. 2008. Web. 22 Jan. 2008

O'Donnel, Pat. The Wall Facebook posting. *Karen Hellekson's Facebook Page*. 24 Jan. 2008. Web. 6 Jan. 2008.

Medium of publication and access date.

Type of text.

The date of the posting.

Citing a post to a discussion group or board, listserv, or newsgroup is basically the same; you need an author, a title, a brief description of the type of text, the date of the original posting and then the typical online citation including date of access and Web address (if needed). A Facebook posting to a Wall and a friend's comments posted on MySpace are very similar to a discussion board posting; therefore, you emulate the citation style.

MLA-59 Hypertext Fiction * Citation Elements: single author, Web site, online, digital

MLA-59

Traditional citation information: author, title, and copyright year; however, notice there is no publisher (n.p.) in this instance.

Medium of publication and access date.

Malloy, Judy. *Revelations of Secret Surveillance*. N.p., 2004. Web. 18 Nov. 2007.

Although hypertext fiction does not change once it is posted (unless the author updates the Web site) the reading experience is different each time a reader moves though the work, selecting different pages in different order.

MLA-60 Video Game on MP3 Player (static) * Citation Elements: no author, video game, digital, edition

MLA-61 Massive Multiplayer Online Role Playing Game (MMORPG) (dynamic) * Citation Elements: no author, video game, digital, online

MLA-60, MLA-61

Version number; treat it as if it were a book edition or volume.

Name of the game.

Sudoku. Version 1.0.0. Video game for iPod. Redwood City: Electronic Arts, 2007. Game.

Brief description of the type of text.

The World of Warcraft: The Burning Crusade. Online video game. Irvine: Blizzard Entertainment, 2007. Web. 22 Jan. 2008 .

City of production company, name of production company, copyright year, and medium of publication.

Access date.

4 Formatting Your Research

MLA-62 Flickr Vision * Citation Elements: map or chart, online, digital, complete Web site, single author

Program designer.   Name of the program.   Brief description of the type of text.

Troy, David. *Flickrvision*. Google maps mash-up. 2007. Web. 22 Jan. 2008.

Copyright date.   Medium of publication and access date.

With the exponentially growing number of software applications, it becomes impossible to provide an example for every type of resource you might find. Therefore, it is up to you to carefully understand the reasoning of a style guide, note the patterns, and then construct the citation, as we did for the Google Map mash-up in example MLA-62.

^ reflect ^

MLA Style: Some Common Errors

☐ Only include the authors' last names in the in-text parenthetical citations.

☐ No commas or other punctuation should appear in the in-text parenthetical citation.

☐ Confusion between the publication, release, or copyright date and the date of access.

☐ Spelled-out names of months. Except for May, June, and July, all months are abbreviated.

☐ Omission of the name of the institution in the citation of a Web site hosted at an academic institution.

☐ Omission of a word or phrase that describes the type of a resource that is not a written document (medium or modality: DVD, weblog, podcast, film, etc.).

☐ Omission of the medium of publication, of delivery, of reception, etc.

For an example of a completed paper formatted in MLA style, see Example 1 in "Research in Progress: Writing a Researched Argument," beginning on page 228.

Figure 12.4 on pages 256–257 and Figure 12.5 on the next page demonstrate what a works cited page should look like using MLA style. ☐

Miller-Cochran 16

Works Cited

Bass, Frank. *The Associated Press Guide to Internet Research and
    Reporting*. Cambridge, MA: Perseus, 2001. Print.

Brockman, Amy S. "Student Research and the Internet."
    Communications of the ACM 48.1 (2005): 35-37. Print.

Evans, Ellen, and Jeanne Po. "A Break in the Transaction:
    Examining Students' Responses to Digital Texts." *Computers
    and Composition* 24.1 (2007): 56-73. Print.

Helms-Park, Rena, Pavlina Radia, and Paul Stapleton. "A
    Preliminary Assessment of Google Scholar as a Source of EAP
    Students' Research Materials." *Internet and Higher Education*
    10.1 (2007): 65-76. Print.

Hewson, Claire, Peter Yule, Dianna Laurent, and Carl Vogel.
    *Internet Research Methods: A Practical Guide for the Social
    and Behavioural Sciences*. Thousand Oaks: Sage, 2003. Print.

Hunt, Tiffany J., and Bud Hunt. "Research and Authority in an
    Online World: Who Knows? Who Decides?" *English Journal*
    95.1 (2006): 89-92. Print.

Kress, Gunther. "Gains and Losses: New Forms of Texts,
    Knowledge, and Learning." *Computers and Composition* 22.1
    (2005): 5-22. Print.

Lunsford, Andrea. "Writing, Technologies, and the Fifth Canon."
    Computers and Composition 23.2 (2006): 169-77. Print.

Tardy, Christine. "Expressions of Disciplinarity and Individuality
    in a Multimodal Genre." *Computers and Composition* 22.3
    (2005): 319-36. Print.

Walker, Billie E. "Google No More: A Model for Successful
    Research." *Teaching Professor* 20.1 (2006): 1-4. Print.

4 Formatting Your Research

APA Citation Style Guidelines

T he *Publication Manual of the American Psychological Association* (APA) is the official style guide of the American Psychological Association. Obviously, the APA's style guidelines apply to those studying psychology; however, APA style is also used in many disciplines that deal with social sciences. APA style is most appropriate to use when writing about topics related to disciplines such as psychology, justice studies, education, linguistics, and sociology. However, many of these disciplines have their own citation styles as well, like those of the Linguistic Society of America and the American Sociological Society.

The scholars who developed APA style emphasize current data. And that preference makes sense; shouldn't a psychologist treating someone be working from the most current information? Therefore, the APA citation style gives the author's name and the copyright date of the text first in a citation. Both pieces of information appear in in-text citations as well as on the references page, which is the APA name for the list of sources at the end of the paper. ▢ However, with the proliferation of resources on the Internet as well as the variety of databases libraries can subscribe to, it is important to include the specific publication information for every resource you work with. For example, if one of your professors gave you a copy of an article about computers and education that led you to an electronic book found online, your citation for the ebook would look like this:

For more information on in-text citations and tracking resources for a references list, regardless of citation style, see Chapter 7.

APA-1 Book Found on Internet (static) ∗ Citation Elements: book, single author, digital, online

APA-1

Information about the core text: author, copyright date, and title. Notice APA does not include author's first name nor capitalize all words in the title.

Tapscott, D. (1997). *Growing up digital: The rise of the net generation.* New York: McGraw-Hill. Retrieved December 31, 2007, from ebrary database.

Print publication information.

Digital access information that includes an access date as well as the location.

Paper Formatting

The APA style guidelines specify details for formatting papers, but they also include details for preparing and submitting various types of articles for publication. Check with your instructor to see if he or she wants you to follow all of the APA guidelines.

Title Page

APA style requires a title page (see Figure 13.1). Centered, and in the middle of the page, you need to include:

- the paper's title
- your name
- your institutional affiliation

APA style also requires running headers that are shortened versions of the title. You introduce this "running head" in the upper left corner of the title page as well as in the upper right corner with the page number.

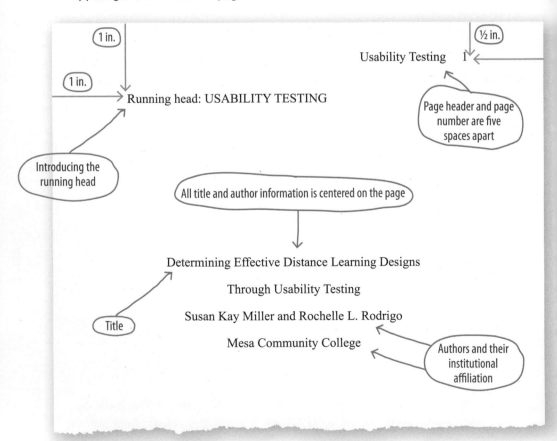

Figure 13.1   A Title Page in APA Style.

Spacing and Margins

APA style requires that you double-space the entire document, including title page information (see Figure 13.1), quotations, and the list of references. You do not need to include extra spaces (i.e., quadruple space) anywhere in the text. Set your top, left, right, and bottom margins for one inch. All paragraphs should be indented by one-half inch.

Headers and Page Numbers

In the upper right corner of each page, include the same page header that was introduced on the title page, with the page number spaced five spaces to the left of the header (Figure 13.1). All pages in the paper should be consecutively numbered (the title page is page 1). The header is placed one-half inch from the top of the page and one inch from the right side of the page on all subsequent pages of the manuscript just like on the title page.

Section Headings

If your paper is long enough and it includes coherent sections, and even subsections, you might consider including section headings in your paper. APA prescribes specific guidelines for section headings. If you have two levels of headings, center the first or highest level, and then format the second level flush left and in italics (see the following example). Make sure that all section titles are syntactically parallel. In other words, if you start your first section title with a noun, start all of your section titles with nouns. For example, the following outline could represent section headings from a paper in APA style.

Technological Advancements

Advancements in Visual Technologies

Advancements in Production and Distribution

Advancements in Interactive Technologies

Narrative Structure

Ideological Differences

Hollywood's Enterprises

Vertical Integration

Further Economic Trends

Conclusions

If you are using more layers or levels of headings, refer to the *Publication Manual of the American Psychological Association*. APA provides guidelines for up to five levels of headings.

Visuals

APA style divides visuals into two categories: tables and figures. Whenever you place visuals into your text, you must place them as close as possible to the paragraph referring to them.

Tables   If you are presenting numerical data in a table format, you should label the table with the word *Table*, an Arabic numeral, and a title. The label and title are placed on top of the table as it appears in your text. If you are reprinting the table from an outside source, you must include the full bibliographic citation for the table directly under the table (not at the end of your paper in the list of references).

Table 5

Instructors' Responses to Question 1[1]

	Presemester survey (level of emphasis on outcome during course)	Postsemester survey (student competence at end of course) Web-based	Postsemester survey (student competence at end of course) face-to-face
Laura	4	3	3
Ann	4	3	2

Figures APA style refers to all other types of visuals like charts, graphs, drawings, and images as figures. You should label each figure with the word *Figure* and an Arabic numeral in italics. The label and caption of a figure are placed below the visual as it appears in your text, along with a reference to the source of the figure if it came from an outside resource.

1. Adaption from Teaching at a Distance: Exploring Instructional Decisions and Learning Perceptions, by S.K. Miller, 2002, unpublished doctoral dissertation. Reproduced by permission of the author.

Indonesian Inflection Phrase   9

Mungkin saya bisa menolong anda?
Perhaps I can help you
"Might I be able to help you?"

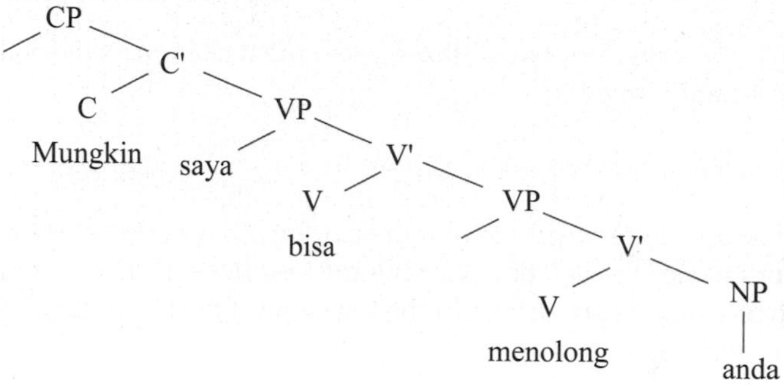

Figure 6. When mungkin is in the C position, the modal cannot move there.

This structural evidence indicates that modals in Indonesian reside in the V position, and that Indonesian contains only root but not epistemic modals. Indonesian does have a specific order for auxiliaries, however, and that makes the complete dismissal of the IP problematic.

Figure 13.2   A Figure in a Paper Using APA Style.[2]

Figure 13.2 shows an example of an APA style figure. In this linguistics paper about how specific words function in a sentence, it is critical to provide sentence diagrams to show how the words work in a sentence. The figure helps the reader to understand the argument being made in the text.

For more information on when to cite sources in-text, what to include in your list of references, and other documentation-related questions that are not specific to APA format, see Chapter 7.

Citation Guidelines

In this section, you will find explanations and examples of how to cite resources that you might use in your research, both in the text of your work (in-text citations) and at the end of your research (references list). ▢

In-Text Citations

You must include an in-text citation in every sentence that includes information from an outside resource. Even if you are only summarizing or paraphrasing the resource, you must include an in-text citation in the same sentence in which you present the

2. Adapted from Heck, S.K. (1999). "Does Indonesian Have an Inflection Phrase?" In Arizona State University Working Papers in Language 1. Reproduced by permission of the author.

material. APA in-text citations require the author's name, the copyright or publication date, and, if you are including a paraphrase or direct quote, a page number with the lowercase letter "p" and a period.

Quotations and Paraphrases   Standard in-text citations in APA format include the author's name, the date, and the page number in the citation.

> Science fiction films "self-consciously foreground their own radicality" of special effects (Freedman, 1997, p. 307).

If the resource was written by two authors, your in-text citation includes the names of both authors, connected by "&."

> (Miller-Cochran & Rodrigo, 2009, p. 294).

If the resource was written by three or more authors, your in-text citation will include all the author's names the first time you cite the resource and any subsequent in-text citations can be shortened by using just the last name of the first author followed by "et al." (which in Latin means "and others").

> (Westman, Linton, Ahrik, Wahlen, & Leppert, 2007, p. 647).
> (Westman et al., 2007, p. 647).

When incorporating short quotations or paraphrases, you can include some of the bibliographic information in the sentence itself. This strategy can be a way to emphasize the name of the author you are citing, highlight the date in which the resource was originally published, or vary the sentence structure in your writing. If you choose to mention the author's name in the sentence, include the copyright or publication date right after the author's name in a set of parentheses. If the author's name and the date are already mentioned in the sentence, you only need to include the page number from which the information or quotation came in the in-text citation. The next example uses the same short quotation from Freedman's work and only needs to provide the page number where the quotation was found because Freedman's name and the date are included in the sentence itself:

> Freedman (1997) criticizes science fiction films for "self-consciously *foreground*[ing] their own radicality" of special effects (p. 307).

APA style calls for authors to be specific about identifying the location of direct quotations and paraphrases. Therefore, if you are citing from an electronic resource without page numbers, such as a Web page, APA requires that you identify the paragraph number your quotation comes from. To distinguish the citation from a normal page marker, introduce the paragraph number with either "para." or a paragraph symbol "¶."

> Introducing his blog posting about "live action" anime, Jenkins (2007) proclaims that this type of event could happen "only at MIT" (para. 1).

Long Quotations   In APA style, text quotations that will be longer than forty words need to be presented in a block quote. Instead of using quotation marks to identify the text being directly quoted, block quotes indent the material so that it stands out on the page. Quotations that are longer than four lines of your paper must be formatted as a block quote, which would be set-off one-half inch from the left margin (Figure 13.3). Because they are direct quotations, block quotes need an in-text citation that includes the author's name and the page number the quotation came from.

Summaries and Multiple Resources   If you are summarizing the main point of a resource and not referencing one particular part of the source, APA style only requires that you provide enough information in an in-text citation to get the reader to the full bibliographic citation in the reference list, which is usually just the author's last name

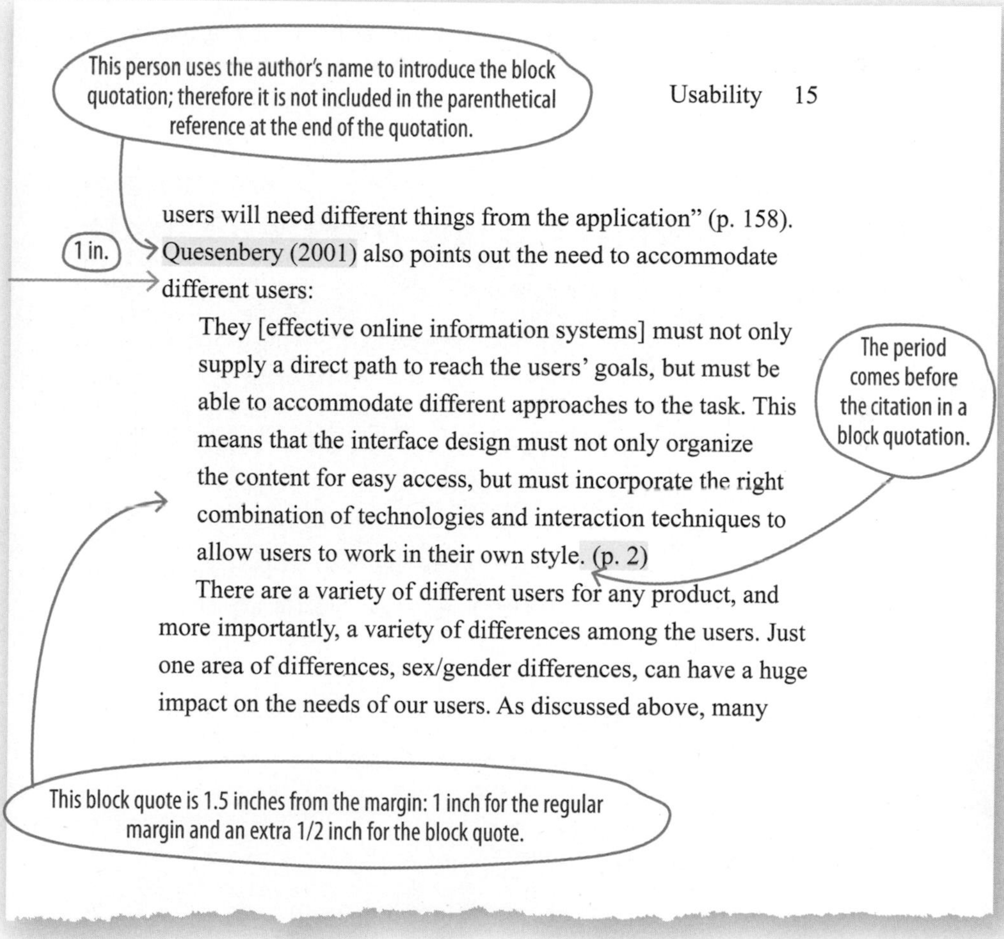

This person uses the author's name to introduce the block quotation; therefore it is not included in the parenthetical reference at the end of the quotation.

Usability   15

1 in.

users will need different things from the application" (p. 158). Quesenbery (2001) also points out the need to accommodate different users:

> They [effective online information systems] must not only supply a direct path to reach the users' goals, but must be able to accommodate different approaches to the task. This means that the interface design must not only organize the content for easy access, but must incorporate the right combination of technologies and interaction techniques to allow users to work in their own style. (p. 2)

There are a variety of different users for any product, and more importantly, a variety of differences among the users. Just one area of differences, sex/gender differences, can have a huge impact on the needs of our users. As discussed above, many

The period comes before the citation in a block quotation.

This block quote is 1.5 inches from the margin: 1 inch for the regular margin and an extra 1/2 inch for the block quote.

Figure 13.3   An Extended Quotation in APA Style[3]

3. Bowie, Jennifer. Beyond the Universal: The Universe of Users Approach to User-Centered Design. In Susan Miller-Cochran & Rochelle Rodrigo, (Eds.), Rhetorically Rethinking Usability. Cresskill, NJ: Hampton Press. Reproduced by permission.

4 Formatting Your Research

and the resource's copyright or publication date. In the following example, the writer briefly refers to multiple texts within the same sentence.

During the 1980s and early 1990s, *Computers and Composition* published many articles discussing methods and criteria for evaluating and choosing instructional software packages (Condon, 1992; Eiler, 1992; Hepler, 1992; Kemp, 1992; Redmond, Lawrence, & Villani, 1985; Taylor, 1992; Wahlstrom, 1985).[4]

Notice that the resources are listed in alphabetical order by the author's last name, not in numerical order by the publication date.

Electronic resources are cited in text in the same way as hard copy resources. If you have the name of the author, you include that information. If there is no author, you include a shortened title.

APA: In-Text Citation Nuts and Bolts

reflect

In APA format, typical in-text citations look like this:

(Author, date, p. number)

If no author is available, use an abbreviated version of the title of the source. The citation would look like this:

(Title, date, p. number)

If no page number is available (e.g., a digital resource), include the paragraph number instead. The citation would look like this:

(Author, date, para. number)

Or like this:

(Title, date, para. number)

---

4. Cahill, Lisa, & Rodrigo, Rochelle. Educational Usability in Online Writing Courses. In Susan Miller-Cochran & Rochelle Rodrigo, (Eds.), Rhetorically Rethinking Usability. Cresskill, NJ: Hampton Press. Reproduced by permission.

Practice In-Text Citations

Use the following sample paragraph, as well as the references list, to practice inserting in-text citations. First, identify where you need to include in-text citations; the sample paragraph contains direct quotes, paraphrases, and summaries. Second, insert the in-text citations where they are required. Be sure to include the appropriate information for each type of in-text citation.

 If you would like to complete this exercise online to more readily insert in-text citations and to check your answers, go to *Student Resources* on the online resource center at www.cengage.com/english/Miller-Cochran/WGTR.

Strauss concludes that "the moral is that unless we show faculty members how technology can meet their needs, they won't consider using it." While studying what community college faculty needed to incorporate technology into their instruction, Quick and Davies found faculty needed time, money, software, classroom computers (professor podium), department computer lab, and faculty technical support and training. In discussing how to prepare college faculty for the incoming net-generation of students, Clayton-Pedersen and O'Neill claim that "much of the learning technology innovation in higher education has been focused on K-12 teacher preparation and development" and that "more focus needs to be placed on preparing existing faculty for the future 'Net Generation students who will populate the twenty-first-century classroom." They continue that call for action in claiming that "faculty's understanding of the teaching and learning power of technology needs to be increased" and "tools need to be developed to help faculty integrate technology into the curriculum." Strauss, Quick and Davies, and Clayton-Pedersen and O'Neill demonstrate that faculty first need blatant introductions to the new technologies themselves: what they are and what they can do.[5]

References

APA-2 Ebook (static) * Citation Elements: Two authors, editors, online, book, digital, anthology/edited collection, section from a book

Clayton-Pedersen, A. R., & O'Neill, N. (2005). Curricula designed to meet 21st-century expectations. In D. G. Oblinger & J. L. Oblinger (Eds.), *Educating the net generation* (chap. 9). Washington, DC: Educause. Retrieved August 22, 2005, from http://www.educause.edu/ir/library/pdf/pub7101.pdf

5. Reproduced by permission of Rochelle Rodrigo.

APA-3 Journal with Continued Pagination (syndicated) * Citation Elements: two authors, journal (pages via volume)

Quick, D., & Davies, T. G. (1999). Community college faculty development: Bringing technology into instruction. *Community College Journal of Research and Practice, 23*, 641-653.

APA-4 Online Weekly Trade Magazine (syndicated) * Citation Elements: single author, online, digital, magazine (weekly or biweekly)

Strauss, H. (2005, June 24). Why many faculty members aren't excited about technology. *The Chronicle of Higher Education, 51*(42). Retrieved December 31, 2005, from http://chronicle.com/weekly/v51/i42/42b03001.htm

Full Bibliographic Citations

APA format requires the inclusion of a list of resources used in the paper, and this list is referred to as "references." This list includes only the names of resources cited in the paper, not resources that you found and read during your research process but did not include in the paper. The references page should start at the top of a new page in your essay; however, it will need to be included in your continuous page numbering. Subsequent references pages do not have a special heading but simply include APA-formatted page numbers. Entries in reference lists are presented in alphabetical order by the author's last name. If you have more than one text by the same author, alphabetize within those author entries by title of the text. If you have texts with no authors, incorporate them into the alphabetical list based on title.

Entries in a reference list should have a hanging indent, a format that looks a bit like an upside-down paragraph. The first line of the citation is left-justified, with no indent. Then all subsequent lines have a half-inch indentation. The examples in Figure 13.4 demonstrate how the hanging indent looks on the page.

Header with continuing pagination.

Usability   33

"References" centered, one inch from the top of the page.

References

APA-5 Section from a Book (static) * Citation Elements: single author, book, section from a book, editors, anthology or edited collection

Bias, R. G. (1994). The pluralistic usability walkthrough: Coordinated empathies. In J. Nielsen & R. L. Mack (Eds.), *Usability inspection methods* (pp. 63–76). New York: Wiley.

Bolter, J. D., & Gromala, D. (2003). *Windows and mirrors: Interaction design, digital art, and the myth of transparency.* Cambridge, MA: MIT Press.

All citations are double-spaced with hanging indent.

APA-6 Journal Article with Continued Pagination * Citation Elements: journal (pages via volume), single author, two or more works by the same author

Blythe, S. (1998). Wiring a usable center: Usability research and writing center practice. In Eric H. Hobson (Ed.), *Wiring the writing center* (pp. 103–116). Logan, UT: Utah State University Press.

Blythe, S. (2001). Designing online courses: User-centered practices. *Computers and Composition, 18*, 329–346.

Notice that multiple works by the same author are organized by year, not the title.

APA-5

APA-6

4 Formatting Your Research

Figure 13.4 The First Page of the References in APA Style.[6]

6. Bowie, Jennifer. Beyond the Universal: The Universe of Users Approach to User-Centered Design. In Susan Miller-Cochran & Rochelle Rodrigo, (Eds.), Rhetorically Rethinking Usability. Cresskill, NJ: Hampton Press. Reproduced by permission.

APA-7 Online Trade Magazine (static) * Citation Elements: two authors, magazine (weekly or biweekly), online, digital

Carnevale, D. (2000, October 6). Arizona plans to create a virtual university. *The Chronicle of Higher Education*. Retrieved January 14, 2001, from http://www .chronicle.com/weekly/v47/i06/06a04901.htm.

Figure 13.4 *Continued*

APA full bibliographic citation style generally provides information in the following order:

1. Name of author (only including initials for author's first and middle names)
2. Copyright or publication year (in parentheses)
3. Title of text (only the first word and proper names are capitalized)
4. Other publication information (usually including publisher's name and location)

For more explanation about static, syndicated, and dynamic resources, see Chapter 4.

Periods are included after each major section of information. For example, a period is included after the name of the author(s), the date, the title of the text, and the complete publication information.

The citation rules for static, periodic, and dynamic resources all follow this general pattern, but each category has some unique characteristics. □

techno_tip >

> Format a Document in APA Style <

If you are using a standard word-processing program to write your paper, you can use its features to write your paper with minimal formatting difficulty. Use the formatting choices to set the following options for your paper.

☐ Double-space your paper throughout. Set this option before you type any text so that your entire paper is double-spaced.

☐ Set your header to include the appropriate heading with your running header and page number. Word-processing programs can automatically insert the page number for you after the running head.

☐ On the references page, use the ruler at the top of the screen to set a hanging indent for your citations so that you don't have to hit "Enter" and "Tab" at the end of each line.

APA Citation Examples

 For more examples of APA citations, go to the online resource center at www.cengage.com/english/Miller-Cochran/WGTR.

Static Resources

Static resources (e.g., books, films, and government documents) are generally easy to cite using APA style.

APA-8 Book with Two Authors (static) ∗ Citation Elements: two authors, book

Notice all the authors' names are listed last name first and the first names are not included, only initials. Also notice the use of the "&" symbol instead of "and."

The copyright date is in parentheses with a period after the closing parenthesis.

Bolter, J. D., & Grusin, R. (1999). *Remediation: Understand-ing new media.* Cambridge, MA: MIT Press.

Title of text with only the first word capitalized. Be sure to include any subtitles; sometimes they are not found on the cover of the book but instead on the title page inside the book. Titles are italicized. You should capitalize the first word of the subtitle.

Publication information: Include the city and state where the publication company resides, followed by a colon, then the name of the publisher, followed by a period.

APA-9 Updated and Expanded Version of a Book ∗ Citation Elements: single author, book, edition

APA-10 Translated Book in a Multivolume Series ∗ Citation Elements: single author, translator, book, books in a series (multivolume)

Author's name and copyright year.

Friedman, T. L. (2006). *The world is flat: A brief history of the twenty-first century* (Updated and Expanded). New York: Farrar, Straus & Giroux.

Bazin, A. (1971). *What is cinema?* (Vol. 2, H. Gary, Trans.). Berkeley: University of California Press.

Title of the book.

Multivolume series information.

Name of the translator.

Publication information: city and publisher's name. When the state is included in the publisher's name, don't include it in the publication location.

When referring to books in multiple editions, use the language you find on the document's title page. Therefore, if it says second or third edition, put the numbers in your citation. If it says "Revised" or "Abridged" put "Rev. ed." or "Abr. ed." in the citation. Similarly, if your book is the fifth in a multivolume work, include "Vol. 5."

APA-11

APA-11 Article from an Edited Collection with an Author, Translator, and Editor * Citation Elements: anthology, single author, translator, editor, section in a book, republished

Author, publication date, and title of the article.

Translator's name (translated the essay, not the entire book).

Name of the anthology.

Heilig, M. (2001). The cinema of the future. (U. Feldman, Trans.). In R. Packer & K. Jordan (Eds.), *Multimedia: From Wagner to virtual reality* (pp. 239–251). New York: Norton. (Reprinted from *Presensce: Teleoperators and virtual environments,* 1(3), 1992)

Editors of the anthology.

Page numbers of the article in the anthology.

City of publisher and publisher's name.

APA-12

APA-12 Introduction to a Republished Book with a Translator * Citation Elements: single author, book, republished, translator, foreword

Author of the introduction.

If the introduction had a title different from "Introduction," you would then put the name of the introduction.

Baynes, W. E. C. (2003). Introduction. In N. Machiavelli, *The Prince* (R. Goodwin, Trans.), (pp. 13–25). Wellesley, MA: Dante University Press. (Original work published 1532)

The author of the book.

The title of the book.

The translator of the book.

The original publication date of the book.

The page numbers of the introduction.

Publisher's city, state, and name.

The citation styles for introductions, prefaces, forewords, and afterwords are basically the same. If you are citing information from one of these, include the title of the ancillary material or include a word that represents the material (i.e., preface, foreword, etc.) before the remainder of the book's citation.

APA-13

APA-13 Book in a Series ∗ Citation Elements: two authors, book, book in a series

Two authors, copyright date, and title of the book.

Name of the series.

Sullivan, P., & Porter, J. E. (1997). *Opening spaces: Writing tech-nologies and critical research practices*. In G. E. Hawisher & C. L. Selfe (Series Eds.), *New directions in computers and composi-tion studies*. Greenwich, CT: Ablex Publishing Corporation.

Series editors.

Publication information.

APA-14

APA-14 Online Annotated Sacred Text ∗ Citation Elements: book, online, digital, sacred text, no author, no date

Name of the sacred text. Treat this citation as if it were a book.

There is no copyright date provided for the material so it is represented with "n.d." in parentheses.

Cascading Bible. (n.d.) Retrieved January 21, 2008, from http://www .verselink.org

The URL of the Web site.

Date of accessing the information on the Internet.

4 Formatting Your Research

APA-15 Entry from a Dictionary ∗ Citation Elements: reference, no author

APA-16 Entry from an Online Dictionary ∗ Citation Elements: reference, online, digital, no author, no date

The title of the entry in the reference work. If the entry has an author, put the author's name first and then the date.

Eclecticism. (1993). *Webster's third new international dictionary of the English language unabridged.* Springfield, MA: Merriam-Webster.

Title of the reference resource.

Eclecticism. (n.d.) *Merriam-Webster online.* Retrieved January 21, 2008, from http://www.m-w.com

Copyright of the reference work.

Access date and URL of the Internet reference entry. For easily searchable reference material, you do not need to include the full URL of the Web page.

For reference resources (a dictionary, thesaurus, encyclopedia, etc.), you should include complete publication information, just as you would for a book or other online resource.

APA-17 Conference Proceedings * Citation Elements: conference proceedings, subscription database, digital, editor, two authors

APA-18 Paper Published in Conference Proceedings * Citation Elements: conference proceedings, section from a book, subscription database, digital, editor, single author

Editors of the proceedings.

Information about the conference that the proceedings come from.

Title of the proceedings.

VanTassel-Baska, J., & Stambaugh, T. (Eds.) (2007). Overlooked gems: A national perspective on low-income promising learners. *Proceedings of the National Leadership Conference on Low-Income Promising Learners*. Williamsburg, VA: National Association for Gifted Children and the Center for Gifted Education, College of William & Mary. Retrieved January 21, 2008, from http://www.eric.ed.gov (ERIC Document Reproduction Service No. ED494579)

Publication information of the proceedings.

Baldwin, Alexinia Y. (2007). Untapped potential for excellence. In VanTassel-Baska, J., & T. Stambaugh (Eds.), Overlooked gems: A national perspective on low-income promising learners. *Proceedings of the National Leadership Conference on Low-Income Promising Learners* (pp. 23-25). Williamsburg, VA: National Association for Gifted Children and the Center for Gifted Education, College of William & Mary. Retrieved January 21, 2008, from http://www.eric.ed.gov (ERIC Document Reproduction Service No. ED494579)

Information about the essay from within the proceedings: author's name, title, and page numbers.

ERIC is an education specific database that has subscription services as well as free online access. If an item or accession number is available, you can include it in your citation after the retrieval information.

APA treats *regularly published* conference proceedings as if they were periodicals. Most professional conferences occur yearly; therefore, if they have regularly printed proceedings, it would be considered a syndicated resource.

APA-19 Published Dissertation ∗ Citation Elements: dissertation or thesis, single author, subscription database, digital

> Author's name and copyright date.

> Title of the dissertation.

Todorovska, V. (2000). *E-mail as an emerging rhetorical space in the workplace.* Retrieved March 21, 2007 from ProQuest Digital Dissertations. (AAT 9965414)

> Most dissertations are published through UMI, which is now accessed through the electronic database by ProQuest. If you accessed the dissertation in this method, then you need to include the document's access number.

To cite an unpublished dissertation, include all of the information from the published dissertation up through the degree title. You then put "Unpublished doctoral dissertation" followed by a comma and the name and location of the degree-granting institution.

APA-20 White Paper ∗ Citation Elements: single author, white paper

> Author and date of the white paper.

> Title of the white paper. This particular title includes the quotation marks.

Bleed, R. (2004). *"Keeping up with technology" strategic conversation* (White paper). Maricopa Community College District, Tempe, AZ: Information Technology Services.

> Description of the resource.

> Location where the white paper was presented as well as the specific department or organization that produced it.

APA-21 Government Web Site * Citation Elements: government publication, online, Web page within a Web site, digital

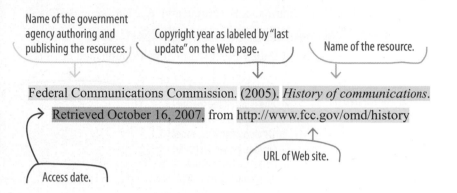

Name of the government agency authoring and publishing the resources.

Copyright year as labeled by "last update" on the Web page.

Name of the resource.

Federal Communications Commission. (2005). *History of communications.*
Retrieved October 16, 2007, from http://www.fcc.gov/omd/history

URL of Web site.

Access date.

Like government agencies, corporations can also author resources. Similarly to APA-21, you can put the corporation's name as the author of a resource (see APA-52 and APA-53).

APA-22 Film * Citation Element: Film

APA-23 Film in DVD Format * Citation Elements: Film, DVD/video, edition, digital

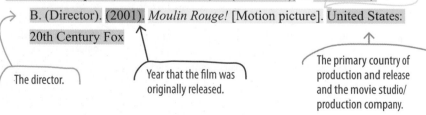

Title of the film. Notice that *Moulin Rouge!* has an exclamation point as a part of its title. You then include "Motion picture" in brackets after the title to identify the form of media.

The names of the individuals who have full producer status.

Baron, F., Knapman, C., & Luhrmann, B. (Producers), & Luhrmann,
B. (Director). (2001). *Moulin Rouge!* [Motion picture]. United States:
20th Century Fox

The director.

Year that the film was originally released.

The primary country of production and release and the movie studio/production company.

The producers' and directors' names and other production information are the same as previous entry.

Mode or media that the recording is published in (DVD, videocassette, HD, etc.)

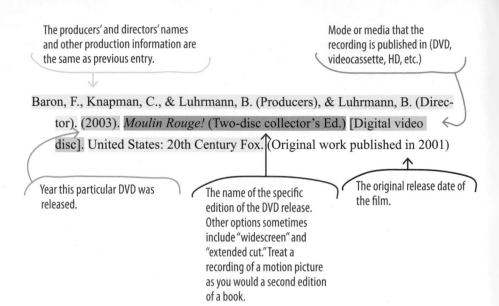

Baron, F., Knapman, C., & Luhrmann, B. (Producers), & Luhrmann, B. (Director). (2003). *Moulin Rouge!* (Two-disc collector's Ed.) [Digital video disc]. United States: 20th Century Fox. (Original work published in 2001)

Year this particular DVD was released.

The name of the specific edition of the DVD release. Other options sometimes include "widescreen" and "extended cut." Treat a recording of a motion picture as you would a second edition of a book.

The original release date of the film.

Consider using the Internet Movie Database (http://www.imdb.com/) to find the names of the producers, directors, and production/distribution companies.

APA-24 A Song from an Album ∗ Citation Elements: sound recording, three to six authors, musical composition, digital

Writers of the lyrics of the song. Notice you do not use the name of the band, in this case, *Deep Purple*.

Copyright year.

Name of the song.

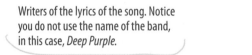

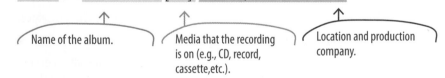

Gillan, I., Blackmore, R., Glover, R., Lord, J., & Paice, I. (1972). Space truckin. On *Machine Head* [CD]. Burbank, CA: Warner Bros.

Name of the album.

Media that the recording is on (e.g., CD, record, cassette, etc.).

Location and production company.

...write...

Practice Full Bibliographic Citations for Static Resources

What if you downloaded a song from iTunes or listened to it as it streamed from XM radio? Using the song information in APA-24, construct two citations with the following information. One citation will indicate that the song was downloaded from iTunes, the other will indicate that it was streamed from XM Satellite radio.

Citation 1

☐ Access date: October 3, 2007

☐ iTunes Store: http://www.apple.com/
itunes/store

Citation 2

☐ XM Radio: http://www.xmradio.com

☐ XM station 41, The Bone Yard

 To view the answers to this exercise along with a discussion of how the citations are constructed, go to *Student Resources* on the online resource center at www.cengage.com/english/Miller-Cochran/WGTR.

APA-25 Map Found on Flickr ∗ Citation Elements: map or chart, online, digital, corporation as author, no date

APA-25

Individual or organization
that produced the data.

Name and description
of the data.

GISuser. (n.d.) LIDAR map of New Orleans flooding from Hurricane Katrina. [map] Retrieved January 22, 2008, from http://www
.flickr.com/photos/gisuser/43339456

Access date and URL.

4 Formatting Your Research

APA-26 Published Interview from a Web site ∗ Citation Elements: published interview, online, Web page in a Web site, digital, single author

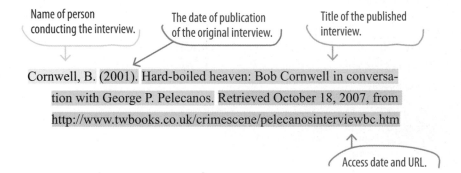

Name of person conducting the interview.

The date of publication of the original interview.

Title of the published interview.

Cornwell, B. (2001). Hard-boiled heaven: Bob Cornwell in conversation with George P. Pelecanos. Retrieved October 18, 2007, from http://www.twbooks.co.uk/crimescene/pelecanosinterviewbc.htm

Access date and URL.

If you conduct an interview, it is considered primary research and you do not include it in the reference list, but you would need to include an in-text citation, providing the first initials and last name of the interviewer, the terms "personal communication", and an exact date. For example: (S. Heck, personal communication, October 5, 2007).

Syndicated Resources

Syndicated resources are a little more complicated because there are usually multiple titles involved. Since many syndicated resources are now found in digital format, their citations are also complicated because they generally include layers of publication information as well. While in school, you will probably find a vast majority of syndicated resources in library databases. If the resource is in a subscription database, provide the homepage of the journal (preferably) or the name of the database you retrieved it from.

APA-27 Newspaper Article Found in a Library Database (syndicated) * Citation Elements: single author, newspaper, subscription database, digital

APA-28 Editorial Found at Newspaper's Web Site (syndicated) * Citation Elements: newspaper, digital, online, no author, editorial

The copyright date—when the article was published in the syndication.

Syndicated resources usually have two titles, the title of the individual text and the title of the syndication.

Access date.

Dutka, E. (2005, May 10). Hollywood caught up in the game: Better technology and a hot video-game market give studios and stars a lucrative movie tie-in. *Los Angeles Times*. Retrieved October 2, 2005, from LexisNexis Academic database.

When citing from a library database, APA style only requires that you include the name of the database.

Swirl, sniff, sip, check the price. (2008, January 19). *Los Angeles Times*. Retrieved January 2, 2008, from http:/www.latimes.com

If there is no author listed you just start with the title of the text you are citing.

When citing from a Web site, APA style requires that you include the date you accessed the material as well as the URL of the Web site. If the Web site is easily searchable, you may list the homepage URL.

APA-29 Journal Article with Continuous Pagination across the Volume ∗ Citation Elements: journal (pages via volume), single author, two or more works by the same author

APA-30 Article by the Same Author with Separate Pagination in Each Issue ∗ Citation Elements: journal (pages via issue), single author, two or more works by the same author

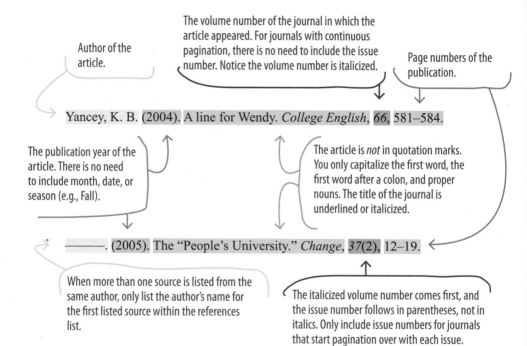

Some journals use continuous page numbers throughout all of the issues in a year, and other journals start each issue with page 1. Check several issues of journals you are citing to see which format they follow, and then use the appropriate format for your references list. However, when you are citing an electronic resource, include both the issue and volume numbers to help readers locate the resource faster. When months are included in a citation, APA style does not abbreviate the names of months.

If your reference list includes more than one entry by an author, you do not need to write the name of the author again (see APA-30). You will need to order the resources based on the publication dates with the earlier dates first.

APA-31 Article in a Monthly or Bimonthly Magazine Found Online *
       Citation Elements: magazine (monthly or bimonthly),
       online, digital, three to six authors

APA-32 Article in a Weekly or Biweekly Magazine Found in a Data-
       base * Citation Elements: magazine (weekly or biweekly),
       subscription database, digital, single author

APA-31, APA-32

Authors' names.

Page numbers.

Norris, D., Bear, L., Leonard, J., Pugliese, L., & Lafrere, P. (2008, January/
February). Action analytics: Measuring and improving performance that
matters in higher education. *Educause Review, 43,* 42–67. Retrieved January
21, 2008, from http://www.educause.edu/ir/library/pdf/ERM0813.pdf

Month, year, and date of the
weekly publications.

Access date and
URL.

Article title.

Magazine title.

Ponnuru, R. (2008, January 10). McCain's independent streak. *Time, 171,*
41. Retrieved January 21, 2008, from LexisNexis Academic.

Access date and the
name of the database.

Page numbers.

When you have four or more authors you can either type out all of their names (APA-31)
or only the first author's name followed by a comma and "et al." (Norris, D., et al.), which
is Latin for "and others." Be careful not to put a period after "et" because it is an entire
Latin word. The Latin abbreviation "al." (with a period) is an abbreviation for "alii" or "alia,"
which means "others."

APA-33 Article That Skips Pages in a Monthly or Bimonthly Magazine * Citation Elements: magazine (monthly or bimonthly), skipped pages, single author

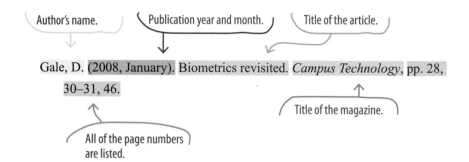

Author's name.

Publication year and month.

Title of the article.

Gale, D. (2008, January). Biometrics revisited. *Campus Technology*, pp. 28, 30–31, 46.

Title of the magazine.

All of the page numbers are listed.

When citing an article that skips pages, you may include the inclusive page numbers if they all run together.

APA-34 Article with a Quotation in the Title * Citation Elements: two authors, quotation in title, journal (pages via volume)

Authors' names and publication date.

Title of the article.

Kahne, J., & Bailey, K. (1999). The role of social capital in youth development: The case of "I have a dream" programs. *Educational Evaluation and Policy Analysis, 21,* 321–343.

Title of the journal.

Journal volume number in italics. Since there is continual pagination, there is no issue number.

The article's page numbers.

APA-35 Review of a Book in an Online Journal • Citation Elements: single author, review, journal, online

Author and copyright date.

Title of the review. When there is no title, leave the title out and continue the citation with the bracketed information.

Always include "Review of the book/film/video game/Web site/etc." and then include the title of the object under review. Notice you do not need to include the author of the text under review.

Drucker, J. (2007). Philosophy and digital humanities. [Review of the book *Humanities Computing*]. *Digital Humanities Quarterly 1*(1). Retrieved November 18, 2007, from http://www.digitalhumanities.org/dhq/vol/001/1/000001.html

Access date and URL.

Information about the journal publishing the review. An online journal has no pages; however, since it posts both volume and issues numbers, include both in your citation.

You can adapt the various journal and magazine article citations for online publications of the journals by just adding the access date and the Web address.

...write...

Practice Full Bibliographic Citations for Syndicated Resources

Using the following information, write a full bibliographic citation for a journal article found in a library's subscription database.

☐ Title: The Relationships Among Perceived Physician Accommodation, Perceived Outgroup Typicality, and Patient Inclinations Toward Compliance

☐ Authors: Christopher Hajek, Melinda Villagran, and Elaine Wittenberg-Lyles

☐ Journal information: Communication Research Reports, September 2007, Volume 24, Issue 4, pages 293–302, 10 pages, 2 charts

☐ Database information: Communication & Mass Media Complete (EbscoHost Research Databases), DOI: 10.1080/08824090701624189; (*AN 27009633*), http://www.ebscohost.com/thisTopic.php?topicID=56&marketID=1

☐ Access date: January 29, 2008

 To view the answers to this exercise along with a discussion of how the citations are constructed, go to *Student Resources* on the online resource center at www.cengage.com/english/Miller-Cochran/WGTR.

The following set of citations offers more examples to help you understand the conventions of APA formatting. The examples are all of the same text, an episode of the television show *Bones*, accessed in three different locations. All three examples have the same basic information about the text and then each has the specific information about when, where, and how it was accessed.

APA-36 Broadcast of Television Episode (syndicated) * Citation Elements: television, broadcast

APA-37 Television Episode Downloaded from iTunes (syndicated) * Citation Elements: television, subscription database, digital

APA-38 Episode from a DVD Season Box Set (static) * Citation Elements: television, DVD/video, digital

Notice that the core information about the individual episode remains the same. For an individual episode from a series, the writer and director are included.

Copyright date.

Benjamin, E. (Writer) & Whitmore, J. (Director). (2006). Superhero in the alley [Television series episode]. In H. Hanson, B. Josephson, & S. Nathan (Executive Producers), *Bones*. Phoenix, AZ: Fox.

Location where the show was broadcast.

Benjamin, E. (Writer) & Whitmore, J. (Director). (2006). Superhero in the alley. *Bones* [iTunes download]. Century City, CA: Twentieth Century Fox Film Corporation. Retrieved August 30, 2007, from http://www.apple.com/itunes/store

Since television broadcasts, Web pages, and database entries can be easily changed (material added or edited out), include the exact date of viewing or access.

Media type of the resource.

Benjamin, E. (Writer) & Whitmore, J. (Director). (2006). Superhero in the alley. *Bones* [DVD]. Century City, CA: 20th Century Fox.

Location of production company.

Although the production company is the same (as these are all citations for the same episode of a show), the name is formatted differently for each resource. Be sure to pay close attention to how names are formatted in/on the resources themselves.

APA includes the following basic information in citations:

1. Name of author

2. Title of text

3. Publication information (including publisher's name, place (city) of publication, and copyright date)

You can find these categories represented in the preceding examples. Notice the following form of the information for the television episode.

1. A television show doesn't specifically list an "author," so the first category you should recognize is the executive producers.

2. The title includes the episode and the show.

3. The second category of information is the publication information, including the production company and the date of publication.

The current *Publication Manual of the American Psychological Association* does not include an example from iTunes, but if you understand the patterns of APA formatting, you can piece together a citation for that resource as well. The citation would need to include the date of access and the URL, just like other electronic resources found in subscription databases (e.g., the library).

Practice a Full Bibliographic Citation for a Streamed Resource

Now many of the broadcast television stations are streaming episodes of television shows on their Internet Web sites. Fox is streaming *Bones* and has posted the "Superhero in the Alley" episode. With the information from the three citations in APA-36, APA-37, and APA-38 and the following information, construct the APA citation.

☐ Access date: January 24, 2008

☐ Web site name: Fox On Demand

☐ URL: http://www.fox.com/fod/player.htm?show=bones

 To view the answers to this exercise along with a discussion of how the citations are constructed, go to *Student Resources* on the online resource center at www.cengage.com/english/Miller-Cochran/WGTR.

...write...

4 Formatting Your Research

APA-39 Blog * Citation Elements: two or more works by the same author, blog, online, digital, single author

APA-40 Specific Posting in a Blog * Citation Elements: two or more works by the same author, blog, online, digital, single author

APA-41 Comment on a Specific Posting in a Blog * Citation Elements: blog, online, digital, comment or reply, single author, entry or post

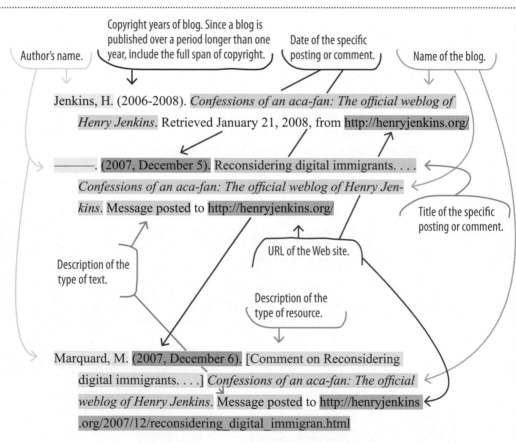

APA does not distinguish between citing an entire blog or a reply posted at a blog from a specific blog entry. If the comment or reply of a weblog has its own title, use that; otherwise, just call it a "comment on" or "reply to" the title of the original blog posting. Since blog and reply posting dates do not change, you do not need to put a retrieval date.

APA-42 Podcast ∗ Citation Elements: podcast, online, sound recording, single author, digital

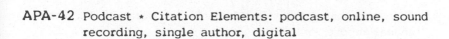

Producer's name.

Date of the podcast's release or posting.

Title of the podcast with the episode or show number.

Fogarty, M. (Producer). (2008, January 11). Yo as a pronoun [Episode 91]. *Grammar girl: Quick and dirty tips for better writing.* Podcast retrieved January 21, 2008, from http://grammar.quickanddirtytips.com/

Title of the podcast series. Many series number their podcasts.

Access date and URL.

APA-43 Online Video ∗ Citation Elements: single author, DVD/video, online, digital

APA-44 Video Reply to an Online Video ∗ Citation Elements: single author, DVD/video, comment or reply, online, digital

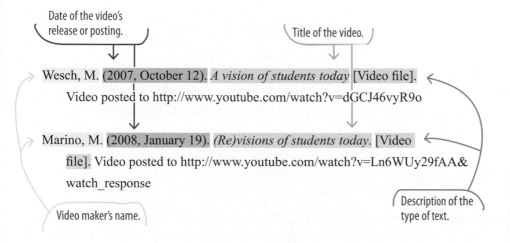

Date of the video's release or posting.

Title of the video.

Wesch, M. (2007, October 12). *A vision of students today* [Video file]. Video posted to http://www.youtube.com/watch?v=dGCJ46vyR9o

Marino, M. (2008, January 19). *(Re)visions of students today.* [Video file]. Video posted to http://www.youtube.com/watch?v=Ln6WUy29fAA& watch_response

Video maker's name.

Description of the type of text.

APA-45 Annual Report ∗ Citation Elements: corporation as author, annual report, online, digital

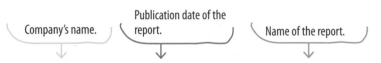

Company's name.   Publication date of the report.   Name of the report.

Payless Shoe Source. (2007). *Inspiring possibilities: 06 annual report.*
Retrieved April 3, 2007, from http://www.annualreports.com/Click/6964

Access date and URL.

Dynamic Resources

Since dynamic resources shift every time you use them, it is critical to cite the date you found, read, or interacted with the resource. APA considers a lot of dynamic resources as primary research (interviews, for example). The APA style calls for citation of the primary resources in the text of your document but not in the reference list.

APA-46 Page from a Wiki (dynamic) ∗ Citation Elements: no author, no date, Web page in a Web site, wiki, digital, online

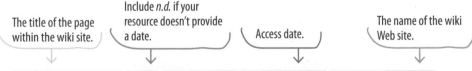

The title of the page within the wiki site.   Include *n.d.* if your resource doesn't provide a date.   Access date.   The name of the wiki Web site.

Tools and platforms. (n.d.). Retrieved November 18, 2007, from the Handbook 700 Wiki: http://handbook700.wikispaces.com/Tools+and+Platforms

The URL of the specific page within the wiki Web site.

Notice there is no author, nor any date. For a resource that lists no author, start with the title. The majority of the "no date" resources tend to be found on the Internet. You still need to include the date you accessed the resource.

APA-47 Public Address * Citation Elements: single author, lecture or public address, live performance

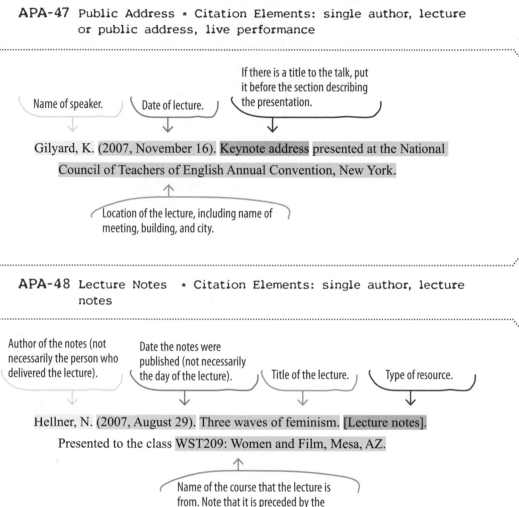

If there is a title to the talk, put it before the section describing the presentation.

Name of speaker.

Date of lecture.

Gilyard, K. (2007, November 16). Keynote address presented at the National Council of Teachers of English Annual Convention, New York.

Location of the lecture, including name of meeting, building, and city.

APA-48 Lecture Notes * Citation Elements: single author, lecture notes

Author of the notes (not necessarily the person who delivered the lecture).

Date the notes were published (not necessarily the day of the lecture).

Title of the lecture.

Type of resource.

Hellner, N. (2007, August 29). Three waves of feminism. [Lecture notes]. Presented to the class WST209: Women and Film, Mesa, AZ.

Name of the course that the lecture is from. Note that it is preceded by the descriptor "Presented to the class."

If the lecture notes were posted on the Web, you would cite them like a Web page.

APA-49 Message Posted to a Discussion Group ∗ Citation Elements: discussion post, online, digital, single author

APA-50 Wall Message on Facebook ∗ Citation Elements: discussion post, online, digital, single author

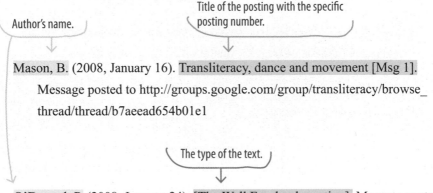

Author's name.

Title of the posting with the specific posting number.

Mason, B. (2008, January 16). Transliteracy, dance and movement [Msg 1]. Message posted to http://groups.google.com/group/transliteracy/browse_ thread/thread/b7aeead654b01e1

The type of the text.

O'Donnel, P. (2008, January 24). [The Wall Facebook posting]. Message posted to http://www.facebook.com/profile.php?id=1038375292&highlight

Citing a post to a discussion group or board, listserv, or newsgroup is basically the same; you need an author, the date of the original posting, a title, a brief description of the type of text, and the date of access and URL of the Web site. Notice that a Facebook posting to a Wall or a friend's comments posted on MySpace are very similar to a discussion board posting; therefore, you emulate that citation style.

APA-51 Hypertext Fiction ∗ Citation Elements: single author, Web site, online, digital

Traditional citation information: author, date and title.

Access date.

Malloy, J. (2004). *Revelations of secret surveillance*. Retrieved November 18, 2007, from http://www.well.com/user/jmalloy/gunterandgwen/titlepage.html

URL.

Although hypertext fiction does not change once it is posted (unless the author updates the Web site), the reading experience is different each time a reader moves though the work, selecting different pages in different order.

APA-52 Video Game on Cell Phone or MP3 Player (static) ★ Citation Elements: video game, digital, edition, corporation as author

APA-53 Massive Multiplayer Online Role Playing Game (MMORPG) (dynamic) ★ Citation Elements: video game, digital, online, corporation as author

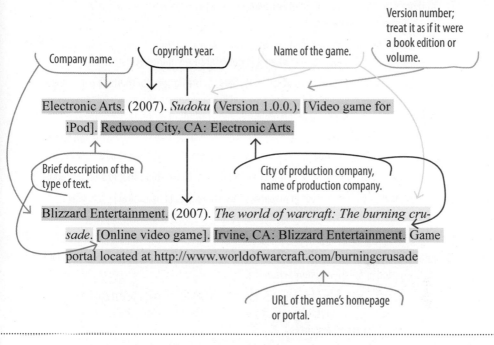

Version number; treat it as if it were a book edition or volume.

Company name.

Copyright year.

Name of the game.

Electronic Arts. (2007). *Sudoku* (Version 1.0.0.). [Video game for iPod]. Redwood City, CA: Electronic Arts.

Brief description of the type of text.

City of production company, name of production company.

Blizzard Entertainment. (2007). *The world of warcraft: The burning crusade*. [Online video game]. Irvine, CA: Blizzard Entertainment. Game portal located at http://www.worldofwarcraft.com/burningcrusade

URL of the game's homepage or portal.

APA-54 Flickr Vision ★ Citation Elements: map or chart, online, digital, complete Web site, single author

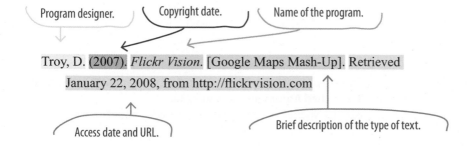

Program designer.

Copyright date.

Name of the program.

Troy, D. (2007). *Flickr Vision*. [Google Maps Mash-Up]. Retrieved January 22, 2008, from http://flickrvision.com

Access date and URL.

Brief description of the type of text.

With the exponentially growing number of software applications, it becomes impossible to provide an example for every type of resource you might find. Therefore, it is up to you to carefully understand the reasoning behind how a style guide works, note the patterns, and then construct the citation, as we did for the Google Map Mash-Up in example APA-54.

APA Style: Some Common Errors

☐ Authors' first and last names in the in-text parenthetical citations. You only need the last name in the in-text citation.

☐ Omission of publication year in the parenthetical in-text citation. Copyright year appears in the parenthetical in-text citation when it is not referenced in the text itself.

☐ "p" and "pp" inserted in citations of journals. These abbreviations for multiple pages appear only in the in-text citation of direct quotes and in magazine or newspaper full bibliographic citations. They do not appear in full bibliographic citations of journals.

☐ Omission of paragraph or Msg. number when quoting from Web sites or discussion boards. A paragraph or Msg. number is required in in-text citations for Web sites or discussion boards.

☐ Spelled-out author's first name in full bibliographic citations. There should be only initials.

☐ Capital letters on all key words in resource titles. There should be capital letters only for the first word in a title, the first word after a colon, and proper nouns.

☐ URLs in an in-text parenthetical citation; URLs never appear in in-text citations.

☐ Insertion of a period after the URL in a full bibliographic citation. URLs are never followed with a period in full bibliographic citations.

☐ Confusion between the publication, release, or copyright date and the date of access. Try to figure out which dates pertain to which situation and be sure to keep good records of when you accessed electronic resources.

☐ Abbreviated names of months. Months are always spelled out completely.

☐ Omission of a word or phrase that describes the type of resource that is not a written document (e.g., media or modality, DVD, weblog, Podcast, etc.). These descriptions are usually put in brackets ([and]).

For an example of a complete paper formatted in APA style, see Example 2 in "Research in Progress: Writing a Researched Argument," on page 236.

Figure 13.6 demonstrates what a complete references page should look like in APA style.

Online Research   16

References

Bass, F. (2001). *The Associated Press guide to internet research and reporting.* Cambridge, MA: Perseus.

Bruckman, A. S. (2005). Student research and the internet. *Communications of the ACM, 48*, 35–37.

Evans, E., & Po, J. (2007). A break in the transaction: Examining students' responses to digital texts. *Computers and Composition, 24*(1), 56–73.

Helms-Park, R., Radia, P., & Stapleton, P. (2007). A preliminary assessment of Google Scholar as a source of EAP students' research materials. *Internet and Higher Education, 10*, 65–76.

Hunt, T. J., & Hunt, B. (2006). Research and authority in an online world: Who knows? Who decides? *English Journal, 95*, 89–92.

Kress, G. (2005). Gains and losses: New forms of texts, knowledge, and learning. *Computers and Composition, 22*(1), 5–22.

Lunsford, A. (2006). Writing, technologies, and the fifth canon. *Computers and Composition, 23*(2), 169–177.

Tardy, C. (2005). Expressions of disciplinarity and individuality in a multi-modal genre. *Computers and Composition, 22*(3), 319–336.

Walker, B. E. (2006). Google no more: A model for successful research. *Teaching Professor, 20*, 1–4.

Figure 13.6   APA References Page.

4 Formatting Your Research

14

CMS Citation Style Guidelines

*T*he *Chicago Manual of Style* (CMS) is the official style guide of the University of Chicago Press, from whom the style takes its name. History is one of the disciplines that most often uses CMS guidelines; however, CMS is generally used by a large number of academic presses dealing with several disciplines. CMS has two basic citation systems that split themselves along disciplinary lines. The notes and bibliography system, which we focus on in this chapter, is primarily used by disciplines in the humanities and some social sciences, and the author-date system is primarily used by the sciences and other social sciences. The notes and bibliography system uses numbered footnotes for in-text citations at the bottom of the page or numbered endnotes for citations at the end of the chapter or article and then has a bibliography at the end of the document with complete publication information. The CMS author-date system resembles the APA's style for in-text citations and bibliographies. If you are interested in using CMS, especially the author-date system, consult the most current edition of *The Chicago Manual of Style* for any larger questions not addressed in this chapter.

If you are using the notes and bibliography system, you need to know how to cite a source in note format as well as how to cite the source as a bibliographic reference. All of the example citations in this chapter include a sample of the CMS footnote or endnote (which are numbered within the paper) as well as the full bibliographic entry that would appear at the end of the paper.

CMS-1 Electronic Book (static) * Citation Elements: book, single author, digital, subscription database

---

Information about the core text: author, and title.

Regular print publication and copyright information.

Complete Footnote

1. Don Tapscott, *Growing Up Digital, The Rise of the Net Generation* (New York: McGraw-Hill, 1997), http://www.ebrary.com/corp/index.jsp.

Complete Full Bibliographic Citation

Tapscott, Don. *Growing Up Digital: The Rise of the Net Generation.* New York: McGraw-Hill, 1997. http://www.ebrary.com/corp/index.jsp.

Include digital access information only for a resource that is likely to change. Electronic versions of books are not likely to change, so no access date is provided here. Notice CMS includes a period at the end of a URL.

Paper Formatting

CMS includes formatting guidelines that are specifically for formal manuscript prepara-tion and submission. In other words, the guidelines are primarily for academic writ-ing that is being submitted for publication in places like scholarly journals. The paper formatting guidelines here are based on Kate L. Turabian's *A Manual for Writers of Term Papers, Theses, and Dissertations* (7th ed. Chicago: University of Chicago Press, 2007), which provides formatting guidelines for college-level writing. Check with your instruc-tor to see if he or she wants you to use all of the following guidelines.

Title Page

The CMS guidelines for title pages are specifically for book manuscript preparation and submission. Turabian style is used for term papers, and it calls for the full title of the paper, the name of the author, the course title, the instructor's name, and the date. Information on the title page is in all caps and each line is centered.

Spacing and Margins

CMS requires that you double-space the entire document (see Figure 14.1 on page 332), including the footnotes or endnotes, quotations, and the bibliography at the end of the paper. You do not need to include extra spaces (i.e., quadruple space) anywhere in the text. Set your top, left, and bottom margins for at least one inch. All paragraphs should be indented by one-half inch.

Headers and Page Numbers

In the upper right corner of each page, you should include a running header with either a shortened version of your title or your last name and the page number (see Figure 14.1 on page 332). All pages in the paper should be consecutively numbered. The header is placed one-half inch from the top of the page and one inch from the right side of the page. You do not need to include the header and page number on the title page of your paper.

Section Headings

If your paper is long enough and it includes coherent sections, and even subsections, you might consider including section headings in your paper. Make sure that all of your section titles are parallel in both syntax and format. In other words, if you start your first section title with a noun, start all of your section titles with nouns. And if the first level of subheads is in bold type, all of the first-level subheads must be bold. If the second level of subheads is in italics, all of the second-level subheads must be in italics. For example, the following outline represents section headings from a paper using CMS.

Technological Advancements

Advancements in Visual Technologies

Advancements in Production and Distribution

Advancements in Interactive Technologies

Narrative Structure

Ideological Differences

Hollywood's Enterprises

Vertical Integration

Further Economic Trends

Conclusions

Visuals

CMS divides visuals into two categories: tables and figures. Whenever you place visuals in your text, you must place them as close as possible to the paragraph referring to them.

Tables   If you are presenting numerical data in a table format, you should label the table with the word *Table*, an Arabic number, and a title. The label and title are placed on top of the table as it appears in your text. Table titles should use an initial capital only. If you are reprinting the table from an outside source, you must include complete bibliographic information for the table directly under the table (not at the end of your paper in the bibliography).

Table 5 Instructors' responses to question 1[1]

Instructor	Presemester survey (level of emphasis on outcome during course)	Postsemester survey (student competence at end of course) Web-based	Postsemester survey (student competence at end of course) face-to-face
Laura	4	3	3
Ann	4	3	2

Figures   According to CMS, all other types of visuals, like charts, graphs, drawings, and images, are treated as figures. You should label each figure with the word *Figure* (or the abbreviation *Fig.*) and an Arabic number (see Figure 14.1). The label and caption of a figure are placed below the visual as it appears in your text, along with a reference to the source of the figure if it came from an outside resource.

---

1. Adaption from Teaching at a Distance: Exploring Instructional Decisions and Learning Perceptions, by S.K. Miller, 2002, unpublished doctoral dissertation. Reproduced by permission of the author.

Heck 9

Mungkin saya bisa menolong anda?

Perhaps I can help you

"Might I be able to help you?"

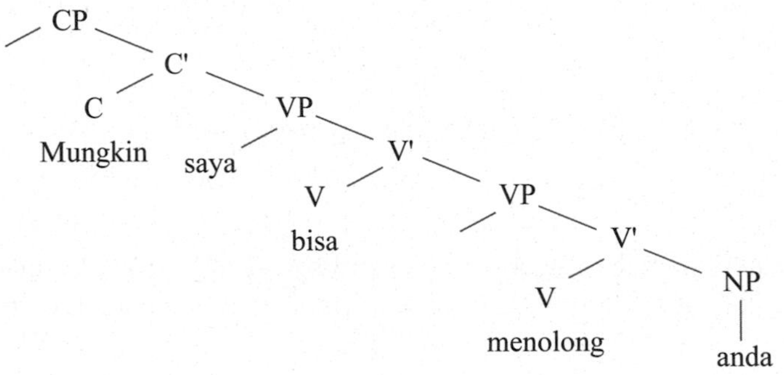

Figure 6. When *mungkin* is in the C position, the modal cannot move there.

This structural evidence indicates that modals in Indonesian reside in the V position, and that Indonesian contains only root but not epistemic modals. Indonesian does have a specific order for auxiliaries, however, and that makes the complete dismissal of the IP problematic.

Figure 14.1   A Figure in a CMS-Formatted Paper.[2]

In a linguistics paper about how specific words function in a sentence, it is critical to provide sentence diagrams to provide evidence of how the words work in a sentence. Figure 14.1 helps the reader to understand the argument being made in the text.

For more information on when to cite resources in text, what to include in your bibliography, and other documentation-related questions that are not specific to CMS format, see Chapter 7.

Citation Guidelines

In this section, you will find explanations and examples of how to cite resources that you might use in your research, both in the text of your work (in-text citations) and at the end of your research (bibliography). ▫

In-Text Citations

You must include an in-text citation in every sentence that includes information from an outside resource. Even if you are only summarizing or paraphrasing the resource, you must include an in-text citation in the same sentence in which you present the material. The in-text citation usually appears at the end of the sentence, but it could also appear at the end of a clause or after the mention of an author's name. CMS in-text citations require a superscript Arabic numeral in the text, which should follow any punctuation (except a dash) with no spacing before

2. Adapted from Heck, S.K. (1999). "Does Indonesian Have an Inflection Phrase?" In Arizona State University Working Papers in Language 1. Reproduced by permission of the author.

it. A corresponding footnote (or endnote) with the same number should appear at the bottom of the page (or the end of the chapter or article), containing the bibliographic information (Figure 14.2). If the paper includes a full bibliography (see Figure 14.3) at the end, the citations in the notes can be concise after the source has been introduced the first time with a full citation (author's name, resource's name, and page number if it is a direct quote); however, if there is no bibliography, the notes must include a full citation.

Lorie and Rodrigo 18

In *A Genealogy of Technical Culture: The Value of Convenience*, Thomas Tierney theorizes how technology functions as a way to overcome the temporal and spatial limits of the body, using technology to promote the Cartesian mind/body split and even overcome death.[1] Obviously in these shows the technologies begin to also overcome the emotional and mental limits of being human. These technofetishized scenes in the *CSI*s, *Bones*, and *ReGenesis* also reenact typical Mulvey[2] moments, with the close-ups of the technology standing in for the close-ups of female body parts; both objectifying, disavowing, and displacing dangerously emotional humanity. In many of these episodes female characters conduct the scientific analyses seeking the truth. The women who play these roles have their "Hollywood beautiful" bodies erased by the lab coat wardrobes they wear; nothing must distract the viewer from focusing on the beautiful infallible technology.

In the same 2000 article that Sawyer claimed science fiction will have to change, he also argued that "The days when you could tell the public that a microwave oven would replace the traditional stove are long gone; we all know that new technologies aren't going to live up to the hype."[3] Maybe Sawyer is focusing on the public that reads science fiction, because the "we" in this statement clearly are not the primary viewers of the various technofetishized murder/mystery dramas. In these shows the technologies do live up to the hype. They are not emotional fallible humans; they can remain "objective" to find "the truth" so that "justice" prevails.

———

[1] Thomas F. Tierney, *A Genealogy of Technical Culture.*
[2] Laura Mulvey, "Visual Pleasure and Narrative Cinema."
[3] Robert J. Sawyer, "The Profession of Science Fiction, 54: The Future Is Already Here," 11.

Figure 14.2 Superscript Numbers for In-Text Citations and Corresponding Numbered Footnotes using CMS. Shortened Notes Used In-Text with Full Bibliography at the End of the Paper.[3]

———

3. Rodrigo, Rochelle. "Technofetishized TV: CSI, Bones, and ReGenesis as Science Fiction Television?" FlowTV, vol. 7, Nov. 16, 2007 (http://flowtv.org/?p=946). Reproduced by permission of the author.

4 Formatting Your Research

CMS-2 Journal with Pagination by Issue (syndicated) ∗ Citation Elements: single author, journal (pages via issue)

CMS-3 Journal with Pagination by Volume (syndicated) ∗ Citation Elements: single author, journal (pages via volume)

CMS-4 Book (static) ∗ Citation Elements: single author, book

Lorie and Rodrigo 23

Bibliography

Mulvey, Laura. "Visual Pleasure and Narrative Cinema." *Screen* 16, no. 3 (1975): 6–18.

Sawyer, Robert J. "The Profession of Science Fiction, 54: The Future Is Already Here." *Foundation: The International Review of Science Fiction* 80 (2000): 5–18.

Tierney, Thomas F. *A Genealogy of Technical Culture: The Value of Convenience*. Albany: State University of New York Press, 1993.

Figure 14.3   Example of Bibliography Page in CMS Format.

Quotations and Paraphrases   Standard condensed notes in CMS format include the author's name, the title of the work, and if referring to a direct quote, the page or paragraph number of the material being cited. Use the condensed note style when you are just including the note to cite a text and will be including a full bibliography at the end of the paper. If you are not including a full bibliography at the end of the paper, make sure your notes include the complete citation information.

Quoted Text with Footnote Reference

Science fiction films "self-consciously foreground their own radicality" of special effects.[8]

Condensed Footnote

8. Carl Freedman, "Kubrick's *2001* and the Possibility of a Science-Fiction Cinema," 307.

CMS-5 Journal Article Paginated via Volume (syndicated) • Citation Elements: single author, journal (pages via volume)

Complete Footnote

8. Carl Freedman, "Kubrick's *2001* and the Possibility of a Science-Fiction Cinema," *Science-Fiction Studies* 25 (1998): 307.

Complete Full Bibliographic Citation

Freedman, Carl. "Kubrick's *2001* and the Possibility of a Science-Fiction Cinema." *Science-Fiction Studies* 25 (1998): 300–18.

When incorporating short quotations or paraphrases, you can include some of the bibliographic information in the sentence itself. This strategy can be a way to emphasize the name of the author you are citing, highlight the date in which the resource was originally published, or vary the sentence structure in your writing. You may also include this type of a discussion in the note itself. If your next in-text citation is of the same resource, you need to give it another note number; however, the note itself can say "ibid."

Quoted Text[4] with Footnote Reference

Science fiction films "self-consciously foreground their own radicality" of special effects.[8] However, it is Freedman's act of disavowing the overt display of technological prowess[9] that best exemplifies Bolter's and Grusin's concept of immediacy: "if immediacy is promoted by removing the programmer/creator from the image, it can also be promoted by involving the viewer more intimately in the image."[10]

Condensed Footnotes

8. Carl Freedman, "Kubrick's *2001* and the Possibility of a Science-Fiction Cinema," 307.

9. Ibid.

10. Jay David Bolter and Richard Grusin, *Remediation*, 28.

You should be as specific as possible about identifying the location of direct quotations and paraphrases. Therefore, if you are citing from an electronic resource without page

---

3. Rodrigo, Rochelle. "Technofetishized TV: CSI, Bones, and ReGenesis as Science Fiction Television?" FlowTV, vol. 7, Nov. 16, 2007 (http://flowtv.org/?p=946). Reproduced by permission of the author.

CMS-5

4 Formatting Your Research

numbers, like a Web page, CMS asks that you include in the note a "descriptive locator" such as a section subhead.

Quoted Text with Footnote Reference

Levine claims that the presentation software Slide "has a good library of templates, backgrounds, [and] effects."[32]

Condensed Footnote

32. Alan Levine, "The Fifty Tools," in the "Slideshow Tools" section.

Long Quotations   In CMS, text quotations longer than 100 words, or longer than eight lines, need to be presented in a block quote (Figure 14.4). Instead of using quotation marks to identify the text being directly quoted, block quotes indent the material one-half inch from the left margin so that it stands out on the page. Because they are direct quotations, block quotes need an in-text citation as well; therefore, they'll have a superscript number at the end of the quotation.

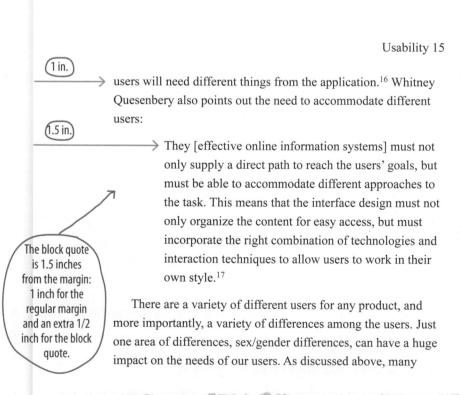

Usability 15

1 in.

users will need different things from the application.[16] Whitney Quesenbery also points out the need to accommodate different users:

1.5 in.

> They [effective online information systems] must not only supply a direct path to reach the users' goals, but must be able to accommodate different approaches to the task. This means that the interface design must not only organize the content for easy access, but must incorporate the right combination of technologies and interaction techniques to allow users to work in their own style.[17]

The block quote is 1.5 inches from the margin: 1 inch for the regular margin and an extra 1/2 inch for the block quote.

There are a variety of different users for any product, and more importantly, a variety of differences among the users. Just one area of differences, sex/gender differences, can have a huge impact on the needs of our users. As discussed above, many

Figure 14.4   An Extended Quotation in CMS Style.[5]

5. Bowie, Jennifer. Beyond the Universal: The Universe of Users Approach to User-Centered Design. In Susan Miller-Cochran & Rochelle Rodrigo, (Eds.), Rhetorically Rethinking Usability. Cresskill, NJ: Hampton Press. Reproduced by permission.

Summaries and Multiple Resources   If you are summarizing the main point of a resource and not referencing one particular part of the source, CMS only requires that you provide the superscript footnote number as the in-text citation and enough bibliographic information in the footnote to get the reader to the entry in the bibliography, which usually includes only the names of the author(s) and the resource. In the following example, the writer refers to multiple texts within the same sentence.

Text with Multiple Footnoted References

During the 1980s and early 1990s, *Computers and Composition* published many articles discussing methods and criteria for evaluating and choosing instructional software packages.[6]

Condensed Footnote

5. William Condon, "Selecting Computer Software for Writing Instruction"; Mary A. Eiler, "Perspectives on Software"; Molly Hepler, "Things to Consider When Evaluating Software"; Fred Kemp, "Who Programmed This?"; Claire Redmond, Cheryl Lawrence, and Frank Villani, "User-Friendly Software"; Paul Taylor, "Evaluating Software"; and Billie J. Wahlstrom, "What Does User-Friendly Mean Anyway?"[4]

Notice that the resources are listed in alphabetical order by the author's last name, the order in which they would appear in the bibliography.

Electronic resources are cited in the notes in the same way as hard copy resources. If you have the name of the author, include that information. If there is no author, include a shortened title.

CMS: In-Text Citation Nuts and Bolts

In CMS format, typical in-text citations include a superscript number that refers to a condensed footnote or endnote that looks like this:

> Number of in-text reference. Author, *Title* (in italics, may be a shortened version), page number (just the numeral itself).

If no author is available, use an abbreviated version of the title of the source. The notation would look like this:

> Number of in-text reference. *Title* (in italics, may be a shortened version), page number (just the numeral itself).

If no page number is available (e.g., a digital resource), include some textual marker like a subhead. The citation would look like this:

> Number of in-text reference. Author, *Title*, "Subhead".

> reflect <

4 Formatting Your Research

---

6. Cahill, Lisa, & Rodrigo, Rochelle. Educational Usability in Online Writing Courses. In Susan Miller-Cochran & Rochelle Rodrigo, (Eds.), Rhetorically Rethinking Usability. Cresskill, NJ: Hampton Press. Reproduced by permission.

Practice In-Text Citations

...write...

Use the following sample paragraph, as well as the bibliography, to practice inserting in-text citations and matching footnotes or endnotes. First, identify where you need to include in-text citations; the sample paragraph contains direct quotes, paraphrases, and summaries. Second, insert the in-text citations where they are required. Be sure to include the appropriate information for each type of in-text citation. Finally, write the appropriate footnote or endnote for the in-text citation.

 If you would like to complete this exercise online and to check your answers, go to *Student Resources* on the online resource center at www.cengage .com/english/Miller-Cochran/WGTR.

Strauss concludes that "the moral is that unless we show faculty members how technology can meet their needs, they won't consider using it." While studying what community college faculty needed to incorporate technology into their instruction, Quick and Davies found faculty needed time, money, software, classroom computers (professor podium), department computer lab, and faculty technical support and training. In discussing how to prepare college faculty for the incoming 'Net-generation of students Clayton-Pedersen and O'Neill claim that "much of the learning technology innovation in higher education has been focused on K-12 teacher preparation and development" and that "more focus needs to be placed on preparing existing faculty for the future 'Net Generation students who will populate the twenty-first-century classroom." They continue that call for action, claiming that "faculty's understanding of the teaching and learning power of technology needs to be increased" and "tools need to be developed to help faculty integrate technology into the curriculum." Strauss, Quick and Davies, and Clayton-Pedersen and O'Neill demonstrate that faculty first need blatant introductions to the new technologies themselves: what they are and what they can do.[7]

Bibliography

CMS-6 Ebook (static) ∗ Citation Elements: two authors, editors, online, book, digital, anthology/edited collection, section from a book

Clayton-Pedersen, Alma R., and Nancy O'Neill. "Curricula Designed to Meet 21st-Century Expectations." Chap. 9 in *Educating the Net Generation*. Edited by Diana G. Oblinger and James L. Oblinger. Washington, DC: Educause, 2005. http://www.educause .edu/ir/library/pdf/pub7101.pdf (accessed August 22, 2005).

CMS-6

7. Reproduced by permission of Rochelle Rodrigo.

CMS-7 Journal with Continued Pagination (syndicated) ∗ Citation Elements: two authors, journal (pages via volume)

Quick, Don, and Timothy Gray Davies. "Community College Faculty Development: Bringing Technology into Instruction." *Community College Journal of Research and Practice* 23 (1999): 641–653.

CMS-8 Online Weekly Trade Magazine (syndicated) ∗ Citation Elements: single author, online, digital, magazine (weekly or biweekly)

Strauss, Howard. "Why Many Faculty Members Aren't Excited about Technology." *The Chronicle of Higher Education*, June 24, 2005. http://chronicle.com/weekly/v51/i42/42b03001.htm (accessed December 31, 2005).

Full Bibliographic Citations

CMS format requires the inclusion of a list of resources used in the paper, and this list is referred to as the "bibliography." This list includes only the names of resources cited in the paper, not resources that you found and read during your research process but did not include in the paper. The bibliography page should start at the top of a new page in your essay, and it should also be included in your continuous page numbering. Subsequent bibliography pages do not have a special heading but simply include CMS-formatted page numbers. Entries in bibliographies are presented in alphabetical order by the author's last name. If you have more than one text by the same author, alphabetize those entries by title of the text, and include three dashed lines for the author's name in the subsequent entries (see CMS-29 and CMS-30). If you have texts with no authors, incorporate them into the alphabetical list based on title.

Entries in a bibliography should have a hanging indent, a format that looks a bit like an upside-down paragraph. The first line of the citation is left-justified, with no indent. Then all subsequent lines have a half-inch indentation. The examples in Figure 14.5 demonstrate how the hanging indent looks on the page.

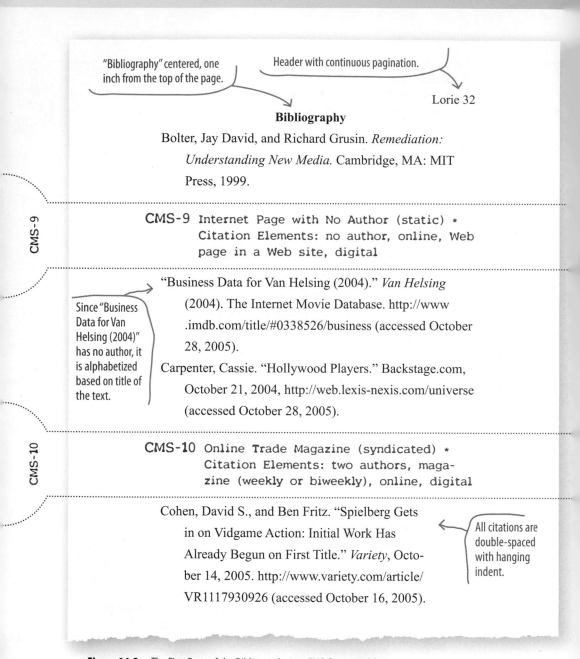

"Bibliography" centered, one inch from the top of the page.

Header with continuous pagination.

Lorie 32

Bibliography

Bolter, Jay David, and Richard Grusin. *Remediation: Understanding New Media.* Cambridge, MA: MIT Press, 1999.

CMS-9 Internet Page with No Author (static) *
Citation Elements: no author, online, Web
page in a Web site, digital

Since "Business Data for Van Helsing (2004)" has no author, it is alphabetized based on title of the text.

"Business Data for Van Helsing (2004)." *Van Helsing* (2004). The Internet Movie Database. http://www .imdb.com/title/#0338526/business (accessed October 28, 2005).

Carpenter, Cassie. "Hollywood Players." Backstage.com, October 21, 2004, http://web.lexis-nexis.com/universe (accessed October 28, 2005).

CMS-10 Online Trade Magazine (syndicated) *
Citation Elements: two authors, magazine (weekly or biweekly), online, digital

Cohen, David S., and Ben Fritz. "Spielberg Gets in on Vidgame Action: Initial Work Has Already Begun on First Title." *Variety*, October 14, 2005. http://www.variety.com/article/ VR1117930926 (accessed October 16, 2005).

All citations are double-spaced with hanging indent.

Figure 14.5 The First Page of the Bibliography in a CMS-Formatted Paper.

techno_tip >

> Format a Document in CMS <

If you are using a standard word-processing program to write your paper, you can use its features to write your paper with minimal formatting difficulty. Use the formatting choices to set the following options for your paper.

☐ Double-space your paper throughout. Set this option before you type any text so that your entire paper is double-spaced.

☐ Set your header to include the appropriate heading with your running header and page number. Word-processing programs can automatically insert the page number for you after the running head.

☐ On the bibliography page, use the ruler at the top of the screen to set a hanging indent for the entries so that you don't have to hit "Enter" and "Tab" at the end of each line.

CMS full bibliographic style generally provides information in the following order:

1. Name of author (spell out the entire name)

2. Title of resource (major words start with capital letters)

3. Publication information (usually including publisher's name and location and the copyright date)

Periods are included after each major section of information. For example, a period is included after the name of the author(s), after the text's title, and after the complete publication information. If there is *no author* for the text, start with the title of the text; however, remember that government agencies and corporations can function as authors. With various online resources you may have to look on other pages to find the name of the author.

Similarly, you may have to search online resources for the date of the last update (like the "history" page in wikis). If you can't find a date, or other publication information, you may use the following abbreviations.

For more explanation about static, syndicated, and dynamic resources, see Chapter 4.

☐ n.p.   No place of publication given

☐ n.d.   No date of publication given

The citation rules for static, syndicated, and dynamic resources all follow this general pattern, but each category has some unique characteristics. ▢

CMS Citation Examples

CMS Citation Examples

 For more examples of CMS citations, go to the online resource center at www.cengage.com/english/Miller-Cochran/WGTR.

Each citation example includes a sample for an extended footnote or endnote as well as a complete entry that you would include in the bibliography.

Dynamic Resources

Static Resources

Static resources (e.g., books, films, and government documents) are generally easy to cite using CMS format.

CMS-11 Book with Two Authors (static) ∗ Citation Elements: two authors, book

Name of author: Notice that in the footnote, both authors' names are listed first name first. In the full bibliographic entry, the first author's name is listed last name first and the second author's name is first name first.

Title of text: Be sure to include any subtitles; sometimes they are not found on the cover of the book but instead on the title page inside the book. Titles are italicized.

11. Jay David Bolter and Richard Grusin, *Remediation: Understanding New Media* (Cambridge, MA: MIT Press, 1999).

Bolter, Jay David, and Richard Grusin. *Remediation: Understanding New Media*. Cambridge, MA: MIT Press, 1999.

Publication information: Include the city where the publishing company is located, followed by a colon, then the name of the publisher, followed by a comma, and the copyright year. Include the state (using postal abbreviation) when the city could be confused with another city.

If there had been three authors, the citation would be similar, but with only the first author's name listed surname (last name) first, for example, "Story, Jonelle, Anne Kroening, and James Anderson."

CMS-12 Article from an Edited Collection with an Author, a Translator, and an Editor * Citation Elements: anthology or edited collection, single author, translator, editor, republished, section from a book

Author, title, and original publication date of the essay.

Translator's name. (Translated the essay, not the entire book.)

12. Morton Heilig, "The Cinema of the Future" (1955), trans. Uri Feldman, in *Multimedia: From Wagner to Virtual Reality*, ed. Randall Packer and Ken Jordan (New York: Norton, 2001), 239–251.

Heilig, Morton. "The Cinema of the Future," 1955. Translated by Uri Feldman. In *Multimedia: From Wagner to Virtual Reality*, edited by Randall Packer and Ken Jordan, 239–251. New York: Norton, 2001.

Name of the anthology.

Page numbers of the resource in the anthology.

Editors of the anthology.

City of publisher, publisher, and copyright year of the anthology.

CMS-13 Updated and Expanded Version of a Book * Citation Elements: single author, book, edition

CMS-14 Translated Book in a Multivolume Series * Citation Elements: single author, translator, book, books in a series (multivolume)

Author's name and title of the book.

Edition and multivolume series information. Notice the difference in capitalization.

13. Thomas L. Friedman, *The World Is Flat: A Brief History of the Twenty-First Century*, exp. ed. (New York: Farrar, Straus & Giroux, 2006).

Friedman, Thomas L. *The World Is Flat: A Brief History of the Twenty-First Century*, Exp. ed. New York: Farrar, Straus & Giroux, 2006.

14. André Bazin, *What Is Cinema?* vol. 2., trans. Hugh Gray (Berkeley: University of California Press, 1971).

Bazin, André. *What Is Cinema?* Vol. 2. Translated by Hugh Gary. Berkeley: University of California Press, 1971.

Publication information.

Translator's name.

When referring to books or other media in multiple editions, use the language you find on the document's title page. Therefore, if it says second or third edition, put the numbers in your citation. If it says "Revised" or "Abridged" put "Rev. ed." or "Abr. ed." in the citation. Similarly, if your book is the fifth in a multivolume work, include "Vol. 5."

CMS-15 Introduction to a Republished Book with a Translator *
Citation Elements: single author, book, republished, translator, foreword

This is the author of the introduction. The book only lists the author's initials; therefore, there is no first name in the citation.

If the introduction had a title different from "Introduction," you would first put the title of the introduction in quotation marks with a period as if it were a chapter in the book.

15. W. E. C. Baynes, introduction to *The Prince* (1532), by Niccolo Machiavelli, trans. Rufus Goodwin (Wellesley, MA: Dante University Press, 2003), 13–25.

The title of the book. If it is a reprint from the original, you may include the year of the original publication as well.

Baynes, W. E. C. "Introduction." In *The Prince* (1532), by Niccolo Machiavelli. Translated by Rufus Goodwin, 13–25. Wellesley, MA: Dante University Press, 2003.

The author of the book.

The page numbers of the introduction.

Publisher's city, name, and copyright year. If the city is not as well known, include the state (abbreviated) as well.

The translator of the book.

The citation styles for introductions, prefaces, forewords, and afterwords are basically the same. If you are citing from one of these, include the title of the ancillary material.

CMS-16 Book in a Series * Citation Elements: two authors, book, book in a series

Two authors and title of the book.

Name of the series.

16. Patricia Sullivan and James E. Porter, *Opening Spaces: Writing Technologies and Critical Research Practices*, New Directions in Computers and Composition Studies (Greenwich, CT: Ablex Publishing Corporation, 1997).

Sullivan, Patricia, and James E. Porter. *Opening Spaces: Writing Technologies and Critical Research Practices*. New Directions in Computers and Composition Studies. Greenwich, CT: Ablex Publishing Corporation, 1997.

Publication information.

CMS-17 Book with a **Title** within the **Title** and a Publisher's Imprint * Citation Elements: single author, book, a title in the title, publisher's imprint

The title of the film within the title of the book is put in quotation marks.

With a publisher's imprint, put the name of the publishing house first, then a comma, and then the name of the imprint.

17. Paul M. Sammon, *Future Noir: The Making of "Blade Runner"* (New York: HarperCollins, Harper Paperbacks, 1996).

Sammon, Paul M. *Future Noir: The Making of "Blade Runner."* New York: HarperCollins, Harper Paperbacks, 1996.

CMS-18 Online Annotated Sacred Text ∗ Citation Elements: online, digital, sacred text, no author, no date

Name of the sacred text.

URL of the Web site.

18. Isaiah. 38: 9–15 (King James Version), http://www.verselink.org/.

Cascading Bible. (King James Version). http://www.verselink.org/.

If the title does not indicate the version, place the name of the version after the title.

CMS does not generally include sacred texts in the bibliography. It only includes the appropriate citation information in the footnote or endnote. Since CMS-18 lists an electronic version of a sacred text with its own title (*Cascading Bible*), however, we demonstrated how you might construct the entry in the bibliography.

CMS-19 Entry from a Dictionary ∗ Citation Elements: reference, no author

CMS-20 Entry from an Online Dictionary ∗ Citation Elements: reference, online, digital, no author, no date

Title of the reference resource.

The title of the entry in the reference work.

"S.v." stands for *sub verbo*, meaning "under the word."

19. *Webster's Third New International Dictionary of the English Language Unabridged*, 3rd ed., s.v. "Eclecticism."

20. *Merriam-Webster OnLine*, s.v. "Eclecticism," http://www.m-w.com/dictionary/Eclecticism (accessed January 21, 2008).

URL of the Internet reference entry and access date.

You only need minimal publication information for the footnote or endnote if the reference resource (dictionary, thesaurus, encyclopedia, etc.) is well known, and then you do not need to include it in the bibliography. If the reference is not well known, include all bibliographic and publication information as for a book or other online resource.

CMS-21 Conference Proceedings * Citation Elements: conference proceedings, subscription database, digital, editor, two authors, book

Editors of the proceedings.

Publication information of the proceedings.

21. Joyce VanTassel-Baska and Tamra Stambaugh, eds., *Overlooked Gems: A National Perspective on Low-Income Promising Learners* (Williamsburg, VA: National Association for Gifted Children and the Center for Gifted Education, College of William & Mary, 2007), http://www.eric.ed.gov/ (accessed January 21, 2008).

VanTassel-Baska, Joyce, and Tamra Stambaugh, eds. *Overlooked Gems: A National Perspective on Low-Income Promising Learners.* Williamsburg, VA: National Association for Gifted Children and the Center for Gifted Education, College of William & Mary, 2007. http://www.eric.ed.gov/ (accessed January 21, 2008).

Title of the proceedings.

Database URL and access date.

CMS treats conference proceedings like books; therefore, if you are citing the entire proceedings (as in CMS-21), treat it like an edited book. If you are citing a particular section of the book, cite it as a work in an anthology or edited collection.

CMS-22 Published Dissertation * Citation Elements: dissertation or thesis, single author

Author's name.

Title of the dissertation in quotation marks.

22. Viktorija Todorovska, "E-mail as an Emerging Rhetorical Space in the Workplace" (PhD diss., Arizona State University, 2000).

Todorovska, Viktorija. "E-mail as an Emerging Rhetorical Space in the Workplace." PhD diss., Arizona State University, 2000.

Degree-granting information: type of document, name of institution, and year of graduation.

CMS-23

CMS-23 White Paper ∗ Citation Elements: single author, white paper

Author of the white paper.

Title of the white paper. The title includes the quotation marks.

23. Ron Bleed, "'Keeping Up with Technology' Strategic Conversation White Paper" (white paper, Maricopa Community College District, Tempe, AZ, 2004).

Bleed, Ron. "'Keeping Up with Technology' Strategic Conversation White Paper." White paper, Maricopa Community College District, Tempe, AZ, 2004.

Location where the white paper was presented.

Date the white paper was presented or published.

Description of the type of document or media.

CMS-24

CMS-24 Government Web site ∗ Citation Elements: government publication, online, Web page on a Web site, digital

Name of the government agency authoring and publishing the resources.

Name of the resource.

24. Federal Communications Commission, *History of Communications*, http://www.fcc.gov/omd/history (accessed October 16, 2007).

Federal Communications Commission. *History of Communications*. 2005. http://www.fcc.gov/omd/history (accessed October 16, 2007).

URL of the Web site.

Date of accessing the resource on the Internet.

Copyright year. If there is a publisher name, include that as well.

Like government agencies, corporations can also be listed as authors. Similarly to CMS-24, you can put the corporation's name as the author of a resource.

CMS-25 Film in DVD Format * Citation Elements: film, DVD/video, edition, digital

Title of the film. Notice that *Moulin Rouge!* has an exclamation point as a part of its title. Normally you would just put a period after the title.

The name of the specific edition of the DVD release. Other options sometimes include "widescreen" and "extended cut."

25. *Moulin Rouge!* two-disc collector's ed., DVD, directed by Baz Luhrmann (2001; Los Angeles: 20th Century Fox, 2003).

Year that the film was originally released.

Moulin Rouge! Two-disc collector's ed. DVD. Directed by Baz Luhrmann. 2001; Los Angeles: 20th Century Fox, 2003.

The director.

Production company, location, and copyright year of the DVD.

Mode or media that the recording is published in (DVD, videocassette, HD, etc.)

You only need to put the original copyright, or release, date of a film if you feel it is important information for the reader to know. Consider using the Internet Movie Database (http://www.imdb.com/) to find the names of the director and production/distribution companies if you cannot find them on the DVD packaging.

CMS-26 Map Found on Flickr * Citation Elements: map or chart, online, digital, corporation as author

Corporate or group author.

Name of the map.

26. GISuser, *LIDAR Map of New Orleans Flooding from Hurricane Katrina*, map, http://www.flickr.com/photos/gisuser/43339456/ (access January 22, 2008).

GISuser. *LIDAR Map of New Orleans Flooding from Hurricane Katrina*. Map. http://www.flickr.com/photos/gisuser/43339456/ (accessed January 22, 2008).

Name of the type of the text or media.

URL of the Web site and access date.

CMS-27 A Song from an Album · Citation Elements: sound recording, four or more authors, musical composition, digital

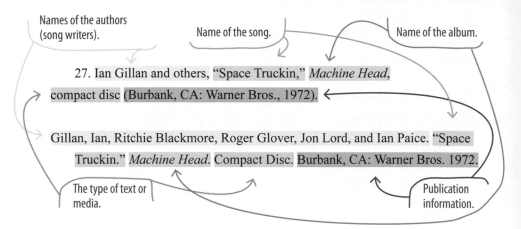

Names of the authors (song writers).

Name of the song.

Name of the album.

27. Ian Gillan and others, "Space Truckin," *Machine Head*, compact disc (Burbank, CA: Warner Bros., 1972).

Gillan, Ian, Ritchie Blackmore, Roger Glover, Jon Lord, and Ian Paice. "Space Truckin." *Machine Head*. Compact Disc. Burbank, CA: Warner Bros. 1972.

The type of text or media.

Publication information.

When there are four or more authors, you can condense the list of names in the note (as in CMS-27); however, be sure to include all the authors' names in the bibliography.

CMS also allows you to choose whether you list the performers or conductors of the music first as opposed to the composer or song writers. You should select which to list first based on the emphasis of your analysis in the paper.

...write...

Practice Full Bibliographic Citations for Static Resources

What if you downloaded a song from iTunes or listened to it as it streamed from XM radio? Using the song information in CMS-27, construct two citations with the following information. One citation will indicate that the song was downloaded from iTunes, the other will indicate that it was streamed from XM Satellite radio.

Citation 1

☐ Access date: October 3, 2007

☐ iTunes Store: http://www.apple.com/itunes/store

Citation 2

☐ XM Radio: http://www.xmradio.com

☐ XM station 41, The Bone Yard

> To view the answers to this exercise along with a discussion of how the citations are constructed, go to *Student Resources* on the online resource center at www.cengage.com/english/Miller-Cochran/WGTR.

CMS-28 Published Interview from a Web Site ∗ Citation Elements: published interview, online, Web page in a Web site, digital, single author

Person who was interviewed.

Title of the published interview.

28. George P. Pelecanos, "Hard-Boiled Heaven: Bob Cornwell in Conversation with George P. Pelecanos," by Bob Cornwell, *Tangled Web UK*, 2001, http://www.twbooks.co.uk/crimescene/pelecanosinterviewbc.htm (accessed October 18, 2007).

The person who conducted the interview.

This is the copyright date—the date of publication of the original interview.

Pelecanos, George P. "Hard-Boiled Heaven: Bob Cornwell in Conversation with George P. Pelecanos." By Bob Cornwell. *Tangled Web UK*, 2001. http://www.twbooks.co.uk/crimescene/pelecanosinterviewbc.htm (accessed October 18, 2007).

The Web site that published the interview, the URL, and access date.

Syndicated Resources

Syndicated resources are a little more complicated because multiple titles are often involved. Since many syndicated resources are now found in digital format, their citations are also complicated because they generally include layers of publication information as well. While in school, you will probably find a vast majority of syndicated resources searching in library databases.

Some journals use continuous page numbers throughout all of the issues in a year, and other journals start each issue with page 1. Check several issues of the journals you are citing to see which format they follow, and then use the appropriate format for your bibliography.

CMS-29 Journal Article with Continuous Pagination across the Volume ∗ Citation Elements: journal (pages via volume), single author, two or more works by the same author

CMS-30 Article by the Same Author with Separate Pagination in Each Issue ∗ Citation Elements: journal (pages via issue), single author, two or more works by the same author

Author of the article. Notice that in the second bibliography entry, the author's name is replaced by dashes if it appears after a citation by the same author.

The volume number of the journal in which the article appeared. For journals with continuous pagination, there is no need to include the issue number.

29. Kathleen Blake Yancey, "A Line for Wendy," *College English* 66 (2004): 581–584.

Page numbers of the publication.

Yancey, Kathleen Blake. "A Line for Wendy." *College English* 66 (2004): 581–584.

30. Kathleen Blake Yancey, "The 'People's University,'" *Change* 37, no. 2 (2005): 12–19.

———. "The 'People's University.'" *Change* 37, no. 2 (2005): 12–19.

The publication year of the article. There is no need to include month, date, or season (i.e., Fall).

The volume number comes first, and the issue number follows, separated by a comma and "no." Only include issue numbers for journals that start pagination over with each issue.

Syndicated resources usually have two titles, the title of the individual text and the title of the syndication. In CMS the title of the actual text is differentiated from the title of the syndication with quotation marks.

If your bibliography includes more than one entry by an author, you do not need to write the name of the author again (CMS-30). You will need to order the resources based on the alphabetical order of the titles, excluding any articles such as "The," "A," or "An."

CMS-31 Newspaper Article Found in a Library Database (syndicated) ∗ Citation Elements: single author, newspaper,
subscription database, digital

CMS-32 Editorial Found at Newspaper's Web Site ∗ Citation Elements: newspaper, digital, online, no author, editorial

This is the copyright date, the actual date the individual text was published in the syndication.

When citing from a library database, CMS requires that you include the general URL of the Web site to access the database and the date you accessed it.

31. Elaine Dutka, "Hollywood Caught up in the Game: Better Technology and a Hot Video-Game Market Give Studios and Stars a Lucrative Movie Tie-in," *Los Angeles Times,* May 10, 2005, http://web.lexisnexis.com/universe (accessed October 2, 2005).

Dutka, Elaine. "Hollywood Caught up in the Game: Better Technology and a Hot Video-Game Market Give Studios and Stars a Lucrative Movie Tie-in." *Los Angeles Times.* May 10, 2005. http://web.lexisnexis.com/universe (accessed October 2, 2005).

32. *Los Angeles Times,* "Swirl, Sniff, Sip, Check the Price," January 19, 2008, http://www.latimes.com/news/opinion/editorials/la-ed-wine19jan19,0,2045726.story?coll=la-news-comment-editorials (accessed January 22, 2008).

Los Angeles Times, "Swirl, Sniff, Sip, Check the Price." January 19, 2008. http://www.latimes.com/news/opinion/editorials/la-ed-wine19jan19,0,2045726.story?coll=la-news-comment-editorials (accessed January 22, 2008).

With unsigned articles, like editorials, the name of the newspaper is used as the author.

CMS-33 Article in a Monthly or Bimonthly Magazine Found Online ∗ Citation Elements: magazine (monthly or bimonthly), online, digital, four or more authors

CMS-34 Article in a Weekly or Biweekly Magazine Found in a Database ∗ Citation Elements: magazine (weekly or biweekly), subscription database, digital, single author

Authors' names. Notice with four or more authors you may use "and others" in the note but not in the full bibliographic citation.

Article title.

33. Donald M. Norris and others, "Action Analytics: Measuring and Improving Performance That Matters in Higher Education," *Educause Review*, January/February 2008, http://www.educause.edu/ir/library/pdf/ERM0813.pdf (accessed January 21, 2008).

Norris, Donald M., Linda Baer, Joan Leonard, Louis Pugliese, and Paul Lefrere. "Action Analytics: Measuring and Improving Performance That Matters in Higher Education." *Educause Review*, January/February 2008. http://www.educause.edu/ir/library/pdf/ERM0813.pdf (accessed January 21, 2008).

34. Ramesh Ponnuru, "McCain's Independent Streak," *Time*, January 21, 2008, http://academic.lexisnexis.com (accessed January 21, 2008).

Ponnuru, Ramesh. "McCain's Independent Streak." *Time*, January 21, 2008. http://academic.lexisnexis.com (accessed January 21, 2008).

Magazine title.

Month and year of monthly publications; month, year, and date of the weekly publications.

Database publication information: general URL of the database and access date.

CMS-35 Article That Skips Pages in a Monthly or Bimonthly Magazine * Citation Elements: single author, magazine (monthly or bimonthly), skipped pages

Author's name.

Title of the article and magazine.

Publication month and year.

35. Doug Gale, "Biometrics Revisited," *Campus Technology*, January 2008.

Gale, Doug. "Biometrics Revisited." *Campus Technology*, January 2008.

When citing an article that skips pages, you may include the inclusive page numbers; however, CMS recognizes the fact there are advertisements in magazines and doesn't require page numbers.

CMS-36 Article with a Quotation in the Title * Citation Elements: two authors, quotation in title, journal (pages via volume)

Title of the article and the journal. Because a quotation is included in the article title, single quotation marks are used.

Authors' names.

36. Joseph Kahne and Kim Bailey, "The Role of Social Capital in Youth Development: The Case of 'I Have a Dream' Programs," *Educational Evaluation and Policy Analysis* 21 (1999): 321–343.

The article's page numbers

Kahne, Joseph, and Kim Bailey. "The Role of Social Capital in Youth Development: The Case of 'I Have a Dream' Programs." *Educational Evaluation and Policy Analysis* 21 (1999): 321–343.

Journal name.

Journal volume number and publication date. Since there is continual pagination, there is no issue number.

CMS-37 Review of a Book in an Online Journal * Citation Elements: single author, review, journal (pages via issue), online, digital

Author of the review.

Title of the review. If there is no title, move on to the next section starting with "review of."

Always include "review of" and then include the title of the book, film, Web site, or other object under review.

37. Johanna Drucker, "Philosophy and Digital Humanities," review of *Humanities Computing*, by Willard McCarty, *Digital Humanities Quarterly* 1, no.1 (2007), http://www.digitalhumanities.org/dhq/vol/ 001/1/000001.html (accessed November 18, 2007).

Drucker, Johanna. "Philosophy and Digital Humanities." Review of *Humanities Computing*, by Willard McCarty. *Digital Humanities Quarterly* 1, no.1 (2007). http://www.digitalhumanities.org/dhq/vol/ 001/1/000001.html (accessed November 18, 2007).

Information about the journal publishing the review. Since an online journal has no pages you don't need to include page numbers; however, since it posts both volume and issue numbers, include both in your citation.

Author of the text under review.

Online reference information: URL of the Web site and access date.

You can adapt the various journal and magazine article citations for online publications of the journals by just adding the reference date and the Web address.

...write...

Practice Full Bibliographic Citations for Syndicated Resources

Using the following information, write a full bibliographic citation for a journal article found in a library's subscription database.

☐ Title: The Relationships Among Perceived Physician Accommodation, Perceived Outgroup Typicality, and Patient Inclinations Toward Compliance

☐ Authors: Christopher Hajek, Melinda Villagran, and Elaine Wittenberg-Lyles

☐ Journal information: Communication Research Reports, September 2007, Volume 24, Issue 4, pages 293–302, 10 pages, 2 charts

☐ Database information: Communication & Mass Media Complete (EbscoHost Research Databases), DOI: 10.1080/08824090701624189; (*AN 27009633*), http://www.ebscohost.com/thisTopic.php?topicID=56&marketID=1

☐ Access date: January 29, 2008

 To view the answers to this exercise along with a discussion of how the citations are constructed, go to *Student Resources* on the online resource center at www.cengage.com/english/Miller-Cochran/WGTR.

The following set of citations offers more examples to help you understand the conventions of CMS formatting. The examples are all of the same text, an episode of the television show *Bones*, accessed in three different locations. All three examples have the same basic information about the text, and then each has the specific information about when, where, and how it was accessed.

CMS-38 Broadcast of Television Episode (syndicated) * Citation Elements: television, broadcast

Notice that the core information about the individual episode remains the same.

Although the production company is the same (as these are all citations for the same episode of a show), the name is formatted differently on each resource. Be sure to pay close attention to how names are formatted in/on the resources themselves.

Since television broadcasts, Web pages, and database entries can be easily changed (material added or edited out), CMS guidelines suggest that the exact date of viewing or access be given.

38. "Superhero in the Alley," *Bones*, TV episode, directed by James Whitmore Jr., Fox, February 8, 2006.

"Superhero in the Alley." *Bones*. TV episode. Directed by James Whitmore Jr. Fox, February 8, 2006.

CMS-39 Television Episode Downloaded from iTunes (syndicated) * Citation Elements: television, subscription database, digital

CMS-40 Episode from a DVD Season Box Set (static) * Citation Elements: television, DVD/video, digital

Notice that the core information about the individual episode remains the same.

Although the production company is the same (as these are all citations for the same episode of a show), the name is formatted differently for each resource. Be sure to pay close attention to how names are formatted in/on the resources themselves.

39. "Superhero in the Alley," *Bones*, TV episode, directed by James Whitmore Jr. (Century City, CA: Twentieth Century Fox Film Corporation, 2006) http://www.apple.com/itunes/store (accessed August 30, 2007).

"Superhero in the Alley." *Bones*. TV episode. Directed by James Whitmore Jr. Century City, CA: Twentieth Century Fox Film Corporation, 2006. http://www.apple.com/itunes/store (accessed August 30, 2008).

40. "Superhero in the Alley," *Bones*, DVD, directed by James Whitmore Jr. (2006; Century City, CA: 20th Century Fox, 2006).

"Superhero in the Alley." *Bones*. DVD. Directed by James Whitmore Jr. 2006. Century City, CA: 20th Century Fox, 2006.

Format of the text or media.

Original release date of episode.

Copyright date.

Downloading something from iTunes is similar to retrieving an article from a library database. You need to include the database's URL and date of access.

CMS includes the following basic information in citations:

1. Name of author

2. Title of text

3. Publication information (including publisher's name, place (city) of publication, and copyright date)

You can find these categories represented in the CMS-38, CMS-39, and CMS-40 examples. Notice the following form of the information for the television episode.

1. A television show doesn't specifically list an "author," so the first person you should recognize is the director; this information is listed after the "title."

2. The title includes the episode and the show.

3. The second category of information is the publication information, including the production company and the date of publication.

The Chicago Manual of Style does not include an example for either television shows or iTunes, but if you understand the common patterns of CMS formatting, you can piece together a citation for all of these resources. The iTunes citation would need to include the date of access and the URL, just like other electronic resources found in subscription databases.

...write...

Practice a Full Bibliographic Citation for a Streamed Resource

Now many of the broadcast television stations are streaming episodes of television shows on their Internet Web sites. Fox is streaming *Bones* and has posted the "Superhero in the Alley" episode. With the information from the three citations in CMS-38, CMS-39, and CMS-40 and the following information, construct the CMS citation.

☐ Access date: January 24, 2008

☐ Web site name: Fox On Demand

☐ URL: http://www.fox.com/fod/player.htm?show=bones

 To view the answers to this exercise along with a discussion of how the citations are constructed, go to *Student Resources* on the online resource center at www.cengage.com/english/Miller-Cochran/WGTR.

4 Formatting Your Research

CMS-41 Blog ∗ Citation Elements: two or more works by the same author, blog, online, digital, single author

Name of the blog.

URL and access date.

41. Henry Jenkins, *Confessions of an Aca-Fan: The Official Weblog of Henry Jenkins*, http://henryjenkins.org (accessed January 21, 2008).

Jenkins, Henry. *Confessions of an Aca-Fan: The Official Weblog of Henry Jenkins.* http://henryjenkins.org (accessed January 21, 2008).

CMS-42 Specific Posting in a Blog ∗ Citation Elements: two or more works by the same author, blog, online, digital, single author

Name of the blog.

Title of the specific posting or comment.

42. Henry Jenkins, "Reconsidering Digital Immigrants. . . . ," *Confessions of an Aca-Fan: The Official Weblog of Henry Jenkins,* posted on December 5, 2007, http://henryjenkins.org/2008/01/last_time_i_offered_some.html (accessed January 21, 2008).

URL and access date.

Jenkins, Henry. "Reconsidering Digital Immigrants. . . ." *Confessions of an Aca-Fan: The Official Weblog of Henry Jenkins.* December 5, 2007. http://henryjenkins.org/2008/01/last_time_i_offered_some.html (accessed January 21, 2008).

Date of the specific posting or comment. Since CMS-41 isn't referring to a specific entry, no date is given.

CMS-43 Comment on a Specific Posting in a Blog ∗ Citation Elements: blog, online, digital, comment or reply, single author

Name of the blog.

Date of the specific posting or comment.

Title of the specific posting or comment.

43. Michelle Marquard, comment on "Reconsidering Digital Immigrants. . . .," *Confessions of an Aca-Fan: The Official Weblog of Henry Jenkins*, comment posted December 6, 2007, http://henryjenkins.org/2007/12/reconsidering_digital_immigran.html (accessed January 21, 2008).

URL and access date.

Marquard, Michelle. Comment on "Reconsidering Digital Immigrants. . . ." Confessions of an Aca-Fan: The Official Weblog of Henry Jenkins. December 6, 2007. http://henryjenkins.org/2007/12/reconsidering_digital_immigran.html (accessed January 21, 2008).

If the comment or reply of a blog has its own title, use that; otherwise, just call it a "comment on" or "reply to" the title of the original blog posting.

CMS-44 Podcast ∗ Citation Elements: podcast, online, sound recording, single author, digital

Title of the podcast episode.

Description of the type of text.

Title of the podcast series.

44. Mignon Fogarty, "Yo as a Pronoun," podcast, *Grammar Girl: Quick and Dirty Tips for Better Writing* 91, http://grammar.quickanddirtytips.com/grammar-yo-pronoun.aspx (accessed January 21, 2008).

Fogarty, Mignon. "Yo as a Pronoun." Podcast. *Grammar Girl: Quick and Dirty Tips for Better Writing* 91. http://grammar.quickanddirtytips.com/grammar-yo-pronoun.aspx (accessed January 21, 2008).

Episode number.

URL of the Web site and access date.

If the individual podcast episodes are numbered, treat the citation more like a journal. If the episodes only include release dates, treat the citation more like a magazine and put the date instead of the volume/issue number.

CMS-45 Online Video * Citation Elements: single author, DVD/video, online, digital

Author's name.

Title of the video.

Description of the type of text.

45. Michael Wesch, *A Vision of Students Today*, online video, posted October 12, 2007, http://www.youtube.com/watch?v=dGCJ46vyR9o (accessed January 21, 2008).

Wesch, Michael. *A Vision of Students Today*. Online video. October 12, 2007. http://www.youtube.com/watch?v=dGCJ46vyR9o (accessed January 21, 2008).

Date of the video's release or posting.

CMS-46 Video Reply to an Online Video * Citation Elements: single author, DVD/video, comment or reply, online, digital

Author's name.

Title of the video.

Description of the type of text.

46. Mark Marino, *(Re)Visions of Students Today*, video reply to online video *A Vision of Students Today*, by Michael Wesch, posted January 19, 2008, http://www.youtube.com/watch?v=Ln6WUy29fAA&watch_response (accessed January 21, 2008).

Marino, Mark. *(Re)Visions of Students Today*. Video reply to online video *A Vision of Students Today*, by Michael Wesch. January 19, 2008. http://www.youtube.com/watch?v=Ln6WUy29fAA&watch_response (accessed January 21, 2008).

Date of the video's release or posting.

Dynamic Resources

Since dynamic resources change regularly, it is very important to include the exact date that you accessed the resource.

CMS-47 Page from a Wiki (dynamic) ∗ Citation Elements: no author, Web page in a Web site, wiki, digital, online, no date

The title of the page within the wiki Web site.

The name of the wiki Web site.

Last date the Web page was updated. Check the wiki page's history.

47. "Tools and Platforms," *Handbook 700*, last updated August 19, 2007, http://handbook700.wikispaces.com/Tools+and+Platforms (accessed November 18, 2007).

"Tools and Platforms." *Handbook 700*. Last updated August 19, 2007. http://handbook700.wikispaces.com/Tools+and+Platforms (accessed November 18, 2007).

The URL of the specific page within the wiki Web site and access date.

Notice there is no author, nor any date for this resource. If your resource lists no author, then start with the title of the resource. Most wiki pages have a "history" or "page history" link or tab that will allow you to see the last time the page was updated.

CMS-48 Live Personal Interview ∗ Citation Elements: personal interview, single author

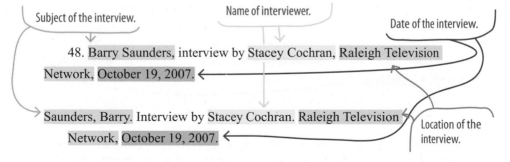

Subject of the interview.

Name of interviewer.

Date of the interview.

48. Barry Saunders, interview by Stacey Cochran, Raleigh Television Network, October 19, 2007.

Saunders, Barry. Interview by Stacey Cochran. Raleigh Television Network, October 19, 2007.

Location of the interview.

Since a personal, unpublished interview is considered primary research, CMS gives you the option of just mentioning it in your paper or including in-text and full bibliographic citations so that you may provide the details of where and when you conducted the interview.

CMS-49 Public Address * Citation Elements: single author, lecture or public address, live performance

Name of speaker.

Location of the lecture; both title of the event and city.

49. Keith Gilyard, keynote address, annual meeting of the National Council of Teachers of English Annual Convention, New York, November 16, 2007).

Gilyard, Keith. Keynote address, annual meeting of the National Council of Teachers of English Annual Convention. New York. November 16, 2007.

If there is a title to the lecture, put it in quotation marks prior to "keynote address."

Date of lecture.

CMS-50 Personal Letter * Citation Elements: letter, single author

CMS-51 Email * Citation Elements: online, digital, email, single author

Name of the individual who sent the message.

Description of the type of text.

Date the message was sent.

50. Devon Adams, letter to the author, June 19, 2007.

Subject line (i.e. title) of the email.

51. Donna Doherty, "Re: Operational Committee," email to Sally Heck, March 14, 2005.

CMS considers personal correspondence primary research; therefore, you would only include a reference in the footnote or endnote and not in the bibliography. Don't forget to get permission for citing someone else's work.

CMS-52 Message Posted to a Discussion Group ∗ Citation Elements: discussion post, online, digital, single author

Author's name.

Title of the posting.

The type of the text along with the specific name of the discussion or email group.

52. Bruce Mason, "Transliteracy, Dance and Movement," discussion group posting to Transliteracy Google Group, January 16, 2008, http://groups.google.com/group/transliteracy/browse_thread/thread/b7aeead6548b01e1 (accessed January 22, 2008).

Mason, Bruce. "Transliteracy, Dance and Movement." Discussion group posting to Transliteracy Google Group. January 16, 2008. http://groups.google.com/group/transliteracy/browse_thread/thread/b7aeead6548b01e1 (accessed January 22, 2008).

URL for the discussion group posting and access date.

The date of the posting.

CMS-53 Wall Message on Facebook ∗ Citation Elements: discussion post, online, digital, single author

Author's name.

URL for the discussion group posting and access date.

The type of the text along with the specific name of the discussion or email group.

53. Pat O'Donnel, posting on the Wall of Karen Hellekson's Facebook page, January 24, 2008, http://www.facebook.com/profile.php?id=1038375292&highlight (accessed January 26, 2008).

O'Donnel, Pat. Posting on the Wall of Karen Hellekson's Facebook page. January 24, 2008. http://www.facebook.com/profile.php?id=1038375292&highlight (accessed January 26, 2008).

The date of the posting.

Citing a post to a discussion group or board, listserv, or newsgroup is basically the same; you need to include an author, a title, a brief description of the type of text, the date of the original posting, and then the typical online citation including date of access and URL of the Web site. Notice a Facebook posting to a Wall or a friend's comments posted on MySpace are very similar to a discussion board posting; therefore, you emulate that citation style.

CMS-54 Video Game on MP3 Player (static) ∗ Citation Elements: video game, digital, edition

CMS-55 Massive Multiplayer Online Role Playing Game (MMORPG) (dynamic) ∗ Citation Elements: video game, digital, online

Name of the game.

Version number; treat it as if it were a book edition or volume.

Brief description of the type of text.

54. *Sudoku*, version 1.0.0, video game for iPod (Redwood City, CA: Electronic Arts, Inc., 2007).

Sudoku. Version 1.0.0. Video game for iPod. Redwood City, CA: Electronic Arts, Inc., 2007.

55. *The World of Warcraft: The Burning Crusade*, online video game, (Irvine, CA: Blizzard Entertainment, 2007) http://www.worldofwarcraft .com/burningcrusade/ (accessed January 22, 2008).

The World of Warcraft: The Burning Crusade. Online video game. Irvine, CA: Blizzard Entertainment, 2007. http://www.worldofwarcraft .com/burningcrusade/ (accessed January 22, 2008).

City of production company, name of production company, and copyright year.

URL and access date.

With the exponentially growing number of software applications, it becomes impossible to provide an example for every type of resource you might find. If you understand the principles of a particular style guide, though, you can construct citations as we did with the video game citations in examples CMS-54 and CMS-55.

> reflect <

CMS Citation Style: Some Common Errors

- ☐ Long notes. If you include a full bibliography at the end of the paper, notes only need minimal citation information (author's name, shortened name of the text, and a page number for a direct quote).

- ☐ The first name goes first in the author/date system; the author's last name is first in the footnote or endnote system.

- ☐ Periods separate elements in the author/date system; elements in the notes system should be separated by a comma.

- ☐ Confusion of publication or release and copyright dates.

- ☐ Abbreviated names of months; all month names should be spelled out entirely.

- ☐ Omission of a word or phrase that describes the type of resource that is not a written document (e.g., media or modality, DVD, weblog, podcast, etc.).

 For an example of a complete paper using CMS, go to *Sample Essays* on the online resource center at www.cengage.com/english/ Miller-Cochran/WGTR.

Figure 14.7 demonstrates what a complete bibliography page looks like using CMS.

Online Research 16

Bibliography

Bass, Frank. *The Associated Press Guide to Internet Research and Reporting.* Cambridge, MA: Perseus, 2001.

Bruckman, Amy S. "Student Research and the Internet."
Communications of the ACM 48 (2005): 35–37.

Evans, Ellen, and Jeanne Po. "A Break in the Transaction:
Examining Students' Responses to Digital Texts."
Computers & Composition 24 (2007): 56–73.

Helms-Park, Rena, Pavlina Radia, and Paul Stapleton.
A Preliminary Assessment of Google Scholar as
a Source of EAP Students' Research Materials.
Internet and Higher Education 10 (2007): 65–76.

Hewson, Claire, Peter Yule, Dianna Laurent, and Carol
Vogel. *Internet Research Methods: A Practical
Guide for the Social and Behavioural Sciences.*
Thousand Oaks, CA: Sage Publications, 2003.

Hunt, Tiffany J., and Bud Hunt. "Research and Authority
in an Online World: Who Knows? Who Decides?"
English Journal 95 (2006): 89–92.

Kress, Gunther. "Gains and Losses: New Forms of Texts,
Knowledge, and Learning." *Computers & Composition* 22 (2005): 5–22.

Lunsford, Andrea. "Writing, Technologies, and the Fifth
Canon." *Computers & Composition* 23 (2006):
169–177.

Tardy, Christine. "Expressions of Disciplinarity and Individuality in a Multimodal Genre." *Computers &
Composition* 22 (2005): 319–336.

Walker, Billie E. "Google No More: A Model for Successful
Research." *Teaching Professor* 20 (2006): 1–4.

Figure 14.7   CMS Bibliography Page.

15

CSE Citation Style Guidelines

Scientific Style and Format: The CSE Manual for Authors, Editors, and Publishers is the official style guide of the Council of Science Editors (CSE), from whom the style takes its name. CSE style is generally used by authors writing in the sciences as the generic formatting that they can then adapt to a specific journal's guidelines, and most of the disciplines in the natural sciences use a style guide that is at least loosely based on CSE guidelines. CSE style has three basic in-text citation systems and only one system for full bibliographies. This chapter introduces all three in-text citation systems and give examples of the full bibliographic entries as well.

Paper Formatting

CSE's formatting guidelines are formal journal and book publication guidelines. Check with your instructor to see if he or she wants you to follow all of the following guidelines.

 Refer to the online resource center at www.cengage.com/english/ Miller-Cochran/WGTR to see a sample paper using the CSE citation style.

Title Page

The CSE style guidelines for journal article title pages specifically ask for the article title, the authors' names, the authors' affiliations, an abstract of the article, and the initial page number. For a course paper, you may want to change "author affiliation" to the names of the instructor and course for which you are submitting the paper. Your instructor may ask for the submission date as well. If there is enough room on the page, feel free to begin the text of your paper on the title page. You will need to check with your professor for specific guidelines on how to format a title page for your course paper.

Spacing and Margins

Your instructor will probably require that you double-space the entire document, including any footnotes you might have and the cited references list at the end of the paper. You do not need to include extra spaces (i.e., quadruple space) anywhere in the text. Set your top, left, and bottom margins for at least one inch. All paragraphs should be indented by one-half inch.

Headers and Page Numbers

CSE does not give specific page header and numbering guidelines for paper submissions. However, in the upper right corner of each page, you should include a running header with either a shortened version of your title or your last name and the page number. All pages in the paper should be consecutively numbered. The header is placed one-half inch from the top of the page and one inch from the right side of the page. You do not need to include the header and page number on the title page of your paper.

Section Headings

If your paper is long enough and it includes coherent sections, and even subsections, you might consider including section headings in your paper. Make sure that all of your section titles are parallel in both syntax and format. In other words, if you start your first section title with a noun, start all of your section titles with nouns. And if the first level of subheads is in bold type, all of the first-level subheads should be bold. If the second level of subheads is in italics, all of the second-level subheads must be in italics. CSE also calls for subheads that are concise and fairly represent the importance of the material.

> For more information on in-text citation, what to include in a references list, and other documentation-related questions not specific to CSE format, see Chapter 7.

Citation Guidelines

This section provides explanations and examples of how to cite resources that you might use in your research, both in the text of your work (in-text citations) and at the end of your research (cited references). ▢

In-Text Citations

You must include an in-text citation in every sentence that includes information from an outside resource. Even if you are only summarizing or paraphrasing the resource, you must include an in-text citation in the same sentence in which you present the material. CSE uses three systems for in-text citations:

- name-year
- citation-sequence
- citation-name

Name-Year In-Text Citation Method   The name-year in-text citation method is similar to the APA citation method. Insert the author's last name and the copyright year in parentheses at the end of the resource you are referencing; this information refers to the full reference that appears in alphabetic order in a cited references list at the end of the paper. Unlike APA style, CSE does not require a comma in between the author's last name and the copyright year.

> If pus under pressure is found at the time of aspiration, surgical evacuation of the abscess should be performed, because an abscess will prevent adequate penetration of antibiotics into the infected tissue (Nade 1983). If the process is diagnosed within 1 or 2 days of the start of the disease before an abscess has formed, antibiotic treat-

ment alone is successful in curing the infections in approximately 90 percent of cases (Cole and others 1982).

To see additional examples of the name-year system for parenthetical references, see the "In-Text Citations" section of Chapter 13 on APA citation style guidelines. These examples work for both APA and CSE styles.

Citation-Sequence In-Text Citation Method   The citation-sequence in-text citation method is a lot like the notes and bibliography citation system used in CMS style. Insert a superscript Arabic number after the phrase or sentence that you are citing, after any punctuation and with no space before the superscript. Entries in your cited references list have the same numbers as the corresponding in-text citations. If you need to refer to a resource again, use the number originally assigned to it.

> If pus under pressure is found at the time of aspiration, surgical evacuation of the abscess should be performed, because an abscess will prevent adequate penetration of antibiotics into the infected tissue.[36] If the process is diagnosed within 1 or 2 days of the start of the disease before an abscess has formed, antibiotic treatment alone is successful in curing the infections in approximately 90 percent of cases.[37]

Citation-Name In-Text Citation Method   The citation-name sequence also uses superscript numbers as in-text citation markers; however, the references are numbered in alphabetical order on the reference list. Therefore, after completing the final draft of the paper, compile the complete publication data of all the resources you cited in the paper and list them in alphabetical order. Once they are in order, number them by author's last name. For example, "Adams" might be number 1; "Ashbeck," number 2; "Cochran," number 3; and "Zimmerman" would be the last number in the sequence. Like the citation-sequence method, no matter how many times you refer to a resource in the paper, the in-text superscript citation number is the same. Since the first text reference in the following example is to Nade and the second is to Cole, the Nade reference has a higher number because, even though it occurs earlier in the paper, it comes later in the alphabet.

> If pus under pressure is found at the time of aspiration, surgical evacuation of the abscess should be performed, because an abscess will prevent adequate penetration of antibiotics into the infected tissue.[28] If the process is diagnosed within 1 or 2 days of the start of the disease before an abscess has formed, antibiotic treatment alone is successful in curing the infections in approximately 90 percent of cases.[4]

Long Quotations   In CSE style, long quotations need to be presented in a block quote. Instead of using quotation marks to identify the text being quoted, block quotes indent the material so that it stands out on the page. Block quotations should be set one-half inch from the left margin. Because they are direct quotations, block quotes need an in-text citation as well.

Summaries and Multiple Resources   If you are summarizing the main point of a resource and not referencing one particular part of the source, CSE style requires that you provide the appropriate in-text citation as well as the appropriate full bibliographic citation in the "Cited References."

...write...

Practice In-Text Citations

Use the following sample paragraph, as well as the cited references, to practice inserting in-text citations. First, identify which in-text citation style you will follow. Next, identify where you need to include in-text citations; the sample paragraph includes direct quotes, paraphrases, and summaries. Third, insert the in-text citations where they are required. Be sure to include the appropriate information for each type of in-text citation. Finally, organize the complete entries for all of the citations into a references list according to the order appropriate to the in-text citation style.

 If you would like to complete this exercise online and to check your answers, go to *Student Resources* on the online resource center at www.cengage.com/english/Miller-Cochran/WGTR.

Strauss concludes that "the moral is that unless we show faculty members how technology can meet their needs, they won't consider using it." While studying what community college faculty needed to incorporate technology into their instruction, Quick and Davies found faculty needed time, money, software, classroom computers (professor podium), department computer lab, and faculty technical support and training. In discussing how to prepare college faculty for the incoming net-generation of students, Clayton-Pedersen and O'Neill claim that "much of the learning technology innovation in higher education has been focused on K-12 teacher preparation and development" and that "more focus needs to be placed on preparing existing faculty for the future Net Generation students who will populate the twenty-first-century classroom." They continue that call for action claiming that "faculty's understanding of the teaching and learning power of technology needs to be increased" and "tools need to be developed to help faculty integrate technology into the curriculum." Strauss, Quick and Davies, and Clayton-Pedersen and O'Neill demonstrate that faculty first need blatant introductions to the new technologies themselves: what they are and what they can do.[1]

Cited References

CSE-1 Ebook (static) • Citation Elements: two authors, editors, online, book, digital, anthology/edited collection, section from a book

1. Clayton-Pedersen AR, O'Neill N. Curricula designed to meet 21st-century expectations. In: Oblinger DA, Oblinger, JL, editors. Educating the net generation [Internet]. Washington: Educause; c2005 [cited 2005 Aug 22]; Chapter 9. Available from: http://www.educause.edu/ir/library/pdf/pub7101.pdf

---

1. Reproduced by permission of Rochelle Rodrigo.

CSE-2 Journal with Continued Pagination (syndicated) * Citation Elements: two authors, journal (pages via volume)

2. Quick D, Davies GD. Community college faculty development: bringing technology into instruction. Community College J Research and Practice. 1999;23:641–653.

CSE-3 Online Weekly Trade Magazine (syndicated) * Citation Elements: single author, online, digital, magazine (weekly or biweekly)

3. Strauss H. Why many faculty members aren't excited about technology. The Chronicle of Higher Education [Internet]. 2005 Jun 24 [cited 2005 Dec 31]; [32 paragraphs]. Available from: http://chronicle.com/weekly/v51/i42/42b03001.htm

Full Bibliographic Citations

CSE format requires the inclusion of a list of resources used in the paper, and this list is referred to as the "Cited References," "References," or "Literature Cited." This list includes only the names of resources cited in the paper, not resources that you found and read during your research process but did not include in the paper. The cited references page should start at the top of a new page in your essay, and it should also be included in your continuous page numbering. Subsequent cited references pages do not have a special heading but simply have CSE-formatted page numbers. References are presented in the order dictated by the in-text citation system you choose to follow. If you are using the name-year method for in-text citation, your entries in the reference list should be alphabetized and use a hanging indent (the first line of the resource is flush left and subsequent lines are indented five spaces). If you are using the citation-sequence or the citation-name methods for in-text citation, your entries in the reference list should be listed in numerical order with the numbers followed by a period and a space before each name that begins the entry. All lines of the reference should be aligned with the left margin. In the citation-name method, alphabetize your list of resources prior to numbering. If you have more than one text by the same author, be sure to write out the author's name each time and organize by publication year. If you have texts with no authors, incorporate them into an alphabetically organized reference list based on title. CSE style requires the cited references list include the page numbers, if available, on which the quotation or paraphrase appears in the resource.

The examples you'll see in this chapter are formatted in the citation-sequence system. To convert these examples to the name-year method, delete the number preceding the citation and move the copyright year of the resource directly after the author's last name. CSE citation-sequence references generally provide information in the following order:

1. Name of author (last name and initials without space or periods separating them)
2. Title of text (capitalize only the first word and proper names and do not italicize or underline the title)

3. Publication information (usually including publisher's name and location and the copyright date)

Periods are included after each major section of information. For example, a period is included after the name of the author(s), the title of the text, and the complete publication information. If there is *no author* for the text, start with the title of the text; however, remember that government agencies and corporations can function as an author. With various online resources you may have to look on other pages to find the name of the author.

For more explanation about static, syndicated, and dynamic resources, see Chapter 4.

Similarly, you may have to search online resources for the date of the last update as well (like the "history" page in wikis). If you can't find a date, or other publication information, you may put the term "date unknown" within square brackets. The citation rules for static, syndicated, and dynamic resources all follow this general pattern, but each category has some unique characteristics. □

CSE Citation Examples

CSE Citation Examples

For more examples of CSE citations, go to the online resource center at www.cengage.com/english/Miller-Cochran/WGTR.

Static Resources

Static resources (e.g., books, films, and government documents) are generally easy to cite using CSE style.

CSE-4 Book (static) ∗ Citation Elements: book, single author

Author's name: Notice no punctuation separating the last name and first initial.

Title: Notice the lack of capitalization beyond the first word of the title and no special formatting of the title.

4. Galison P. Image and logic: a material culture of microphysics. Chicago: University of Chicago Press; 1997.

Basic publication information: City of publisher, publisher's name, and publication year.

CSE-5 Book with Two Authors ∗ Citation Elements: two authors, book

Notice there is no "and" between the authors' names. Also notice that no punctuation is inserted between first and middle initials of the authors' names.

Title of the text and publication information. If the city is well known, the state or country do not need to be included.

5. Foreman JK, Stockwell PB. Automatic chemical analysis. Chichester (UK): E. Horwood; 1975.

If there are more authors, the citation would appear similar to example CSE-5 but with the additional authors' last names and first initials included.

CSE-6

CSE-6 Edition of a Book ∗ Citation Elements: two authors, book, edition

Author and title.

6. Mohapatra RN, Palash BP. Massive neutrinos in physics and astrophysics. 3rd ed. River Edge (NJ): World Scientific; 2004.

Edition information comes after the title.

Publication information.

When referring to books or other media in multiple editions, use the language you find on the document's title page. Therefore, if it says second or third edition, put the number in your citation. If it says "Revised" or "Abridged," put "Rev ed." or "Abr ed." in the citation. Similarly, if the book is the fifth in a multivolume work, include "Vol. 5."

CSE-7

CSE-7 Article from an Edited Collection ∗ Citation Elements: two authors, editor, book, section from a book, anthology/ edited collection

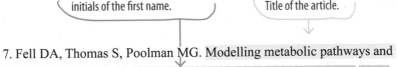
Editors' names: last name and initials of the first name.

Title of the article.

7. Fell DA, Thomas S, Poolman MG. Modelling metabolic pathways and analyzing control. In: Bryant JA, Burrell MM, Kruger NJ, editors. Plant carbohydrate biochemistry. Oxford (UK): BIOS Scientific; 1999. p. 17–28.

Title of the edited collection.

Publication information.

Page numbers of the article.

If you are citing an introduction, preface, foreword, or afterword, treat it like a section from a book.

CSE-8 Book in a Series with an Organization as the Author ∗ Citation Elements: corporation as author, book, series

Name of the organization that is the author. If it is a vague name, you might need to put the country the organization is from.

8. Agricultural Research Council (UK). Methods for the detection of the viruses of certain diseases in animals and animal products. Brussels: Commission of the European Communities; 1976. (Information on agriculture; no. 16).

Information about the series.

CSE-9 Translated Book ∗ Citation Elements: single author, book, translator

Author's name and book title.

9. Trinh, XT. Chaos and harmony: perspectives on scientific revolutions of the twentieth century. Reisinger A, translator. New York: Oxford University Press; 2001.

Name of the translator.

Publication information.

According to CSE, you do not need to include the information about a translator unless it is relevant to what you are writing about.

CSE-10 Published Dissertation ∗ Citation Elements: dissertation or thesis, single author

Title of the thesis with the type of resource in brackets.

10. Amir A. Industry technology roadmapping of nonwoven medical textiles [master's thesis]. Raleigh (NC): North Carolina State Univ; 2006 Nov 6.

Basic publication information that includes school location, school name, and date of the degree.

CSE-11 Film in DVD Format ∗ Citation Elements: film, DVD/video, digital

Title of the film with description of media in brackets.

Mode or media that the recording is published in (DVD, videocassette, HD, etc.) with brief description as well.

Names of editors and producers separated by a semicolon.

11. Life after people [digital video disc]. Wakabayashi M, Yaskin K, editors; Cohen D, Tarantino L, producers. Los Angeles: Flight 33 Productions; 2008. 1 digital video disc: 94 minutes, sound, color. Available from: The History Channel: http://store.aetv.com/html/product/index.jhtml?id=110900&name=Life%20After%20People

Production company, location, and copyright year of the DVD.

Description of where reader can obtain a copy of the film.

Consider using the Internet Movie Database (http://www.imdb.com) to find the names of editors and producers, information about the production and distribution companies, as well as the other details required by the citation.

CSE-12 Government Web site ∗ Citation Elements: complete Web site, government document, digital, online

In this case the author name is the name of the Web site. Also include a description of the mode of access within brackets prior to the period.

Publication information with "c" before the copyright date to distinguish it from other dates in the entry.

12. Centers for Disease Control and Prevention [Internet]. Atlanta (GA): Department of Health and Human Services; c2008 [modified 2008 Mar 14; cited 2008 Mar 16]. Available from: http://www.cdc.gov

Last known date that Web site was updated.

Access date.

URL of Web site, always preceded by "Available from:". Notice that no punctuation follows the URL.

CSE-13 Web Page from within a Government Web Site * Citation Elements: Web page in a Web site, government document, digital, online

Author name or agency name followed by the name of the overall Web site the Web page is posted within. Mode of access is included in brackets.

Publication information with "c" before the copyright date to distinguish it from other dates in the entry.

13. Centers for Disease Control and Prevention. Autism Information Center [Internet]. Atlanta (GA): Department of Health and Human Services; c2008. Autism Spectrum Disorders Overview; 9 Feb 2007 [cited 2008 Mar 16]; [about 3 screens]. Available from: http:// www.cdc.gov/ncbddd/autism/overview.htm

Name of the specific Web page and the last date that page was updated.

Access date.

URL of Web site.

Approximate length of the article within brackets, followed by a period.

Syndicated Resources

Syndicated resources are a little more complicated to cite in CSE style because there are usually multiple titles involved. Since many syndicated resources are now found in digital format, their citations are also complicated because they generally include layers of publication information as well. Some journals use continuous page numbers throughout all of the issues in a year, and other journals start each issue with page 1. Check several issues of journals you are citing to see which format they follow, and then use the appropriate format for your cited references list.

CSE-14 Article in a Journal * Citation Elements: journal (pages via issue), single author

Name of the article in the journal.

Name of the journal. Abbreviate the title when possible. In this case, "Science" has been abbreviated to "Sci". Note that no punctuation follows the abbreviation.

14. Azawi OI. Postpartum uterine infection in cattle. Animal Reprod Sci 2008;105(3/4):187–208.

Publication year, followed by a semicolon, no space, the volume number, and the issue numbers of the journal in parentheses.

Page numbers of the article. Note there is no space between the colon and the numbers.

CSE-15 Article in a Magazine * Citation Elements: magazine (monthly or bimonthly), single author

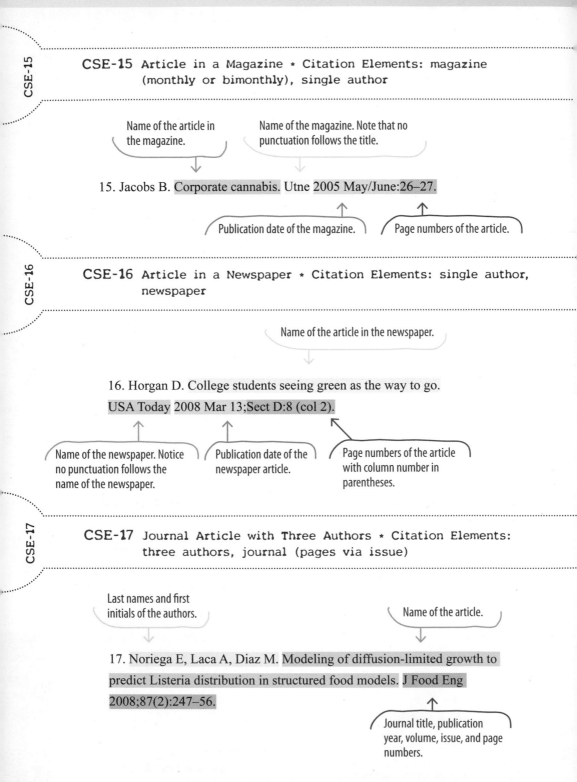

Name of the article in the magazine.

Name of the magazine. Note that no punctuation follows the title.

15. Jacobs B. Corporate cannabis. Utne 2005 May/June:26–27.

Publication date of the magazine.

Page numbers of the article.

CSE-16 Article in a Newspaper * Citation Elements: single author, newspaper

Name of the article in the newspaper.

16. Horgan D. College students seeing green as the way to go. USA Today 2008 Mar 13;Sect D:8 (col 2).

Name of the newspaper. Notice no punctuation follows the name of the newspaper.

Publication date of the newspaper article.

Page numbers of the article with column number in parentheses.

CSE-17 Journal Article with Three Authors * Citation Elements: three authors, journal (pages via issue)

Last names and first initials of the authors.

Name of the article.

17. Noriega E, Laca A, Diaz M. Modeling of diffusion-limited growth to predict Listeria distribution in structured food models. J Food Eng 2008;87(2):247–56.

Journal title, publication year, volume, issue, and page numbers.

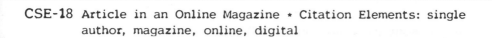

CSE-18 Article in an Online Magazine * Citation Elements: single author, magazine, online, digital

Author's name.

Name of the article, name of the online magazine, and the mode of access of the text.

Publication date of the magazine.

18. Pain E. Playing well with industry. Science [Internet] 2008 Mar 14 [cited 2008 Mar 16]; 319(5869):1548–51. Available from: http://www.sciencemag.org/cgi/content/full/319/5869/1548

Access date within brackets.

URL of Web site. Note there is no period at the end of the URL.

Volume, issue, and page numbers.

CSE-19 Blog * Citation Elements: single author, blog, online, digital

Author's name.

Title of the blog entry and the mode of access of the text.

19. Latter J. Support or sponsor "evolution research" [blog post on the Internet]. 2006 Jul 17 [cited 2008 Mar 17]. [12 paragraphs]. Available from: http:// evolutiontest.blogspot.com/2006/07/support-or-sponsor-evolution-research .html

Publication date of the blog entry and access date within brackets.

URL of blog post.

Description of the Internet text in screens, paragraphs, or lines within brackets.

CSE-20 Reply to a Blog Entry ∗ Citation Elements: single author, blog, comment or reply, online, digital

Author's name.

Title of the blog entry and the modality of the text.

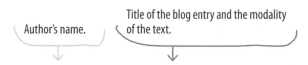

20. Adams D. Reply to "cyber salon, the reality" [reply to blog post on the Internet]. 2008 Mar 9 [cited 2008 Mar 17]. [1 paragraph]. Available from: http://www.committedtechnofile.com/index .php/application/comments/cyber_salon_the_reality

Publication date of the blog entry response followed by date of access.

URL of blog post.

Description of the Internet text.

CSE-21 Podcast ∗ Citation Elements: no author, podcast, sound recording, online, digital

Title of the specific episode.

Description of the media, including running time and mode of access.

The name of the podcast series.

21. TWiT 130: Microhoo? [podcast on the Internet]. In: This Week in Tech. Laporte L, Calacanis J, Scoble R, hosts; Laporte L, producer. [place unknown]: This Week in Tech TV; 2008 Feb 4. Episode 130 [cited 2008 Mar 17.] 1:16 min. Available from: http://twit.tv/130

Names of key people in production.

Access date and URL.

Production company information, including date of release and episode number. If publication location is unknown, include "place unknown" in brackets as shown here.

Dynamic Resources

Since dynamic resources change regularly, it is very important to include the exact date that you accessed the resource. CSE considers personal correspondence (e.g., letters, email, and live interviews) as primary research that you would describe in the text. No citation is required for primary research resources.

CSE-22 Web Page from within a Wiki ∗ Citation Elements: Web page in a Web site, no author, wiki, digital, online

Name of the overall Web site the Web page is posted within.

Type of resource.

22. Classrooms for the future: CFF science. [Wiki on the Internet]. [unknown place]: Classrooms for the Future; c2008. Anatomy; 29 Jan 2008 [cited 2008 Mar 16]; [about 2 screens]. Available from: http://cffscience.wikispaces.com/Life_Science

Title of the specific part of the wiki you are referencing followed by date of publication or the most recent update.

Publication information with "c" before the copyright date to distinguish it from other dates in the entry.

Access date.

URL of Web site.

Approximate length of the article.

Notice there is no author listed. If you cannot find an author for your resource, then start with the title of the resource. Most wiki pages have a "history" or "page history" link or tab that will allow you to see the last time the page was updated.

CSE-23 Conference Presentation on the Internet ∗ Citation Elements: conference proceedings, lecture or public address, single author, online, digital

Description of the text.

Information about the conference title, mode of access, date, and location.

15. Scott J. Surgical management of gynecomastia [conference presentation on the Internet]. In: Proceedings of the 2008 Miami Breast Cancer Conference [Internet]; 2008 Feb 20-23; Orlando, FL. Dallas: Physician's Education Resource; 2008 Apr [cited 2008 Apr 10]. p. 95–9. Available from: http://www.cancerconf.com/media/2008/wednesday.php

Proceedings publication information.

Access date and URL of Web site.

Specific page numbers of the presentation.

CSE treats conference proceedings like books; therefore, if you are citing the entire proceedings, treat it like an edited book. If you are citing a particular section of the book, cite it as work in an anthology or edited collection.

> reflect <

CSE Style: Some Common Errors

☐ Entries in your cited reference list fail to correspond to citations or are in the wrong format. The style of the cited references list is dictated by the in-text citation style you use.

☐ Punctuation in the author's name. The author's first initial is not separated from the last name with punctuation. The author's initials have no periods after them (except after the last one, which is the end of the category "author" in the entry).

☐ Confusion of publication or release and copyright dates.

☐ Spelled-out names of months. Most month names are condensed to three letters.

☐ Omission of a word or phrase that describes the type of resource that is not a written document (e.g., media or mode of access, DVD, weblog, podcast, etc.).

 For an example of a complete paper formatted in CSE style, visit the online resource center at www.cengage.com/english/Miller-Cochran/WGTR.

Figure 15.1 demonstates what a complete cited references page looks like in CSE style.

Online Research 16

Cited References

1. Hunt TJ, Hunt B. Research and authority in an online world: who knows? who decides? English Journal 2006;95:89–92.

2. Hewson C, Yule P, Laurent D, Vogel C. Internet research methods: a practical guide for the social and behavioural sciences. Thousand Oaks (CA): Sage; 2003.

3. Evans E, Po J. A break in the transaction: examining students' responses to digital texts. Computers and Composition 2007;24(1):56–73.

4. Bass F. The Associated Press guide to internet research and reporting. Cambridge (MA): Perseus; 2001.

5. Tardy C. Expressions of disciplinarity and individuality in a multimodal genre. Computers and Composition 2005;22(3):319–36.

6. Lunsford A. Writing, technologies, and the fifth canon. Computers and Composition 2006;23(2):169–77.

7. Kress G. Gains and losses: new forms of texts, knowledge, and learning. Computers and Composition 2005;22(1):5–22.

8. Walker BE. Google no more: a model for successful research. Teaching Professor 2006;20:1–4.

9. Helms-Park R, Radia P, Stepleton P. A preliminary assessment of Google Scholar as a source of EAP students' research materials. Internet and Higher Education 2007;10:65–76.

10. Bruckman AS. Student research and the internet. Communications of the ACM 2005;48:35–7.

Figure 15.1   A Complete References Page Using CSE Style.

Invention Activities

Invention was the way that ancient rhetors referred to the practice of developing different ideas and arguments about a given topic. Writers, as well as writing instructors, have continued to develop a variety of writing activities to generate ideas. You may be used to thinking about using these kinds of activities only at the beginning stages of working on a research or writing project, but the majority can be used at many points in your writing process. Of course, several of these activities can be particularly useful as you are choosing and defining the scope of your topic and argument.

Brainstorming or Listing

Brainstorming, or listing, is generating a list of ideas on a certain topic. Sometimes brainstorming takes place for a set period of time, and sometimes the goal is to come up with a certain number of possible ideas (or as many as possible). When we brainstorm, we know that some of the ideas might be discarded, but the purpose is to open up our minds to possibilities.

Many writers use brainstorming or listing activities to explore what they already know about a given topic. For example, when a student is first assigned a paper topic, she might brainstorm everything she knows about it. While brainstorming or listing, do not let your internal sensor keep you from adding something to your list; in other words, keep your mind open to all ideas that might relate to your topic. You should write down everything, no matter how far-fetched it may seem.

Brainstorming or listing can be helpful at the beginning of a project to choose a topic or to identify what you already know. It can also be useful during the middle of a research project so that you can list everything you have learned. It may even be useful to compare your preresearch brainstorming with your postresearch listing; you will be able to identify what you've learned, what you may still want to research, and how your thinking has begun to shift.

Imagine that you are researching air pollution in the city that you live in. You could try brainstorming a list of possible causes that you know about, and it might look something like this:

- car exhaust
- poor mass transit in city
- lack of rain this year
- increased population
- industrial emissions

If these were the first things that came to mind when you started brainstorming, then you could look at a few resources to see what you should add to your list.

Listing can also be useful when thinking about your writing project's purpose and audience, especially when identifying all of the purposes and audiences that your topic might address. It is critical to list all of the specific wants and needs of your various rhetorical purposes and audiences. Lists can then become checklists to verify that your writing project includes all of the information that your specific purpose and audience might require.

Brainstorming and listing can easily be done with traditional pen and paper or on the computer. Either way, it's a good idea to save your results in a notebook or computer file so that you can return to them later in your project.

Using Brainstorming or Listing in Your Research Process

The following are examples of brainstorming or listing activities that you might find helpful in your research process.

- Chapter 3: page 38, "Write: Analyze the Rhetorical Situation" is an example of using listing within a structured space; the activity asks you to fill in the blanks of a chart.

- Chapter 3: page 39, "Write: Find Out What's Important to You"

- Chapter 3: page 44, "Write: Focus Your Research Topic"

- Chapter 4: page 72, "Write: Develop a List of Search Terms"

Journaling

Journaling can be very helpful in organizing a research project. A journal is a collection of writing, composed of multiple entries, all generally related to the same topic. Therefore, it is a good idea to start a journal for any major research project that you undertake. In the journal (or you might try a blog if you would like to journal electronically), you can keep the following types of entries:

- any of the other writing activities listed in this appendix

- an annotated bibliography or other notes about the resources you find

- timelines and checklists to help organize your research process

- reflections on research and/or writing sessions

- notes about discussions you've had with other people on the topic

- drafts of your writing

- any other ideas that you find relevant or interesting as you work through your research

By using a journal, you will keep everything related to your research project in one place. Whenever you are stuck on your project, look over the various entries in your journal to remind yourself of what you need to do and why this project is important to you.

To help keep your journal entries organized, it is generally a good idea to include the following information in every entry:

- the date of your entry

- a title that briefly describes your entry

- blank space to make more comments about the entry at a later date

Therefore, if you are using a traditional paper journal, don't feel that you have to start the next entry right after the last. Even consider skipping a page between entries. If you use a blog, the reply feature will allow you, or others, to provide more feedback about your entry. Or if you use a three-ring binder or a single word-processing document, you can add pages as needed.

Using Journaling in Your Research Process

Nearly all of the activities included in the "Reflect" and "Write" sections in this book could be considered journaling activities. Here are a few examples that could help you get started on journaling and see some of the ways that it can be used in your research.

- Chapter 1: page 6, "Reflect: How Have You Conducted Research Before?" (journaling as reflection)

- Chapter 2: page 26, "Reflect: What Are Your Writing Idiosyncrasies?" (journaling as reflection)

- Chapter 2: page 30, "Write: Discover Disciplinary Patterns and Conventions"

- Chapter 3: page 35, "Write: Identify Kairos"

- Chapter 3: page 43, "Reflect: How Can I Make a Topic Manageable?"

- Chapter 5: page 109, "Reflect: What Does Your Research Plan Look Like Now?"

Freewriting

At one point or another, most writers have had writer's block. And almost all writers agree that the way to get over writer's block is just to write. Freewriting is a strategy to get yourself "just writing"—you simply sit down at your computer (or with a pen and paper) and write anything that comes to mind on your topic. During freewriting sessions, like brainstorming and listing, turn off your internal sensor and just get words on the page or screen. To get going, many writers give themselves a brief topic or question and then set a time limit (like 5 to 15 minutes). Then they force themselves to write during that entire time. It doesn't matter if their mind wanders. And if they get stuck, they can just write the same word or phrase over and over until they get new ideas or go back to the beginning idea or question and start over. The purpose of freewriting is just to get words down.

Much of the writing produced during a freewriting session will never see final print or publication. Instead, this writing is meant to help the author think through elements of his or her project. At the beginning stage of a project, freewriting can be useful for exploring initial thoughts and feelings about a topic. During the research process, freewriting can help researchers make connections among multiple resources. And during the drafting stage, freewriting can help authors work through writer's block and get started with different sections of their projects.

Although you can easily freewrite with pen and paper, there are definitely some advantages to freewriting with a word processor on the computer. For example, some writers turn off the monitor when they freewrite, or they might make the font color white so that they can't see what they are writing on the screen. When the text is not visible, writers are not distracted by what they've already typed, and they are not looking for misspellings or grammatical errors. Instead, writers just focus on writing. Once you realize that freewriting is pure invention work, it doesn't matter if it looks messy!

Using Freewriting in Your Research Process

The following are examples of freewriting activities that you might find helpful in your research process.

- Chapter 3: page 40, "Write: Consider Audience and Purpose"

- Chapter 3: page 41, "Techno Tip: Use Technology to Explore What You Already Know"

- Chapter 11: page 214, "Write: Draft an Effective Introduction"

- Chapter 11: page 215, "Write: Develop Closure"

Looping

Looping is an activity that writers usually use after freewriting, brainstorming, or listing. Once a writer has concluded one of these writing sessions, she could read the paragraph or list and look for one or two "hot spots" that resonate with her. They might spark her interest or surprise her. The point of looping is to discover a new perspective on your topic or to focus your thinking by taking that idea or phrase and making it the focal point for another round of freewriting, brainstorming, or listing. Looping is also another way to combat writer's block, and it's a good way to focus a topic if your initial subject matter is too broad. Looping might also help you work through connections in ideas and resources so that you can better arrange them in your writing.

Let's imagine that you were going to do a looping exercise with your list about air pollution from earlier in the appendix. The list of possible causes for air pollution looked like this:

- car exhaust

- poor mass transit in city

- lack of rain this year

- increased population

- industrial emissions

After completing this list, you might choose one of these to explore in more detail. You could copy and paste it and then freewrite or list for a while and see what you come up with. For example, if you chose to pursue increased population, you might write something like this:

> Phoenix, Arizona, has one of the fastest growing populations in the country, especially in the suburbs surrounding the city. Several of the other items on the list come from the increase in population. For example, with more people driving, we have an increase in car exhaust that is contributing to the pollution problem. People are also resistant to carpooling here.

You can see that some of the ideas in this section overlap with ideas in the original list—that's okay. A looping activity might reveal ideas you hadn't considered, and it might help you come up with connections between ideas that you hadn't thought of before.

You can use any technology for looping: paper and pen, computer, blackboard, or whiteboard. Loop in whatever technology you used for your initial writing. If you use a word processor, you can use different colors, fonts, or highlighting tools to identify hot spots, and then you can cut and paste before you start writing again.

Using Looping in Your Research Process
The following are examples of looping activities that you might find helpful in your research process.

- Chapter 3: page 40, "Write: Generate Topic Ideas"

- Chapter 11: page 214, "Write: Draft an Effective Introduction"

- Chapter 11: page 215, "Write: Develop Closure"

Cluster Mapping
Writers use cluster mapping to help organize their thoughts or resources. Clustering is a more visual activity than the methods already discussed; it helps writers see their work in a different manner. After producing a brainstorm or list, writers group like elements from their lists. After conducting research, writers cluster resources that contain similar perspectives or ideas. If juggling multiple purposes and audiences, writers cluster the results of a detailed analysis of wants and needs.

Cluster-mapping exercises help writers and researchers not only to group like elements but also to understand connections among the groups. After grouping like elements, writers can draw lines connecting groups and describe the types of connections. Some cluster maps show hierarchies, like family trees. Others show working relationships, like flow charts. Some writers represent the size of each cluster in relation to other clusters so they know whether an area might not have enough ideas or examples to support it.

If we were to draw a cluster map of our air pollution example, it might look something like the following figure.

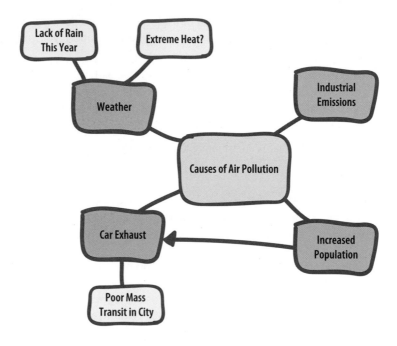

Cluster mapping can be done in a variety of modes. You can easily use paper and pen, maybe even many different colored pens, to group elements and map out connections. There are also a variety of computer and Web-based programs that allow you to develop different types of cluster maps. Sometimes it helps to physically work with the elements, or groups of elements, by putting them on index cards or sticky notes that you can shuffle and rearrange as you explore different groups and connections.

Using Cluster Mapping in Your Research Process

The following are examples of cluster-mapping activities that you might find helpful in your research process.

- Chapter 1, page 12, "Reflect: How Do Rhetorical Situations Compare?" (Although this is not technically a cluster map, this activity shows another way you might use graphic representations throughout your research process.)

- Chapter 3: page 44, "Write: Focus Your Research Topic"

- Chapter 9: page 174, "Write: Define the Rhetorical Situation"

- Chapter 9: page 176, "Write: Create a Cluster Map"

- Chapter 10: page 202, "Write: Draw a Cluster Map"

- Chapter 10: page 203, "Techno Tip: Create Clusters on the Computer"

Outlining

Like cluster mapping, outlining is an activity that helps you to organize materials into meaningful patterns and relationships. Outlines hierarchically group like topics, and detailed outlines begin to describe relationships between the groups. Writers might take the results of an initial brainstorming activity that explored what they already knew about a topic and try to outline the results so they can identify areas they need to learn more about. Many researchers use outlines as a predrafting technique to lay out what they are going to say and then plug in the various resources that they will include. A writer could then take that outline and start writing from it because it has already sectioned the paper into easily manageable parts. For example, Chapter 8 developed from this outline:

Formal Outline of Chapter 8

I. Copyright
   A. Fair Use
   B. Ideas vs. Words
II. Plagiarism
   A. Blatant Plagiarism
   B. Careless Plagiarism
III. Integrating Resources into Your Argument
   A. Introducing the Resource
   B. Incorporating the Resource
      1. Quoting from Resources
      2. Summarizing and Paraphrasing Revisited
   C. Interpreting the Resource
   D. Documenting the Resource
      1. When Should You Cite?
      2. How Should You Cite?
      3. In-Text Citations
      4. Full Bibliographic Citations

By breaking the chapter into smaller parts, the authors were able to make the task manageable instead of being overwhelmed by it.

You might choose to write your outline in one of three ways: a formal outline, a sentence outline, or a scratch outline. The outline from Chapter 8 is a formal outline, with Roman numerals and carefully numbered headings and subpoints. You might choose instead to write a sentence outline, where each point is developed into a full sentence. Such an outline will really help you get started on drafting. Written as a sentence outline, the first part of the Chapter 8 outline would look like this:

Sentence Outline of First Part of Chapter 8

I. Copyright laws regulate the use of a particular expression of an idea.

     A. Fair Use allows individuals to copy small portions of texts so that they may use them in other contexts, especially research and education.

     B. Copyright technically protects the expression of an idea, not the idea itself.

II. Plagiarism is copying work from another resource without documenting it.

     A. Blatant plagiarism is knowingly copying sections of other resources and submitting them as your own work.

     B. Careless plagiarism is using information from an outside resource without documentation because you think it is common knowledge or you do not adequately document the source.

At early stages of your writing and research, you might find a scratch outline to be sufficient. A scratch outline casually lists ideas in the order that you would discuss them without concern to headers and subpoints. A scratch outline for that same section of Chapter 8 might look something like this:

Scratch Outline of First Part of Chapter 8

Copyright laws
Fair use
What copyright protects
What copyright doesn't protect
Types of plagiarism
Blatant
Careless

You might experiment with a more formal outline and a less formal one to see what works best for you, and you might find that different kinds of outlines work at different stages of your research and writing process.

As with cluster mapping, outlining helps you not only to organize your materials but also to evaluate the amount of ideas, resources, or support that you have for each category. If you only have one or two pieces of evidence for a particular category, and all the rest have more support, you may need to do more research or alter your inclusion of that category in your final project.

Most word processors have numbering or listing tools that begin to label subcategories that you make in your outline when you indent the appropriate lines.

Using Outlining in Your Research Process

The following are examples of outlining activities that you might find helpful in your research process.

- Chapter 9: page 190, "Write: Construct an Argument"

- Chapter 10: page 202, "Write: Draw a Cluster Map"

- Chapter 11: page 212, "Write: Develop an Outline"

Asking Journalistic Questions

Whereas brainstorming and freewriting are open forms of idea generation, journalistic questions focus writers and researchers on specific aspects of their topics. Traditional journalistic questions use the following words to develop a list of information-seeking questions.

- who

- what

- when

- why

- where

- how

Dedicated writers and researchers might critically explore their topics with multiple questions from each category. The purpose of using journalistic questions is to try to see and understand the topic from a variety of perspectives.

The invention tactic of asking questions can be more generalized, however. Exploring the topic in any structured manner will help a writer and researcher get to know a topic and the relevant resources much better. Other organized methods of exploring include the following perspectives.

- spatial: inside to outside, top to bottom, left to right

- oppositional: for and against, compare and contrast, denotation and connotation

- relational: cause and effect, parts to a whole

As you are writing and researching, be sure to keep and revisit any focused questioning activity. Many times thinking gets stuck in a rut; however, if you revisit your focused activity a few hours or days later, you might come up with different questions as well as different answers. Since it is so useful to revisit questioning activities, it is important to be sure to leave either lots of blank space or the electronic ability to add and revise later.

Using Journalistic Questions in Your Research Process

The following are examples of activities that use journalistic questions that you might find helpful in your research process.

- Chapter 3: page 45, "Write: Write a Research Question"

- Chapter 7: page 131, "Write: Track Bibliographic Information"

Photo Credits

Chapter 1, page 4: © BrandX/Getty Images

Chapter 1, page 13: Copyright 2008, Linden Research, Inc. All Rights Reserved.

Chapter 1, page 14: Reprinted by permission of Alan Levine.

Chapter 2, page 16: © Blair Fethers/Getty Images

Chapter 3, page 34: © Bonnie Kamin/PhotoEdit

Chapter 4, page 64: © 2008 Estate of Pablo Picasso/Artists Rights Society (ARS), New York. Photo © Scala/Art Resource, NY.

Chapter 4, pages 70 and 74: Google Brand Features are trademarks or distinctive brand features of Google Inc.

Chapter 4, page 71: From Gale. Screen shot from ACADEMIC ONEFILE. ©Gale, a part of Cengage Learning, Inc. Reproduced by permission. www.cengage.com/permissions

Chapter 4, page 78: Artwork by Robert A. Rohde/Global Warming Art

Chapter 5, page 92: © Kharidehal Abhirama Ashwin/Shutterstock

Chapter 6, page 112: © David McNew/Getty Images

Chapter 6, page 113: Reprinted by permission of GunCite. http://www.guncite.com/

Chapter 6, page 118: American Honda Motor Co., Inc.

Chapter 6, page 121: Reprinted by permission of Rebecca Lueckenotte and LiveJournal (www.livejournal.com)

Chapter 6, page 122: Copyright Edmunds.com, Inc. Reprinted with permission.

Chapter 7, page 128: © Harry Sieplinga/Getty Images

Chapter 7, page 132: Copyright © 2008 Elsevier B.V. ScienceDirect(R) is a registered trademark of Elsevier B.V. Zotero material reprinted by permission of the Center for History and New Media, George Mason University.

Chapter 7, page 136 top: © Adobe Systems Incorporated. All rights reserved. Adobe and the Adobe logo are either registered trademarks or trademarks of Adobe Systems Incorporated in the United States and/or other countries.

Chapter 7, page 136: Reprinted with permission of CNET.

Chapter 8, page 140: © Steve Dunwell/Getty Images

Chapter 9, page 172: © Photofusion Picture Library/Alamy

Chapter 10, page 194: © Ken Hurst/Shutterstock

Chapter 11, page 206: © Gazimal/Getty Images

Chapter 12, page 251: Warner Bros./The Kobal Collection

Text Credits

This page constitutes an extension of the copyright page. We have made every effort to trace the ownership of all copyrighted material and to secure permission from copyright holders. In the event of any question arising as to the use of any material, we will be pleased to make the necessary corrections in future printings. Thanks are due to the following authors, publishers, and agents for permission to use the material indicated.

Chapter 6, page 123: Copyright Edmunds.com, Inc. Reprinted with permission.

Chapter 9, pages 181–182: "A Frank Statement to Cigarette Smokers" from The New York Times, January 4, 1954.

Citation Sample Index

What features of citation are you looking for?	See these sample citations for examples containing that feature.	
Two to Three Authors	MLA-2, MLA-3, MLA-4, MLA-7, MLA-8, MLA-11, MLA-16, MLA-22, MLA-38	APA-2, APA-3, APA-7, APA-8, APA-13, APA-17, APA-34
Four or More Authors	MLA-29, MLA-35	APA-24, APA-31
No Author	MLA-6, MLA-13, MLA-14, MLA-15, MLA-32, MLA-50	APA-14, APA-15, APA-16, APA-28, APA-46
Corporation as Author	MLA-28, MLA-49	APA-25, APA-45, APA-52, APA-53
Two or more Works by the Same Author	MLA-33, MLA-34, MLA-43, MLA-44	APA-6, APA-29, APA-30, APA-39, APA-40
Translator	MLA-9, MLA-10	APA-10, APA-11, APA-12
Editor	MLA-1, MLA-3, MLA-9, MLA-16, MLA-17, MLA-22, MLA-27	APA-2, APA-5, APA-11, APA-17, APA-18
Quotation in the Title	MLA-38	APA-34
Book	MLA-1, MLA-2, MLA-3, MLA-8, MLA-10, MLA-11, MLA-12, MLA-27	APA-1, APA-2, APA-5, APA-8, APA-9, APA-10, APA-12, APA-13, APA-14
Online or Electronic Book	MLA-1, MLA-3	APA-1, APA-2, APA-14
Anthology/Edited Collection	MLA-3, MLA-9	APA-2, APA-11
Section from a Book	MLA-2, MLA-3, MLA-9, MLA-17, MLA-27	APA-2, APA-5, APA-11, APA-18
Foreword, Afterword, Introduction, or Preface	MLA-10	APA-12
Edition	MLA-23, MLA-25, MLA-27, MLA-60	APA-9, APA-23, APA-52
Book in a Series (Multivolume)	MLA-11	APA-10, APA-13
Reference	MLA-14, MLA-15	APA-15, APA-16
Sacred Text	MLA-13	APA-14
Republished	MLA-9, MLA-10	APA-12
Magazine	MLA-5, MLA-7, MLA-35, MLA-36, MLA-37	APA-4, APA-7, APA-31, APA-32, APA-33
Magazine (monthly or bimonthly)	MLA-35, MLA-37	APA-31, APA-32, APA-33
Magazine (weekly or biweekly)	MLA-5, MLA-7, MLA-36	APA-4, APA-7
Magazine (skip pages)	MLA-37	APA-33
Digital Magazine	MLA-5, MLA-7, MLA-35	APA-4, APA-7, APA-31
Journal	MLA-4, MLA-33, MLA-34, MLA-38, MLA-39	APA-3, APA-6, APA-29, APA-30, APA-34, APA-35

CMS-6, CMS-7, CMS-10, CMS-11, CMS-16, CMS-21, CMS-36	CSE-1, CSE-2, CSE-5, CSE-6, CSE-17
CMS-27, CMS-33	
CMS-9, CMS-18, CMS-19, CMS-20, CMS-32, CMS-47	CSE-22
CMS-26	CSE-8
CMS-29, CMS-30, CMS-41, CMS-42	
CMS-12, CMS-14, CMS-15	CSE-9
CMS-6, CMS-12, CMS-21	CSE-1, CSE-7
CMS-36	
CMS-1, CMS-4, CMS-6, CMS-11, CMS-13, CMS-14, CMS-15, CMS-16, CMS-17, CMS-21	CSE-1, CSE-4, CSE-5, CSE-6, CSE-7, CSE-8, CSE-9
CMS-1, CMS-6, CMS-18	CSE-1
CMS-6, CMS-12	CSE-1, CSE-7
CMS-6, CMS-12	CSE-1, CSE-7
CMS-15	
CMS-13, CMS-25, CMS-54	CSE-6
CMS-14, CMS-16	CSE-8
CMS-19, CMS-20	
CMS-18	
CMS-12, CMS-15	
CMS-8, CMS-10, CMS-33, CMS-34, CMS-35	CSE-3, CSE-15, CSE-18
CMS-33, CMS-35	CSE-15
CMS-8, CMS-10, CMS-34	CSE-3
CMS-35	
CMS-8, CMS-10, CMS-33	CSE-3, CSE-18
CMS-2, CMS-3, CMS-5, CMS-7, CMS-29, CMS-30, CMS-36, CMS-37	CSE-2, CSE-14, CSE-17

Citation Sample Index

What features of citation are you looking for?	See these sample citations for examples containing that feature.	
Journal (pages via issue)	*MLA-34	APA-30
Journal (pages via volume)	*MLA-4, MLA-33, MLA-38	APA-3, APA-6, APA-29, APA-34
Digital Journal	MLA-39	APA-35
Newspaper	MLA-31, MLA-32	APA-27, APA-28
Online Newspaper	MLA-32	APA-28
Editorial	MLA-32	APA-28
Review	MLA-39	APA-35
Map or Chart	MLA-28, MLA-62	APA-25, APA-54
Musical Composition	MLA-29	APA-24
Sound Recording	MLA-29, MLA-46	APA-24, APA-42
Film	MLA-23, MLA-25	APA-22, APA-23
DVD/Video	MLA-23, MLA-25, MLA-42, MLA-47, MLA-48	APA-23, APA-38, APA-43, APA-44
Broadcast	MLA-40	APA-36
Television Recording	MLA-40, MLA-41, MLA-42	APA-36, APA-37, APA-38
Live Performance	MLA-52, MLA-54	APA-47
Lecture or Public Address	MLA-52	APA-47
Lecture Notes	MLA-53	APA-48
Conference Proceedings	MLA-16, MLA-17	APA-17, APA-18
Government Publication	MLA-21	APA-21
White Paper	MLA-20	APA-20
Dissertation or Thesis	MLA-18, MLA-19	APA-19
Published Interview	MLA-30	APA-26
Personal Letter	MLA-55	
Email	MLA-56	
Personal Interview	MLA-51	
Online Subscription Database	MLA-16, MLA-17, MLA-19, MLA-31, MLA-36, MLA-41	APA-17, APA-18, APA-19, APA-27, APA-32, APA-37
Complete Web Site	MLA-59, MLA-62	APA-51, APA-54
Web Page in a Web Site	MLA-6, MLA-21, MLA-30, MLA-50	APA-21, APA-26, APA-46
Discussion Post (Listserv Posting, Discussion Board/ Group, or Newsgroup Posting)	MLA-57, MLA-58	APA-49, APA-50
Wiki	MLA-50	APA-46
Blog	MLA-43, MLA-44, MLA-45	APA-39, APA-40, APA-41
Comment or Reply on a Web Site	MLA-45, MLA-48	APA-41, APA-44
Podcast	MLA-46	APA-42
Video Game	MLA-60, MLA-61	APA-52, APA-53

*MLA guidelines no longer make a distinction between journals that are numbered continuously or numbered separately. According to current MLA guidelines, no matter how journals are paginated, all of them must contain volume and issue numbers (if available). (See MLA-33 and MLA-34 on page 273.)

CMS-2, CMS-30, CMS-37	CSE-14, CSE-17
CMS-3, CMS-5, CMS-7, CMS-29, CMS-36	CSE-2
CMS-37	
CMS-31, CMS-32	CSE-16
CMS-32	
CMS-32	
CMS-37	
CMS-26	
CMS-27	
CMS-27, CMS-44	CSE-21
CMS-25	CSE-11
CMS-25, CMS-40, CMS-45, CMS-46	CSE-11
CMS-38	
CMS-38, CMS-39, CMS-40	
CMS-49	
CMS-49	CSE-23
CMS-21	CSE-23
CMS-24	CSE-12, CSE-13
CMS-23	
CMS-22	CSE-10
CMS-28	
CMS-50	
CMS-51	
CMS-48	
CMS-1, CMS-21, CMS-31, CMS-34, CMS-39	
	CSE-12
CMS-9, CMS-24, CMS-28, CMS-47	CSE-13, CSE-22
CMS-52, CMS-53	
CMS-47	CSE-22
CMS-41, CMS-42, CMS-43	CSE-19, CSE-20
1S-43, CMS-46	CSE-20
1S-44	CSE-21
1S-54, CMS-55	